AF606005

THE NETHERLANDS EAST INDIES AT THE TROPENMUSEUM

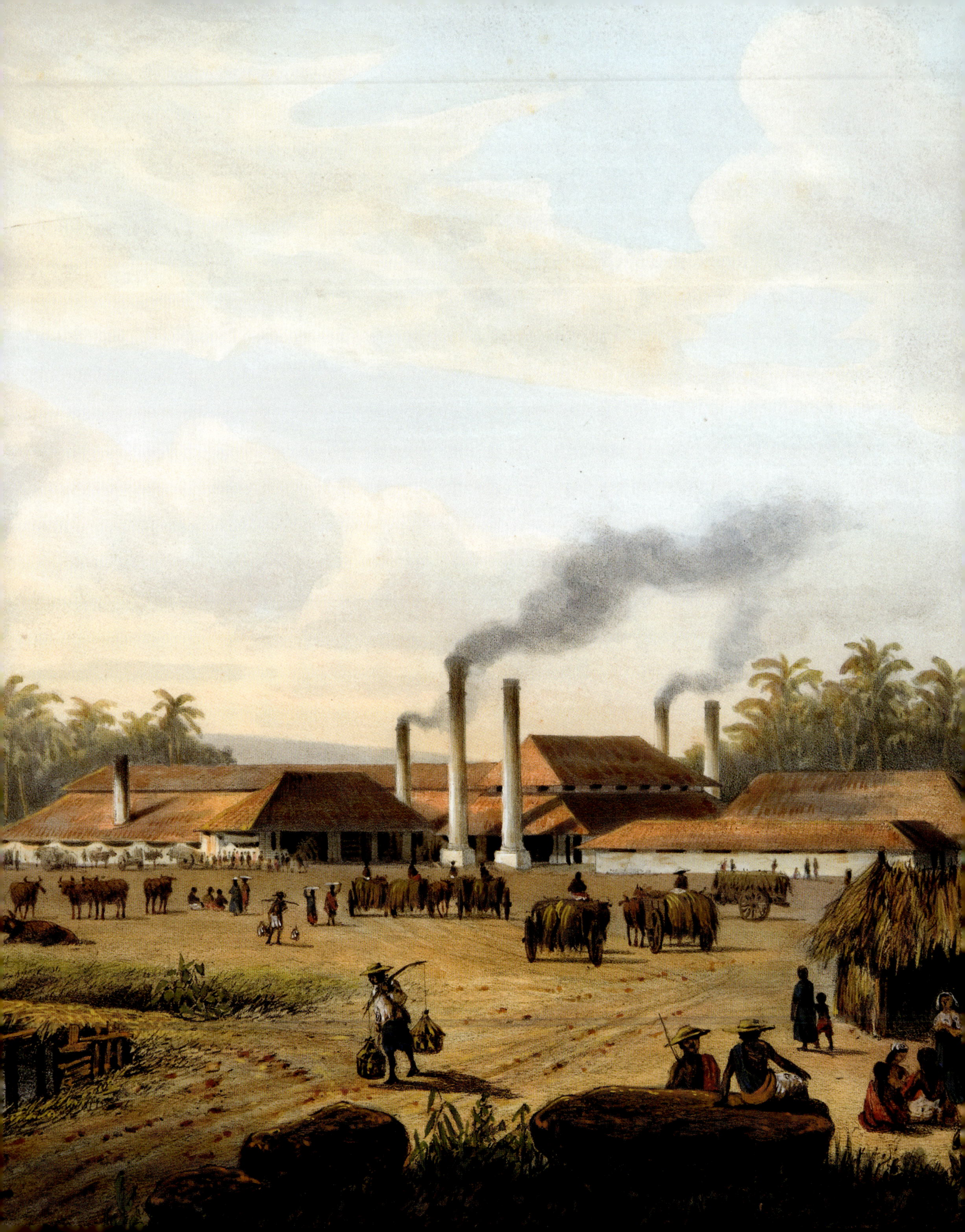

THE NETHERLANDS EAST INDIES

at the Tropenmuseum

A colonial history

SUSAN LEGÊNE
JANNEKE VAN DIJK
(EDS)

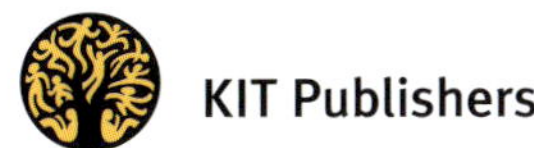

CONTENTS

6 Foreword
Lejo Schenk

7 Preface

9 Introduction: The Netherlands East Indies, a colonial history
Susan Legêne and Janneke van Dijk

The Netherlands Eastward Bound

29 The resonance of violence in collections
Harm Stevens

39 Equal and free: Indonesian demands in education and politics
Elsbeth Locher-Scholten

53 Enterprises
J. Thomas Lindblad

67 Domestic servants in colonial times
Ratna Saptari

81 The Javanese and Balinese dance theatre as community art
Margareta Dorila

97 Expeditions, collection, science. The Dutch fascination for the Papuans of New Guinea
David van Duuren

Colonial collections at the Tropenmuseum

113 Ten collectors, ten collections
Susan Legêne and Janneke van Dijk

123 Ten collectors
123 The colonial civil servant: Johan Ernst Jasper
124 The entrepreneur: Théodore F.A. Delprat

126 The missionary: Petrus Vertenten
128 The artist: Hendrik Paulides
129 The artists couple: Mr and Mrs Quirien A.A. Krijnen and Petronella Maria Helena (Nellie) Krijnen-Surie
131 The photographer: Margaretha Mathilde ('Thilly') Weissenborn
134 The scientist/museum director: Johan Christiaan van Eerde
135 The soldier and his wife: Henri N.A. Swart and Victorina M.G. Stadlmair
137 The founder of the Koloniaal Museum: Frederik Willem van Eeden
138 The music collector: Jaap Kunst

141 Ten collections
141 Wood
142 Maps
144 Family photographs
145 Films
146 Clothes
149 Paintings
150 The library collection
152 Weapons
153 Yogya silver
155 Models and miniatures

Colonial imagination and reflection

161 Collective memory. The interactions between literature, museums, cinema and photography
Pamela Pattynama

171 The arrows aim. Coloured comments on Dutch colonial drama
Edy Seriese

186 Notes

188 References

193 About the authors

198 Index

FOREWORD

A museum collection is much more than a collection of objects. Considerable history is attached to each and every object. Viewed in this light, a museum collection serves as a gateway to an endless number of stories. Some of the stories concern the cultural world in which these objects originally functioned. They say something about the people that made them, saw them, used them and experienced them. Other stories concern the manner in which the objects passed from their initial owners into the hands of, for example, traders, colonial officials and missionaries, collectors, anthropologists and art lovers. And there are also stories about the way in which the objects made their way to their (temporary) final destination, where they are continually given new significance. These stories are about curators and educators, restorers and designers, viewers and readers.

The Tropenmuseum is an exceptional museum. Located in the unique historical building of the Koninklijk Instituut voor de Tropen (Royal Tropical Institute), it manages a collection of some 180,000 objects and 270,000 historical photographs. This collection is closely linked with both Dutch history and world history and documents the numerous types of contact that occur between different peoples, cultures and nations.
In the course of history, the museum has reinvented itself several times. It traces its origin back to a 19th century colonial collection that was brought together in a museum in Haarlem. In 1910, this collection became a part of the Vereniging Koloniaal Instituut (Colonial Institute Association), newly founded at the time, which had a new building built in Amsterdam. The museum then gained great renown as the Koloniaal Museum (Colonial Museum). After the Second World War, it was rechristened the Indisch Museum (Indies Museum), and in 1950 became the Tropenmuseum. As a part of the Koninklijk Instituut voor de Tropen, the museum profiled itself as a post-colonial museum with a global focus on economics, trade and culture. In the 1970s the museum was radically transformed into a presentation centre for development issues and was supplemented with an active theatre and a still much talked about children's museum.

The most recent transformation was completed in 2009: the Tropenmuseum as a dynamic institution focused on world culture, a place where a richly variegated balance is sought between colonial collections, classic ethnography, contemporary art, intangible cultural heritage and *popular art*. It is a museum that continually strives to play a significant role in society, a museum that seeks contact with people and communities which recognize themselves in the heritage that the museum manages and the stories that it tells.
A museum collects, studies and exhibits. Yet a museum also continually reflects on its own mission and provides access to its knowledge. For several years now, this has meant that the collections have been made available online so that they can be searched through. The museum has also felt a strong need to publish the most important pieces in the collection, stories and the museum's history in book form. The structure of this ten-volume series is based on the areas of specialization embedded in the institute, including cultural regions and several themes.
Of course, the books will reveal only the tip of the iceberg. We are nonetheless convinced that publishing these books in all their glory might well entice the reader to seek out and enjoy all the objects and stories that the museum houses.

The Netherlands Indies at the Tropenmuseum is the first volume of the series. The choice was not arbitrary. The volume underlines the relationship between colonialism and the creation of a collection. Thousands of objects produce a picture of the era and bear witness to the diversity and complexity of this relationship. Since the 1950s, most of these objects have been stored away in the museum's depots. It is a sleeping collection that has played an active role in the semi-permanent exhibition 'Netherlands East Indies, a colonial history' (Nederlands-Indië, een koloniaal verleden) since 2003. Research into collections and collection histories, into collectors and the circumstances under which they gathered the collections throw a different light onto the objects. It continues to produce new stories to tell.

I would like to extend a word of thanks to all authors, researchers, photographers and designers in and around KIT-Tropenmuseum and KIT-Publishers who have helped to bring this vast project to life. Immense appreciation should be expressed to the Ministry of Foreign Affairs/Development Cooperation, which has made our museum's work possible for so many years. A word of thanks is also owed to the BankGiroLoterij, which has allowed us to use a part of the funds that we have received since 2006 for the further development of the collection and specifically for the creation of this historical series of books on the museum's huge collection.
I wish you all a lot of reading pleasure and hope to see you inside the museum soon.

Lejo Schenk
Director of the Tropenmuseum

PREFACE

Around the turn of the twentieth century, almost all staff members of the Tropenmuseum in Amsterdam were involved, in one way or another, in the renovation process of the museum. Not even visitors could escape this process, since the museum was open to the public, with only a few galleries temporarily closed. Researchers, curators, technicians, educators, restorers, museum guards, photographers, ICT staff, all of them participated in this process. Support from freelance researchers, architects, designers, focus groups and collectors played a crucial part as well. The process of renovation not only required a concerted effort on the part of the many different professionals involved in the management of the museum and the creation of exhibitions, it also relied heavily on the collective knowledge of the staff, on the personal experiences that contribute to the creative process of making an exhibition, and on a respect for the different perspectives, emotions and choices of all those concerned with the visualization of the range of views held on the colonial past in contemporary society. Acknowledging the importance of this colonial past for today's Tropenmuseum was regarded a precondition for the renovation of any gallery in the museum.
The decision to address this issue explicitly for the coming decades in one of the new galleries, 'The Netherlands Indies, a colonial history', received general support both inside and outside the museum.

The Netherlands Indies at the Tropenmuseum is one of the outcomes of an elaborate process in which many people have been involved. The book follows the overall concept of the exhibition 'The Netherlands Indies, a colonial history' with a focus on the many aspects of colonialism as a history, a culture and a legacy. The introductory chapter provides an historical sketch of the Tropenmuseum's institutional past as it relates to colonialism and decolonization. It also explains some fundamental choices made in the conceptualization of an exhibition on the colonial past, such as the choice of a perspective that employs the Tropenmuseum/Koloniaal Museum as the main actor to present the history of its own colonial views and practices. After this introduction, the first part of the book contains six essays that discuss the main themes of the exhibition related to expansion, education, economics, social relations, culture and science. These essays discuss the exhibition concept and add views that differ from the museum's interpretation of the collections. The second part of the book focuses on the creation of these collections. It introduces the new collection category of 'colonial collections': collections that up to now have largely gone unnoticed, but that apparently can be found all over the museum: in the storage rooms, in museum offices, attics, in the library and even in the architecture of the building itself. Three types of colonial collections emerged: (1) objects related to the culture of colonialists overseas; (2) objects that express the colonial relationship at home in the Netherlands, and (3) objects that visualize the colony. Subsequently, brief explorations of ten collectors and ten collection genres relevant to the Tropenmuseum are described. The last part of this book consists of two essays that reflect on the centrepiece of the exhibition 'The Netherlands East Indies, a colonial history', i.e. a colonial theatre with seven historical archetypes, some based on real and some on fictional characters. The two authors discuss the implications of this mixture of references for history and fiction, how it connects to past exhibition practices and what it means for the future policy of the Tropenmuseum.
Throughout the book, hundreds of images of objects are included. Some are photographs of historical objects, others are prints of historical photographs or images of exhibitions. And all of them refer to many more objects, images and scenes. These visual sources support the stories and provide a comment or contrasting image. Moreover, they invite the reader to reflect on the process of imparting meaning, which began when the first objects were collected and continues up to the present day.

The editors of this book are grateful to the Tropenmuseum and to KIT Publishers for the book's realization. We would like to thank the many authors involved for their individual contributions, ranging from full chapters to single captions and everything in between. And we sincerely hope that this book will serve as an invitation to readers in the East and the West to further explore the many legacies and the heritage of the colonial past.

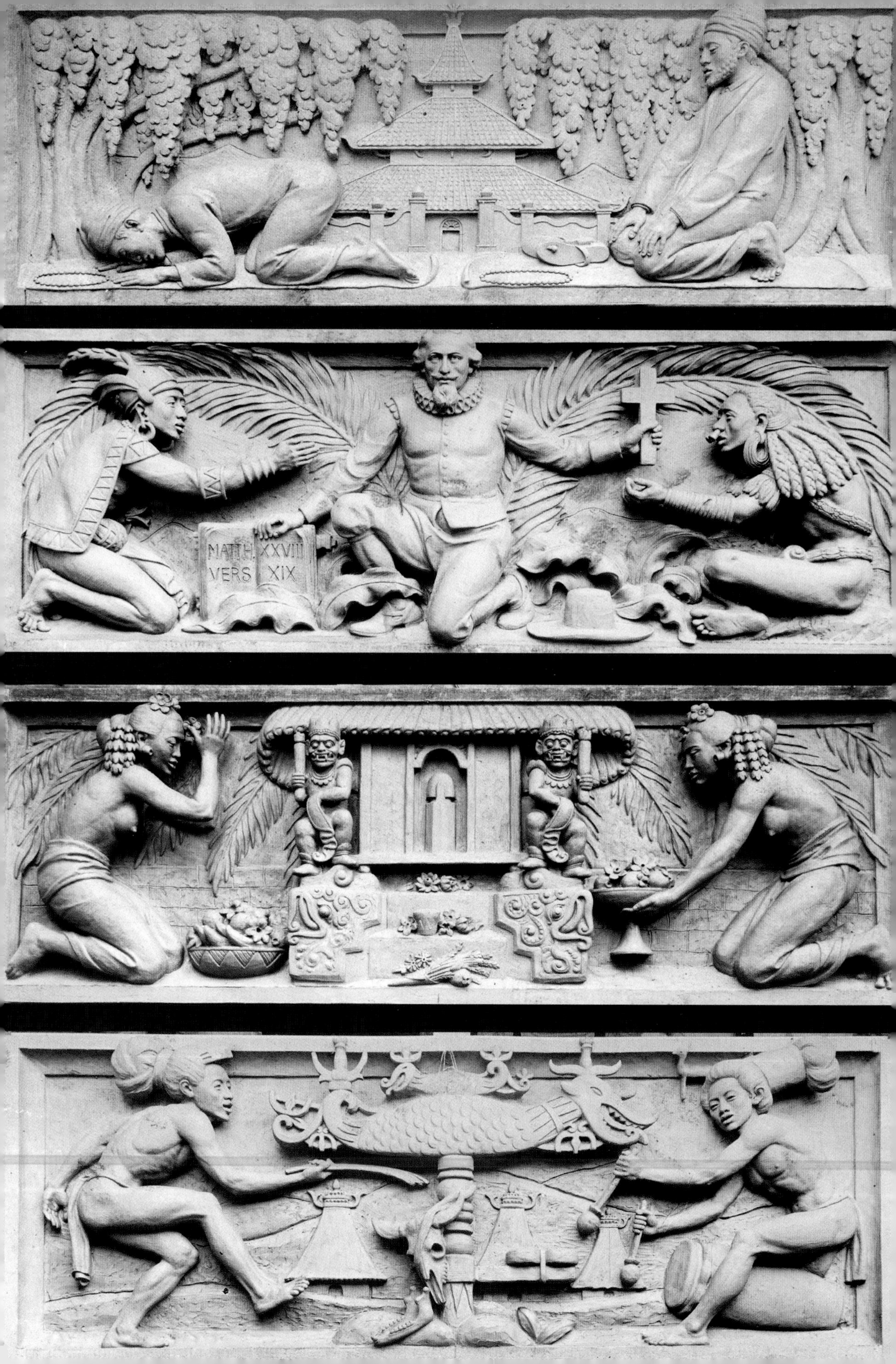
MATTH. XXVIII
VERS XIX

INTRODUCTION
The Netherlands East Indies, a colonial history

SUSAN LEGÊNE AND JANNEKE VAN DIJK

1
Relief depicting Islam, Java, facade Tropenmuseum
W.O.J. Nieuwenkamp
(1874-1950)
c. 1923
60054458

2
Relief depicting Christianity, Nias and Papua, facade Tropenmuseum
W.O.J. Nieuwenkamp
(1874-1950)
c. 1923
60054459

3
Relief depicting Hinduism, Bali,facade Tropenmuseum
W.O.J. Nieuwenkamp
(1874-1950)
c. 1923
60054460

4
Relief depicting animism, Alor, facade Tropenmuseum
W.O.J. Nieuwenkamp
(1874-1950)
c. 1923
60054461

The West – The East – The collaboration: a building with a history

It is obvious that the museum's access to the Koninklijk Instituut voor de Tropen, KIT (Royal Tropical Institute) is not the main entrance to this impressive building. Anyone approaching the Tropenmuseum from Amsterdam's inner city first passes a long façade with half-reliefs and statues depicting the planting and harvesting of rice, sugar cane, of rubber and tobacco, or references to religion (animism, Hinduism, Islam, and Christianity), to shipping and trade, spinning and weaving, science and missionary work. At the main entrance, a sculpture of the city's patroness positions the Institute in Amsterdam; Jan Pieterszoon Coen gives it a place in history; a relief with the Bible, opened at the Gospel of St. Mark provides a Christian foundation, while a geographer holding a globe refers to Western science. The head quarters of the Koninklijk Instituut voor de Tropen invite for an encounter with a colonial past that is still topical. (Fig. 1-4)
Inside the building, this encounter proceeds with images of past colonialism in a contemporary setting. The marble hall at the main entrance shows a large mural, as a triptych above the doors leading to the auditorium. To the left is *The West*, with next to it *The East* and to the right *The Collaboration*. *The West* does not represent the West Indies, but symbolizes the Institute and the dynamic modernity of the Netherlands or, more probably, Europe. *The East* represents the static agrarian Netherlands East Indies. *The Collaboration* shows how Western scientific, technological and industrial knowledge creates dynamic economic change in overseas society. Through Dutch initiative and the help of a large and eager to learn Eastern workforce, progress and economic prosperity awaits on both sides of the ocean.[1] (Fig. 5-7)
With this mural, the painter Hendrik Paulides has provided an idealistic picture of the mission of the Koloniaal Instituut (Colonial Institute), that was founded in 1910 at the initiative of wealthy colonial entrepreneurs and with the warm support of the Dutch Society for the Advancement of Industry, the Municipality of Amsterdam, the Amsterdam Zoo Natura Artis Magistra or 'Artis', and others. In letters of gold the names of all the founders are chiselled into the marble of the wall of this entrance hall. Already in 1864 the influential Dutch Society for the Advancement of Industry had founded in Haarlem a Museum of the East and West Indies Natural Resources, soon renamed the Koloniaal Museum (Colonial Museum), which had opened

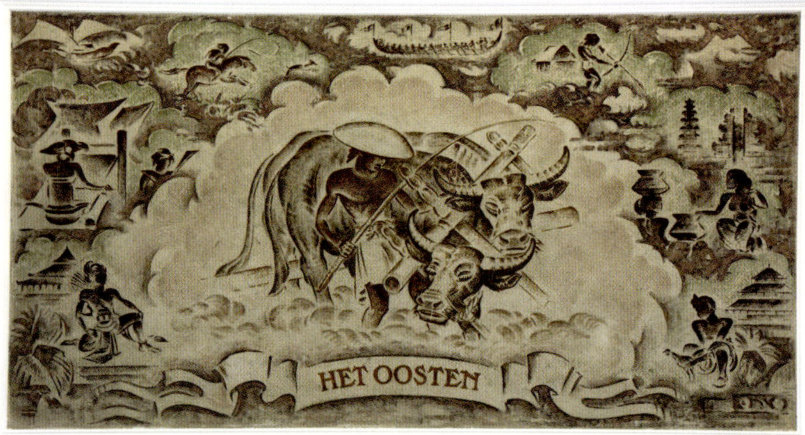

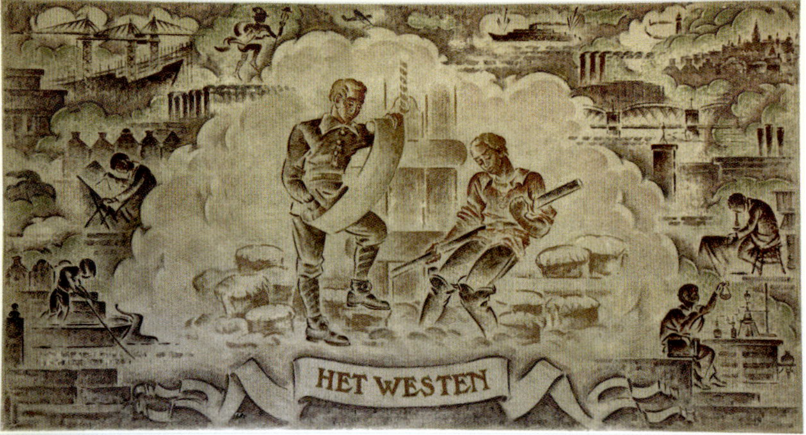

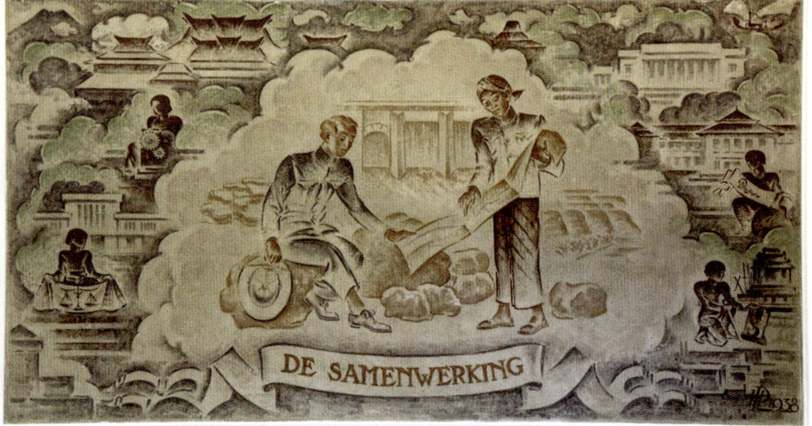

5, 6, 7
Murals **Het Oosten, Het Westen** and **De Samenwerking** in the marble hall of the Koninklijk Instituut voor de Tropen
Hendrik Paulides (1892-1967)
1938
10016339-10016341

its doors in 1871. Artis had been collecting for its own ethnographic museum in Amsterdam since the end of the 1850s. In 1861 Artis opened to the public its first solely ethnographic museum, in 1888 followed by the larger museum in the building "De Volharding". After 1910 both the Haarlem and the Artis collection were transferred to the Koloniaal Instituut. The Koloniaal Museum in Amsterdam thus started with two collections, that originated from 19th century colonial and scientific expansion and exploration, with a focus both on tropical products in the broadest sense (Haarlem) and on ethnographic objects (Artis).

The initiative to this Koloniaal Instituut was in line with the so-called *Ethische Politiek*, that was officially introduced in the colonies by the Netherlands in 1901. According to the principles of this Ethical Policy, the Netherlands as an enlightened coloniser was duty-bound to develop colonial society overseas not only for its own benefit, but also for the benefit of its colonial subjects. In this context, the Koloniaal Instituut was meant to be a centre of expertise for entrepreneurs and government in the area of colonial trade, tropical medicine and physical and cultural anthropology. The immense building provided space for research departments and regional institutes, a library, laboratories, a greenery, collections of seeds, wood samples and other tropical products, maps and picture archives. Its Koloniaal Museum presented this collective colonial knowledge to the Dutch public. In one section of the museum, tropical products were on display. The other section showed the art and culture of the native population of the Dutch colonial empire within the Netherlands East Indies and the Caribbean.

Because the completion of the building ran into delays due to the First World War and the subsequent economic dip, its inauguration by Queen Wilhelmina finally took place in 1926. (Fig. 8) By that time the Netherlands was confronted overseas with an emerging Indonesian nationalist movement, and the Ethical Policy had adopted a conservative and more openly repressive nature. Nevertheless, at home in the Netherlands, the ethical principle committed to edifying the peoples of the Indonesian archipelago, continued as the dominant colonial discourse. To the general public this message of a civilizing mission was convincing, also because it was inextricably linked with the building and the programme of the Koloniaal Instituut in Amsterdam. Regardless of developments overseas, the building and exhibitions contained a reassuring message of great things to be achieved in the sphere of economic and cultural knowledge, development, exchange and progress. Today the KIT is the descendant of this Koloniaal Instituut, just as the Tropenmuseum is counterpart to the original Koloniaal Museum. Much has changed in the Institute's field of work since decolonisation ensued after 1945, and thus in the meaning of the word *Collaboration* in the Paulides mural of the entrance hall, but the concept as such remained leading in the mission of the institution.

Shortly after the end of the German occupation of the Netherlands, but before the unilateral Declaration of Independence by Soekarno on 17 August 1945, the Executive Board of the Koloniaal Instituut already decided that the word 'Colonial' should be removed from the Institute's name. It was argued that the connotation of that word was not longer acceptable for the Institute's 'Indies friends' and Indonesian counterparts, whereas, according to the President of the Board, in the United States as well the word 'colonial' no longer would be appreciated. In this respect reference was made to the Atlantic Charter of 1941 and the 1945 United Nations Charter.[2] As a result of these considerations, the Institute was renamed the Indisch Instituut and the museum the Indisch Museum. It remained 'neutral', or better did not express any political opinion, during the years of conflict and the two Dutch Military Aggressions following Indonesian unilateral Declaration of Independence. When the transfer of sovereignty to Indonesia finally was signed by the Netherlands on 27 December 1949, institute and museum broadened the geographical focus and were renamed Koninklijk Instituut voor de Tropen and Tropenmuseum.

After 1950, the KIT gradually shifted its attention to other areas in what would successively be referred to as the Third World or the South. The former close ties between the Institute and the former Dutch colonial enterprises that by now had become large Dutch international and multinational companies became more casual. The ties with the government however became more closely-knit, especially since in the 1960s Dutch government encouraged the Institute to expand its international activities in the fields of tropical agriculture, health care and cultural anthropology. Following United Nations' policy 'collaboration' became development cooperation, with a focus on providing 'technical assistance' in the context of 'developmental aid'. The Institute sent its staff members (sometimes called 'volunteers') to tropical

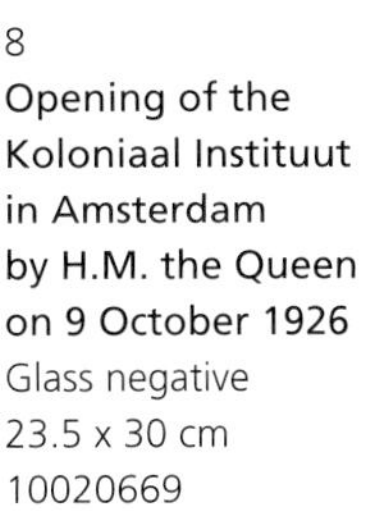

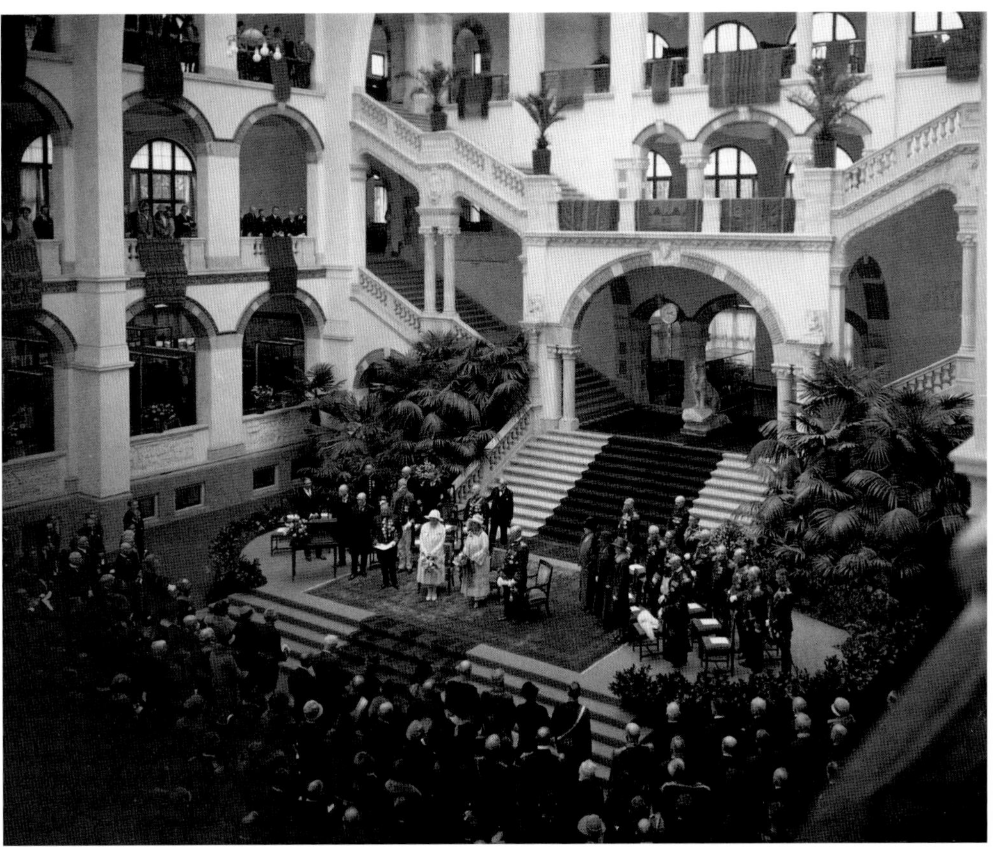

8
Opening of the Koloniaal Instituut in Amsterdam by H.M. the Queen on 9 October 1926
Glass negative
23.5 x 30 cm
10020669

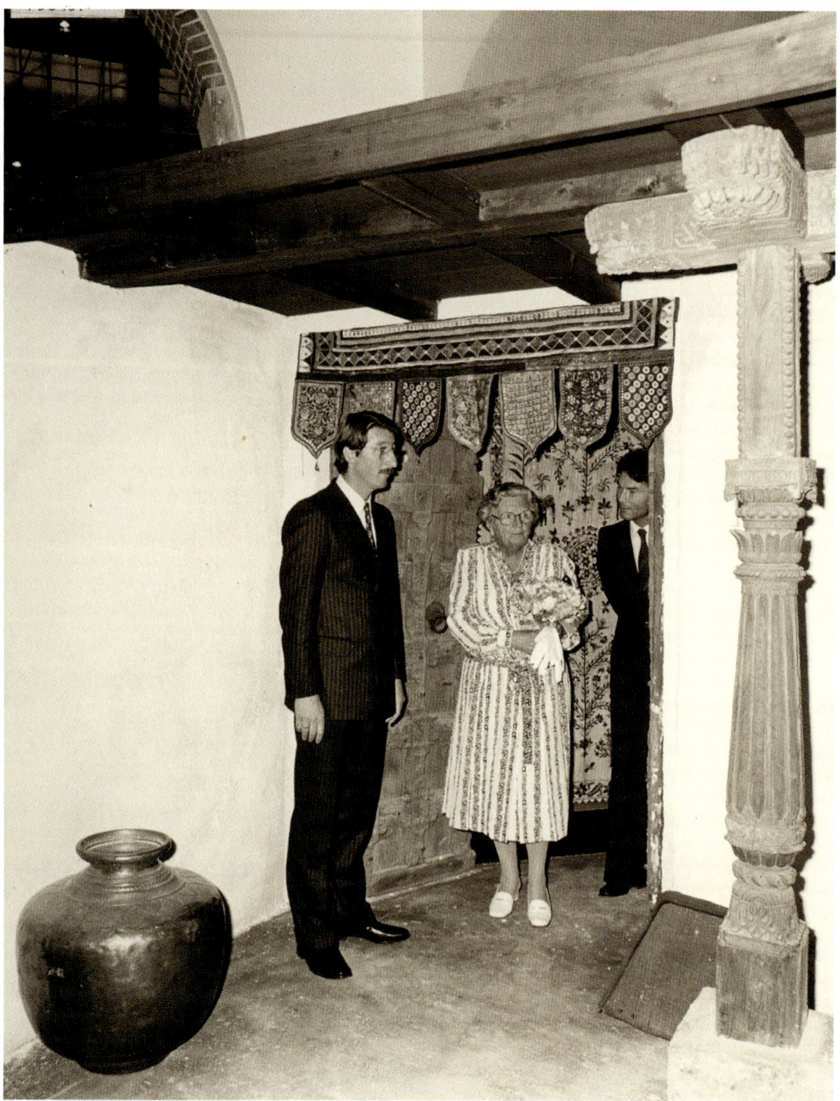

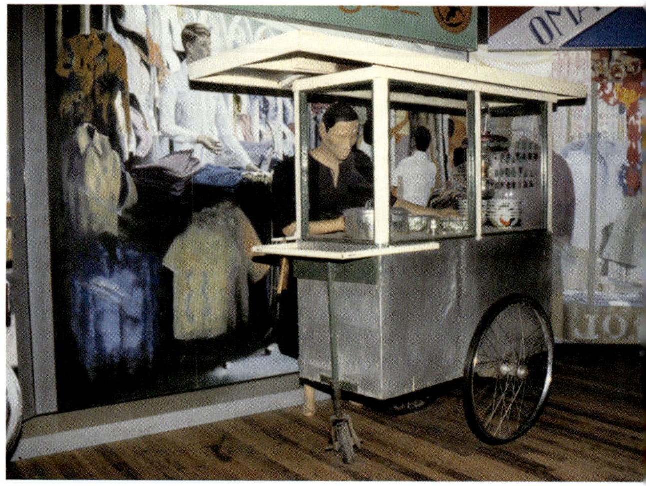

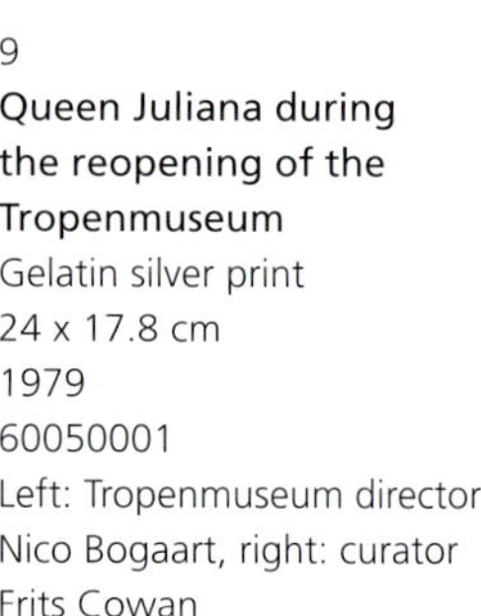

9
Queen Juliana during the reopening of the Tropenmuseum
Gelatin silver print
24 x 17.8 cm
1979
60050001
Left: Tropenmuseum director Nico Bogaart, right: curator Frits Cowan

countries all around the world. As in colonial times, they were experts in agricultural techniques, crop research, erosion control, tropical diseases or primary health care. Meanwhile in the museum the permanent displays from the colonial era became more and more obsolete. The 'traditional' ethnographic objects gradually disappeared into the museum's depot. By the end of the 1960s, with full government support, the museum embarked on a complete refurbishment. As a result, an entirely modernised and renovated Tropenmuseum in 1979 assumed the task of presenting the public at large with information about development processes and the frictions and tensions at stake in what was then called the Third World.[3] (Figs 9, 10)

When in 1979 Queen Juliana inaugurated this modernised Tropenmuseum, most of the colonial reliefs, murals, motifs and ornaments that were part of the building and an integral part of the context of the museum's displays, had become an unacknowledged frame for a story about change around the world. The storyline of the exhibitions focused on the concept of 'modernisation' and the constraints that incongruous world relations brought to the people in developing countries. It was well received by the public, particularly because of an innovative museological approach based on a *mise-en-scène* of 'almost real' daily life scenes in the tropics, including smell, noise, and daily use artefacts. People could enter a *desa* (village/countryside) house from Indonesia, walk in a slum in Bombay (Mumbai), or visit an African market. The objects as well as the stories that were presented in the exhibitions, had become unrelated to both the objects stored in the depot and to the building itself. Even the stately stairway at the entrance to the museum was removed, motivated by a wish to bring the entrance to street level. The colonial authority of the building thus was downplayed, the long façade with its colonial reliefs gradually darkened from exhaust fumes.
Three decades after the reopening of the museum in 1979, this refurbishment had become outdated as well. Already in the 1980s, a critical debate arose about the principles of development cooperation, such as the blue print approach or top-down imposition of development models and the continuing unbalanced North (centre)-South (periphery) relations based on dependency. The changing political

< 10
Impression of modern Indonesia at the semi-permanent Southeast Asia exhibition
Colour slide
2.4 x 3.6 cm
1980
20043280

relations on the world stage that ensued after 1989 and the ending of the Cold War contributed to a further reassessment of Dutch policy concerning development cooperation. Gradually the presentation in the Tropenmuseum of modernisation processes in the Third World no longer reflected or supported contemporary approaches to what was by then called 'international cooperation'. Besides, the context for displaying 'the tropics' had changed as well with respect to Dutch society. For instance, due to colonial, postcolonial and labour immigration, increasing numbers of Dutch citizens had personal connections to those 'tropics' that in the Tropenmuseum were on display, whereas it became more easy as well, to visit 'tropical countries' as holiday destination. It became evident that the manner in which the Tropenmuseum in the 1970s had musealised Third World problems in itself could be regarded as an expression of how the Netherlands had dealt (or better, had *not* dealt) with its *own* decolonisation process. For the museum, time had come for another approach to collections and audiences, implying a new refurbishment of the museum's semi-permanent exhibitions.
Between 1994 and 2008 throughout the museum and department by department, this second complete refurbishment was realised. This book discusses the first floor, where this happened under an umbrella title 'Eastward Bound! Art, culture and colonialism'. The title was taken from the travelogue *Oostwaarts* by the famous Indo-Dutch writer Louis Couperus about his trip to the Netherlands East Indies, China and Japan in 1923. The four 'Eastward Bound!' exhibitions took as a starting point the museum's core collections originating from South and Southeast Asia, and Oceania and collected since the 19th century, with one exhibition, called 'The Netherlands East Indies, a colonial history', addressing the history

OOSTWAARTS

11
Oostwaarts
Louis Couperus
Published by N.P. Leopold, The Hague
Paper, linen
24.5 x 17.5 x 4.5 cm
1923
6043-1a. Purchase: Antiquariaat Bestebreurtje, 2002

Oostwaarts, the book that inspired the Tropenmuseum to chose 'Eastward Bound!' as the umbrella title of four exhibitions on South and Southeast Asia, is the report of the trip made by the Dutch writer Louis Couperus (1863-1923) and his wife to the Netherlands East Indies. The trip, from October 1921 to May 1923, was made on the invitation of the weekly newspaper *De Haagsche Post* and, apart from the Netherlands East Indies, also included visits to Hong Kong and Japan. The report was initially published as a serial. It was published as a book four months after the death of Couperus in October 1923.
Louis Couperus, who was born into an East Indian family, spent his youth on the island of Java. His work is embedded in the Dutch colonial culture around 1900, both in its content and design. The artist Chris Lebeau (1878-1945), several of whose batik designs are owned by the Tropenmuseum, designed the batik cover for the famous work of Couperus, *De stille kracht*, in 1901. Other artists who made covers and illustrations for the work of Couperus included Jan Toorop (Metamorfoze, 1897), Julius de Praetere, Jan Rotgans and H.P. Berlage. The cover of *Oostwaarts*, designed in red buckram (a stiff type of linen) with gold lettering, was made by Tjipke Visser (1876-1955). A great many photographs in the book were taken by Thilly Weissenborn (1889-1964). She was the owner of the photography studio Lux in Garut (Garoet), Java. SL

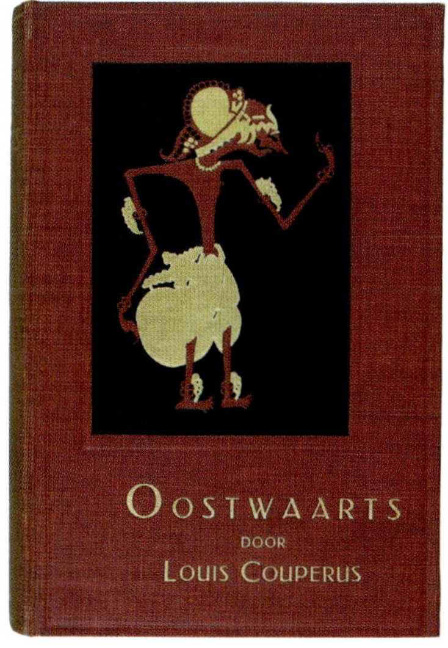

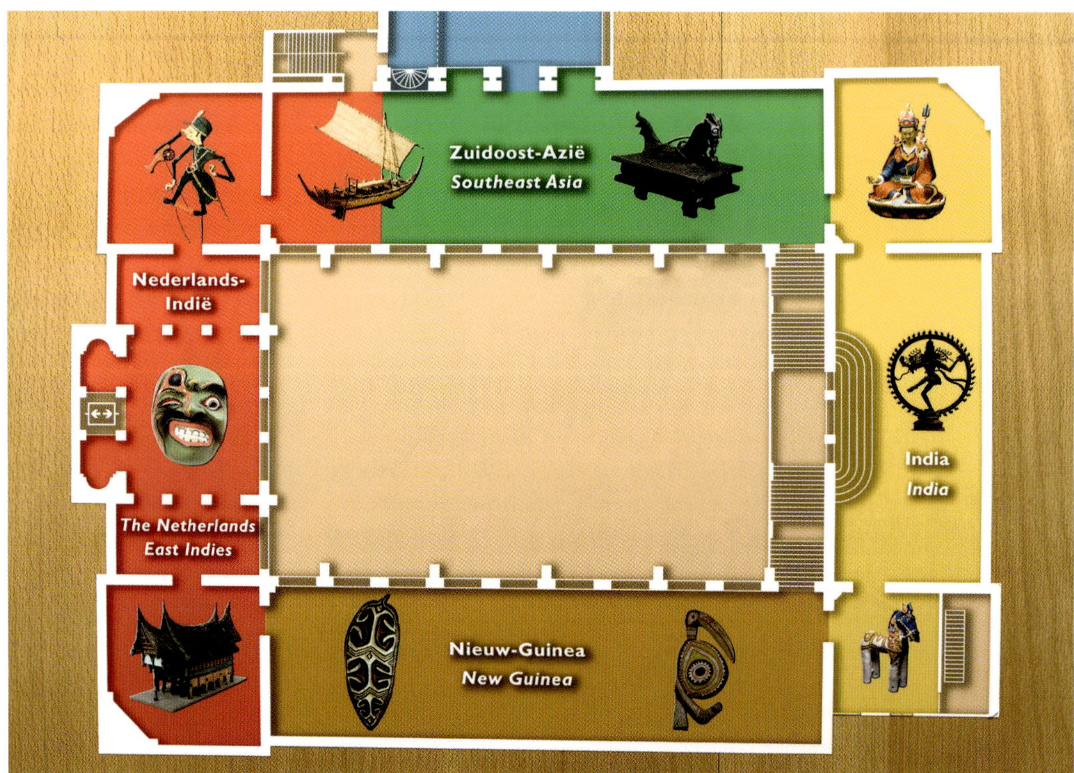

12
Schematic layout of the exhibition 'Eastward bound! Art, culture and colonialism'

13
Artist's impression of the exhibition 'The Netherlands East Indies, a colonial history'
Architect Jowa, Amsterdam
2.4 x 3.6 cm
2002
20043279

of collection formation. It opened in January 2003. The return of some two thousand ethnographic objects in 'Eastward Bound!', after their removal from the museum floor in the wake of decolonisation, put renewed emphasis on the meaning of ethnographic traditions in contemporary culture. It was not intended as just a restoration of a colonial order of things. While the Tropenmuseum in its refurbishment programme explored the relationships between ethnography and contemporary art as an expression of contemporary developments in a local, national and international setting, it also linked the objects on display to their collection histories. In 'The Netherlands East Indies, a colonial history' this approach was mirrored. The display was conceptualized as a performative setting for three intersecting stories related to the current Tropenmuseum, and to the institutional and museological history of the museum and its building, placed in the context of a broader colonial history of the Netherlands and the Netherlands East Indies. It is this exhibition on the colonial past of the Netherlands and the museum, that is the focus of this book. (Fig. 11-13)
'The Netherlands East Indies, a colonial history' starts from the idea that the museum collections,

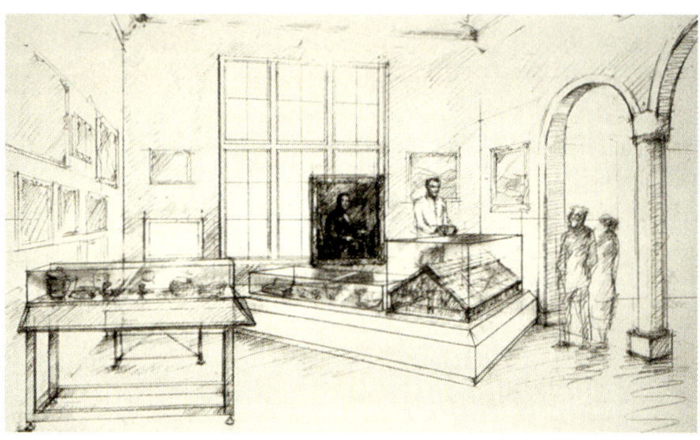

along with their provenance, the history of how they have been collected and displayed in the museum, are a unique source to knowledge about Dutch attitudes, actions and frames of reference regarding colonialism and decolonisation. The museum used to display its authority by classifying, arranging and explaining objects and by typecasting people. The collections from colonial times and the exhibitions about peoples colonized, maybe told more about the perceptions of the colonizers/collectors, than about those other people. 'The Netherlands East Indies, a colonial history' focuses on these colonizers/collectors and how, through the museum, they were engaged in home-colonialism as well.

Collectors and the reappraisal of the collection and display tradition

This concept for a new semi-permanent exhibition about collection formation as a colonial history has contributed to a reappraisal of many collection items. Most objects presented in the exhibitions of 'Eastward Bound!' are masterpieces from the Southeast Asia, Oceania and South Asia core collections. In addition, in the theme exhibition of 'The Netherlands East Indies, a colonial history', hundreds of pieces are on display that until recently were barely considered to have any authentic ethnographical origin or value. It concerns objects from natural history (animal skulls, shells, minerals etc.) or, for instance, 'almost real' tropical plants made in plaster or wax, and full size statues or facial masks of real people. (Figs. 14-16) Cultural objects belong to this category as well, like diorama's, miniatures and models of colonial scenes, of houses, boats and people; or paintings by Western painters and objects from daily life of colonialists, like furniture or clothing, food samples, historical films and photograph albums. The museum has gathered and kept thousands of such objects. For decades they were not seen as collectables, but merely as 'stage props', leftovers or archival materials, made or commissioned for exhibitions in the Netherlands about the Netherlands East Indies. Ethnographic collections from the various peoples of the Netherlands East Indies combined with these 'stage prop' collections about these people and with the material culture of the colonialists themselves, make it easier to reflect on a centuries-old Western fascination for Eastern crafts, art, religion and culture beyond the established classifications that have developed into a kind of art historical and ethnographic canon in museums around the world. The museum has staged Georg Everhard Rumphius (1627-1702) as an early exponent of this Western collectors' 'unbiased' engagement with these unknown worlds. His posthumously published *d'Amboinsche Rariteitkamer* of 1705 is a case in point. But he was not unique in his curiosity and dedication to get to know and explain what he found in an unfamiliar world. In the course of time numerous men and women for various reasons started collections which ended up in the stores of the Tropenmuseum. Based on current computer data, we estimate the number to come to c. 3000 families.

These collectors came from all layers and political socio-religious 'pillars' of Dutch society and were involved in the widest range of functions within the colonial system. Some had recently moved to or visited the Netherlands East Indies; others were the first generation born there, or had lived there for generations. Most collectors belonged to the Indo-Dutch community or to the Dutch colonial elite, but many Indonesians contributed to the collections as well.

As an imagined community of 'collectors' from all ranks, positions, ethnic groups, political persuasions or religious beliefs, they were active in a dynamic colonial society. In the Netherlands the museum was one of the places where they gave shape and colour to what can be labelled a 'home colonial culture'.

Of this culture, Louis Couperus is one of the most distinguished exponents, witness his novels and travelogues, among which *Oostwaarts*. Based on professional careers, personal ties or cultural affiliation, anyone, also someone who never travelled to the Netherlands East Indies, could become a donator of a collection to the Koloniaal Museum, including artists who were inspired by Indonesian culture.

Until today the 'East Indies' live on in the family histories of many people in the Netherlands, based on a wide range of experiences and perspectives.

Regularly the museum acquires new objects, donated by postcolonial generations to whom the Tropenmuseum apparently seems to be the best place to

14
Model of a sailing boat
Wood, cotton
39 x 69 x 15.5 cm
c. 1885
A-4788a. Gift: Natura Artis Magistra, 1920

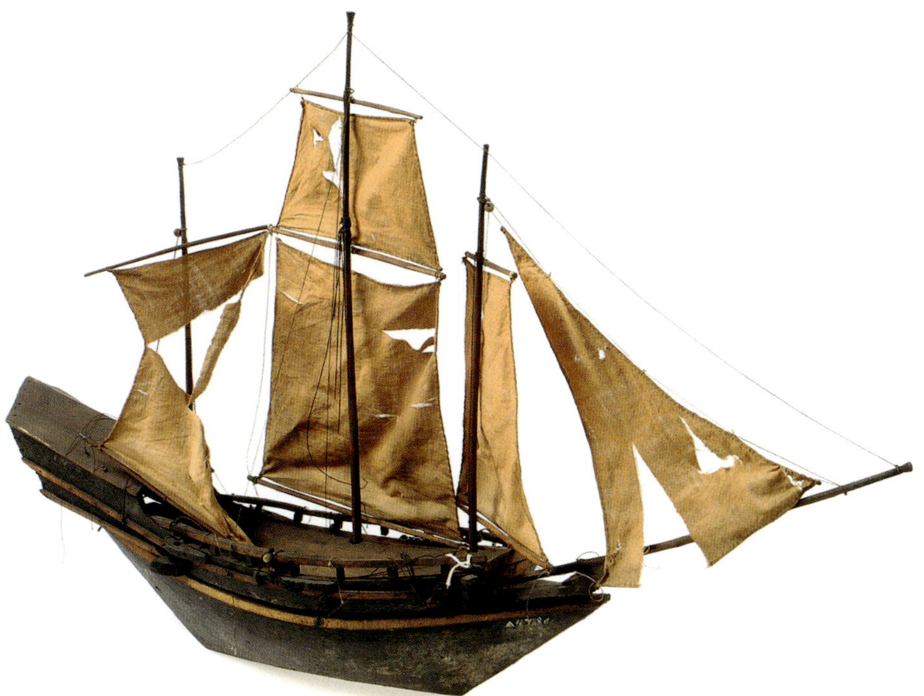

PLASTER MODELS

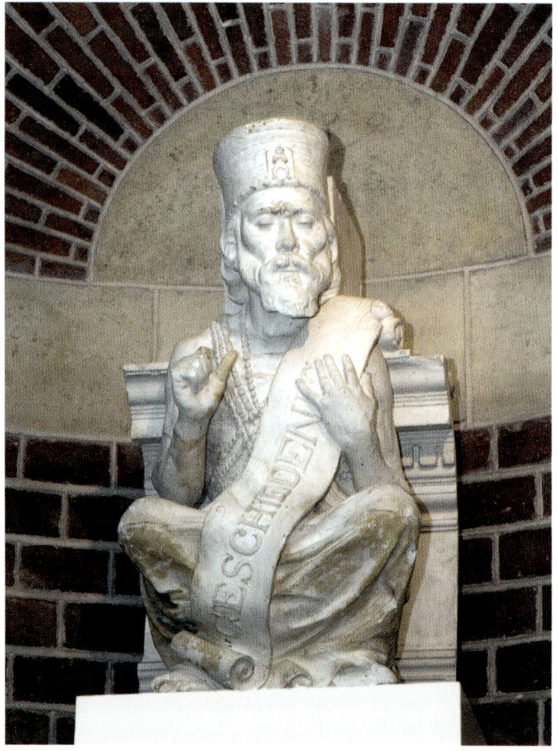

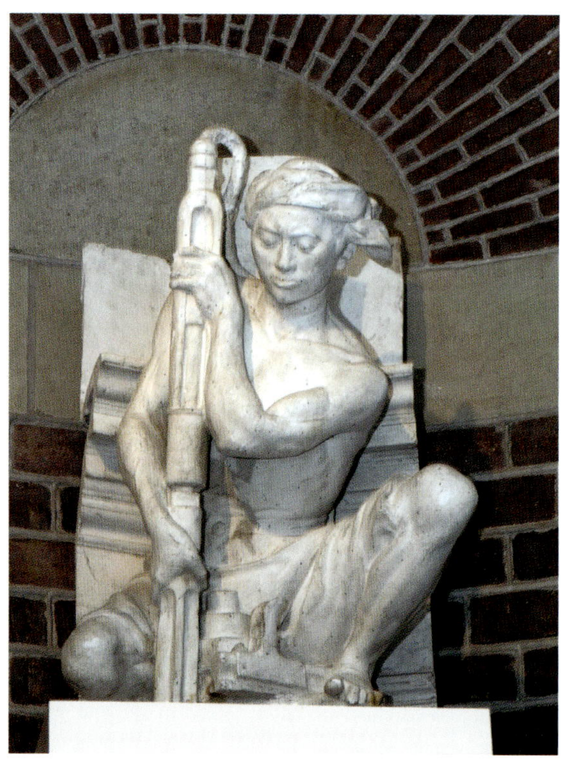

15
Model of a Balinese priest who passes on history
L.J. Vreugde (1868-1936)
Commissioned by the Koloniaal Instituut, c. 1922
Plaster
6333-2

16
Plaster model of an Acehnese man with drill bit for petroleum extraction
L.J. Vreugde (1868-1936)
Commissioned by the Koloniaal Instituut, c. 1922
Plaster
6333-3

The Koninklijk Instituut voor de Tropen is richly decorated with scenes and ornaments. Many of them were produced by the sculptor Louis Vreugde. Vreugde became involved in the construction of the building through the influential businessman, banker and politician J.T. Cremer, who was also the initiator and founder of the Koloniaal Instituut. The bust of Cremer, prominently displayed in the marble hall next to the bust of co-founder H.F.R. Hubrecht, was made by Vreugde. On friezes and capitals in the museum, he also depicted the stories about the Indonesian mouse deer Kancil and the story of 'the first expedition to the East' by Dutch ships under the command of Cornelis de Houtman (1595).

For the reading room of the Institute, Vreugde produced ten wooden carvings that represented the expertise of the Koloniaal Instituut. Two of these carvings are included as plaster casts in the exhibition 'The Netherlands East Indies, a colonial history' – a reciting Balinese priest, symbolising the passing on of history, and an Acehnese man with a bit used for petroleum extraction. Vreugde was educated at the Koninklijke School voor Nuttige en Beeldende kunsten (Royal School for Practical and Visual Arts) in Den Bosch and learned woodworking from his father. After holding posts at the studio of the architect Josephus Hubertus (Pierre) Cuypers, among others, Vreugde started working in his own studio in Haarlem in 1900. From 1903 to 1919 he was also a teacher in figure modelling at the School voor Kunstnijverheid (School for Applied Arts). MTH

deposit these inherited objects. This reaffirms that it is probably the most important Dutch public institution where colonial history, the development of colonial society and decolonization can be traced in a tangible form, and from many perspectives. The museum has intended to present this self-reflection to its visitors in the new exhibition 'The Netherlands East Indies, a colonial history'. The centre of the exhibition is staged as a 'colonial theatre' with seven characters who, as historical archetypes, represent a community of collectors. By a range of examples, this imagined community of colonialists and their objects are present in this book as well.

Colonial culture, politics and citizenship in the Netherlands

The renewed appreciation in the Tropenmuseum's exhibitions of the collection and its reorientation towards the history of how these objects came together during the colonial era, aims to achieve a double goal. Museologically, the museum intends to put cultural objects in the spotlight as a universal heritage with great aesthetic value and historical/ethnographic meaning. It also aims to provide insight into the circles of collectors, their mutual relationships, motives for and views about a colonialism within which many specific relationships developed between the different population groups, their art and culture. This historical approach aims at a new form of 'collaboration', intended to share histories through new connections with source communities in Indonesia whose histories are also kept in the objects collected in Amsterdam. And this approach has topical significance for Dutch postcolonial society as well. By addressing colonial history as a history of the once colonizers, the Tropenmuseum tries to recall how views of 'citizenship' and belonging – concepts of what it means to be Dutch – have changed between colonial and postcolonial times. Dutch citizenship perhaps initially got its clearest outline within the transnational colonial context of the Netherlands East Indies. Overseas and far from home, the Dutch easily could identify with a Dutch nation beyond the political or religious fragmentation that existed at home. As the members of a minority European community, it was easier to identify themselves by what they shared with one another in terms of values and standards, culture and physical appearance. Both satisfaction and discomfort about their role in Indonesian society was part of being Dutch in the colony.[4]

Many members of this 20th-century colonial elite from Europe lived and worked in the colony with dedication and a full appreciation of both the Indonesian population and the great (economic) potential of the area. However, colonial society knew many mechanisms of exclusion, especially regarding the indigenous Indonesian and the Chinese people. Only a minority of the Europeans were conscious and open to what was at stake for that population, and few joined their cause. The nationalist leader Soetan Sjahrir who had studied in the Netherlands, and was exiled to Upper Digul after his arrest in 1934, wrote to his fiancée in the Netherlands about 'the colony of the Europeans, (...) who are as distant from us as the continent of Europe, perhaps even farther removed, since Europe can at least be reached by ship and air. But the social barriers, racial segregation in colonial society, are much more difficult to bridge.'[5] Sjahrir analysed this situation as a major problem created by the existence of sharp ethnic contrasts that developed as a result of consciously created social barriers. This problem was ignored or even maintained by the Dutch. As a result most colonialists had no feeling, let alone sympathy for the broad support for the Indonesian independence movement among the native population. (Fig. 17, 18)

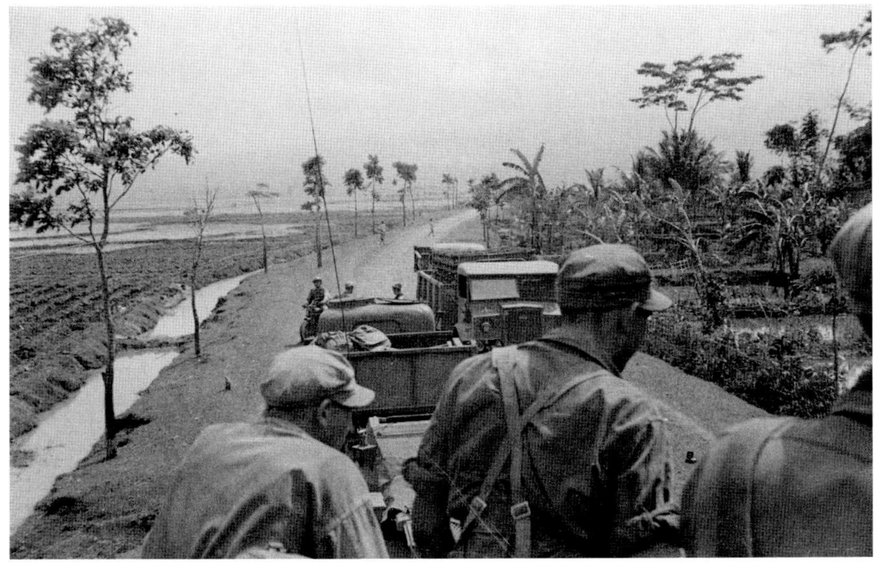

17
Agresi militer Belanda or military column during the first Police Action, Java 1947
Photographer: Cees J. Taillie (1920-2005)
Acetate negative
2.4 x 3.6 cm
10029179. Gift: C.J. Taillie, 2004

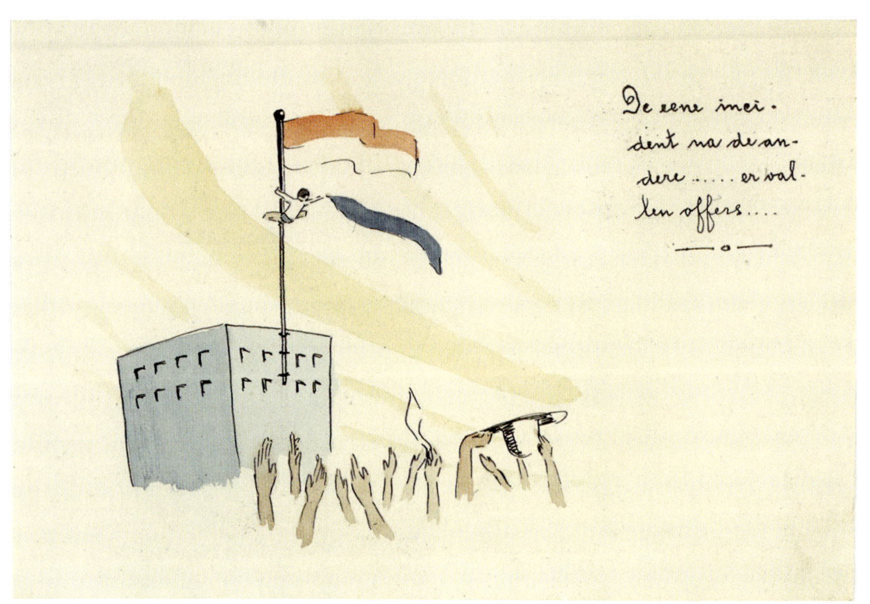

18
Dutch flag from which the blue is being removed
Paper
16 x 23 cm
East Java, Madiun
1949
5635-6. Purchase: C.J. Littel, 1996

19
Poster
Hendrik Paulides (1892-1967)
Jubilee Exhibition in the Koloniaal Instituut 1938
Paper
105.1 x 74 cm
5877-149. Gift: KIT Library, 2004

In those years, the Koloniaal Museum did not explicitly pay attention to this topic either. Although focused on Indonesian art and culture, it was in the Netherlands one of the exponents of the growing gap between Europeans and Indonesian people in overseas colonial society. (Fig. 19) And the museum was criticized for that role. When in the Netherlands East Indies the Ethical Policy turned repressive in view of the emerging Indonesian nationalism, supporters of Indonesian nationalism in the Netherlands, among whom Indonesian students, challenged the Koloniaal Museum as well. In that context the progressive cultural magazine *Links Richten* in 1933 published the poem 'Colonial Institute': 'They organized Beauty and Crafts / Coolly on view, with label, behind glass / They stole the dreams of a people / To put them on display for only a dime...'[6]
Today, in 'Eastward Bound!', in which these same objects returned in the glass showcases with new labels by the current museum staff, this critique is presented as a historical critique. The same objects are now staged for entirely different visitors in a social environment entirely different from the one that existed in the Netherlands in the 1930s. It is in this present day context that the museum has historicized its own display tradition by showing how the Koloniaal Museum highlighted the Netherlands as a colonial power through colonial art. This is connected to issues of citizenship through the challenge it poses to today's discourse about Dutch society, which suggests that the Netherlands used to be a homogenous society that for the first time was confronted with ethnic and cultural diversity due to recent immigration. In this discourse, the colonial experience in Dutch society is ignored and 'colonialism' reduced to just a political history that ended when the Netherlands recognised Indonesian sovereignty at the Round Table Conference in December 1949.
The history of the collectors of the Tropenmuseum shows, however, how before the second world war, just one or two generations ago, colonialism implied a cultural diversity and transnational orientation with peculiar modes of inclusion and exclusion not only overseas but in Dutch society as well. The many recent donations to the Tropenmuseum collection confirm that in many families these historical experiences extend into the present day. The same can be said about contemporary literary, film and art productions that also address the cultural diversity of and the often problematic memories about the colonial past. (Fig. 20)

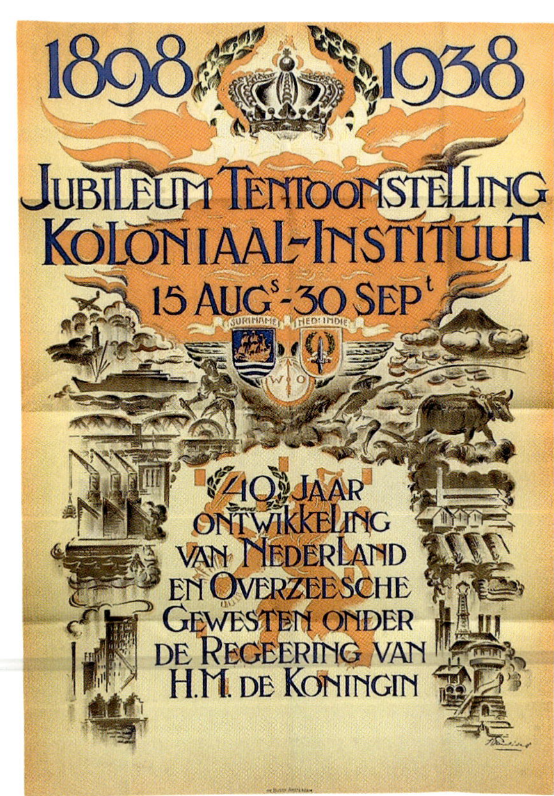

CHAIR FROM PASSENGER SHIP

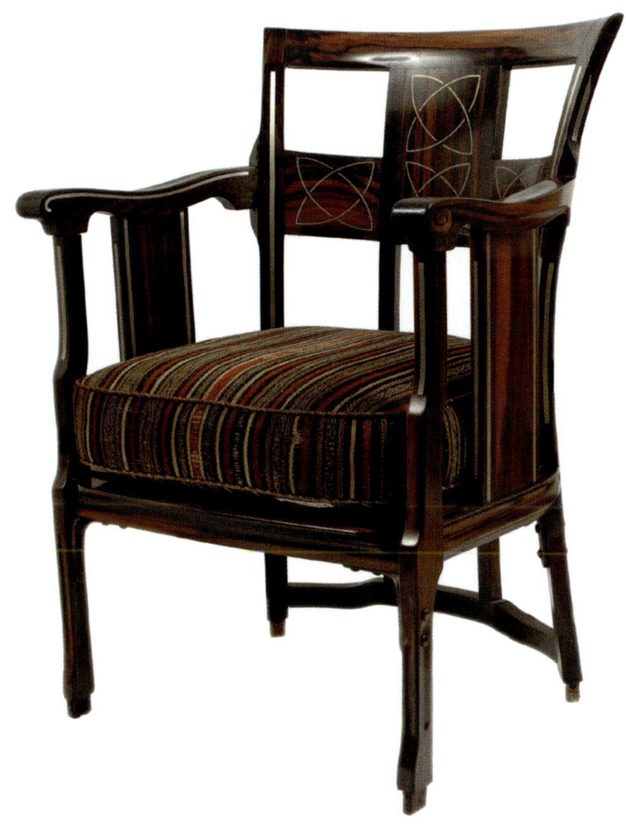

20
Chair from the passenger ship
MS *Johan van Oldebarnevelt*
C.A. Lion Cachet (1864-1945)
Wood
87 x 58 x 61.5 cm
1928-1930
3344-1a/b. Gift: Stoomvaart Maatschappij Nederland N.V., 1963

From 1928 to 1930, the Stoomvaart Maatschappij Nederland built the passenger ship MS Johan van Oldebarnevelt. C.A. Lion Cachet (1864-1945) designed the entire lounge: furniture, wooden wall ornaments, carpets and gobelin tapestry. It was one of the most luxurious ships to sail between the Netherlands and the Netherlands East Indies. It could accommodate up to 338 1st class passengers, 281 2nd class passengers and 64 3rd class passengers. In 1951 it was converted into an emigrant ship and sold to a Greek ship owner in 1963. That same year it caught fire and sank.
This oriental chair had legs that were reinforced with lead to hold it in place during stormy weather. It is one of the many objects from the category of colonial furniture in which the influence of Indonesian artisans/artists in the Netherlands was made visible. Lion Cachet and his colleagues from the Arts and Crafts movement experimented in the Koloniaal Museum with batik and Indonesian motifs, and integrated them into their designs for chairs, lamps, wallpaper, book covers, banknotes and ornamentation in architecture (also Fig. 78, 102). SL

After Indonesian independence, the notion of 'transnational' citizenship that existed in the colonial context of the Netherlands and the Netherlands East Indies could disappear from the public sphere because so few of the Dutch had thought about this fundamental change in what it would mean to be Dutch without the vast colony in the East. The Koloniaal Instituut had anticipated that it would be appropriate to abandon the term 'Colonial' and establish a new kind of Commonwealth relationship. But nearly five years of diplomatic and armed struggle had followed. While many postcolonial migrants came or returned to the Netherlands, as a rule there was little appetite for a public debate on the social-cultural history of the Dutch presence in the former colony and its impact on contemporary society. Most people simply kept quiet about the past, and the former Koloniaal Museum moved with the current. The fact that by the 1970s the majority of the collection from Indonesia had been quietly stored in depots to make way for a presentation about developing countries was part of this silence. In retrospect, we can see that the 1970s policy change at the Tropenmuseum reflected the way in which colonial culture disappeared from Dutch public life in general, surviving mainly in the private sphere of family experiences.

Museological interpretations of colonial history

When the Tropenmuseum decided to present this history as the institutional history of a former Koloniaal Museum, the first step was to decide what was colonial about the museum. Colonialism was defined as the settlement of people in foreign regions, the subsequent colonisation (use, exploitation and development) of the natural resources and the domination by the colonizing country of its inhabitants. In the

COLONIAL THEATRE

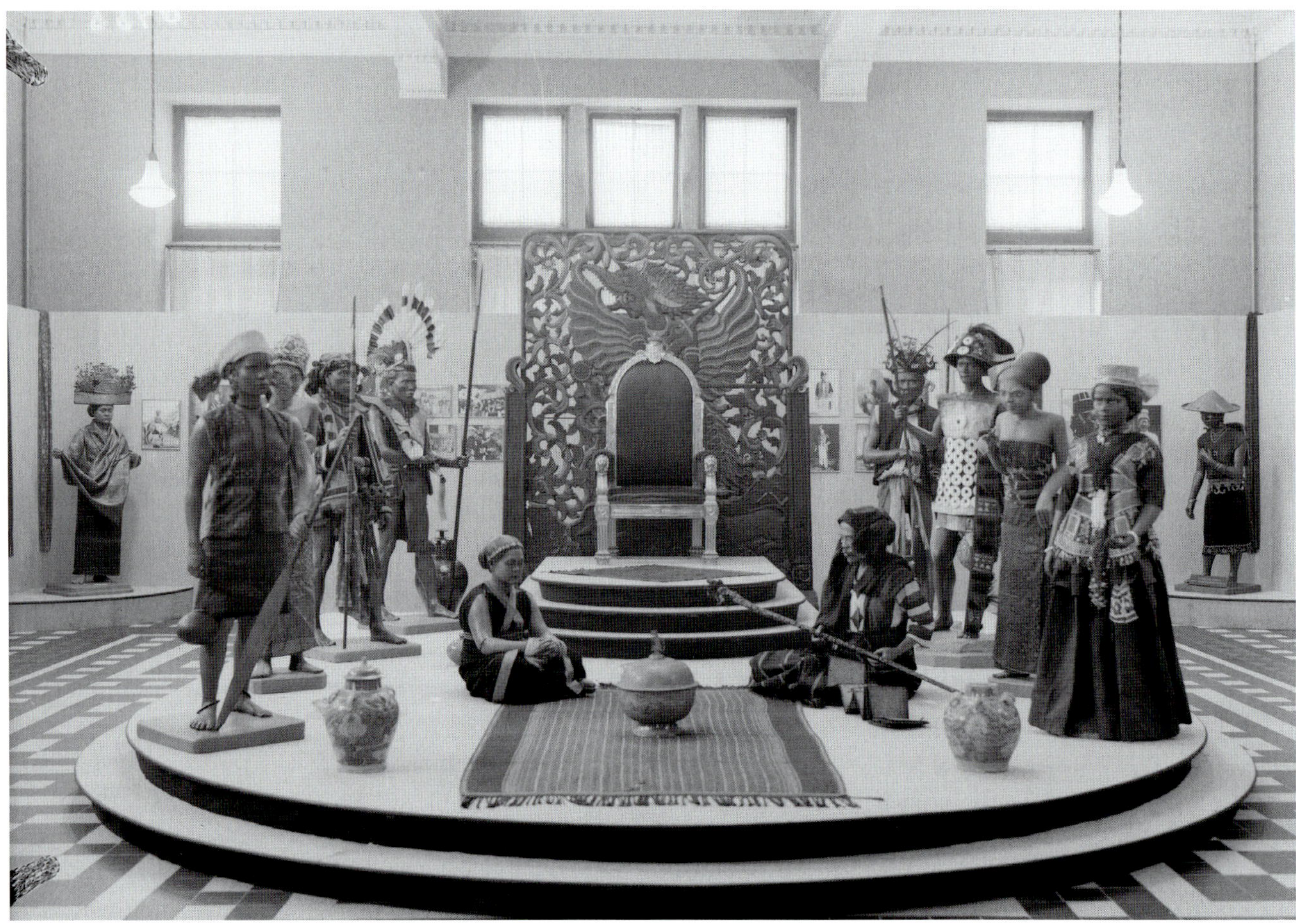

21
The symbolic throne of Queen Wilhelmina surrounded by peoples of the Netherlands East Indies, exhibited at the Jubilee Exhibition in the Koloniaal Instituut of 1938
Glass negative
13 x 18 cm
10000091

How to display the collectors that contributed to the collections of the Koloniaal Instituut? Essential in this conceptualization process has been this photograph of an exhibition in 1938, mounted to celebrate the 40 years jubilee of Queen Wilhelmina who in 1898 had ascended to the throne. At the centre of that exhibition was a throne referring to the Queen. It was surrounded by various life sized wax figures. They are idealized ethnic types representing those Indonesian people who had become colonial subjects during her 40 years of rule. Ethnographic museums have a long tradition in displaying such representations of ethnic types. Although almost real in their appearance, it was never suggested that these were individuals. In the 1970s they were removed from the museum displays; black and white photographs of persons blown up to life size (and sometimes cut out from the context of the photograph to bring them closer to the exhibition scene) took their place. In the exhibition 'The Netherlands East Indies, a colonial history', this photograph has been mirrored, decentralized, and turned into a historically specific image. The Queen now has a positive image, presented in the form of her sculpted portrait in the museum collection, of the 'W' on the buttons of the colonial uniforms, as well as the Dutch national flag that until 27 December 1949 belonged to the port authorities office of Tanjung Priok. It was donated to the Tropenmuseum in 2003, by the widow of the Dutch administrator who had lowered it there for the last time.

Another reversal exists in the seven life size figures. They are no longer ethnic types, as in 1938, but seven historical archetypes, with individualized traits, representing seven positions within the colonial order: the highest colonial official, the artist, the soldier in the Koninklijk Nederlandsch-Indisch Leger (Royal Netherlands Indies Army, KNIL), the 'inlandse' (indigenous) administrator, the European house wife, the missionary wife and the tobacco planter. Three of these characters represent real historical persons: Governor General Bonifacius de Jonge; tobacco planter Jacob Theodoor Cremer who also was one of the founders of the Koloniaal Instituut; and visual artist Charles Sayers. Two others are famous characters from literary fiction by Dutch authors who lived in the East Indies: the indigenous administrator Toewan Anwar from the novel *De raadsman* (1958) by H.J. Friedericy and the KNIL-soldier Willem Kleyntjes from Maria Dermoût's *De tienduizend dingen* (1955). Two women, finally, represent life stories based on a compilation of a number of memoires and autobiographies: the (fictive) nurse-missionary Anna Elink-van Maarseveen and the (likewise fictive) wive of a Dutch military officer Margaretha Engelen-Koets. They are surrounded by three persons from the historical exhibition, who have been restored and dressed up in order to play a historical role in the colonial theatre, instead of representing an ethnic type: a teacher, a seamstress, and a clerk. And in the two flanks of the display two other characters are staged: the blind Georg Everhard Rumphius from the end of the 17th century, and the anthropologist Charles Le Roux with his photo camera from the early 20th century.

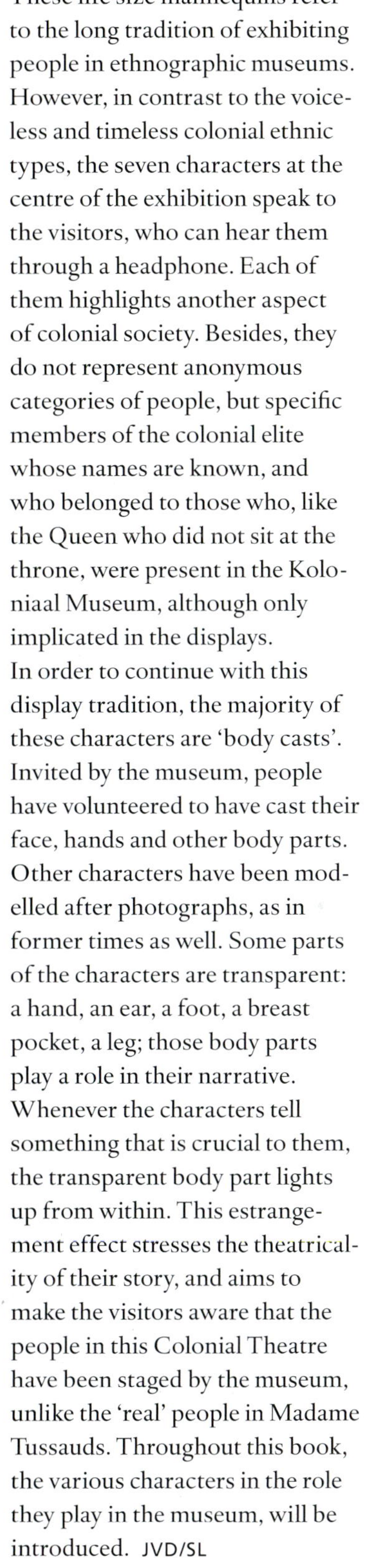

These life size mannequins refer to the long tradition of exhibiting people in ethnographic museums. However, in contrast to the voiceless and timeless colonial ethnic types, the seven characters at the centre of the exhibition speak to the visitors, who can hear them through a headphone. Each of them highlights another aspect of colonial society. Besides, they do not represent anonymous categories of people, but specific members of the colonial elite whose names are known, and who belonged to those who, like the Queen who did not sit at the throne, were present in the Koloniaal Museum, although only implicated in the displays.

In order to continue with this display tradition, the majority of these characters are 'body casts'. Invited by the museum, people have volunteered to have cast their face, hands and other body parts. Other characters have been modelled after photographs, as in former times as well. Some parts of the characters are transparent: a hand, an ear, a foot, a breast pocket, a leg; those body parts play a role in their narrative. Whenever the characters tell something that is crucial to them, the transparent body part lights up from within. This estrangement effect stresses the theatricality of their story, and aims to make the visitors aware that the people in this Colonial Theatre have been staged by the museum, unlike the 'real' people in Madame Tussauds. Throughout this book, the various characters in the role they play in the museum, will be introduced. JVD/SL

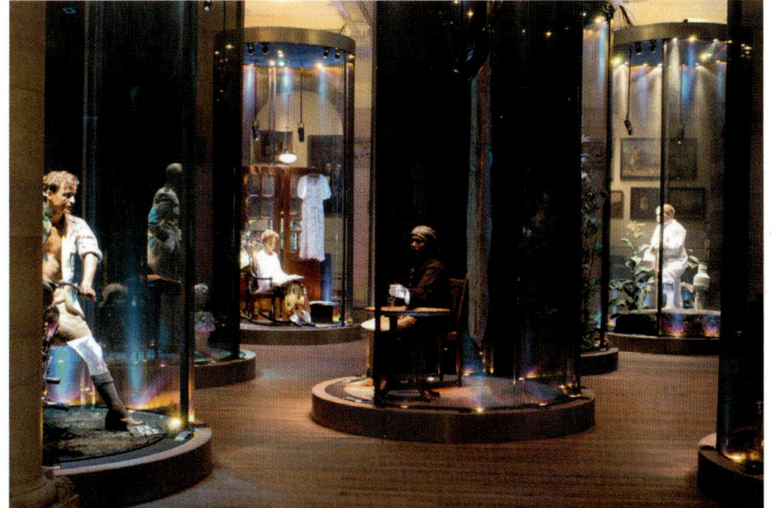

22
Overview of the colonial theatre in the exhibition 'The Netherlands East Indies, a colonial history'
2002

context of the Netherlands East Indies, the term refers to the settlement and expansion of the Dutch in the Indonesian archipelago, starting around 1600 and ended around 1949 (Indonesia) and 1963 (Irian Jaya/Papua). From the objects and the history of their collection, four periods can be distinguished, with transitions marked by various kinds of military conflict. First is the period of trade-driven colonialism of the Republic of the Seven United Provinces of the Netherlands, exercised by the Verenigde Oost-Indische Compagnie (Dutch East India Company, VOC, 1600-1799). Jan Pieterszoon Coen at the main entrance of today's KIT refers to this first period of trade colonialism. Second is the period of colonial expansion after the defeat of Napoleon and the restoration of the authority of the now Kingdom of the Netherlands in the East. It resulted in the establishment and expansion of a political, military and legally defined colonial administration during the 19th century (1800-1900), with the Aceh war as the last campaign for what was called the territorial 'completion' of the Netherlands East Indies. In those years the Ethical Policy was formulated, lasting until the end of effective Dutch administration in the Second World War (1901-1940/2), followed by decolonisation, which in military terms began with the Japanese invasion in 1942 and politically ended with the transfer of sovereignty in 1949, though the process had begun much earlier (at the start of the 20th century) and maybe continues to the present day.

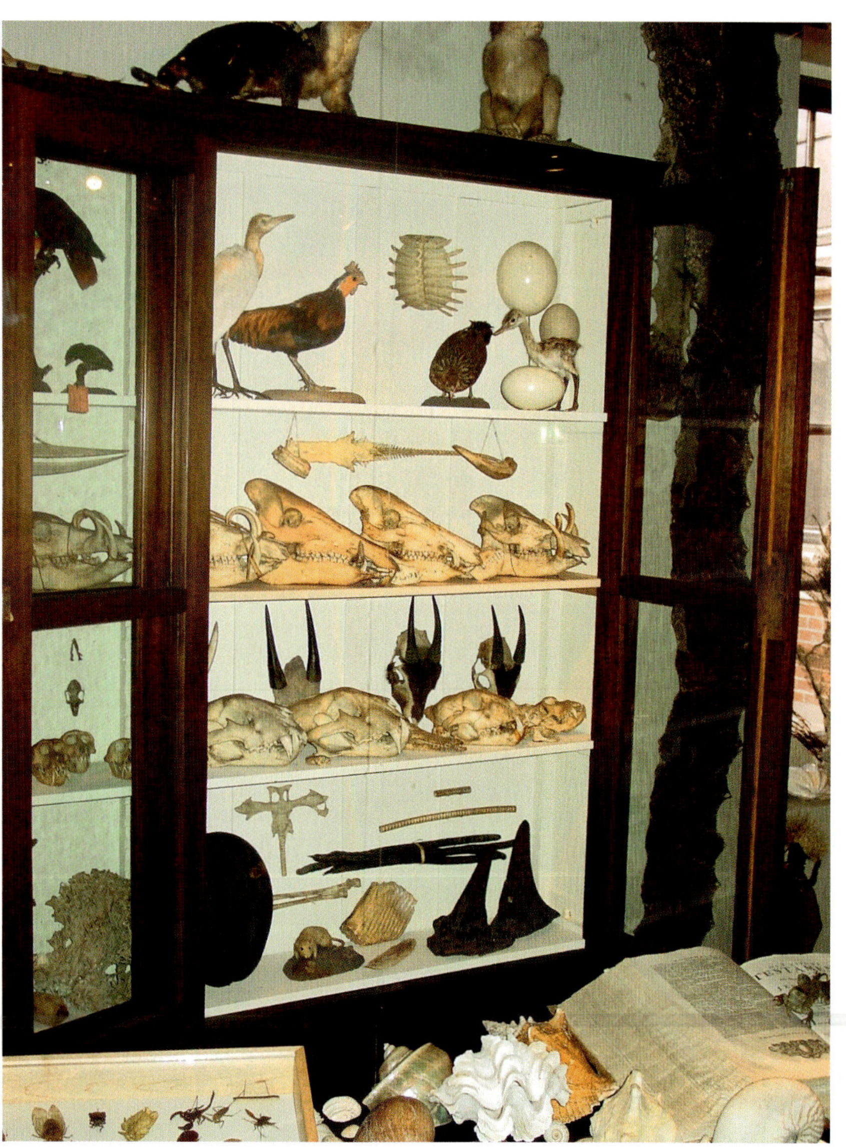

23
Impression of Rumphius' Cabinet of Curiosities in the exhibition 'The Netherlands East Indies, a colonial history'
2002

The Tropenmuseum focused its historical exhibition on the third period, 1901-1942. It is the period that in Indonesia and the Netherlands today still is remembered from firsthand experience, and the period in which most of the ethnographic collections were acquired. The recent acquisition of objects from European colonial culture often dates from this period as well. In these years the Dutch were most confident about their colonial policy, in which the museum building itself takes shape, and at the same time they did not acknowledge that they also were losing contact with Indonesian society.

Next to this periodization, the Tropenmuseum defined different types of collection history, addressing different but overlapping 'spheres' of collecting. Acquisition of objects in the colonial context could be the result of the collectors' amazement and wonder as they learned about other peoples and cultures, but also of conflicts associated with their desire to exchange, to possess and to control. Other forms of collecting happened as an aspect of cohabitation and intercourse, of the blending of cultures and the inspiration this generated, and in the process of exchange of knowledge. Or the act of collecting was interlinked with economic exploitation and scientific and cultural appropriation.

In the exhibition on Dutch colonialism, a grid with on the one hand historical periods and on the other 'spheres' of colonial collecting, has served as a means to present different perspectives on colonial society. Rumphius' Cabinet of Curiosities from the first phase of the colonial history, for instance, was chosen as icon for collecting as a strategy to explore unknown worlds. (Fig. 23)

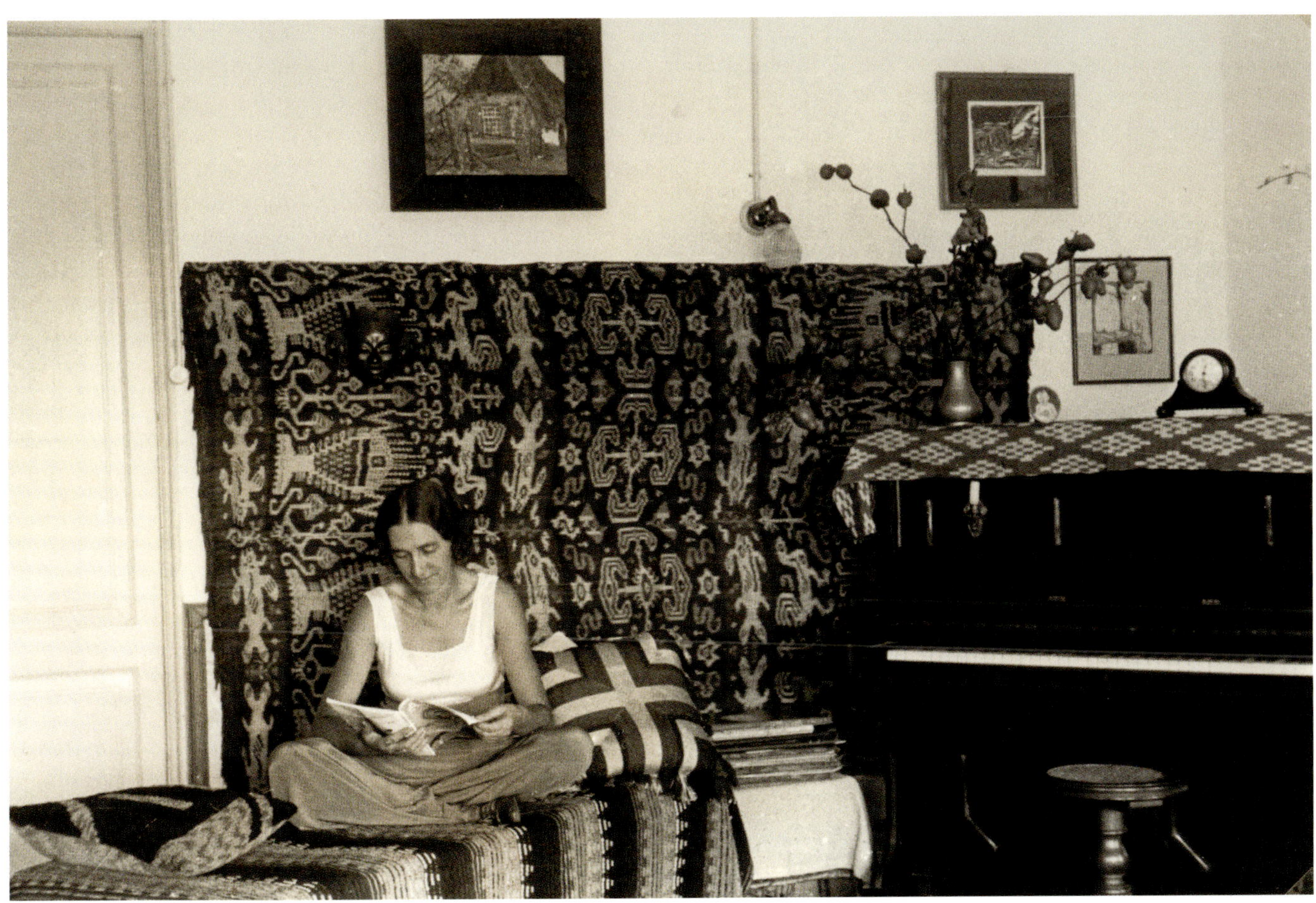

24
Photograph from a family album, woman reading on divan, Java
Gelatin silver print
8.3 x 12.2 cm
c. 1935
60045205. Gift: G.A. de Mol, 1954

A display case with the museum's collection of precious weapons reflects the ambivalences of the endeavour to discover, conquer and establish administrative control in the 19th century. Some weapons bear witness to the disarming of the local population. Other weapons, such as an honorary sabre, reflect the appreciation of the brave actions of a Dutch soldier during an open colonial conflict. Living together – the intimate contact between the coloniser and the colonised and the personal position of women and children in the colonial system – is presented in connection to the East Indies colonial household. The family album, with photographs that were meant to provide the people back home with a picture of life overseas, best represents the collection associated with it. (Fig. 24) The inspiration generated by Indonesian culture as a source and a model for individual creativity, leading to all kinds of culturally hybrid objects, is represented by the rich batik collections, the Yogya silver, or the East Indies Western style paintings. (Fig. 25) On display as well are scaled objects, like a boat model, that served as conversation pieces and visual proof during interviews of local craftsmen by ethnographers. Other objects testify how language politics and education policy were at the same time instruments for strengthening contact and instruments of alienation. Objects like sample collections are euphemisms of economic exploitation, linked to scientific research into natural resources, for instance, food, industrial raw materials or energy sources, linked as well to the development of the transport sector, communication technology, and medical science. And finally, presenting the Netherlands as a colonial power by exhibiting the Netherlands East Indies at international exhibitions in Europe, resulted among others into rich collections of models and miniatures of people, houses, animals, scenes from daily life or special occasions. As a colony in miniature, they became a kind of index of the expertise and the many objects brought together in the Koloniaal Museum.

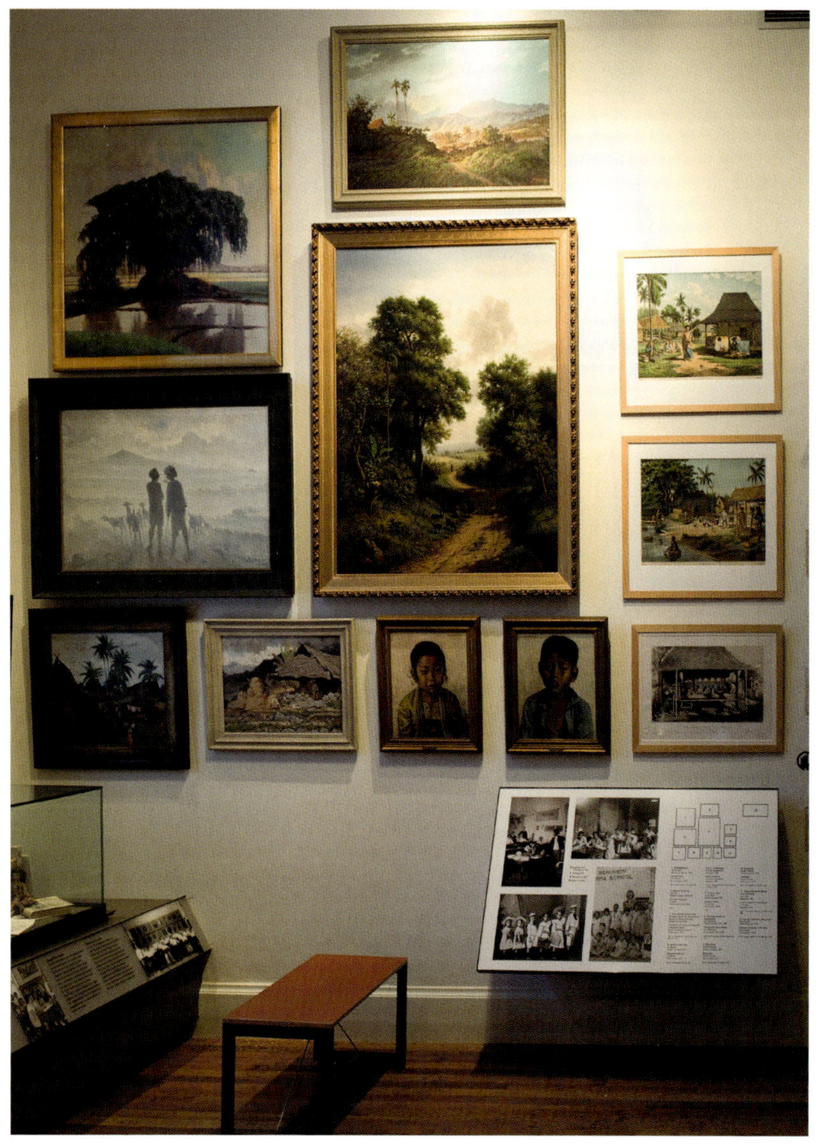

The essays in this book elaborate on these 'collection spheres' that organize the exhibition in the Tropenmuseum: on control and warfare, contact and cultural exchange, exploration and exploitation, education and exposition. Eight invited authors have each chosen a different perspective on these subjects, responding to the representation of colonial history in the Tropenmuseum as a history of collecting objects. Their essays are supplemented by descriptions of specific objects, collections and collectors. Through this multifaceted structure, this publication is meant to be a contribution to what might become the next phase in the 'decolonisation' of the Tropenmuseum's collections, beyond the colonial perspective. This next phase is important because the most outspoken (and contested) conceptual decision in 'The Netherlands East Indies, a colonial history' has been to present colonial society from the museum's own institutional perspective. The exhibition is first and foremost an interpretation of the colonizers' perspective on colonial society during the era of Ethical Policy. Colonial views are centre stage, linked to those who gave shape to the Koloniaal Instituut, provided information and objects, and helped shape the interpretations of art, culture and society in Indonesia that accompanies the objects until today. Of course some collectors were outspoken in their anti-colonialism, and some also will have disagreed with the statement made by Governor General De Jonge in 1936 (and repeated in the display) that the Dutch would need to remain in the Netherlands East Indies for another 300 years. (Fig. 26) Visitors who

25
Wall with paintings in the exhibition 'The Netherlands East Indies, a colonial history'
2010

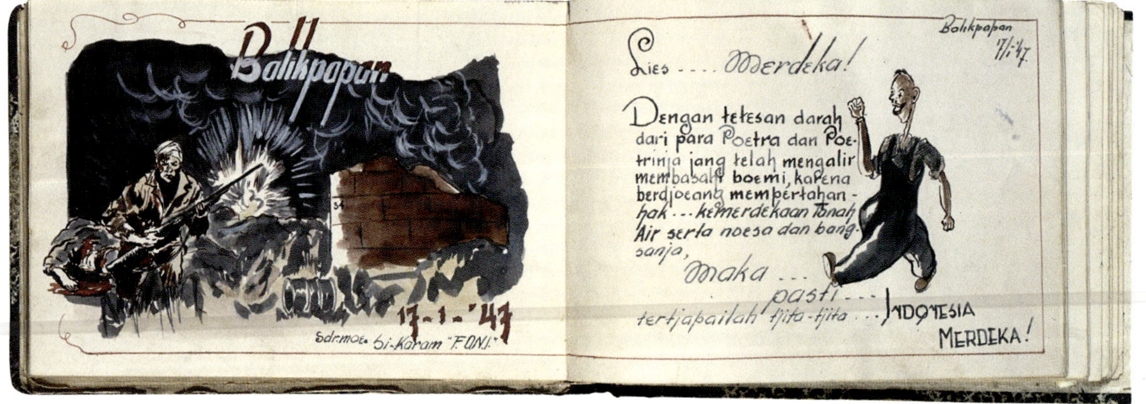

26
Indonesia Merdeka! Free Indonesia. Album amicorum of Lies Aini
Paper, paint
14 x 21 x 2 cm
Indonesian. Jakarta
1946
6065-5. Through the mediation of M.J. Hillerström, 1970s

ANNA ELINK-VAN MAARSEVEEN – MISSIONARY WIFE (1887-1961)

She attended teacher training college in Leeuwarden, followed by nurse's training. They were training programmes which she hoped would enable her to make a practical contribution to improving the welfare of the Indonesian people.
She left for the Netherlands East Indies in 1917 to join her husband Johan Elink, whom she had married 'by proxy' when she was still in the Netherlands and he was already working in the East Indies as a minister.
The Dutch Reformed Church sent the couple to a new missionary area in South-east Sulawesi. Anna Elink-Van Maarseveen was included in the exhibition as a model representing people who went to the Netherlands East Indies full of idealism. JVD

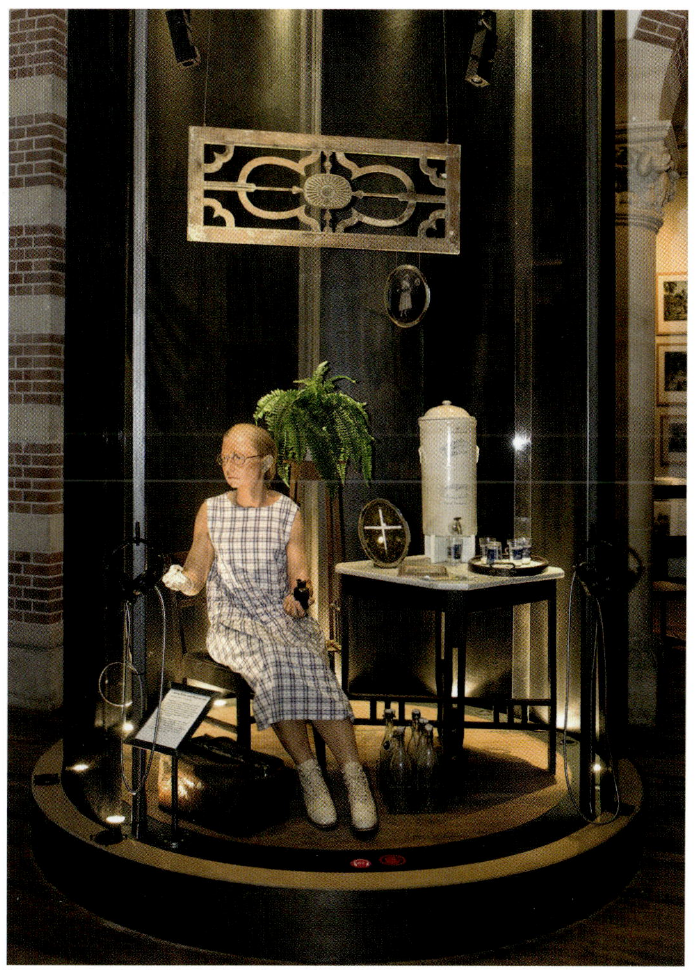

want to hear those voices can find them in the exhibition, like those of the Indonesian nationalists, leaders of rebellions or idealistic Indonesian resistance members. They are present in the picture created by the Tropenmuseum in its galleries. But their presence is deliberately an implied one, just as was the case in the dominant image of the Netherlands East Indies in the Netherlands at the time.
With this dedicated representation of a colonial perspective, the Tropenmuseum is marking time for now and for a new interpretation of collaboration as sharing histories. In the stories that lie hidden behind the collections, one can find not only a history of contact and control, but also a history of resistance and protest; a history not only of affectionate cultural blending and the inspiration it generated, but also of brutal oppression and annexation. Developing one side of the story without on beforehand filling in the other side of the story as well, is intended to weaken the authority of the institution by making it vulnerable for critique and offer possibilities for counter narratives and a dialogue on history. The structure of this collection book is intended to contribute to this dialogue.

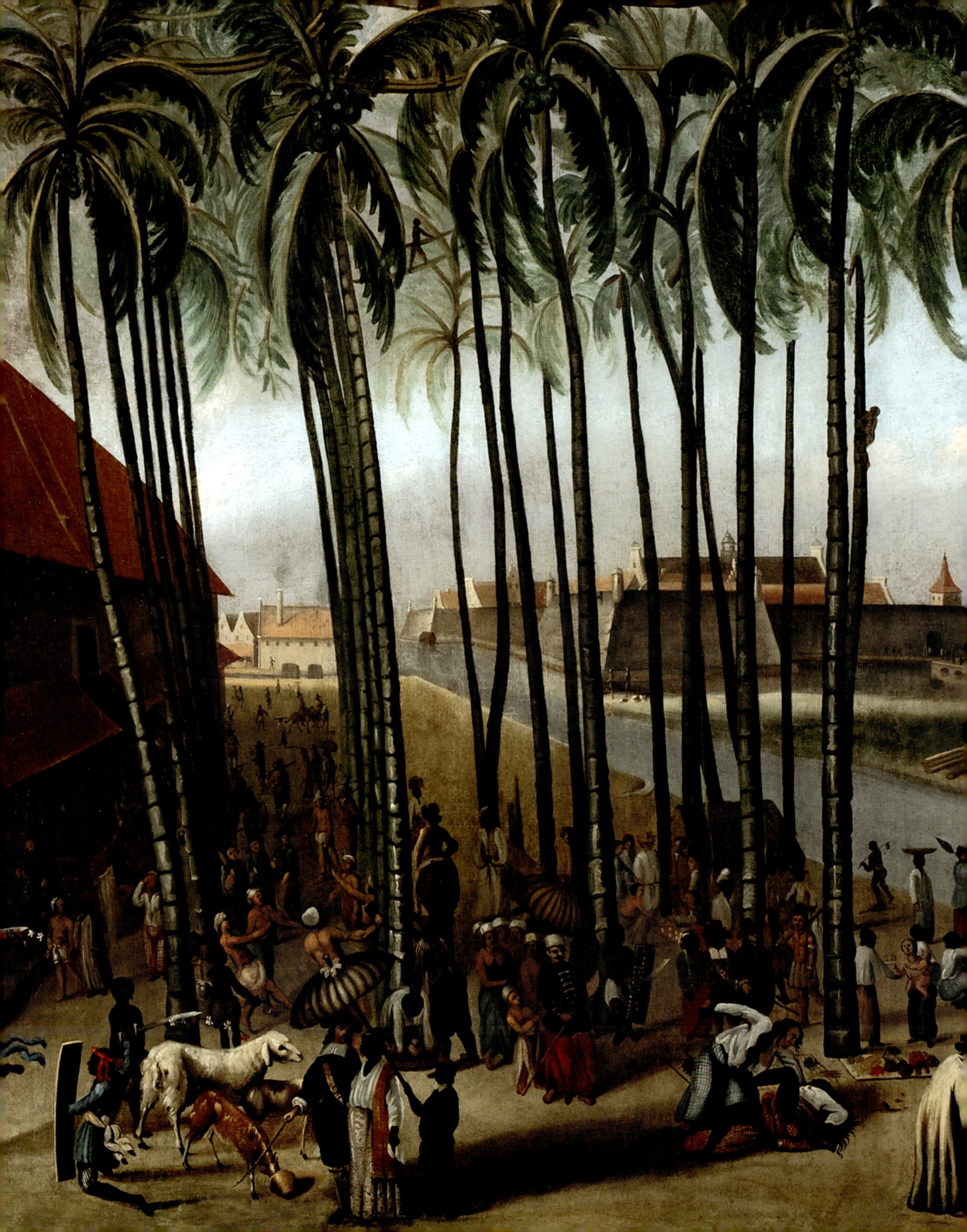

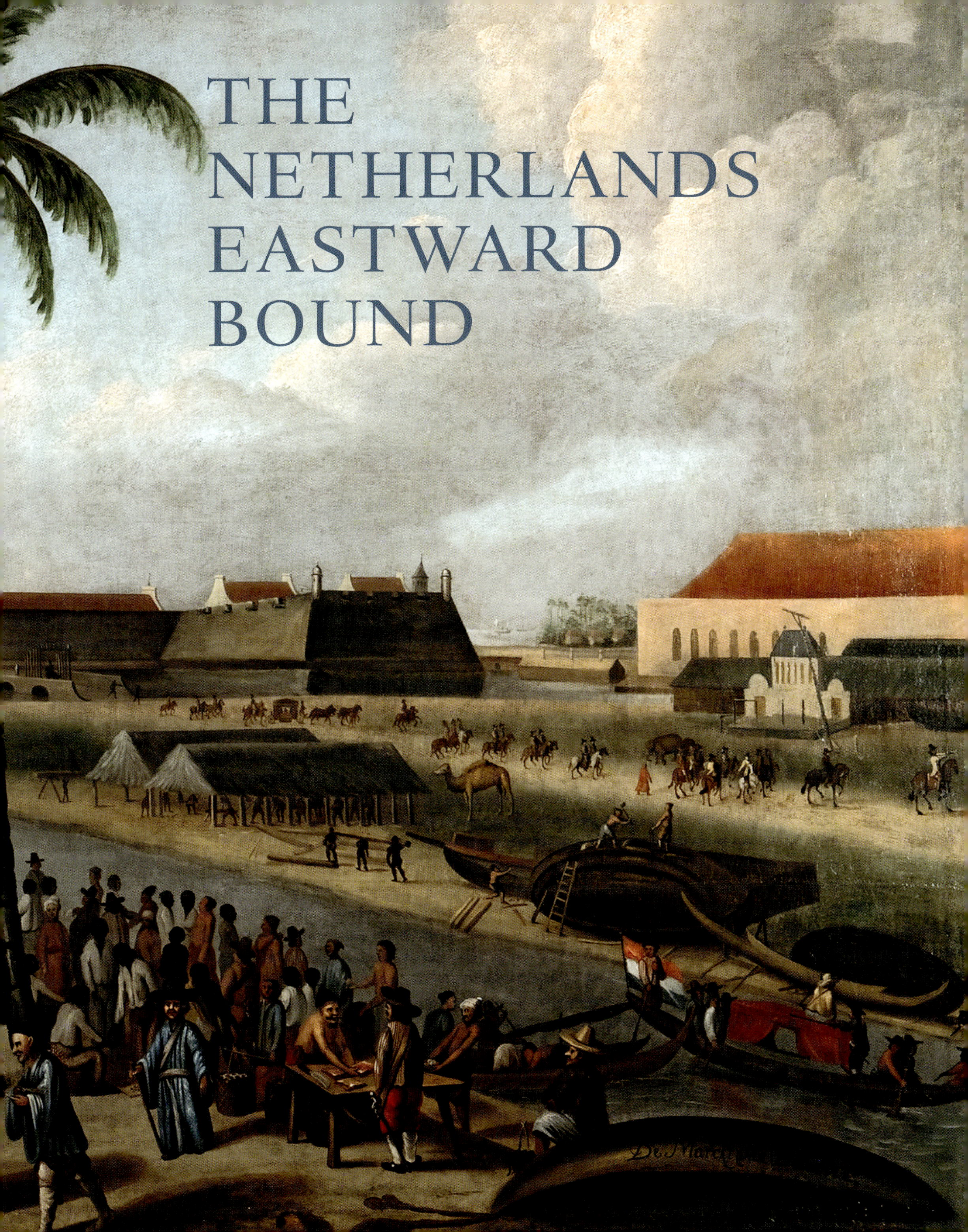
THE
NETHERLANDS
EASTWARD
BOUND

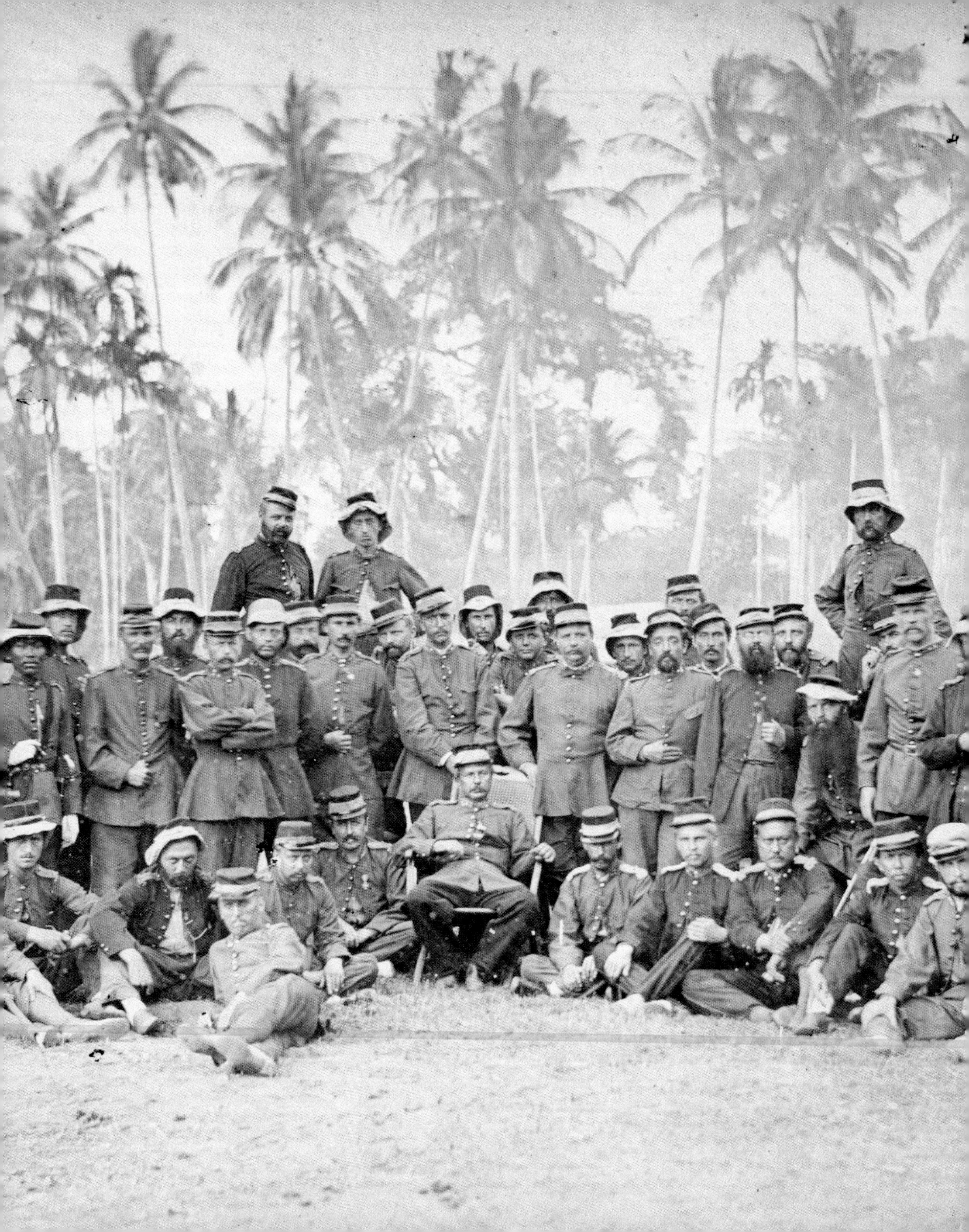

THE RESONANCE OF VIOLENCE IN COLLECTIONS

HARM STEVENS

Repression and violence may be seen as significant cornerstones of the display of power by the Dutch in the East Indian archipelago. A museum that wants to focus on this unpleasant aspect of Dutch colonialism is faced with a difficult task. Established museums in the Netherlands, and the Tropenmuseum in particular, are institutes that have traditionally presented an idealised image of the colony rather than a picture that reveals the sharp edges of this Dutch overseas adventure. The museums of today are the inheritors of institutions that were originally intended to legitimise Dutch colonial rule to the public. Interest in the darker sides of this rule is simply not embedded in the fibre of these institutes. Anyone wanting to show that occasionally a certain type of nightmare emerged from the dark heart of the colony – in contrast to the colonial dream of benevolent progress and a beneficial alliance between East and West – must row against the strong current of this museum tradition.

To illustrate the aggressive, intimidating character of Dutch colonialism, the historian Henk Schulte Nordholt cites an incident in May 1886 in his article 'A genealogy of violence' in which a protest by farmers near Bogor (former Buitenzorg) on the island of Java was nipped in the bud by the fatal gunfire of the colonial troops deployed. These troops proceeded to amuse themselves by pretending the protest was a shooting competition and that the people in the crowd were targets. Within minutes, 40 of the unarmed farmers lay dead and seventy were wounded. The soldiers and even several civilian vigilante marksmen were passionately encouraged by the local *assistent-resident*. The soldier who shot the leader of the protest march was personally treated to a dinner that evening by a prominent representative of the colonial administration. Just an incident, perhaps, but it was an incident that was full of significance because, according to Schulte Nordholt: '[...] in just a few sentences, the door of the colonial club is opened, showing a glimpse of the brutal colonial mentality that lies hidden behind the bureaucratic decency of the archives'.[7]

The question is whether the exhibition entitled 'Eastward Bound!' in the Tropenmuseum, and particularly the section named 'Cloves and powder', provides what Schulte Nordholt observed in that singular incident: admission to the 'colonial club' and a revealing glimpse of colonial use of violence. The door of the colonial club will, in any case, briskly be thrown open to museum visitors. The museum building itself can be seen as the brick edifice of the old colonial club. The institute was created at the high point of Dutch colonialism in the first quarter of the 20th century

<< See Fig. 216

27
Officers of the 3rd Brigade of the KNIL, Aceh
Albumin print
23.6 x 30.4 cm
1874
60003282

as Koloniaal Instituut. The architecture and décor unavoidably express the ideology of the colonial club. This auspicious message is borne in the polished and stylised version that befits this cathedral of Dutch entrepreneurship overseas: a historical façade of colonial civility that pushes colonial violence and oppression into the background with a grand and forceful gesture.

The affected civility of the building is then continued without problem in the displayed collection, a significant part of which was meant as a monument to the envisaged colony. The painting created by Nicolaas Pieneman in the 1830s on the commission of H.M. Baron de Kock is a striking example of such an idealised memorial. (Fig. 28) The title of the painting, a loan from the Rijksmuseum to the Tropenmuseum, is placed on the gilded list in a cartouche: 'The subjection of the chief rebel Diepo Negoro to Lieutenant General De Kock. At the end of the war on Java, 1825-1830'.[8] It is the triumphant language that people loved to see in the colonial club.

The image presented on canvas made the picture complete. Prince Diponegoro (1785-1855), was justly reprimanded in a dignified way by the colonial authority in the person of Lieutenant General Baron de Kock, standing on a landing as he gestures with his right arm, his steely eyes fixed on Sergeant Major De Stuers. Diponegoro descends the steps of the landing and looks out dejectedly over the crowd. In utmost exaltation, two figures kneel at his feet. The background of the dramatic scene is filled by the house of the resident of Magalang on the island of Java. Above the entrance to the building is a Dutch coat of arms. In the middle of the scene, the Dutch flag flies at the summit.

In reality, the scene inside and in front of the resident's house was less 'dignified' than Pieneman and his client De Kock wanted to believe. Under a promise of safe conduct from the Dutch, De Kock had Diponegoro arrested after the latter, in the opinion of De Kock, made much too far-reaching demands on the colonial government during negotiations.

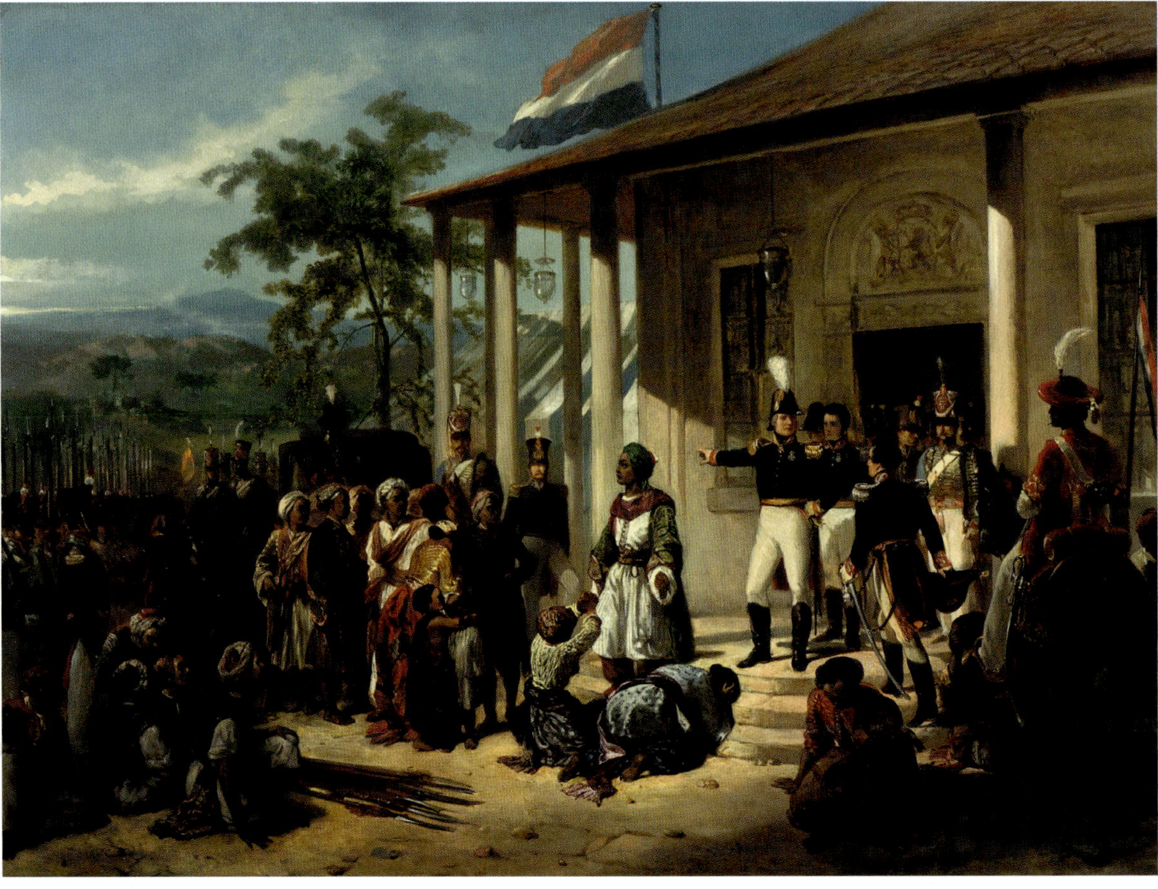

28
The arrest of Prince Diponegoro
Nicolaas Pieneman
(1809-1860)
Paint, linen
77 x 100 cm
1830-1835
6001-3. On loan: Collection Rijksmuseum Amsterdam

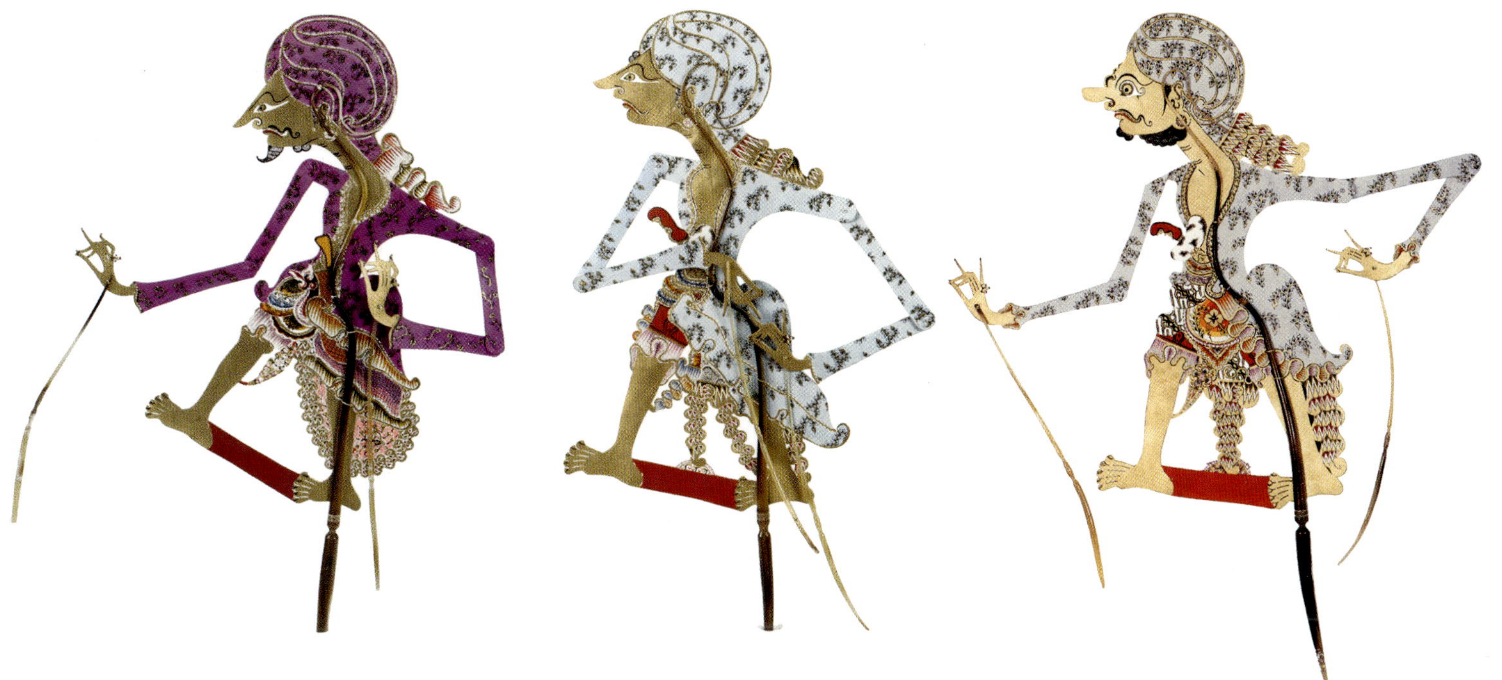

29, 30, 31
Wayang puppets depicting figures from the Java War
Suprapto Amosutijo
From left to right: spiritual leader Kyai Maja, Prince Diponegoro, army leader Sentot
Horn, parchment
74 x 30 cm, 78 x 28.5 cm, 75 x 27 cm
Javanese, Yogyakarta
c. 1979
4551-25, 4551-15, 4551-9
Purchase: Suprapto Amosutijo, 1979

This painting is a product of colonial 'civility', a façade that obscures the view of a less rosy reality. In this painting, the visitor to the 'Eastward Bound!' exhibition is made to feel especially welcome in the colonial club. But does the visitor to 'Eastward Bound!' subsequently also catch a glimpse of 'the brutal colonial mentality that lies hidden behind the bureaucratic civility'? In other words: does the colonial club provide a window from which to view the brutal practices used in the Java War, which in Pieneman's painting seemed to be brought to a close so neatly a war that had cost the lives of some 200,000 Javanese? (Fig. 29-32)

Yes, the window is there, but to open the shutters one has to descend into the cellar of a screen presentation entitled 'Colonial Wars'. A couple of steps removed from Pieneman's idealised picture, a watercolour entitled *Maron in Baglen Anno 1829* (Maron is a village in the Javanes district of Baglen) appears on the screen. A path winds through the hilly landscape to a cemetery located to the right of a settlement. To the left in the foreground, next to the road, eight human heads are perched atop lances. The heads are probably on display as a fearful warning to the adversary. Written in ink is 'the cut-off heads of rebels'.[9] The drawing is not the work of a famous artist, but probably the hurriedly sketched drawing of an eye-witness of Dutch nationality – which can be gleaned from the captions. This provides a direct view of the harsh practices used in the struggle during the Java War. The amateurish watercolour, with the unpolished language of the handwritten caption – 'the cut-off heads of rebels' – is a striking contrast to the academic painting bearing the obligatory language of the conqueror in gilded letters ('the subjection of the chief rebel, etc.'). An idealised, colonial façade of civility and, hidden behind the façade, a glimpse of the violence that was linked with the colonial adventure – that is what these two works of art represent.

We return to the colonial club and take another look at the painting of Pieneman. Lying on the ground, at the feet of the conqueror, we see an indefinable number of lances. They are the weapons of Diponegoro's followers. This theme is clearly meant to be a sign of surrender and subjection to the colonial authorities, whose armed troops stand ready in the painting at left, their bayonets raised proudly in the air, in contrast to the Javanese lances thrown to the ground.

Anyone who keeps the significance of these Javanese lances on Pieneman's canvas in the back of his mind will perhaps look less innocently at the Indonesian weapons which are displayed in horizontal stacks, as a central part (in this exhibition hall) of 'Eastward Bound!', just a few metres away from the painting. (Fig. 33) Do these weapons hang there, too, as a sign of the surrender and subjection to Dutch colonial

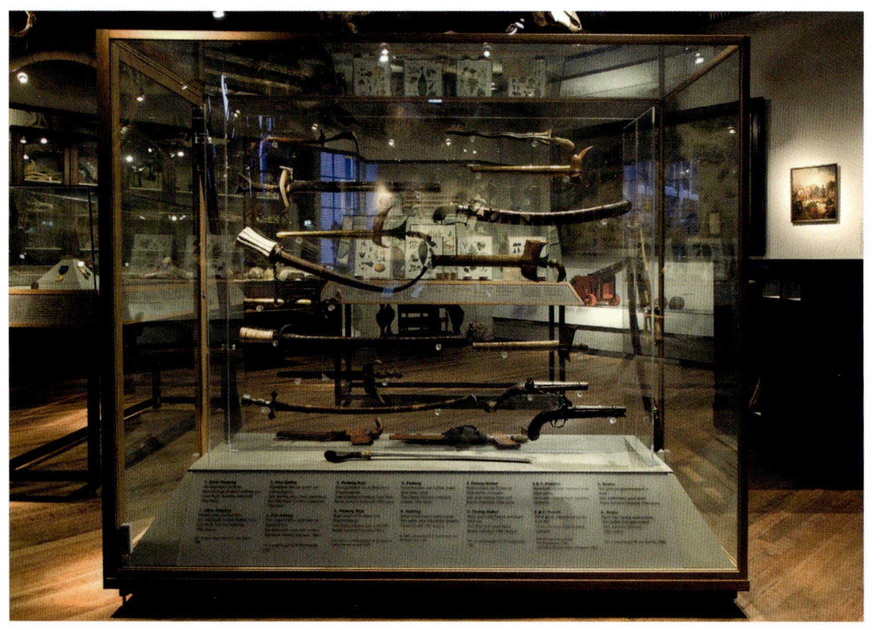

authorities? Are they war trophies, something which also always represents a sign of surrender to the enemy? Or are they the remnants of a bureaucratic measure of the colonial administration (which is a token of dominance in itself), i.e. the structural disarming of the local population, especially in regions that were hotbeds of rebellion? In any case, piece for piece, these weapons bear testimony to the impulse to collect things, which was a fixed part of the Dutch colonial adventure from the very beginning. Thus the display case containing military attributes fits seamlessly with the largest part of the section, which is literally filled to the brim with curiosities from the East. This creates a type of retro-curiosity gallery consisting of a range of flora and fauna and a cross-section of all types of products of native industriousness. Within the colonial club, the systematic interest

WAYANG PUPPET

32
Wayang puppet
Suprapto Amosutijo
Parchment, horn, paint
87.5 x 32 cm
Yogyakarta
c. 1979
4551-20. Purchase: Suprapto Amosutijo, 1979

This wayang puppet is a part of the Wayang Dupara, the wayang theatre that presents historical figures from Java. The puppet depicts the Dutch Lieutenant General Hendrik Merkus Baron de Kock, who imprisoned the Javanese prince Diponegoro and thus brought the Java War to an end. De Kock is wearing a fantasy uniform from the 19th century; on his head sits a three-cornered hat with a feather. His face shows the hallmarks of a Javanese interpretation of Dutchmen: round eyes, a big nose, an open mouth with visible teeth and a prominent beard, moustache and hair on his forehead. According to the iconography of the traditional Javanese wayang, these are the external features of someone with a self-assured and rough or hot-headed character. Official Dutch portraits of De Kock do not show him with a moustache or beard. His golden complexion, lowered gaze and the position of his hands point to the fact that he has self-control, is probably scheming and is from a noble family. His external appearance and size stand out against the delicate, small figures of the Javanese princes. (Fig. 29-31) Two separate attributes belong to this puppet: a cannon and a rifle.
PW

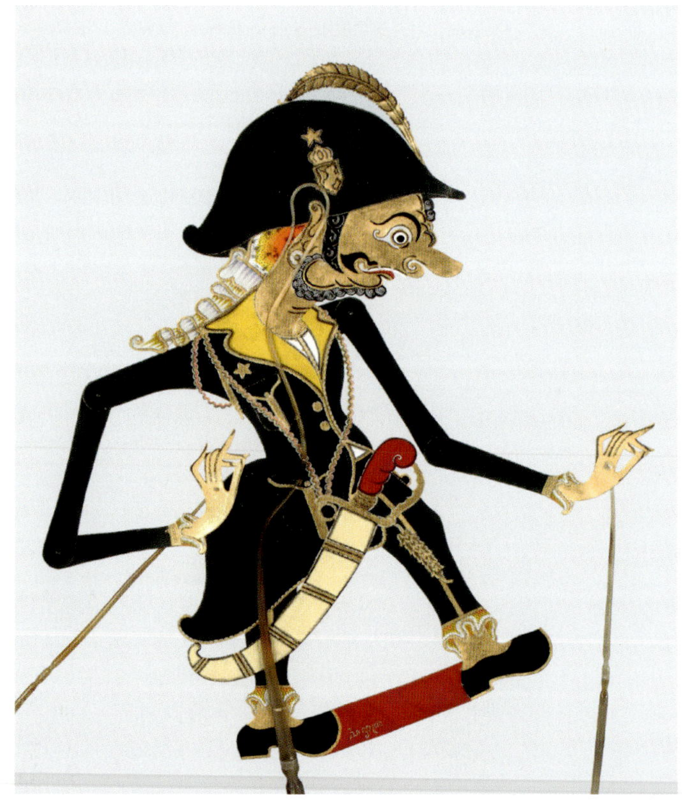

in the unknown world and the associated impulse to collect things is always presented as recommendations for colonialism. Rumphius, the famous naturalist, who is represented by a mannequin sitting at his desk, seems to give his blessing to the spirit of exploration, discovery and study. Rumphius is commonly considered as the personification of the warm interest in the exotic world. (See p. 165)
Nonetheless, this world of colonial civility runs up against its limits with the displayed collection of Indonesian weapons. These military attributes are also a silent witness to the military violence linked with the Dutch colonial enterprise. The echoes of that din of arms are fairly well muffled by the façade of civility that was erected by the aesthetic arrangement of these weapon display cases. (Fig. 33)
A vague echo of the colonial war's violence is faintly audible from the short caption accompanying one of the weapons on display: 'Rudus, often-used military sword in Aceh'. (Fig. 34) Another weapon, which looks beautiful with its carved wood sheath and a grip of ivory, is referred to in the accompanying text as 'Podang Raja, Imperial Sword of the Batak Prince Singamangaraja'. Apparently, this is the only weapon in the display case that can be attributed to an original owner. But who is this Singamangaraja, the Batak prince? (Fig. 35)
The answer to this question brusquely opens a window onto a view of the colonial practice of violence and repression. Si Singamangaraja (born in 1849) was the central figure in the struggle against the colonial rule and the Christian missions in the area of the Toba-Bataks on the island of Sumatra. His special position as the spiritual head of the ritual order, combined with the increasing infiltration of foreigners ensured that Si Singamangaraja was able to bring about a hitherto unknown Batak solidarity among the various clans. His contacts with Islamic fighters from the neighbouring war area of Aceh, spanning nearly a quarter of a century, made him a formidable adversary to the colonial power. On 17 June 1907, Si Singamangaraja was killed in a jungle on Middle Sumatra by a brigade of the Marechaussee of the Netherlands East Indian Army. With this final blow, the Batak community was finally brought under the subjection of Dutch colonial rule. For the Toba-Bataks, this day marked a watershed in their history that is commemorated annually up to the present day in the region located south of Lake Toba on Sumatra. Following decolonisation, the anti-

< 33
Display of weapons in the exhibition 'The Netherlands East Indies, a colonial history'
2002

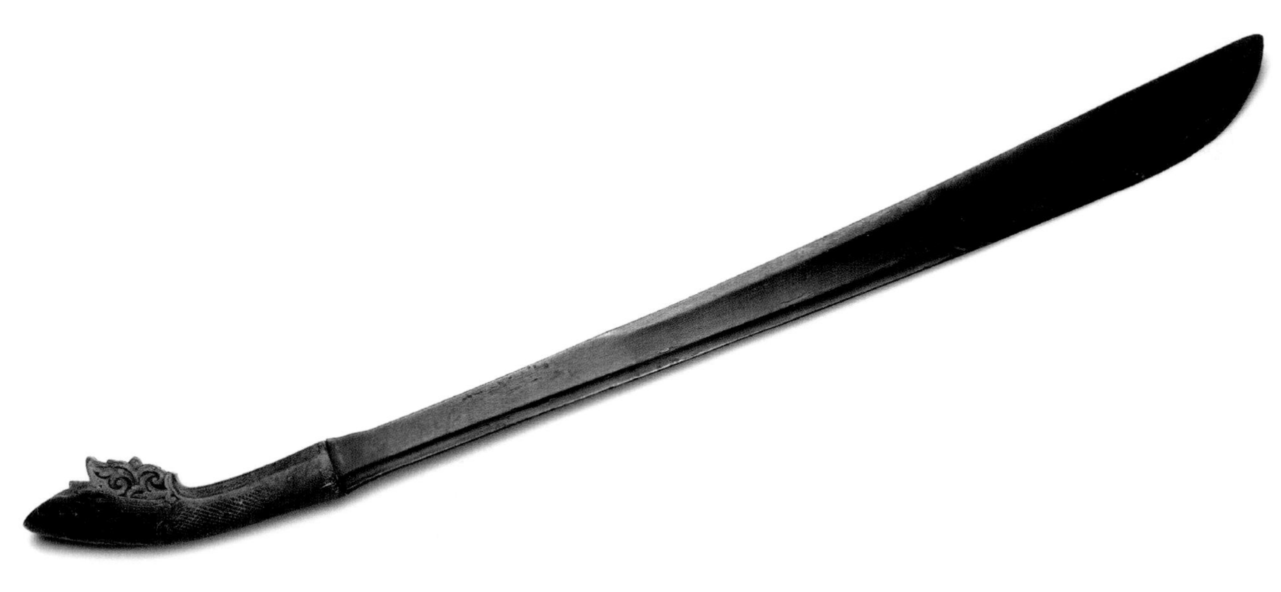

34
Sword
Metal, wood
77 x 71 x 3.3 cm
Aceh. Sumatra
214-24. Gift: H. J. Hoogeveen, 1924

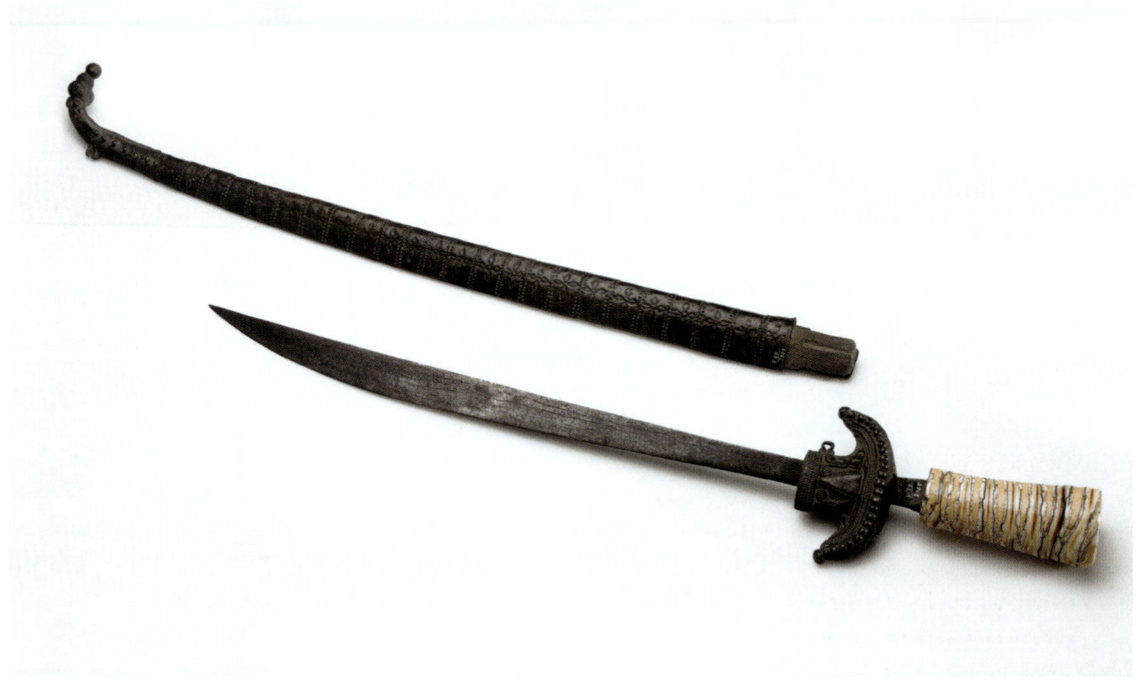

35
Sabre with ivory hilt
podang
Iron, ivory, silver alloy
62 x 5.5 x 5.5 cm
Toba. Tapanuli. North Sumatra
2761-62a. Gift: Vrije
Evangelische Gemeente, 1959

36 >
Letter from Si Singamangaraja to the Government, November 3rd, 1904
Paper. 34 x 21 cm
687-73. Purchase: F.W.
Stammeshaus, 1931

colonial struggle of the Bataks under the leadership of their prince was recognised as an authentic, regional contribution to the independence of the Republic of Indonesia. In 1961, Si Singamangaraja was officially given the honorary title of 'hero of the struggle for independence' by presidential decree, a title that he shares with Diponegoro, among others. The window onto this panorama remains closed in the 'Eastward Bound!' exhibition. The fact that the accompanying caption states that the imperial sword was a gift made in 1959 by the Vrije Evangelische Gemeente (Free Evangelical Church Congregation) in Amsterdam can perhaps be considered a sign of the earlier-mentioned bureaucratic decorum. Anyone who, nonetheless, wants to have a metaphorical glimpse of the 'brutal colonial mentality', must consult the archives of the Tropenmuseum. There, one will find a letter written in Batak writing dated 3 November 1904 on the instruction of Si Singamangaraja. The letter was written, from a hiding place, to the government as a response to the continual hostilities of colonial troops. In the letter, a reference is made to earlier correspondence with the local *resident*. (Fig. 36) A translated fragment: '[...] and now I say to the Lord Lieutenant General: turn back, do not continue to make war against me and those whom I govern, because as I said in my letter [...] it is unacceptable for the company [the colonial government, HS] to harass me and those whom I govern. [...] so remove yourselves from this place.' This raw, desperate cry – 'Remove yourselves from this place' – remains unseen in 'Eastward Bound!'. Colonial violence and the struggle itself remain pretty much invisible. Anyone viewing the collection of Indonesian weapons stands metaphorically with their back to the colonial wars.

That is also literally the case. A 180-degree turn of the body is enough to put you face to face with a display case that, according to the accompanying text, focuses on the 'colonial wars'. (Fig. 37) Here again we come across weapons, but this time weapons of the type that keep the rough practice of the colonial war at a safe distance. The official honorary military sword is a Royal honour awarded to the First Lieutenant C.J. Boon. On the blade, in gilded letters, it reads 'Koningin Wilhelmina/Voor betoonde dapperheid' ('Queen Wilhelmina/in Recognition of demonstrated Bravery'). On the reverse side of the blade stands the rank and name of the donee, and the heroic deed underscoring the tribute 'Aceh 1897'. The sword is housed in an oak case lined with blue velvet. (Fig. 38)

Everything about this weapon – from the royal crown on the lion's head to the prominent blue of the case's lining – breathes out an atmosphere of the colonial

CEREMONIAL JACKET

37
Ceremonial jacket of Teukoe Oemar Djohan
Wool, cotton, gold
63 x 43 cm
Aceh, Sumatra
1893-1899
674-722. Purchase: F.W. Stammeshaus, 1931

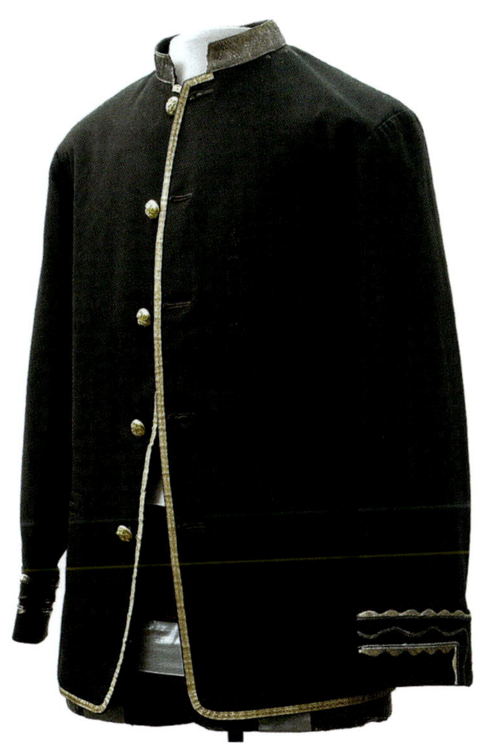

Teukoe Oemar Djohan (1840-99) is one of the most famous resistance heroes in Indonesian history. Memories of him in Indonesia are still very vivid and in many cities streets have been named after him. During the Aceh war (1873-1914), Teukoe Oemar initially fought against the Dutch. In 1893, he was bribed with money, opium and weapons to turn against his own people. He became a warlord in colonial service. But in 1896, he and his men switched their loyalties back to the Aceh camp. Teukoe Oemar was lured into a Dutch ambush in 1899 and killed. It is said that he was wearing this jacket at the time, which, in design and ornamentation, including the brass buttons bearing the letter 'W' (referring to Kings Willem 1, 2 or 3 or, after 1898, to Wilhelmina), is reminiscent of the uniform of administrative officers.
In 1930, Teukoe Radja Lehman, Teukoe Oemar's son, gave the jacket to F.W. Stammeshaus (1881-1957). Stammeshaus fought as a soldier in the Koninklijk Nederlandsch-Indisch Leger (KNIL) in Aceh, later became an administrative officer and was an enthusiastic collector of ethnographic items. In Koetaradja (present-day Banda Aceh) he was one of the first curators of the Aceh Museum. A year later, he and his family left for the Netherlands. He transferred his personal collection to the Aceh Institute, which was a part of the Koloniaal Instituut at the time. Up to 1946, Stammeshaus was the curator of the Cultural Anthropology Department at the Koloniaal Museum. Today, the Tropenmuseum collaborates with the Museum of Banda Aceh. JVD

club. The royal letters, the martial language ('in Recognition of demonstrated Bravery') and the Royal Decree no. 32 of 10 November 1898 that underscores the award of the decoration – everything points to the bureaucratic civility which is the centre of focus. The sword of honour is a ceremonial accessory that is used during military ceremonies, at parades and at receptions in colonial society. Gold gilt, i.e. not a weapon that was used to fight the vicious guerrillas in Aceh in 1897.
The same also goes for the non-military sword that floats rather frivolously, obliquely above Boon's sword of honour. According to the caption, this is the 'state sword of General J.B. van Heutsz' (Fig. 39) (this claim is in some doubt because the sword that Van Heutsz wore with his official uniform in his civil

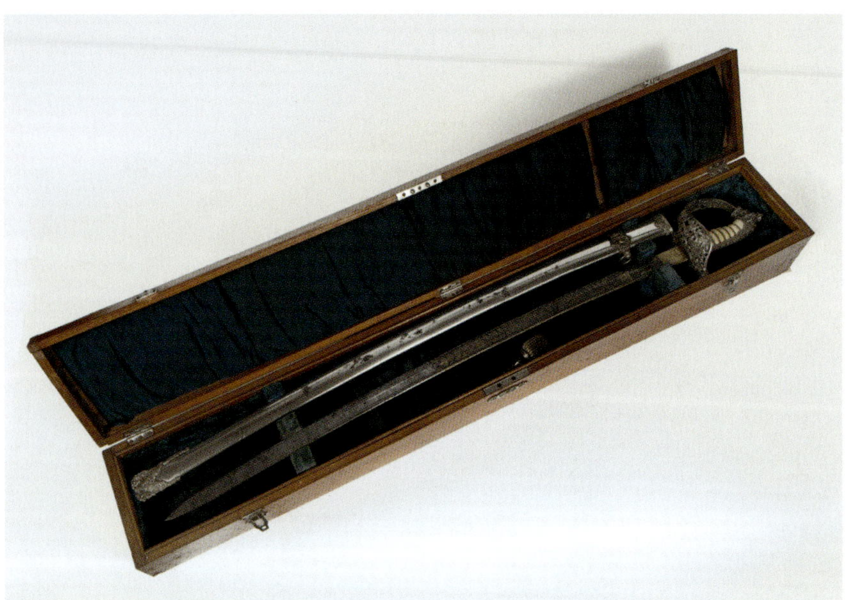

38
Sword of honour for C.J. Boon
Gold, iron, wood.
16 x 130 x 17.5 cm
1897
1655-1. On loan:
C. Brummelhuis, 1945

capacity as Governor General, as prescribed, and according to his official portrait in the Rijksmuseum, should have had a white sheath). Van Heutsz, the celebrated pacifier of Aceh (and later the reviled imperialistic bogeyman), may not of course be left out of the colonial club. He was in fact one of the pacesetters, as is testified to by the decisive role he played in creating the Koloniaal Instituut.
Yet for those visiting the colonial club, the figure of Van Heutsz should also be seen as pointing the way to the dark cellar of the colonial enterprise: the Aceh battle scene where the establishment of Dutch authority was achieved over the decades at the cost of many lives. Behind the frail sword, which, hanging vertically next to the gold braid of the official uniform, imparted to the wearer a little something of the ancient allure of a knight, the dark heart of Dutch colonialism lies hidden. To reveal this violent dark side just a little, we must again consult the screen presentation where earlier we saw the 'cut-off heads'. From the colonial club, we step into the world of Aceh in 1897, coincidentally the same place and year as the 'bravery demonstrated' by First Lieutenant C.J. Boon (see the sword of honour). (Fig. 40)
The photograph shows a group of soldiers from the colonial army soon after the overpowering of Koeta Teungkoh, a village in Aceh. The man standing to the far right is Van Heutsz, at the time still bearing the rank of Lieutenant Colonel and in the trained physical condition that is necessary to service in the field. At the feet of the future governor lie the bodies of three slain Aceh men – 'rebellious elements' that were violently subdued by colonial supremacy. It is an archetypal example that is seen in more extreme form in the series of photos that H.M. Neeb made during the notorious military expedition through Gayo and Alas lands under the command of Lieutenant Colonel G.C.E. van Daalen. These photos are also a part of the screen presentation in 'Eastward Bound!'. Each of them bears striking witness to the colonial use of violence. (Fig. 41)
The picture taken on 14 June 1904, soon after the capture of the *benteng* (fort) Koeto Reh, shows the feared Marechaussee of the KNIL above the stockade – at their feet lie the bodies of Aceh men. The photo provides a rare intimate look into the horror story of the Aceh War. At the same time, in the horrifying images in the photo, an analogy can be found to the idealised image in the painting by Pieneman. They are images of colonial supremacy, hegemony and

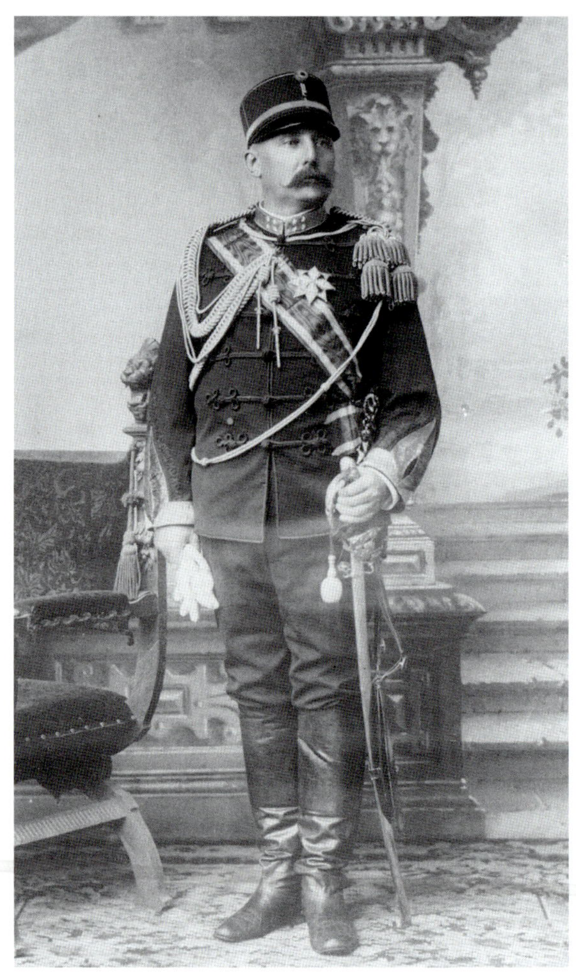

39
Lieutenant General J.B. van Heutsz as civil and military governor of Aceh
Glass negative
9 x 12 cm
1904-1909
10018730

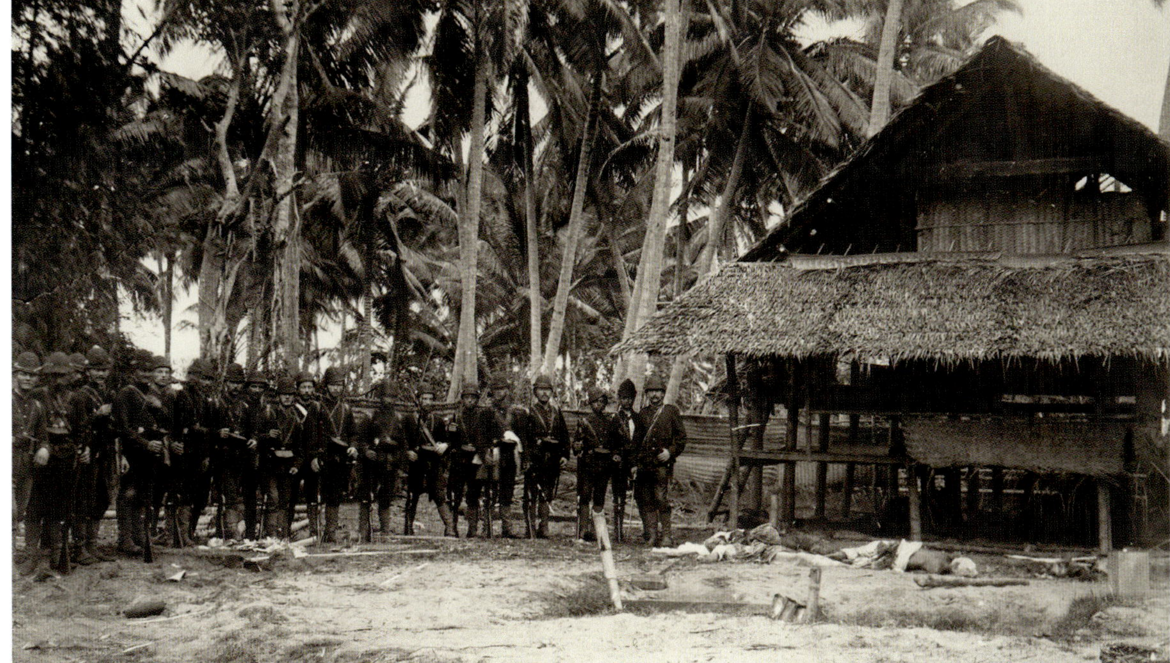

40
Soldiers with killed inhabitants of a compound; at the far left Lieutenant Colonel J.B. van Heutsz, Aceh
Photographer: M. Neeb
Gelatin silver print
16.8 x 22.7 cm
1897
60029845. Gift: J.A. van Rijn van Alkemade, 1925

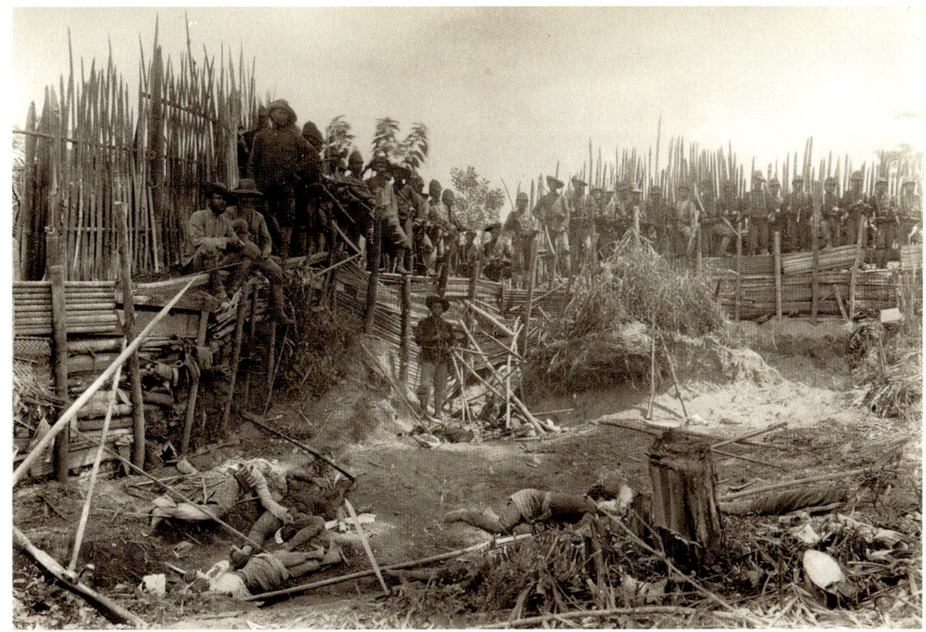

41
Military police, with Lieutenant Colonel Van Daalen, with killed inhabitants of the reinforced compound Koeto Reh, Aceh
Photographer: H.M. Neeb
Gelatin silver print
11.6 x 17 cm
1904
60009090

the surrender of native peoples – dead or alive.
It is a good thing that the images in these photographs, the picture of Koeto Reh and that of Koeta Teungkoh, will perhaps remain longer in the minds of onlookers – because of the disgust they elicit amongst most viewers – than the more deceitful, theatrical images presented in the painting of Pieneman.

If this is the case, then it can be said that the Tropenmuseum, through the 'Eastward Bound!' exhibition, has paddled against the overwhelming current of its own museum tradition. As a result, the comfortable and cheerfully respectable atmosphere of the colonial club is disrupted sporadically. The shutters on the windows that provide a view to the violent and repressive side of Dutch colonial rule have been set ajar.

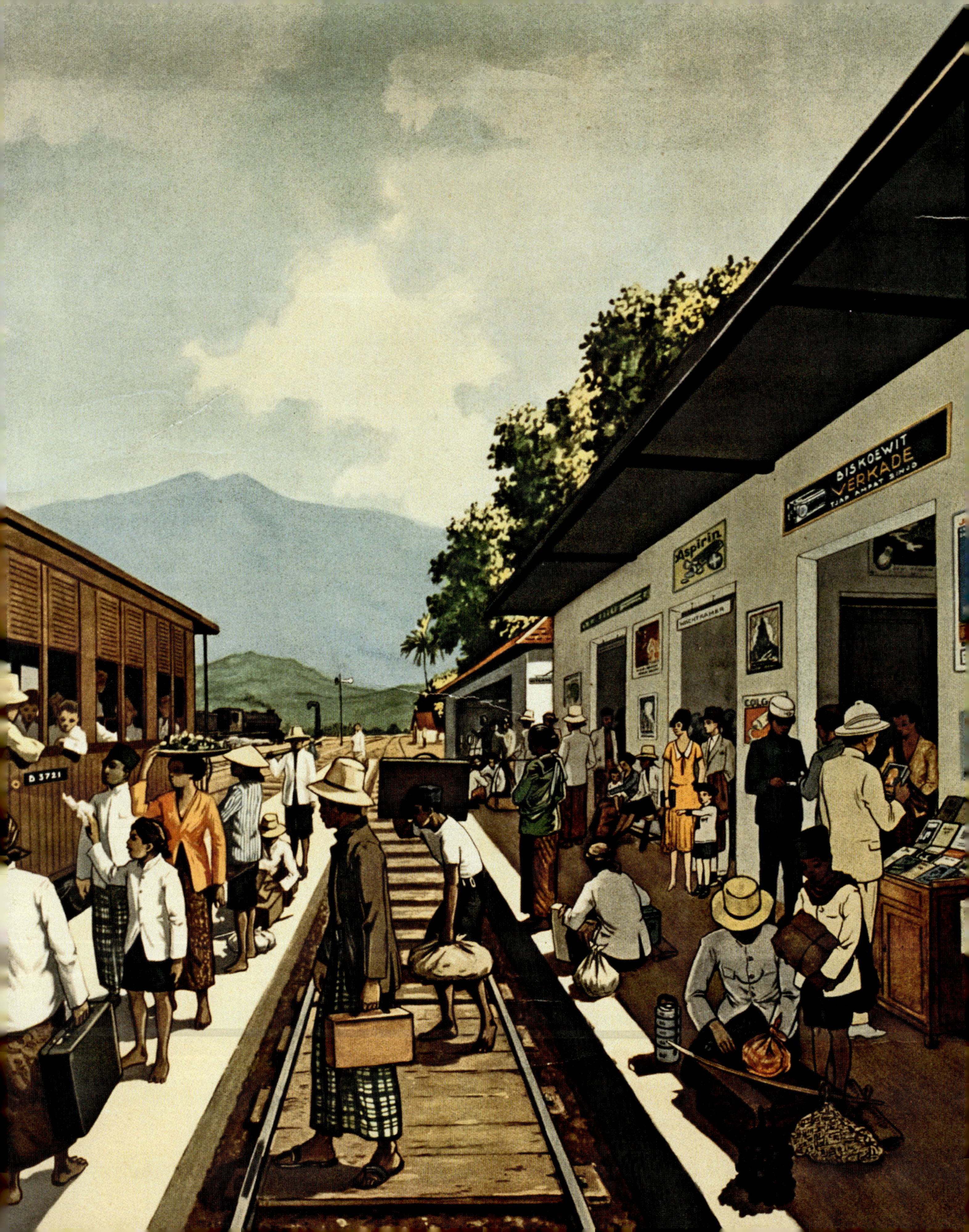
B 3721
BISKOEWIT
VERKADE
TJAP AMPAT SINJO
Aspirin
WACHTKAMER

EQUAL AND FREE: INDONESIAN DEMANDS IN EDUCATION AND POLITICS

ELSBETH LOCHER-SCHOLTEN

42
Detail Fig. 54

43
Autographed portrait of the three sisters: Kartini, Kardinah and Roekmini, Java
Photographer: Charls & Co
Gelatin silver print.
10 x 14.5 cm
c. 1900
60033327. Purchase: H. L. van der Kamp 1999

Wanting to know

A present-day teenager who loathes going to school might be surprised: over a century ago Kartini (1879-1904),[10] the daughter of a Javanese prince (a *regent*), wanted to do just that, to attend a Dutch high school. (Fig. 43) She longed to learn about the world, just like the Dutch girls around her; yet her father refused to give his permission. The fact that he had allowed his three daughters to visit Dutch primary education had already been exceptionally progressive for the time. Now, at the age of twelve, Kartini had to prepare herself at home for an arranged marriage. However, Kartini did not lose her longing for education. She was finally able to accomplish this within the limits of her social position and culture. Once she was respectably married, she started a pre-school in her home in the regent's residence. But this experiment was short-lived, as she died in childbirth soon after.

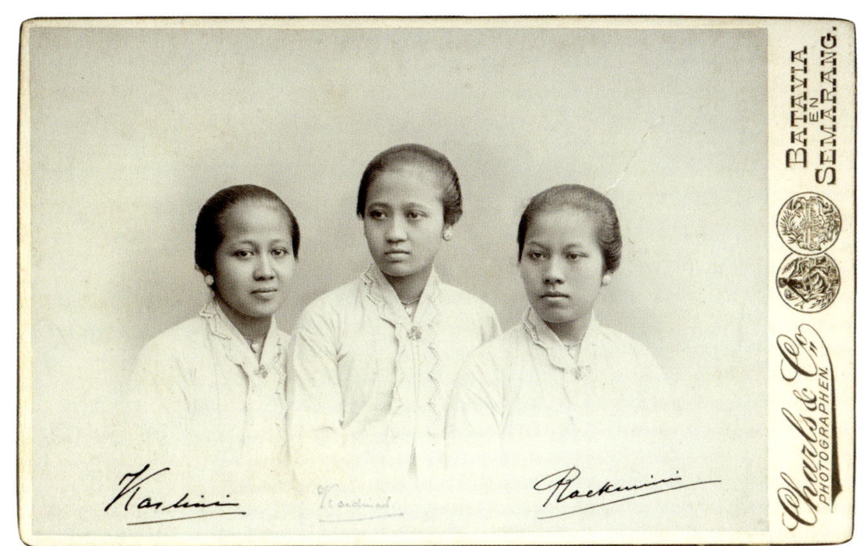

Almost forty years later – in hindsight close to the end of the colonial era – another Indonesian woman, Soewarsih Djojopoespito (1912-77), wrote the autobiographical novel entitled *Buiten het gareel*.[11] Unlike Kartini, she had attended secondary education; indeed, she had loved every minute of it. In Surabaya she had visited the mulo (roughly equivalent to junior high school). She continued her studies to become the first Javanese to earn a teaching certificate from a European teacher-training college.
Once graduated, she started teaching at a Taman Siswo (Pupil's garden) school in Bandung, which was a primary school and a mulo combined. (Fig. 44) This school was one of the so-called Wilde Scholen (Wild Schools), private schools who had no relation with the government – whether financial or inspection wise. Their aim was to make pupils aware of

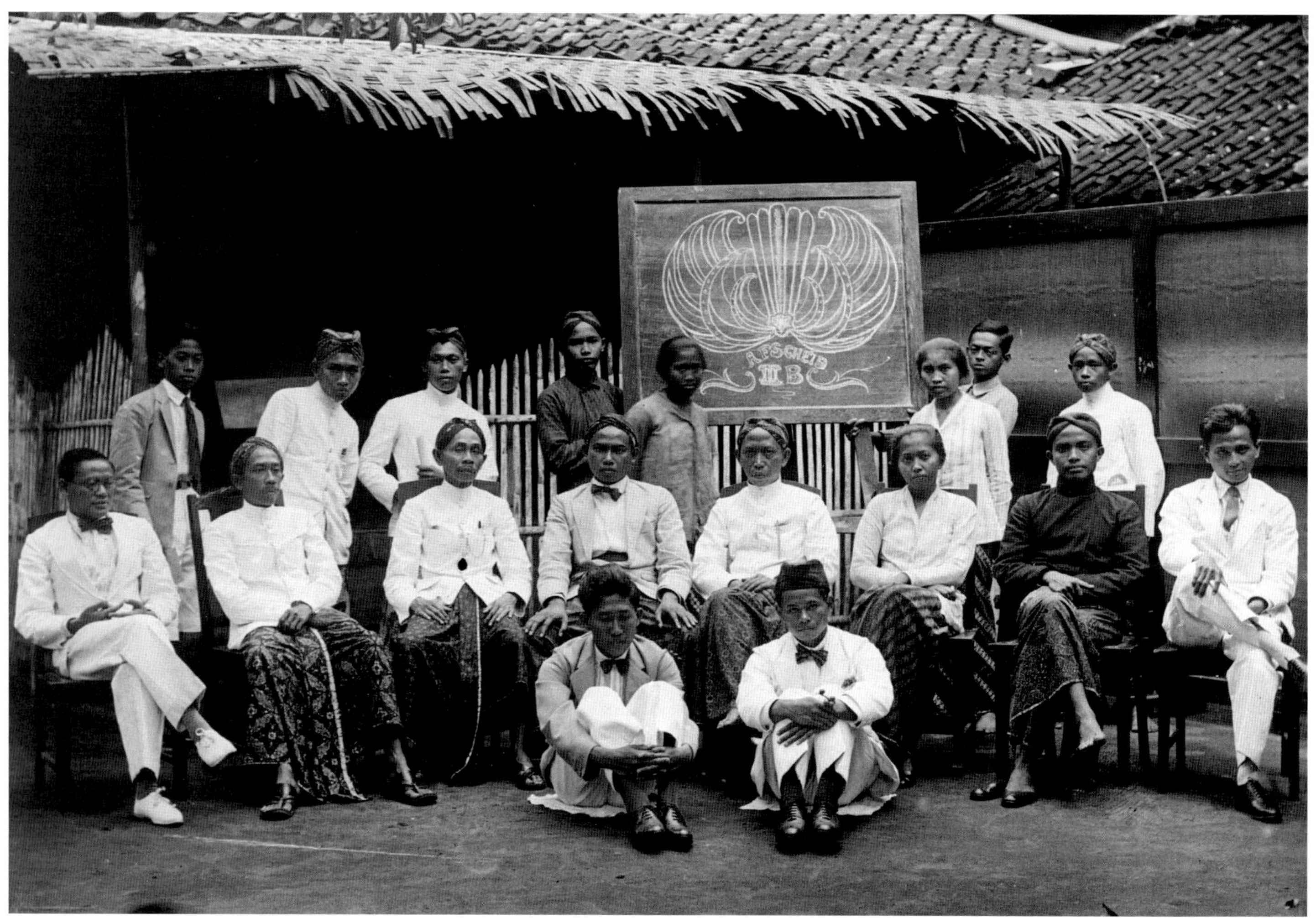

44
Teaching staff of the Taman Siswo school in Yogyakarta
Glass negative
9 x 12 cm
1920-1930
10002264. Gift: L.D. Petit

their Indonesian roots and identity. At the Taman Siswo schools, western-style education was given with an emphasis on Indonesian culture. Because of the nationalist ideals of these schools, the colonial government did not trust them; it had them searched sometimes by the police, as Soewarsih Djojopoespito describes in her book.
Kartini and Soewarsih Djojopoespito marked the beginning and the end of an era of education in the Netherlands East Indies. Their divergent life stories keenly illustrate this. As for Kartini, assertive but also respectable, her destination was the Javanese regent's house. Soewarsih Djojopoespito lived in a modern world. In addition to their desire for Western education as a gateway to progress and development, the two women shared a love for their country Java/Indonesia and a striving to see women gain greater autonomy. In Indonesia Kartini is honoured nowadays as a pioneering leader of the nationalism movement and one of the first champions of the Indonesian women's movement. Soewarsih voiced both ideals in her book. In the exhibition 'Eastward Bound!' both women can be found in photographs while Soelastri, the main character in Soewarsih's novel, is depicted by a life-sized model.

Education

Education was one of the showpieces of the colonial Ethical Policy. This policy, launched around 1900, declared that the Netherlands was responsible for the development of the archipelago. The Ethical Policy focused on the economic, cultural and political 'elevation' (development) of the native population, though the Dutch never forgot their own interests.

SOEWARSIH DJOJOPOESPITO (1912–1977)

Soewarsih Djojopoespito was born in the vicinity of Buitenzorg/ Bogor. Her father was a Javanese nobleman and her mother came from a wealthy Chinese family engaged in business. She and her two year older sister attended Dutch education at the Kartini School in Buitenzorg, a school for girls from the native aristocracy. Remembering her youth, she writes fondly about her Dutch teacher: "She did her best to teach us proper standard Dutch, to instil in us good eating, drinking and sleeping habits and to monitor the formation of our character." The sisters were boarders. In Buitenzorg they also attended the mulo, which was very unusual for 'native' girls at that time. It was their father who thought a good, Western-oriented education was important for his six children. Following the mulo, Soewarsih attended the European teacher-training college in Surabaya. Out of the thirty students in her class, she and a Javanese student were the only Indonesians. She remembers that in the eyes of a number of her fellow students, a 'dark stain' had been placed on the prestige of the school by their presence. She was thus confronted with a colonial society that made her aware that she was different. "From a lower class", as she put it, and: "As young as we were, we knew that intellect and knowledge were the only weapons we had to conquer the many obstacles we faced."

In her search for her own identity, Soewarsih joined the national youth movement. Her meeting, when she was sixteen, with Soetan Sjahrir marked an important moment in her life. He was leading a group of young nationalists in Bandung, and from that time on she knew that, after teacher-training college, she would go to work at the nationalist school, a school for Indonesian children taught by Indonesian teachers. In her eyes, the education of her own people took priority over a reasonably paid teaching job under the strict control of the Dutch government.

In 1931, Governor General De Jonge took office. He saw the growth in the number of native 'unofficial schools' as a threat to peace and order, and issued the 'unofficial school decree'. Inspectors of education were given the authority to refuse the opening of a 'Taman Siswo school' ('Pupils garden') or to withdraw existing permits. The decision ran up against considerable opposition and De Jonge was forced to rescind the decree. It was a victory for the nationalist movement over the rigid Dutch authorities.

In the book *Buiten het gareel*, Soewarsih Djojopoespito tells about her years as a teacher at different 'unofficial schools'. She relates how she and her colleagues tried to serve their fatherland at a time when the Dutch government and the Indonesian nationalist movement were at loggerheads. The 'unofficial schools' were kept under strict control by the Political

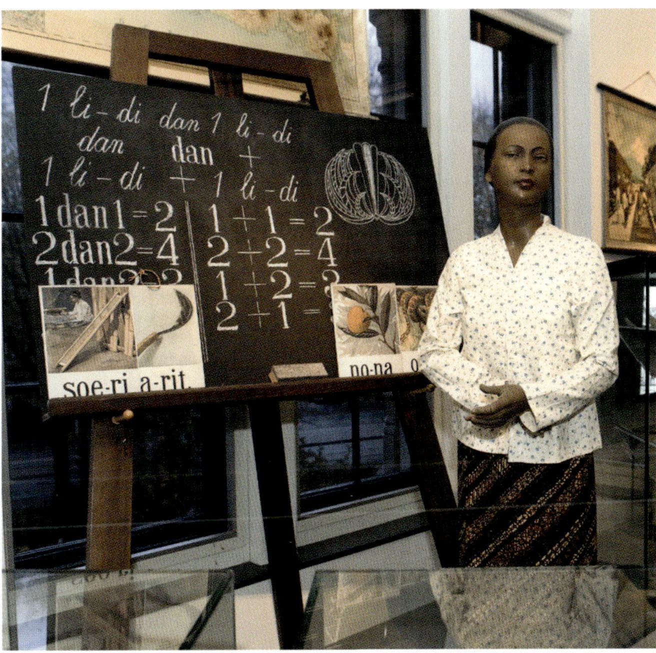

Intelligence Service. Arrest or a ban on teaching continually hung above the teachers' heads. Often the school fees were not received from the largely poor parents, so they had to improvise to keep the school and themselves afloat.

They were years of bitter poverty. She does not avoid writing about her own feelings and the internal conflict she had. She also stresses her fight for emancipation.

The model of Soewarsih Djojopoespito was one of the first wax figures in the Koloniaal Museum; up to 1950 she could be seen in different capacities. JDJ/JVD

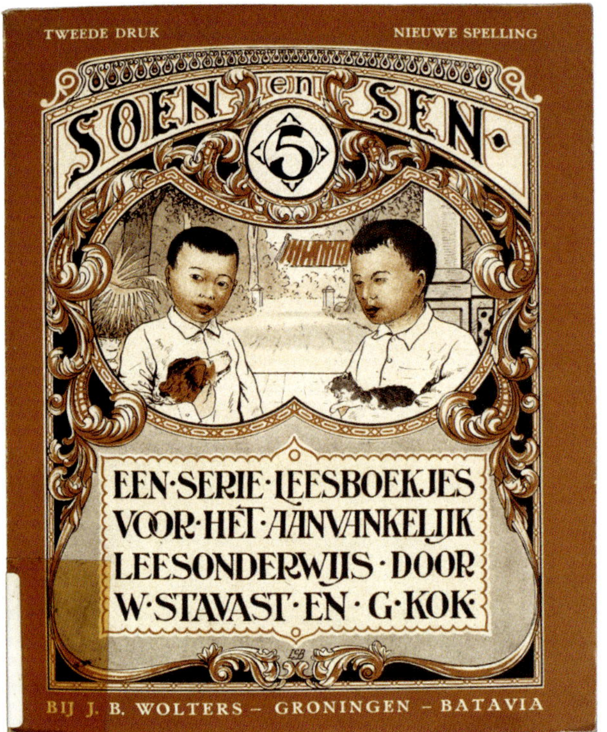

45
Cover of Soen and Sen Textbook for reading lessons at Dutch-Chinese elementary schools
By W. Stavast and G. Kok
Published by J.B. Wolters, Groningen, Batavia
2th. ed., 1936

Colonial government and business, for example, benefited from an educated workforce that could speak and write Dutch. (Fig. 45) For this reason, Dutch-language education was increasingly expanded. In the 19th century it was still uncommon for Dutch civil servants to speak Dutch with Indonesians. A simple form of Malay was considered enough to communicate. Indonesians that spoke the language of their superiors might, after all, get the idea that they were equal to Dutchmen. That attitude changed after 1900. Governor General J.B. van Heutsz (1904-09) in particular, known for his hard actions during the Aceh War (1873-1903/1914), promoted the use of the Dutch language. By expanding access to Western education the colonial government not only met its own needs. It also answered to a growing demand from Indonesians, who saw Western, Dutch-language education as 'a ticket to the West', a way to achieve modernisation and progress.[12]
Racial or ethnic differences permeated colonial society, including the structure of education. Different types of schools developed for different ethnic groups. European/white children (and a very limited number of children of the native elite) visited the Europese Lagere School (European Elementary School). European secondary education according to the Dutch model (lyceum, HBS and gymnasium) awaited this group as teenagers. These schools were primarily found in the large colonial cities. The Hollands-Inlandse School (Dutch Native School), established in 1914, was meant for Indo-European children (children with Dutch and Indonesian ancestry) and Indonesian children from more affluent environments, as can be seen in the photographs at the exhibition. In 1917, the Hollands-Chinese School or HCS (Dutch Chinese School) opened its doors to Chinese children. At all these school types, Dutch was the language of education. Native children in the country received elementary 'public education' in three-year desa (village/countryside) schools, which the government cautiously launched in 1907. Here the children of village leaders and rich farmers got a basic education in the regional language. The desa communities were themselves responsible for establishing and maintaining these schools; the colonial government only funded the start-up and unexpected shortfalls. To make the transition from a desa school to further education possible, a complex system of additional classes and schools was gradually designed.[13] The result of this proliferation of educational institutions is visible in the films at the exposition. These show white children wearing white clothes and dark shoes (and socks) leaving urban gymnasia; classes of the HCS, filled by Chinese children with short hair; and desa schools, where bare foot Javanese children fill their slates with Javanese letters.
Yet all these different types of schools had one thing in common: from public school to university, they adopted Western teaching forms and methods based on Western pedagogy and didactics (such as class, grades and remuneration systems).[14] (Fig. 46)

Education was not completely new for Indonesians. Islamic schools (*pesantren*) had been established in the archipelago when Islam became the dominant religion centuries previously. The sons of the elite learnt to read and write there; they subsequently learnt the skills they needed for a future in (government) administration on the job. *Pesantren* also trained religious teachers. This type of education was not open to Indonesian girls. As a rule, it was only after 1900 that they were allowed to attend school, when Western schools were established for them as well, the so-called Kartini schools for daughters of the native Indonesian elite. (Fig. 47)

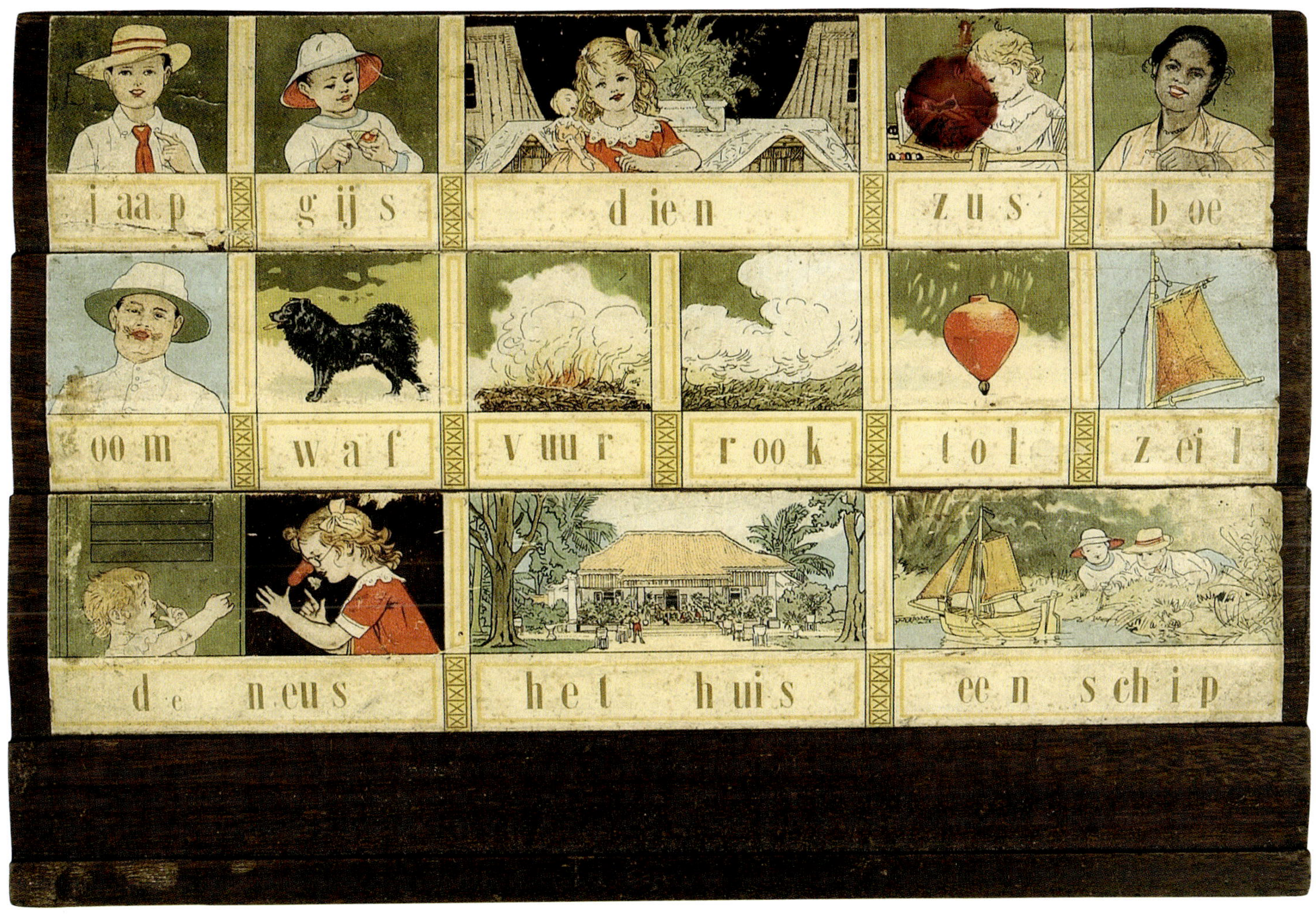

46
Wooden primer
Paper, wood
20.5 x 30 cm
West Javanese
European. Jakarta
c. 1925
5505-1. Gift: H. Verburg, Wormer, 1993

The Christian missions also encouraged the participation of girls in education. Particularly in the areas beyond Java, the so-called *Buitengewesten* (Outer Regions), these missions (Protestant and Catholic) were responsible for education. They received government subsidies for their efforts, just like private schools in the Netherlands. Islamic organisations that wanted to establish religious schools also received subsidies. They then were obliged to observe the government regulations and accept official inspection. In the 1920s and 1930s expenditures for Islamic education lagged way behind those for Christian education, reason for Indonesians to distrust the colonial government's educational efforts.
The slow expansion of Western secondary education explains the rapid growth of the Wild Schools in this period: thousands of them existed in the archipelago by the 1930s. Did the government fail to meet the growing demand for Western education? Then Indonesians themselves would take care of it: education was part and parcel of nationalist struggle. The desire for education did not stop at secondary school. Vocational and higher education were the real targets of students as well as the labour market; colonial society was urgently in need of trained professionals. Teacher-training schools, technical and vocational education, plus secondary education for native civil servants, doctors and lawyers were developed to meet this demand. (Fig. 48) Yet, the highest form of education, a full-fledged university, was never established in this colony; education at university level remained restricted to some separate faculties. Launched by private initiative, a Technical College was founded in 1920 in Bandung. In 1924, the government opened a Faculty of Law in Batavia (present day Jakarta), in 1927 a medical faculty in

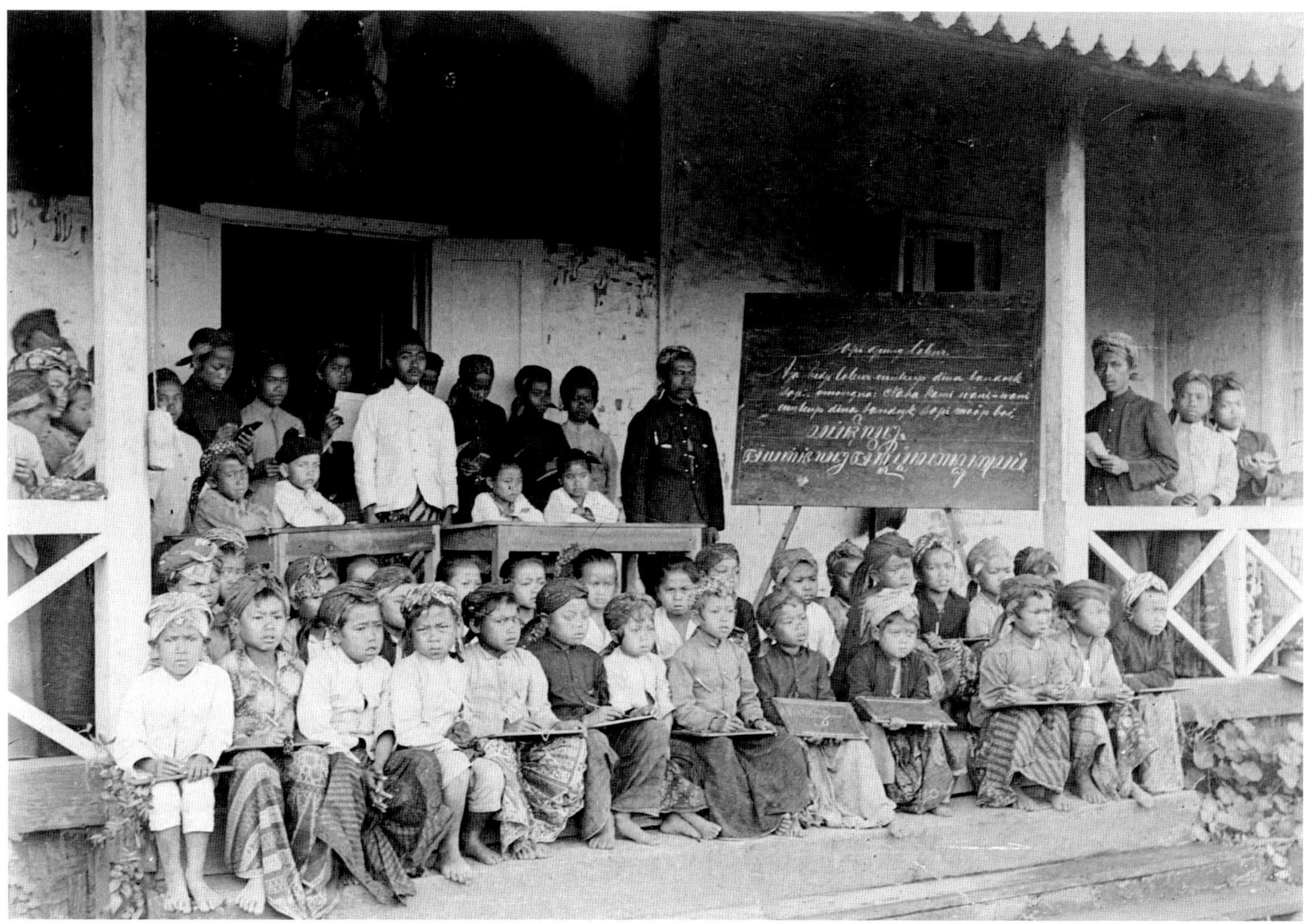

47
School for children of labourers at the Malabar teaplantation, Java
Glass negative
9 x 12 cm
c. 1915
10002299

Surabaya, and in 1940 a Faculty of Arts in Batavia. In a rapidly growing society, where the population nearly doubled between 1900 and 1940, education was a bottomless pit according to some Dutch opinion leaders. Around 1930, a wide-ranging debate broke out: some feared that an ever expanding Western education would lead to unemployment among native Indonesians, as the labour market would not be able to absorb them. This in turn would lead to what was called a native intellectual 'white-collar' proletariat (comparable to the industrial blue-collar proletarians). And that could only result in the much feared rise of nationalism.

In the world economic crisis around 1930, which hit the Netherlands East Indies hard, education was sacrificed when government expenditures were gradually reduced with fifty percent. Education for Indonesians suffered the most: expenditures were reduced to one-fifth. Western education and higher education were relatively best off. The colonial government did not want to tamper with the 'concordance' between Western education in the East Indies and education in the Netherlands. A Dutch child who attended school in the East Indies, had to be able to enter the same class without any problems on returning to the Netherlands.

Did the Dutch colonial administration have much reason to be proud of the 'ethical' show horse, the colonial education system? It does not appear so. The number of school attendees did grow exponentially: in 1900, some 134,000 pupils took their places on the school benches, in 1940 it was nearly 20 times that many, over two million (2,380,000). But the figures for literacy point in a different direction. In 1930, no more than 10 per cent of native Indonesian men and a little more than 2 per cent of women were literate. Among European men and women in the Netherlands East Indies, literacy was nearly 80 and over 70 per cent respectively; among Chinese men and women, literacy counted for 40 and 12 per cent respectively. Of the total population of sixty million people, 7.2 per cent could read and write. Of this small minority, less than 10 per cent (400,000 persons) had a mastery of Dutch, less than half of whom were Indonesian (188,000). There were therefore fewer than two hundred thousand native Indonesians (0.3 per cent of all Indonesians) who could achieve a position equal to Europeans based on their language skills.[15]

Another dramatic figure was the number of university graduates in the Netherlands East Indies – in 1938, 71 people fell into this group (15 Europeans, 38 Indonesians and 18 so-called *Vreemde Oosterlingen* (Foreign Orientals: Chinese and Arabs). So it was not surprising that a high-level Dutch East Indian civil servant, just prior to the Second World War, observed: 'Compared with the countries around us, we lag shamefully behind in the fight against illiteracy; also with respect to the capacities of our further education we do not lead the pack.'[16] Figures backed up this view. In the 1930s, 50 per cent of Filipinos, 12 per cent of India's population and 10 per cent of the Vietnamese were literate. At a little more than 7 per cent, Indonesians were last in the line. Foreign observers had little respect for Dutch education efforts in the colony, and rightly so.

Why did the colonial government not promote literacy through education more fervently? In the dilemma between quality (concordance) and quantity (increasing literacy), the colonial administration chose the former and did not want to make any concessions. It suffered from Dutch perfectionism, to the detriment of the Indonesian population. Besides Dutch perfectionism, the colonial vision of education for Indonesians played a major role as well. Western education was considered suitable for the native elite only. The farming population was not allowed to be 'uprooted' by education that would detach it from the economic roots of its existence. After independence, the brand new Indonesian government tackled the education problem very differently: it took the road to universal literacy.

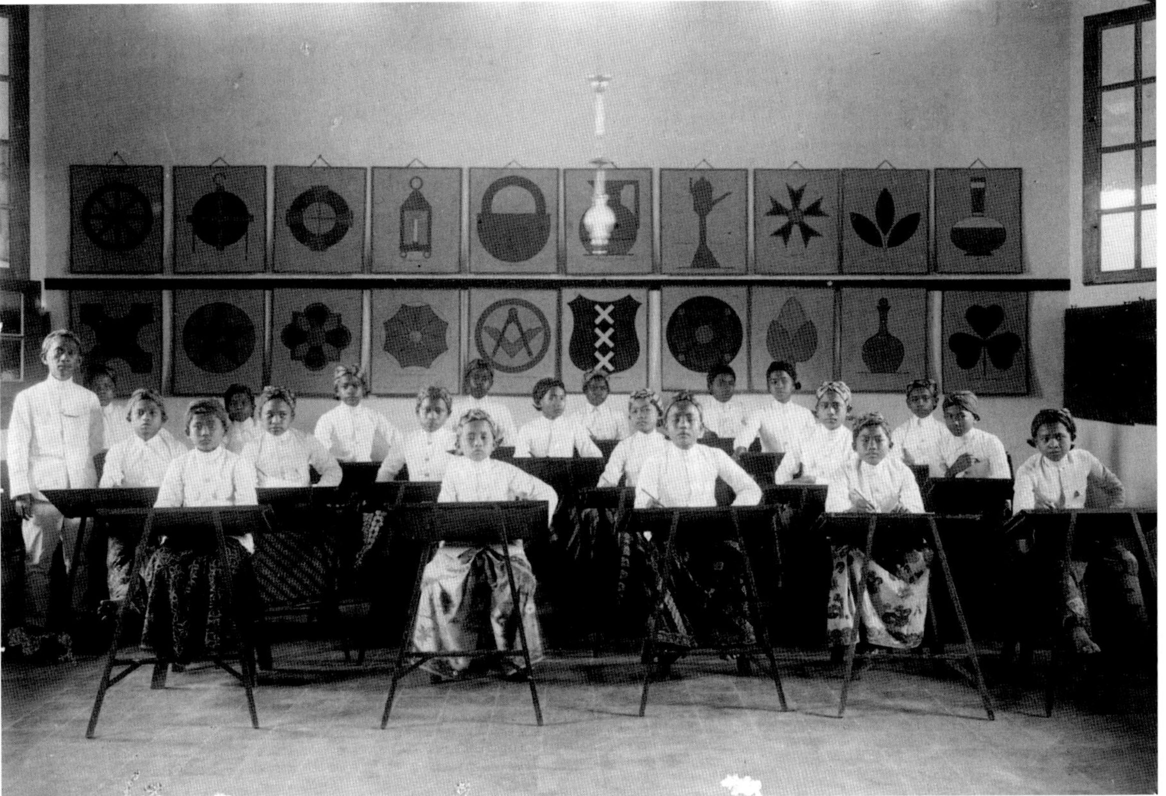

48
Drawing lesson at the 'Inlandsche Normaal School' which trained native teachers, Java
Glass negative
9 x 12 cm
c. 1920
10002338. Gift: G.J. Nieuwenhuis

Equality in education / freedom in administration

As mentioned above, Soewarsih Djojopoespito worked as a teacher at a Wild School. The ideal she strove to achieve was equality: gender equality within marriage and racial equality by independence in politics, administration and society at large. For her feminism and nationalism went hand in hand and education was a means to achieve both. Nationalist Indonesian leaders recognised the importance of education from personal experience.[17] Indonesian nationalism was born among native students enrolled in medical studies in Batavia. In 1908, they founded the first national association of Boedi Oetomo (Lofty Intent). (Fig. 49) Their goal was to achieve greater participation and a greater say for Indonesians. Yet Western education was not the only engine driving the founding of Boedi Oetomo. The national movement in British India and Japan, which in 1905 was the first Asian country to defeat a Western power (Russia), provided encouraging examples.

Indonesian nationalism began in a moderate form as a new cultural and political awareness among the Javanese elite. Regional sentiments and loyalties were to have the upper hand until the end of the 1920s. Groups of students from Sumatra, Ambon and other regions started their own movement. This new direction was known as *beweging* or *pergerakan* (movement) until late in the 1920s. The different associations and parties also were given political substance

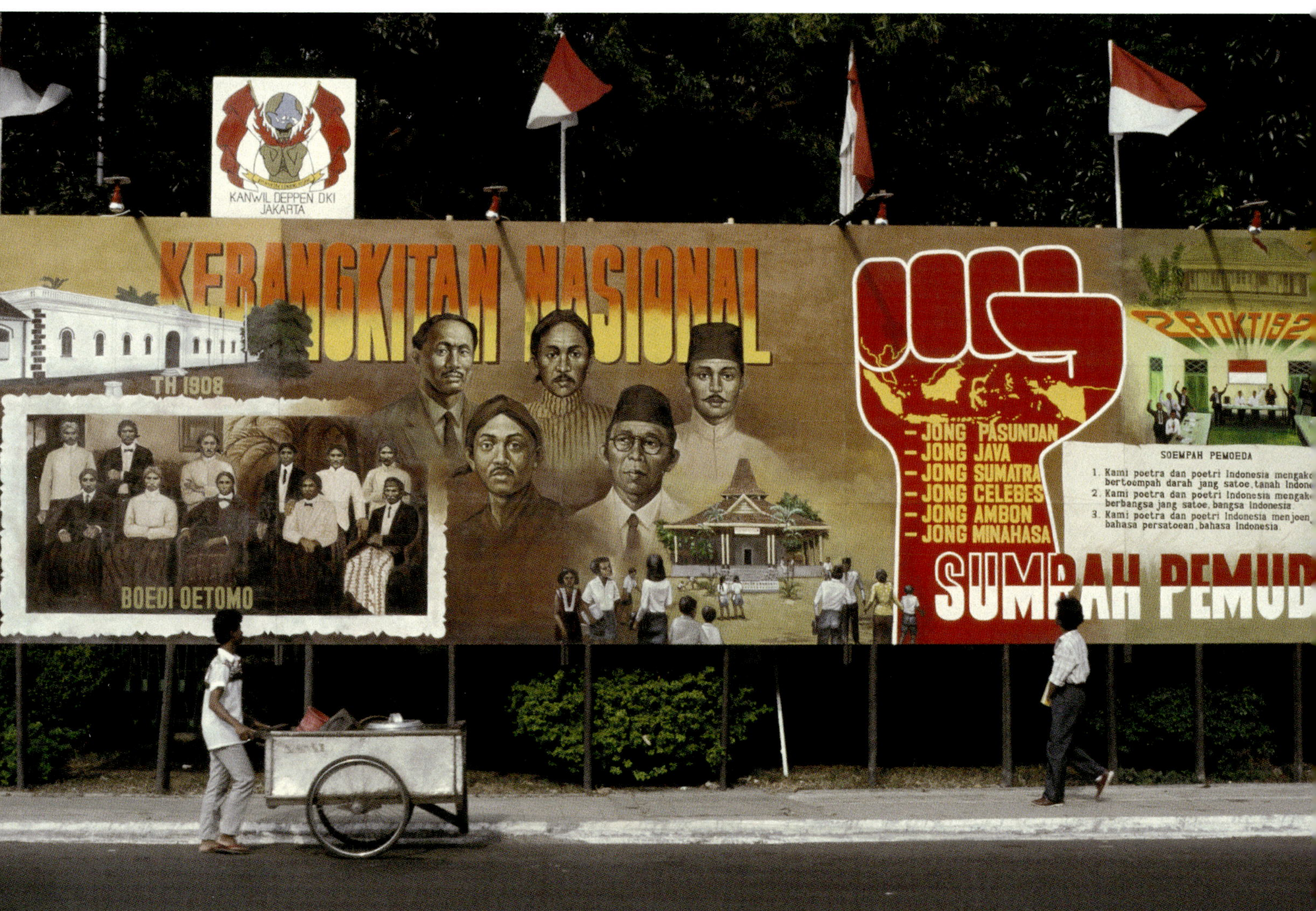

JHR. MR. BONIFACIUS CORNELIS DE JONGE – GOVERNOR GENERAL (1875–1958)

He was the eighth of eleven children. Following a career as the Dutch Minister of War (1917-18), he served as the Director of the Bataafsche Petroleum Maatschappij (Batavian Petroleum Company) (BPM) in London (1920), then held a seat on the Board of Supervisory Directors at BPM. In 1931 he was appointed as the Governor General of the Netherlands East Indies (1931-36). He was the last Governor General to serve out his full term.

De Jonge was an opponent of the Ethical Policy and a supporter of the Rijkseenheidsgedachte (movement promoting the unity of the Dutch Empire). He brought about a complete break with the Indonesian nationalists. His term as Governor General was hampered by drastic cutbacks that he was forced to introduce on orders from The Hague as a result of the economic depression that enveloped the world at the time. He took decisive action against the mutineers on the navy ship De Zeven Provinciën (1933).

De Jonge is included in the exhibition as the head of government in the Netherlands East Indies, an office he exercised in the name of the king/queen. He had 65 predecessors dating back to 1610. JDJ

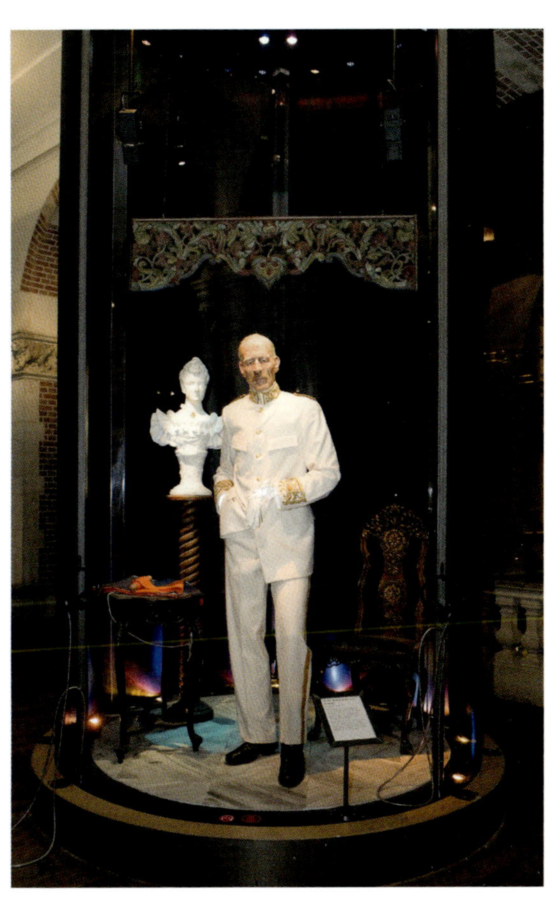

< 49

Painting made on the occasion of the 40th anniversary of the celebration of Independence Day, Jakarta

H.W. van Rinsum
Colour slide
2.4 x 3.6 cm
August 1985
20019401

Painting along the Jalan Medan Merdeka Barat at the National Monument (Monas) in Jakarta. Figures that can be distinguished include members of Boedi Oetomo, the first national political movement in Indonesia, founded in 1908. The right-hand side recalls the Sumpah Pemuda, the 'Youth Pledge', which took place on 28 October 1928.

through the introduction of the East Indian proto-parliament, de Volksraad, in 1918. At the end of the 1920s, the *pergerakan* changed in the nationalist movement striving for independence.

Apart from originally being a regional movement, nationalism was also a young people's movement. Associations such as Jong-Java (Young Java), de Jong Sumatranen Bond (the Young Sumatrans Union), de Jong Islamieten Bond (the Young Islamite Union), Jong Ambon (Young Ambon), Jong Celebes (Young Celebes) and the Jong Bataks Bond (Young Bataks Union) bore the name 'Young' with pride and united in 1930 under the name Jong Indonesië. The nationalist movement was therefore characterised as a revolt of sons against fathers who had often collaborated with the Dutch as administrative civil servants. Nationalism was also seen as a movement of the lower nobility against the higher nobility on Java. High nobility was (with some exceptions) more reluctant to take part in nationalism or it organized its own associations. At the four royal courts of Central Java, the movement had a varying following. The colonial government had watched the founding of Boedi Oetomo with sympathetic enthusiasm. The parties founded shortly thereafter, were received with a critical eye. The Sarekat Islam (1911/1912) was inspired by a new Islamic self-awareness fed by Egypt. The Indische Partij (East Indian Party), founded in 1912, focused on Indo-Europeans and Indonesians, and its platform was the first to clearly set national independence as its goal.

With the radicalisation of these parties around 1918, the vigilance of the government increased. A politically motivated intelligence service was established which, in the eyes of politically aware Indonesians, quickly gave the East Indies the character of a police state. The Netherlands East Indian government was open to calls for moderate reform, but it had little patience for anything that directly threatened the colonial relationship, as the Indonesian Communist Party (Partai Komunis Indonesia – PKI) did. The revolts organised by this party in November 1926 and January 1927 led to heavy repression, death sentences, and the establishment of the feared prison camp of Boven-Digoel on the island of New Guinea. The banning of the PKI opened the way for ir. Soekarno, then a young architect in Bandung. He founded a new, non-religious (secular) party, the Partai Nasional Indonesia (PNI, 1927). This party formulated independence of Indonesia as its objective, a permanent part of the nationalism programme since then.

In the 1930s, Soekarno and other nationalist leaders were repeatedly arrested, convicted, freed, re-arrested and exiled. Governor General B.C. de Jonge (1931-36), had deep contempt for these leaders and so he tried to ban the Wild Schools, but was forced to rescind the ban. Yet he was largely successful in 'decapitating' the nationalism movement. The remaining leaders of secular nationalism (to which Soewarsih Djojopoespito also belonged) joined forces after 1935 and forged two political parties. Under pressure from the approaching war, they moderated their stances and were ready to cooperate with the East Indian government. Islamic parties also united in 1938 to form their own nationalist 'pillar'. A year later, the three organisations collaborated in an action to establish an East Indian parliament, the first successful form of national unity in the movement.

The European public was largely unaware of these changes in nationalism. Newspapers reported on the feared Indonesian 'extremism', but the movement did not encroach upon the daily lives of Europeans. Its ideals were considered far-fetched and unrealistic.

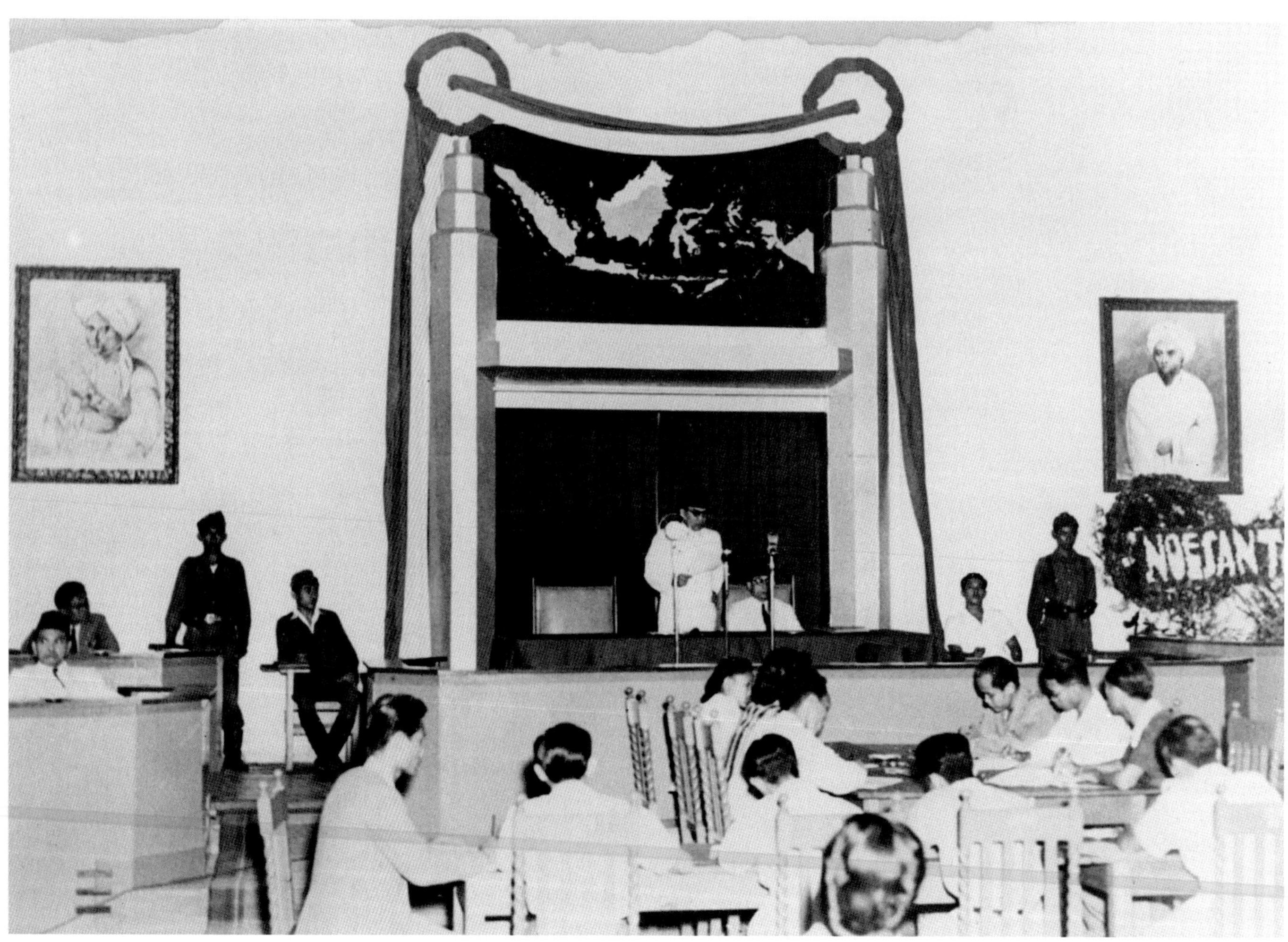

50
President Soekarno opens the session of the Republican Parliament in Malang on 18 March 1947
Glass negative
9 x 12 cm
10001279. Gift: Gemeente Archief Den Haag, 1952

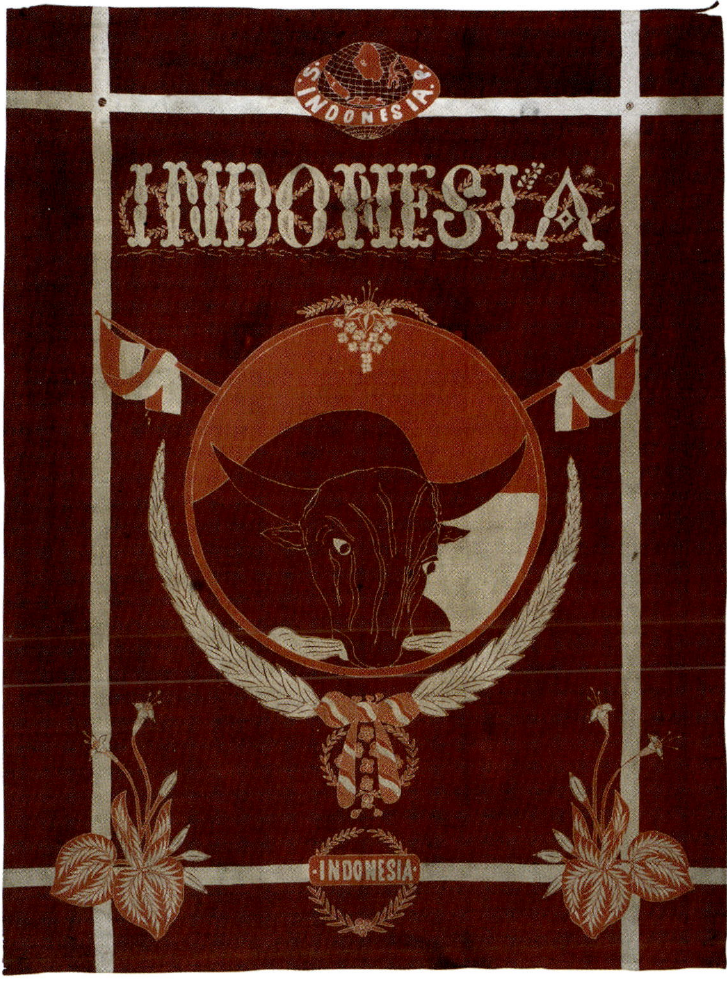

BAGI TJÉTAKAN JANG KEDOEA.

Doea boelan sadja tjétakan jang pertama telah habis terdjoeal. Terpaksalah dengan segara kami mengeloearkan tjétakan jang kedoea. Adalah beberapa lagoe² jang telah kami oebah, demikian djoega pantoen dan sja'irnja banjak ditoekari dan ditambah, hingga djaoeh sempoernanja dari tjétakan jang pertama. Lagoe „*Moelai Beladjar*" kami ganti dengan lagoe „*Asam paja*" seboeah lagoe jang dimana-mana sadja kedengaran dinjanjikan serta ditarikan orang.

BAGI TJÉTAKAN JANG KETIGA.

Isinja tiada beroebah dari pada tjétakan jang kedoea.

PENGARANG.

1. WILHELMUS.

2. Boelan jang kedelapan diinilah waktoe,
Tiga poeloeh satoe bilangan tertentoe;
Hari lahir Baginda Poeteri Ratoe,
Mengoetjapkan selamat kami sekoetoe.

5

1930s. In its view, it had tamed nationalism. Had not the nationalist leaders in May 1940 declared their willingness to support the Dutch when Germany invaded the Netherlands? The hatchet seemed to be buried. But the disappointment of the Indonesian nationalists was great when the East Indian government refused to grasp their outstretched hand and instead simply put all plans for reform on ice. The government wanted to wait until the war was over, by which time the Dutch parliament could take part in negotiations.

This colonial optimism was a serious miscalculation. The peace of the late 1930s proved to be the quiet before the storm. (Fig. 51) The Japanese occupation of the Indonesian archipelago changed everything. Japanese soldiers freed Soekarno, who collaborated with them in order to achieve his ideals. This enabled him to develop into a leading national figure whose compelling speeches via the radio's in trees, the 'singing telephone poles', became known all the way to the villages. Two days after the surrender of Japan on 15 August 1945, Soekarno declared the independence of the Republic of Indonesia. Following many negotiations, two focused military actions and a bloody guerrilla war, Queen Juliana and Vice President Hatta signed the transfer of sovereignty on December 27, 1949 in the Royal Palace on the Dam Square in Amsterdam. Indonesian nationalism, launched in 1908 as a student movement, had won its political struggle and had become equal and free in little more than forty years. (Fig. 50)

51
Cotton cloth with nationalist emblems
Cotton, paint
78.5 x 106 cm
Pekalongan. c. 1944
5663-1090. Purchase: H.C. Veldhuizen, 1996

52
Dutch national anthem, Wilhelmus, translated into the Malaysian language from Taman Kesoema, boekoe njanji oentoek sekolah rendah boemi-poetera
By Madong Loebis, A. Chalik
Published by J.B. Wolters
Groningen-Batavia, c. 1933

Even the most progressive Dutchmen at the time thought that Indonesians would need a generation, i.e. some thirty years, before they were ready to stand on their own feet. In other words, the politically aware Dutchman thought the colonial administration would last a long while. As can be expected, this topic did not figure in the children's books, on exposition in 'Eastward Bound!'. These books paid attention to idyllic images of Indonesian nature, of the lives of colonial children and their friendly servants. These images tallied with the positive harmony that dominated ideals of the perfect family of those years. Even in present-day interviews with Dutch people about this period in the East Indies, nationalism is never discussed as a main point of focus.

The conservative East Indian government monitored the nationalism movement through its intelligence services. Yet, it saw no reason to panic in the late

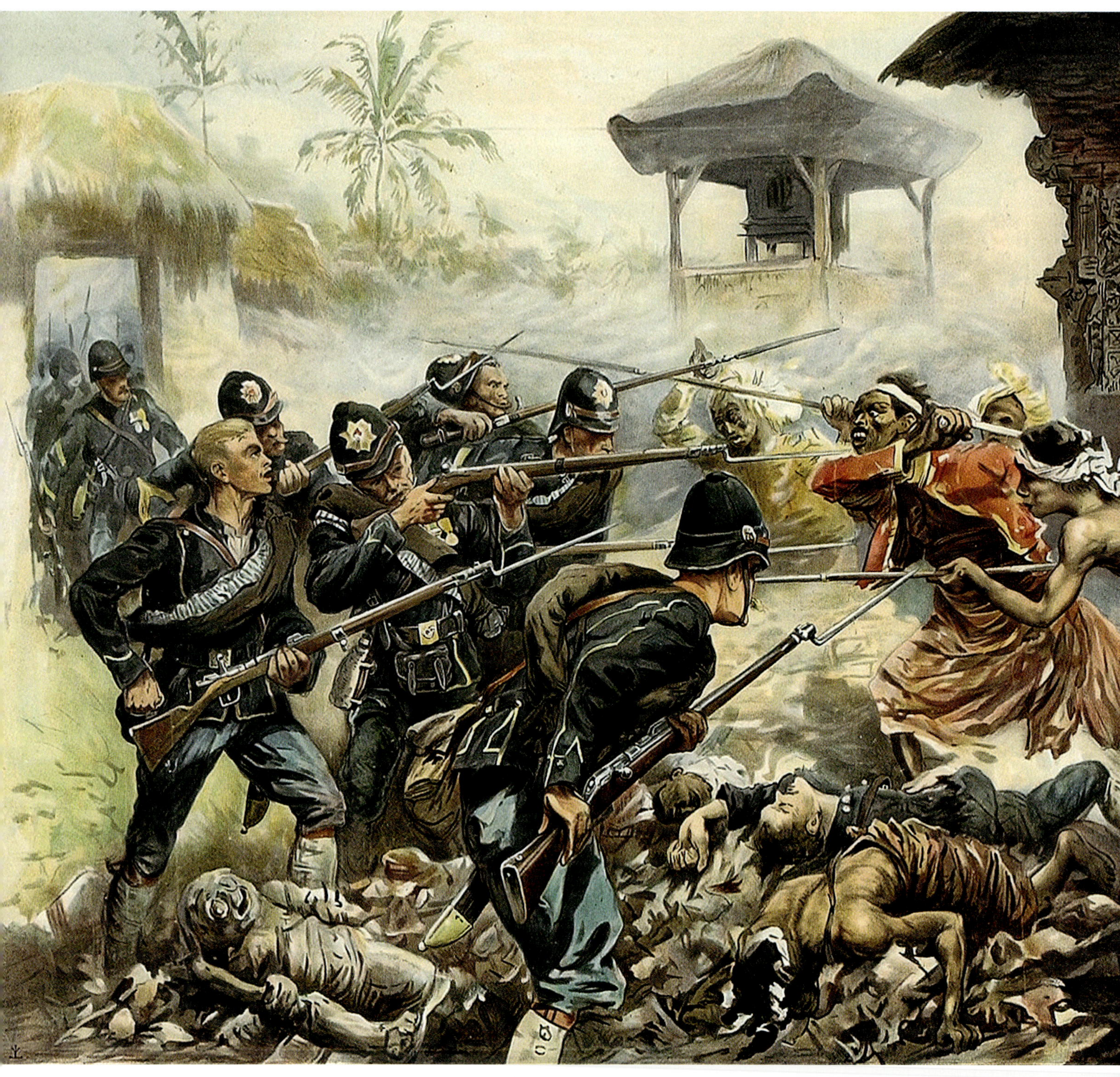

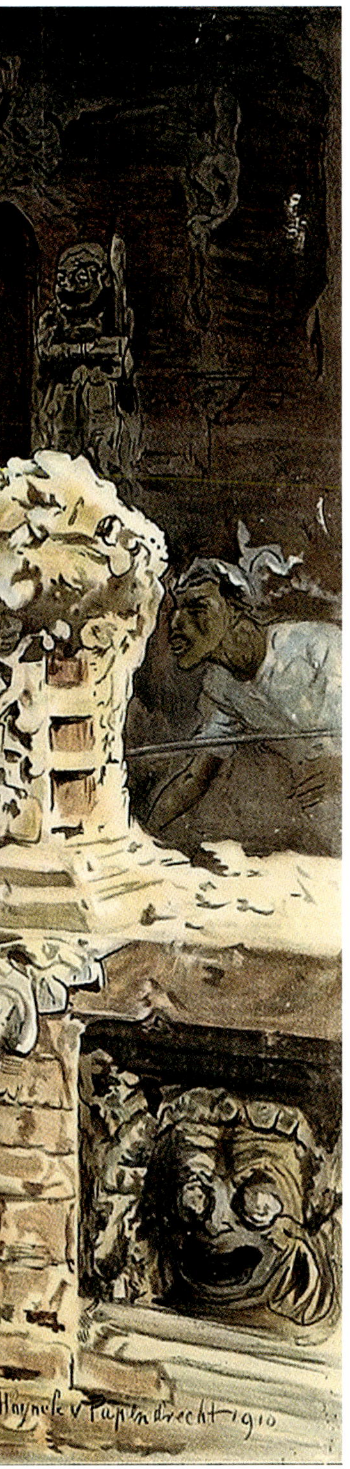

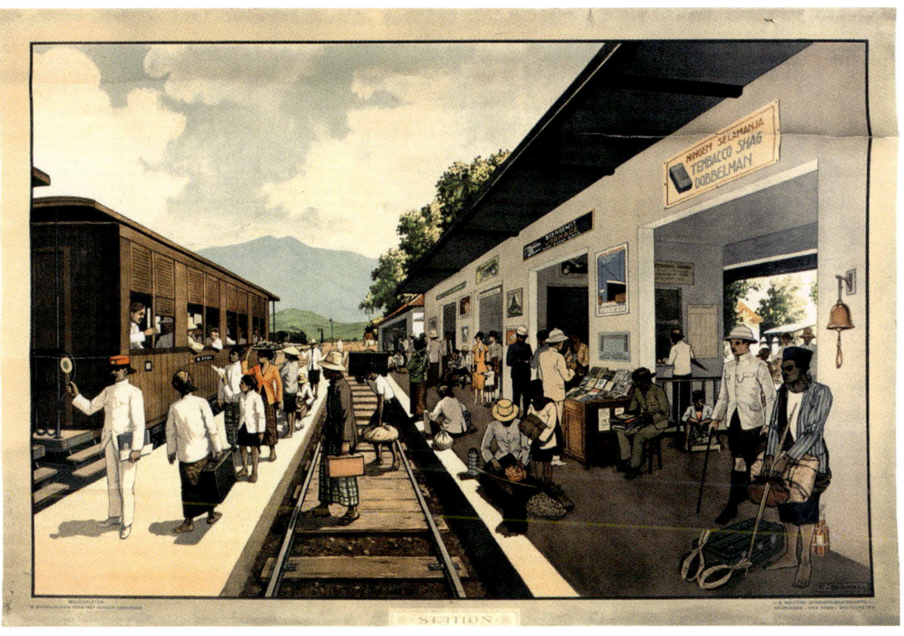

In 1894-1895, the Koninklijk Nederlandsch-Indisch Leger (KNIL) conquered the island of Lombok, east of Bali. This school poster shows the attack on the palace of the Prince of Cakranegara, a Balinese prince that ruled Lombok. Hoynck van Papendrecht never visited the Netherlands East Indies, but his drawing is remarkably detailed nonetheless. The Dutch can be recognised by their outfits; they included fusiliers, regular soldiers and a corporal. Two of the soldiers are wearing military decorations. Despite the battle, they look well groomed, with combed hair, cleanly shaven faces and handsome features. They are a paragon of a calm and disciplined army. The native army of the Prince of Cakranegara is at the opposite end of the spectrum: their clothing is rumpled, their hair and eyes are wild and chaos reigns. The message of this school poster from 1910 can be nothing other than an assurance that the Dutch colonial army was doing good work and that the Dutch authorities were necessary to keep the wild elements in Indonesian society in check.

The school poster was published by J.B. Wolters in the series *Schoolplaten voor de Vaderlandse geschiedenis* (School posters for Dutch history). It was taken off the market in 1928 due to declining sales. But perhaps the picture on it was too violent for tender young schoolchildren and no longer accorded with the feeling that the colonial history was meant to elicit. PW

53
School poster,
De verovering van Tjakranegara op Lombok 1894
J. Hoynck van Papendrecht (1853-1933)
Paper
82.5 x 110 cm
1910-1911
5976-2. Purchase: Firma De Kantlijn, 2003

54
School poster of a railway station
F. van Bemmel
Paper
1.14 x 81.5 cm
Indonesia / The Netherlands
1913
4108-814. Gift: 1973

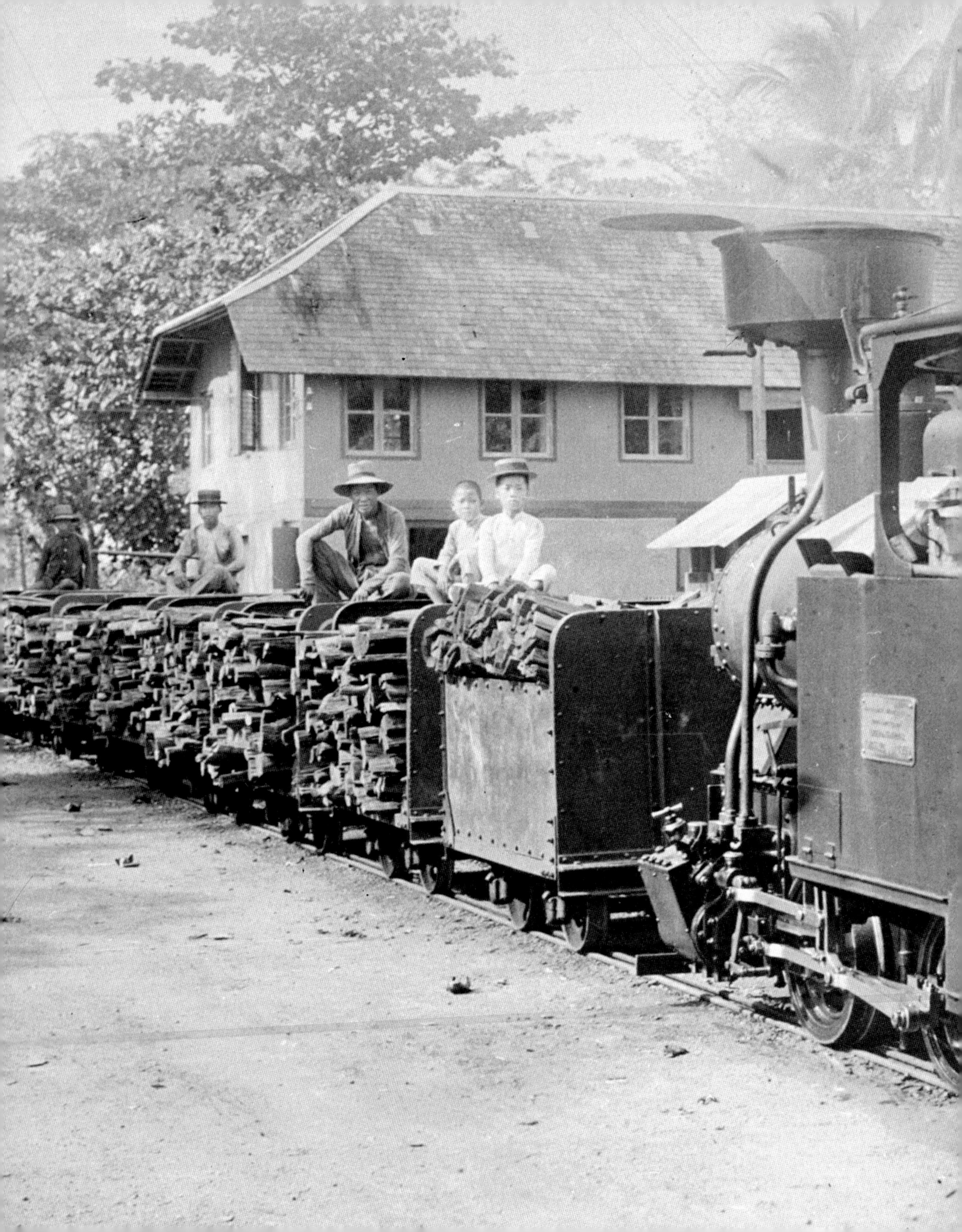

ENTERPRISES

J. THOMAS LINDBLAD

'I would like to warn you, dear friend, that here on Sumatra anything goes. The world you have now entered is a land of impossibilities. It is perhaps the only place in the world where you can make something from nothing.'

With these words, the planter Van Braakel, a heavyset man with a red face, welcomed his new assistant, the twenty-two year-old Hungarian Lászlo Székely, when he arrived on Sumatra's east coast in 1914. At least, these were the words embedded in Székely's memory when, years later, he wrote a story about the occasion.[18] Székely – whose wife, Madelon Lulofs, acquired wider fame as a novelist than he did – thus expressed the unbridled optimism that characterised the colonial economy in the Netherlands East Indies at the time. Yet, did everyone share this optimism?
In photographs from the colonial era, we often see Indonesian clerks sitting at their desks diligently at work in offices of Dutch plantation and trading companies. They were just as much a part of the colonial economy as the planters and the newly arrived assistants from Europe. This contribution provides a rough profile of the colonial business culture, with special attention given to the position of the indigenous Indonesian in this culture. We delve into matters such as the structure of the colonial economy, the position of Indonesians in this economy, enlightened or unenlightened (as the case may be) Dutch entrepreneurship and the 'Indonesianisation' of economic life in the aftermath of the Dutch presence in the Indonesian archipelago in the 1950s.
Dutch colonial capitalism experienced its heyday in the Indonesian archipelago from approximately 1870 until the Japanese invasion in 1942, with an extension until late in the 1950s, when numerous Dutch companies continued to operate in the independent Republic of Indonesia.
The leading symbol of this economic system was the large agricultural company, the plantation where tobacco, rubber, sugar, coffee or tea was grown. Doing business in the colony involved the combination of external and internal production factors. Natural riches, land and labour were present locally while the investment capital, modern technology and management were brought in from abroad. The most fertile of this combination of production factors took shape in the thinly populated areas outside Java, especially in the plantation region of Deli on Sumatra's east coast, where labour had to be brought in from outside. This created a pioneering society that had little or nothing to do with the society surrounding it.[19] A place where, in the words of Székely's planter, something was created out of nothing.

55
Detail Fig. 75

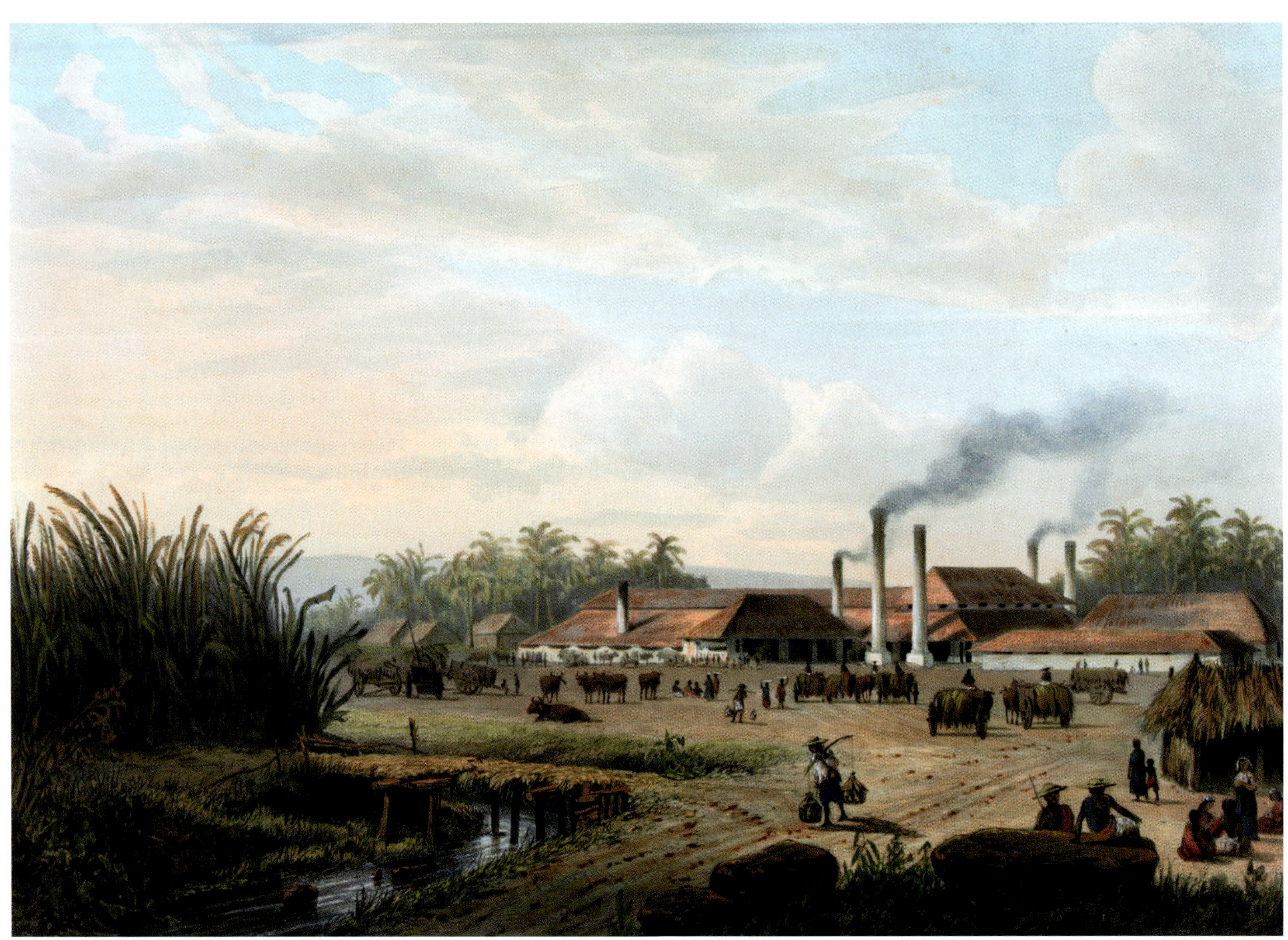

56
Sugar factory in Pangkah
Reproduction of a painting by Abraham Salm (1857-1915)
Litho
26 x 35.9 cm
1865-1872
3728-412. Gift: KIT Library, 1977

The development of Java by private Dutch capital took off after 1870 when the *Cultuurstelsel* (Cultivation System) based on forced deliveries to the government, was abolished. At the same time, the other islands, the so-called *Buitengewesten* (Outer Regions), were opened up to private investment from the West. The capital initially came from the Netherlands, then later also from Great Britain, the United States and Belgium. These firms invested their money primarily in sugar, petroleum and rubber, and later in palm oil as well. The private investments were supported by a steady expansion of effective Dutch authority over the entire archipelago, a process often accompanied by the violence deemed necessary to accomplish it. This brought about a colonial economy with its own characteristics which was closely linked to the colonial state and society which extended from the administrative centre on the island of Java over the entire island empire.[20]

Virgin soils were claimed from the rainforest, roads were built and houses, workers' sheds and warehouses were erected. In the hills of Priangan (Dutch: Preanger) behind Batavia (present-day Jakarta), emphasis was placed on tea cultivation, while in Central and East Java sugar refineries were set up in the vicinity of wetland rice fields where sugar cane was also grown. The pioneering society set up on a tea plantation in Priangan in the late 19th century is eloquently described in Hella Haasse's historical novel *Heren van de thee.*[21]

(Fig. 56) Java emerged as one of the three largest producers of cane sugar in the world and its more than hundred sugar refineries were designated by experts as 'a First World factory in a Third World field'.[22] Here productivity (amount of sugar produced per hectare or worker) increased in the early 20th century by leaps and bounds due to the use of modern technology. Yet what most caught the imagination were the many vast plantations for tobacco, rubber and palm oil planted on formerly uncultivated land in the sparsely populated areas on Sumatra's east coast and elsewhere on the islands beyond Java.

In 1869, the Deli-Maatschappij (Deli Company) was founded on Sumatra's east coast on an agricultural concession granted some years previously by the Sultan of Deli in Medan to the tobacco grower Jacobus Nienhuys. (Fig. 57, 58) The leading financer in the company's establishment was the Nederlandsche Handel-Maatschappij (Netherlands Trading Society, NHM),[23] which at that time was increasingly shifting its activities from trading into banking.

The Deli-Maatschappij grew rapidly and eventually embraced more than twenty separate agricultural businesses with a combined surface area of 120,000 hectares. Around 1920, the company employed nearly 40,000 Indonesian labourers and 150 European staff. The operating capital increased from an initial 300,000 Dutch guilders to 30 million Dutch guilders around 1920 and 40 million Dutch guilders in the 1930s. The dividend percentage was very high, averaging 76 per cent in the 1880s, and reaching 125 per cent in the mid-1920s although the total capital had been greatly increased in the intervening years.[24] The example of the Deli-Maatschappij clearly indicates how much could be earned in the colony. The company's head office in Indonesia is still a prominent landmark in the city centre of Medan.

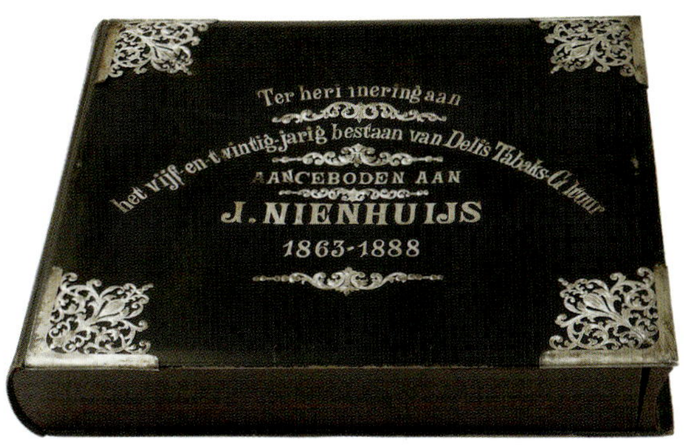

57 >
Photo album on Deli Tabaks Maatschappij 1863-1888 offered to Jacob Nienhuys on the occasion of the company's 25th anniversary
Paper, cardboard, silver
10 x 55 x 44.5 cm
1888
ALB-1466

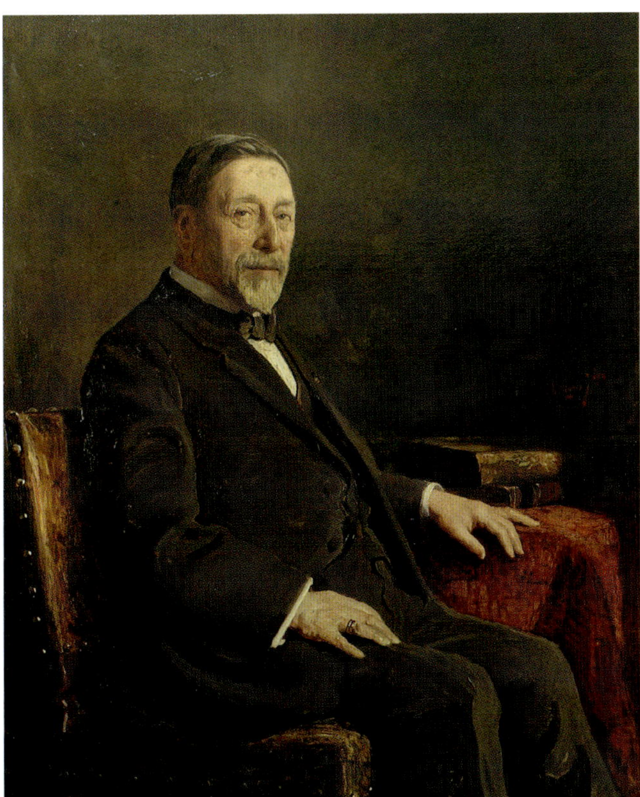

58
Jacob Nienhuys (1836-1927)
Willem Maris (1844-1910)
Pigment, wood
150 x 120 cm
1890-1910
4219-1. Gift: J. Nienhuys, 1974

Optimism, opportunities to earn unknown profits (which were not always realised in the end), use of the production factors present in the colony, a strong orientation towards exports and an increasingly broader package of export products – these were several important features of the colonial economy as it took shape in the late 19th and early 20th centuries. Another feature was the close link between private capital and the colonial government. But one must also realise that the colonial government had its own priorities which, particularly after the inauguration of the so-called Ethical Policy[25] in 1901, did not always coincide with the interests of the business community. In 1925, the oil and sugar industries even financed an alternative training programme for colonial administrative civil servants in Utrecht intended as a counterweight to the more ethically inspired education given at the University of Leiden.[26] However, the most important feature of the colonial economy was the segmentation of activities by ethnic origin, which particularly comes to the fore when we focus on the position of indigenous Indonesians in this structure and on initiatives to introduce change. (Fig. 59, 62)

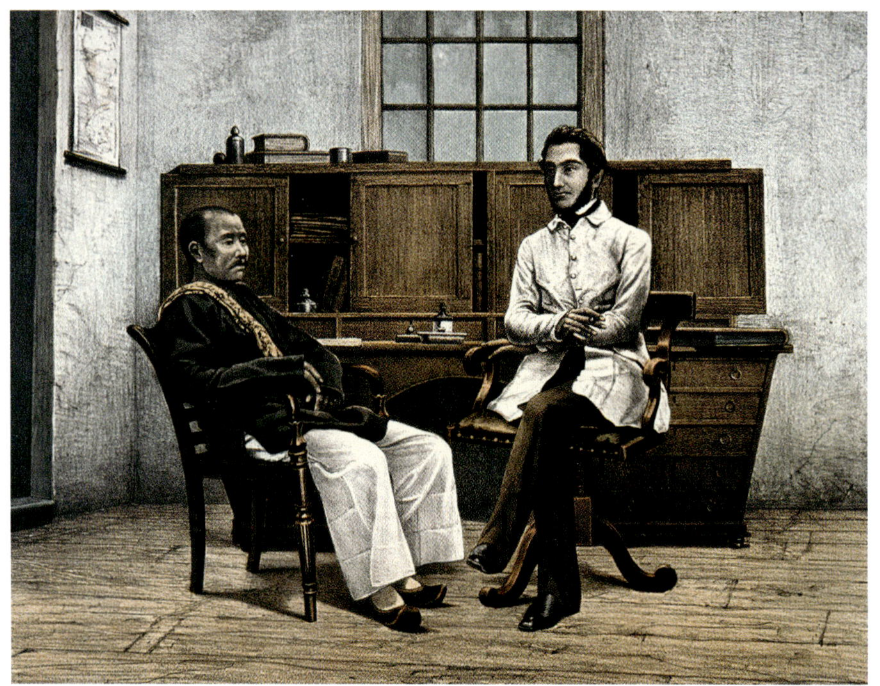

59
Chinese man at the office with a European
Reproduction of a work by A. van Pers (1815-1871)
Litho
20 x 25.7 cm
Indonesia
1854
3728-169. Gift: KIT Library, 1977

Segregation by ethnic origin was laid down in the *Regeeringsreglement* (Government Regulation) of 1854, which can be considered as the colony's constitution. In this regulation, a careful distinction was drawn between Europeans (and those equated with them), so-called Vreemde Oosterlingen (Foreign Orientals, largely ethnic Chinese) and 'inlanders' or 'natives', a term with a pejorative undertone, which is now usually replaced by 'indigenous Indonesians'.[27] For each category, special laws, customs and economic functions applied. Legal segregation by ethnic origin did not as such prescribe a division of economic activity between the various population groups but it constrained the possibilities of people to move across economic sectors thus preserving the existing structure. The 'modern' sector of the economy, including international and long-distance trade, was dominated by Europeans. The ethnic Chinese controlled the regional and local trade networks, while the indigenous Indonesians primarily worked in food crop production, particularly rice cultivation, and as untrained labourers or as office personnel in Western and Chinese companies. In the financial world, Western and Chinese interests were interwoven to a high degree. The most successful indigenous Indonesian enterprises were found in small-scale rubber plantations in Sumatra and Kalimantan and in the cultivation of coconut palm trees on Sulawesi.[28] Another example of successful non-Western entrepreneurship can be found in the tobacco industry in Kudus (Central Java), where both Javanese and Chinese businessmen set up factories for *kretek* (clove) cigarettes.

Segregation by ethnic origin in the structure of economic life in the colony had clear consequences for the development of income and prosperity among the different population groups. The 1920s experienced a boom in the export industry, which saw the incomes of Europeans and Chinese rise by in total 50 and 80 per cent respectively, while the majority of indigenous Indonesians benefited hardly if at all from the boom – with the significant exception of the small-scale rubber cultivators in Sumatra and Kalimantan. In the 1930s, the worldwide economic depression ensued. All incomes fell, as did prices. The decline brought Europeans and Chinese back to the income level of 1920, while the native Indonesians earned half the level of this. On average, calculated over the entire period of the 1920s and the 1930s, the income of a European in the colony was equal to the incomes of 45 indigenous Indonesians or eight Chinese.[29] Such sharp differences in income were only made possible by the far-reaching segmentation in the colonial economy.

Indigenous Indonesian labour was hired in a wide range of different ways for the export production driven by Western capital and Western technology. On the *sawah* (wet rice fields) in Java, a symbiosis developed between rice farming and the cultivation of sugar cane in which the Javanese peasant made land and labour available to the sugar refinery. Rice and sugar co-existed as separate lines of production but were planted on the same land and used the same labourers and the same sources of irrigation. A controversial point in the assessment of this system is the question of who profited the most from the investments made by the colonial government in facilities for the irrigation of the fields: the Javanese farmer or the sugar refinery? Although the land remained inalienable from the village community and the peasant retained his status as a free labourer, his negotiation position vis-à-vis the managers of the sugar refineries was not strong, especially since the supply of manpower was usually abundant due to the high population density in Java.[30] On the plantations outside Java, the situation was very different.

TUBES AND CYLINDERS WITH OPIUM SAMPLES

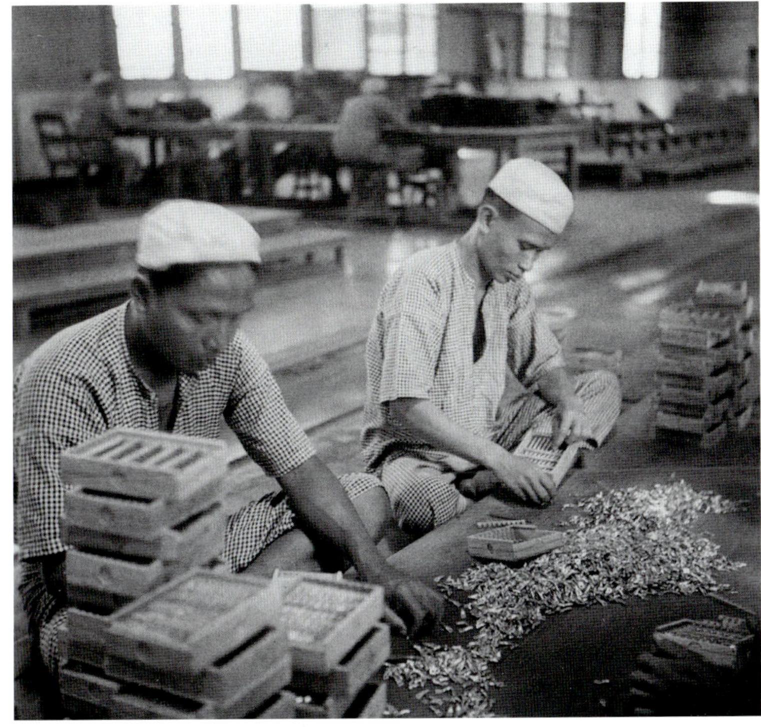

60
In an opium factory in Batavia tubes are packed into boxes
Glass negative
9 x 12 cm
May 1936
10012174. Gift: Opium factory Batavia, 1936

61
Tubes and cylinders with opium samples
Wood, lead
5 x 25 x 27 cm
Batavia
c. 1930
3401-1147a/k
Former collection KIT
Tropical Products, 1964

As early as 1676, the Verenigde Oostindische Compagnie (VOC) obtained a monopoly on the import and processing of poppies from India and the trade in opium. The drug began to play an important role in the development of 19th-century imperialism when the English, despite protests from the Chinese Manchu rulers, used it as an 'exchange medium' for desirable Chinese products such as tea. It resulted in the first opium war (1839-42) and the Treaty of Nanking that humiliated the Chinese. In the meantime, the Dutch colonial government in Batavia had an opium monopoly. It was an important source of income, partly because so-called opium smoking also increased in popularity in the Netherlands East Indies. Opium became a proven method of binding the contract labourers to the colonial businesses; because so many of these labourers used opium, it was often given a Chinese inscription. The existence of different rules and laws within the archipelago also resulted in a range of different opium packaging. A number of modern equipped factories had stood in Batavia since 1894 for the processing of opium. The opium was packed in tin cylinders for export – the same type of cylinders used for paint. The factories were entirely legal and were under the strict supervision of the colonial government. The Netherlands was also a member of the Opium Commission of the League of Nations. It was not until after the Second World War and Indonesian independence that this trade came to an end. The Tropenmuseum possesses a number of wooden boxes that contain cylinders of different sizes containing opium samples which were meant to be used as demonstration material for (potential) customers. This is the reason the museum has an opium permit. PW

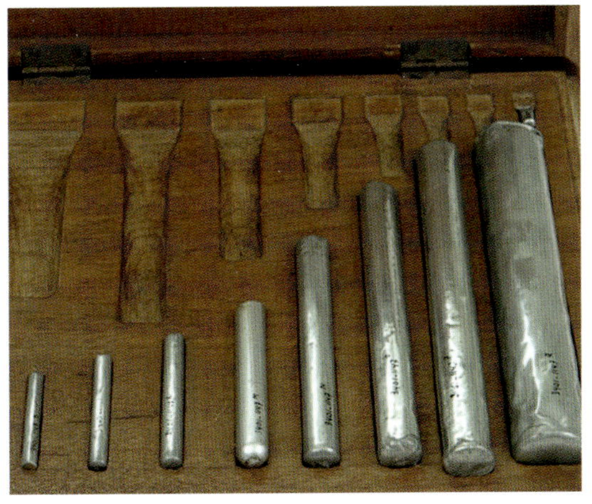

Here workers had to be brought in either because the areas in question were thinly populated or because the local population preferred not to work on Western plantations (the latter was the case in Aceh). This brings us to the so-called *koelievraagstuk* (coolie question), one of the most controversial issues in colonial economic life, even at the time. It also brings us back to the Deli-Maatschappij.
Jacob Theodoor Cremer (1847-1923) (see p. 62), who figures prominently in the exhibition 'The Netherlands East Indies, a colonial history' of the Tropenmuseum, was appointed as the administrator of the Deli-Maatschappij in Medan at the tender age of twenty-three. He oversaw the stormy expansion in the initial years of the Deli-Maatschappij. At the instigation of the planters in Deli the so-called *koelie-ordonnantie* (Coolie Ordinance) was issued in 1880. Initially this regulation only applied to Sumatra's east coast. Later it applied to all Outer Regions while, ironically enough, a similar regulation had just been abolished in Java. The ordinance gave far-reaching authority to the employer (the company), over the employee (the coolie), who initially had been imported from South China, and was later recruited in Java. By virtue of the hated *poenale sanctie* (penal sanction), non-compliance with contractual obligations, even on minor points, was made a criminal offence. The penal sanction was considered necessary by planters such as Cremer due to the investments that the company had made for the recruitment and transport of coolies from Java.[31] Until its abolition under international pressure in 1931, the penal sanction was fervently defended by the leading employers' organisation on Sumatra's east coast, the Deli Planters Vereniging (Deli Planters Association), where Cremer served as chairman for a long period. Cremer eventually became director of the NHM and entered politics serving as a member of the Dutch Parliament and as Minister of Colonial Affairs. In 1910 he was one of the founders of the Koloniaal Instituut in Amsterdam.[32] As director of the Deli-Maatschappij, he was succeeded by his son Herbert Cremer.
The coolie issue continued to dominate passions among planters. In 1902, a small book entitled *De millioenen uit Deli* by J. van den Brand, a lawyer in Medan, was published. It made an allegation against the planters, linking them to the many instances of violence and abuse committed at the plantations.[33] An investigation was ordered by the colonial author-

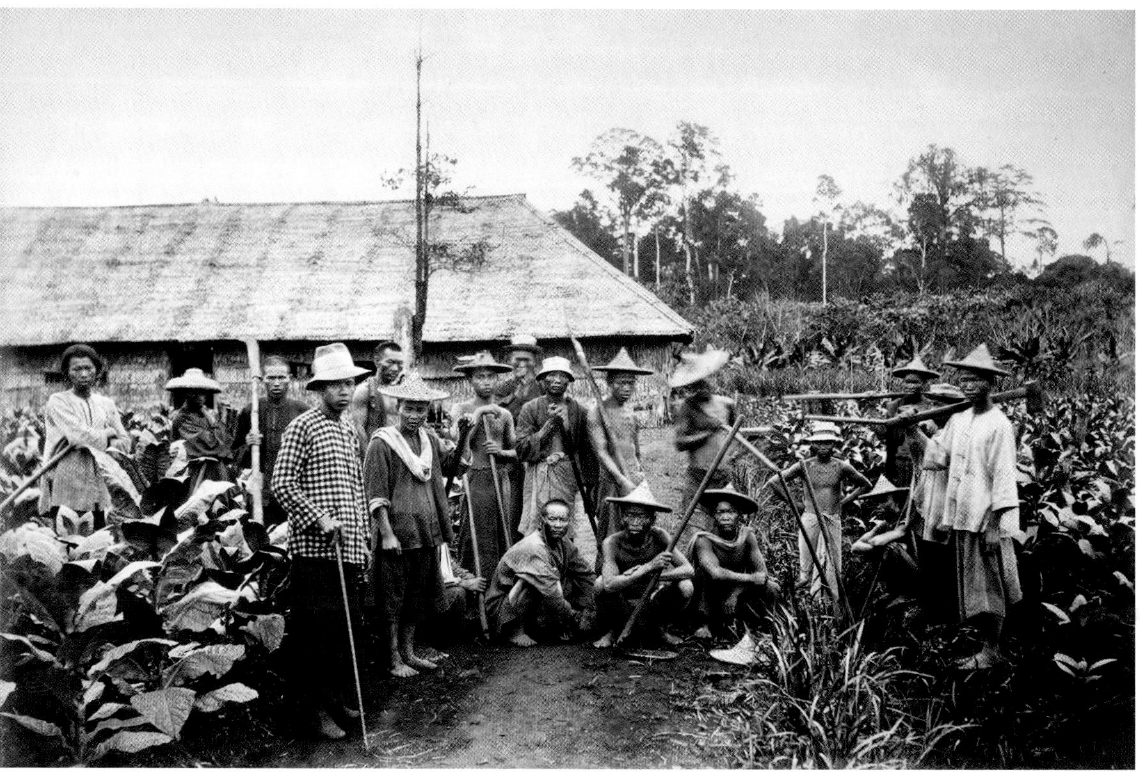

62
Chinese coolies on a tobacco plantation
Deli, Sumatra
Photographer: G.R. Lambert & co. (1880-1910)
Albumen print
26.7 x 35.5 cm
1880-1890
60001834

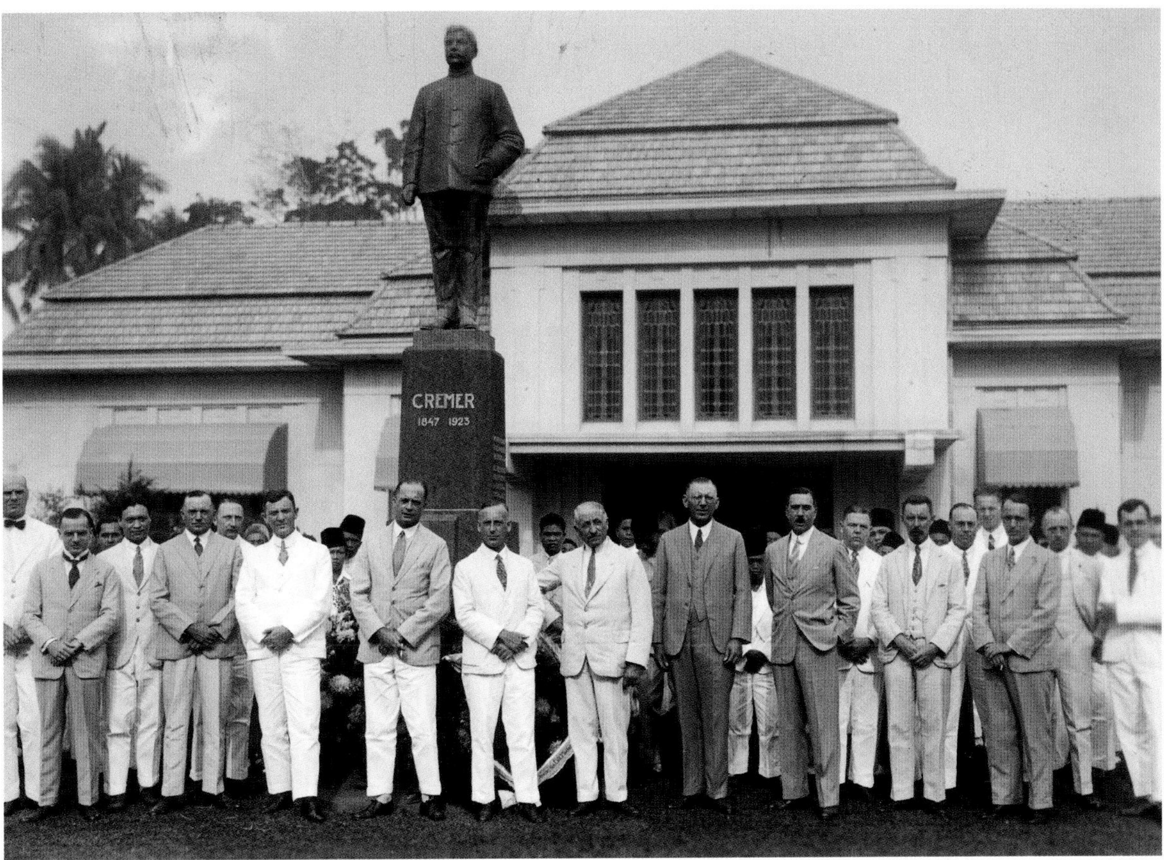

63
Group portrait around the statue of J.T. Cremer, Medan, on the occasion of the fiftieth Jubilee of the Deli Planters Association
Photographer: W.T. Uhlenhuth
Gelatin silver print
11.8 x 16.3 cm
1929
60039579

ities. The report of the investigation was not made public until some 80 years later.[34] The investigation prompted the colonial government to set up a separate labour inspectorate for the Outlying Isles. Despite this, until late in the 1920s, scandals continued to occur which involved cases of excessive violence perpetrated against coolies – cases that apparently went unnoticed by the labour inspector. Increasingly, publicity was given to the violence committed by coolies against Chinese or Javanese supervisors and European assistants or administrators in the extremely segregated plantation society, which was closed to the outside world.[35] Contemporary novels such as *Rubber* and *Koelie* by Madelon Székely-Lulofs described how violence and the fear of violence were an inseparable part of the daily life of planters and coolies.[36]

The Western companies frequently displayed pride about those things that were brought about in the small pioneering communities in isolated locations. There are many examples – the quays in the harbour of the coal mine Poeloe Laoet (Pulau Laut in current spelling) on the island of the same name off the south-east corner of the island of Kalimantan, schools and cinemas on the terrain of the refineries of the oil company BPM,[37] local railway lines and telephone services provided by the Deli Spoorweg Maatschappij (Deli Railway Company) that Cremer founded in 1883. On the island of Belitung (former Billiton) east of South Sumatra, the local population could ride on the tram maintained by the Billiton Maatschappij, market leader in tin mining, free of charge. (Fig. 75) The vast majority of these investments was focused on the physical infrastructure and intended to facilitate the production process. Little was invested in imparting knowledge to native Indonesian employees.

The most famous example of enlightened Dutch entrepreneurship dates from the years preceding the large-scale flight of export production from the colony. His name was Karel Frederik Holle (1829-96). (Fig. 76) He began his career as a clerk in the

64-73
Several opium pipes
Java
19th and early 20th century
From left to right: 3401-1058a, -1070a, -1095a, -1066a, -1036, -1032, -1057a, -1062a, -0055, -1060, 405-5
Former collection KIT Tropical Products, 1964

> 74
bottom right **Opium pipe**
Chinese, Indonesia
c. 1925
405-5. Gift: A. Coster-de Roo, 1927

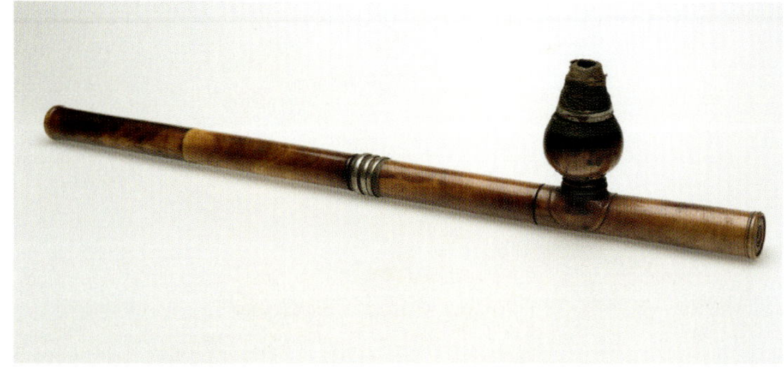

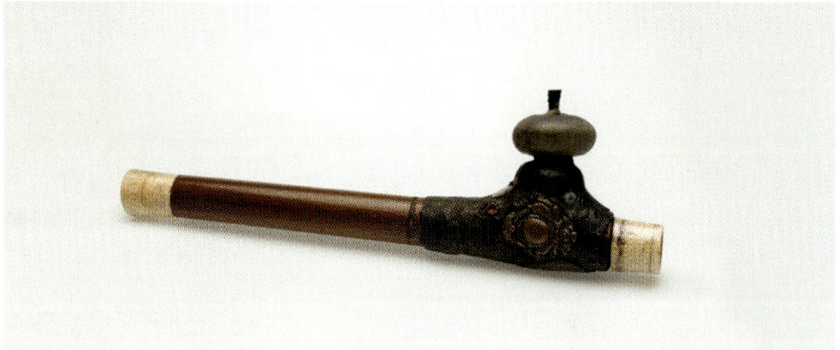

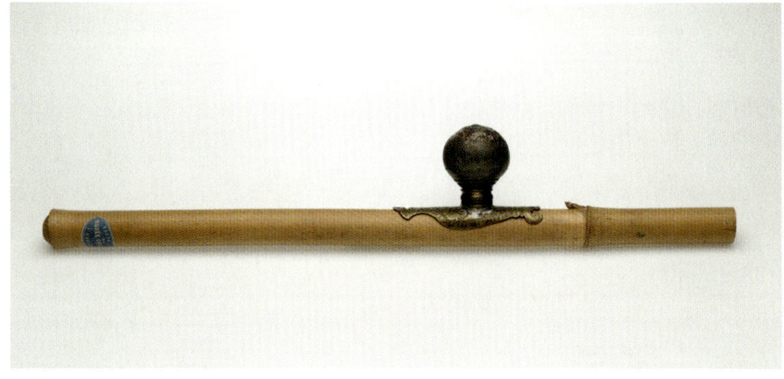

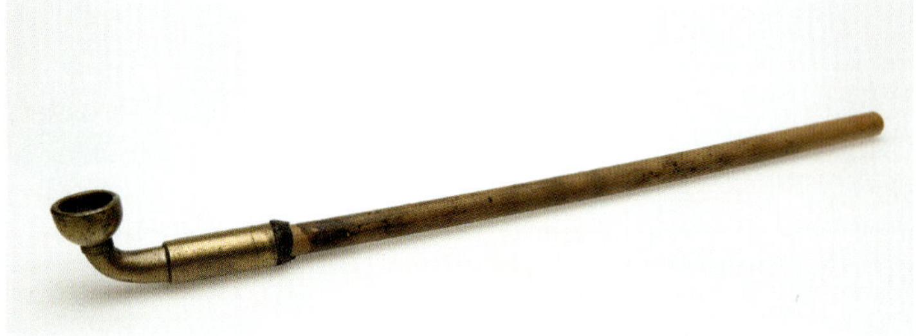

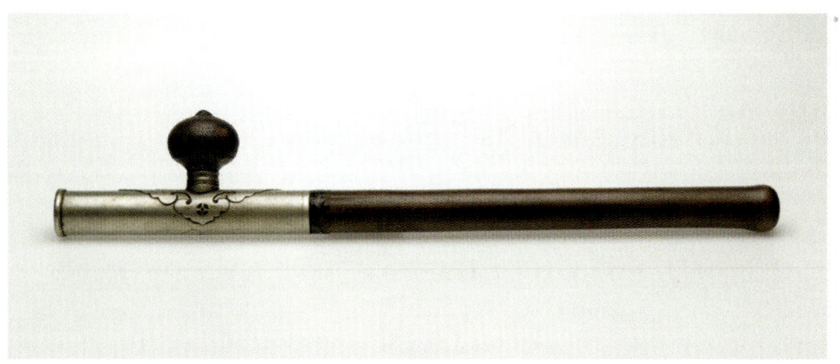

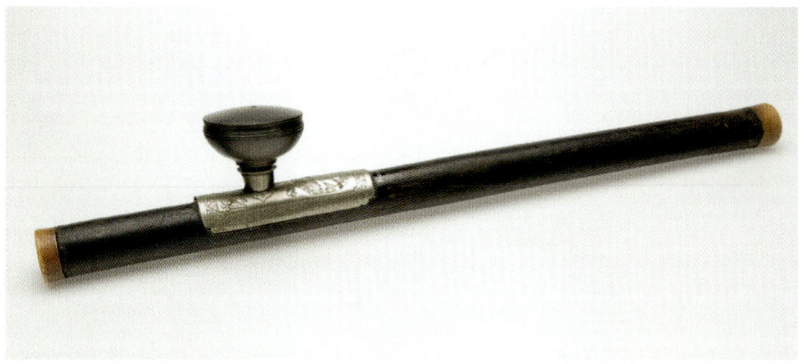

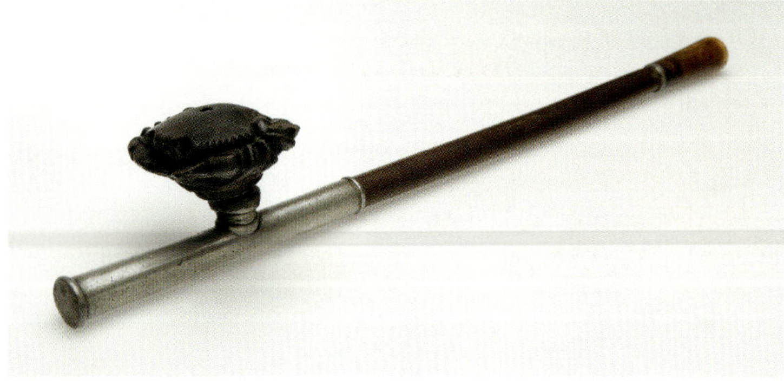

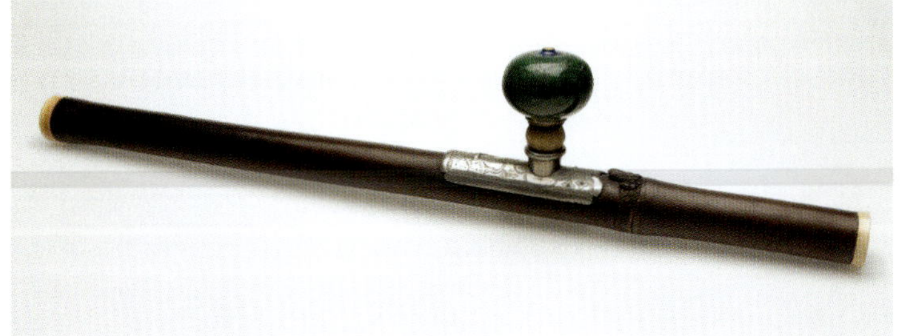

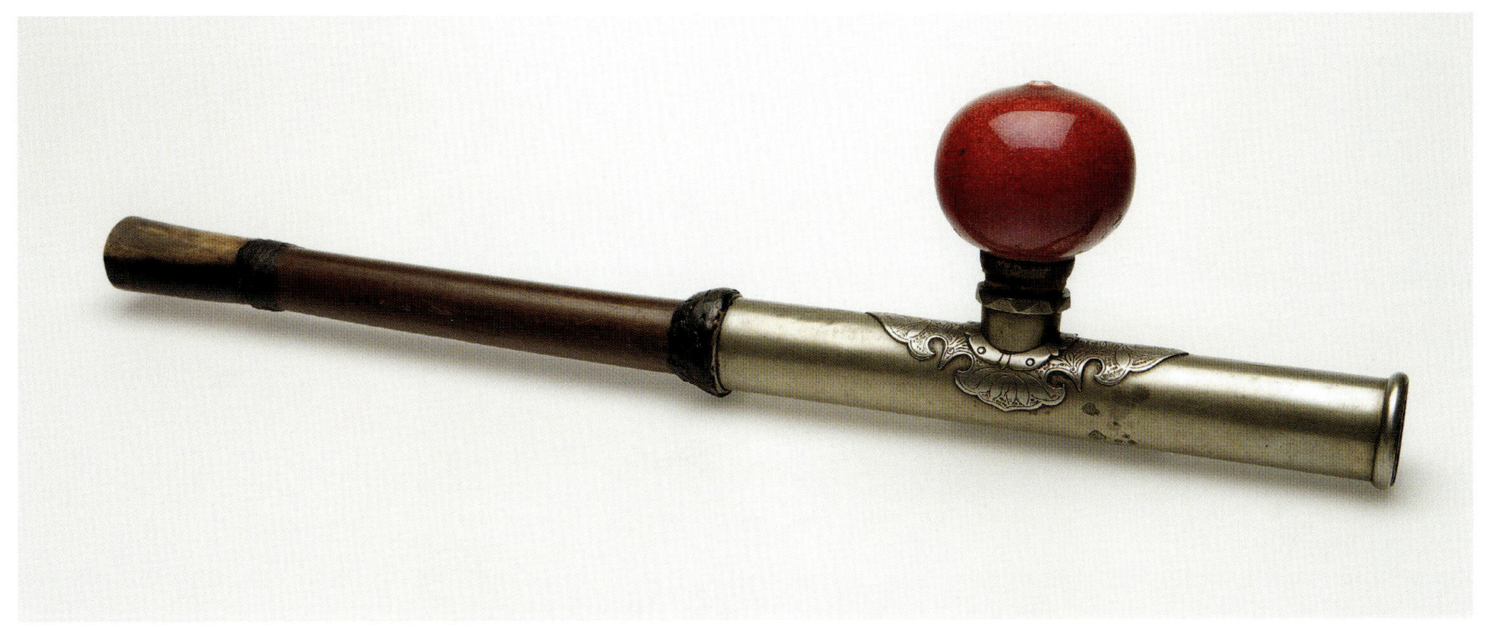

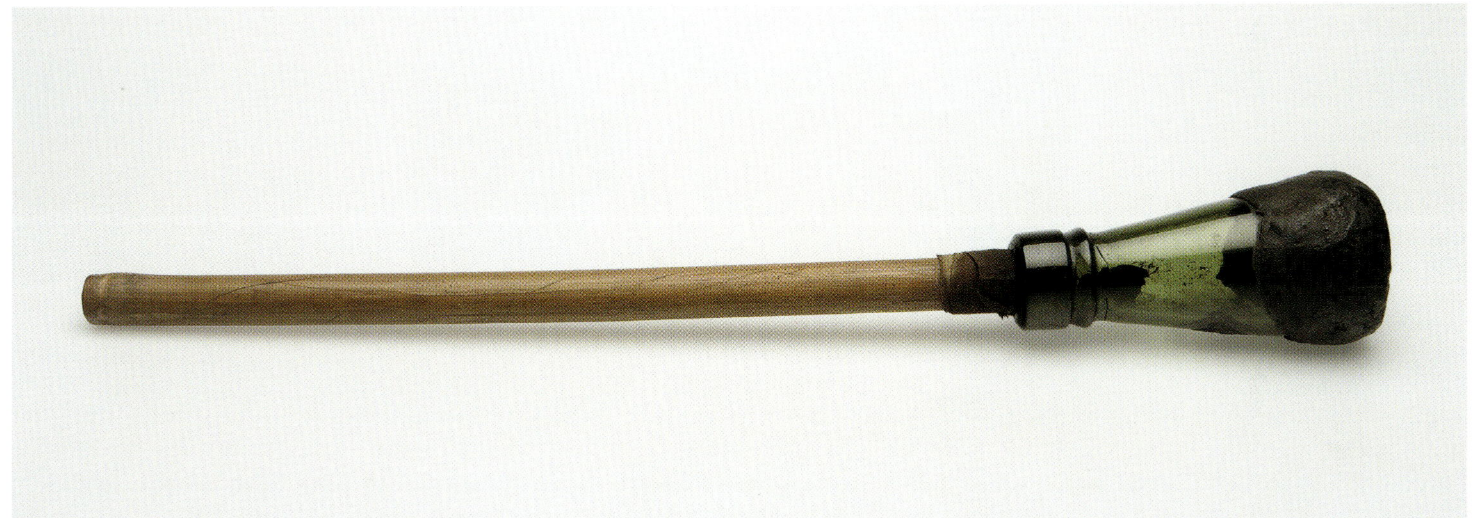

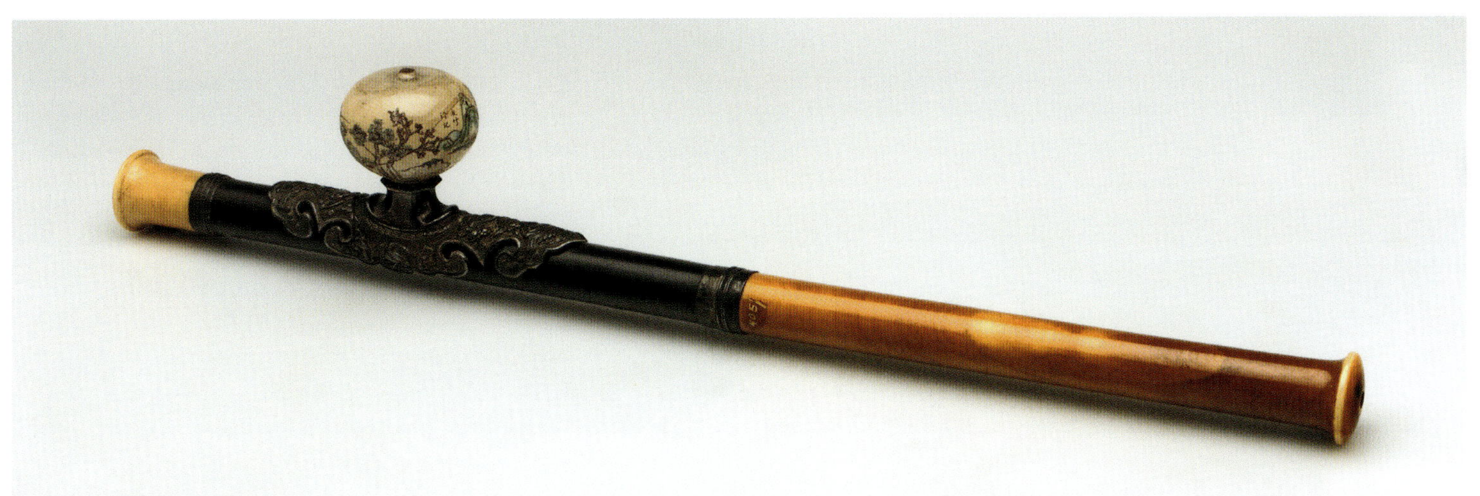

JACOB THEODOOR CREMER – PLANTER AND MORE (1847–1923)

He attended secondary school in Zwolle and Arnhem and in 1868 entered employment with the Nederlandsche Handel-Maatschappij (NHM), Batavia (Java). Later he was a tobacco planter and administrator in Deli (Sumatra). He was co-initiator of the koelie-ordonnantie (Coolie Ordinance). Back in the Netherlands, he successively became a Member of Parliament (Lower Chamber, Uni-Liberals 1884-97), Minister for the Colonies (1897-1901), President of the NHM (1907-12) and co-founder of the Koloniaal Instituut, Amsterdam (1910).Cremer was a mover and a shaker among the colonial elite.
JDJ

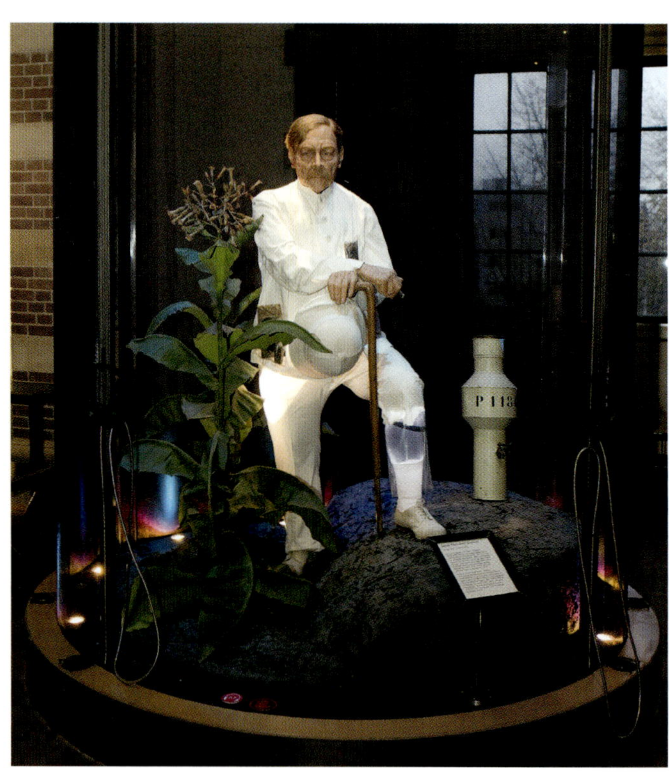

colonial government, but at the age of twenty-seven he moved into business. He became an administrator and later the owner and director of tea plantations in West Java. Holle immersed himself in the language and culture of the Sundanese population in the area and actively tried to promote the wellbeing of indigenous Indonesians. He did this, among other ways, by establishing a teacher-training college for schools attended by indigenous children. From 1871 he served as an advisor for 'native affairs' to the colonial government.[38] Holle actually anticipated the Ethical Policy that was generally defined by its three pillars: 'irrigation, education and emigration'. According to critical observers, only the first objective achieved anything.[39]

The strict ethnic segregation between the sectors of the economy and within individual companies was maintained by language barriers. Knowledge of Dutch was indispensable for every higher position in a commercial enterprise while access to Dutch language education was limited to a very small circle of indigenous Indonesians, often from the nobility, as well as to Europeans and a handful of Chinese. At the end of the colonial era, following four decades of implementing Ethical Policy, less than one thousand students, of whom only 220 indigenous Indonesians, sat final exams each year out of a total population of 60 million.[40] The pattern is clearly visible when we look at the staff of De Javasche Bank (the Java Bank), the private bank that functioned as central bank for the colony and was responsible for the circulation of money. All management positions at the bank were occupied by Dutchmen, while the lower ranks were almost exclusively occupied by Indonesians, with the striking exception of all the bank tellers, who were almost all ethnic Chinese. Such a division of tasks by ethnic origin had developed over several decades.[41] The situation was much

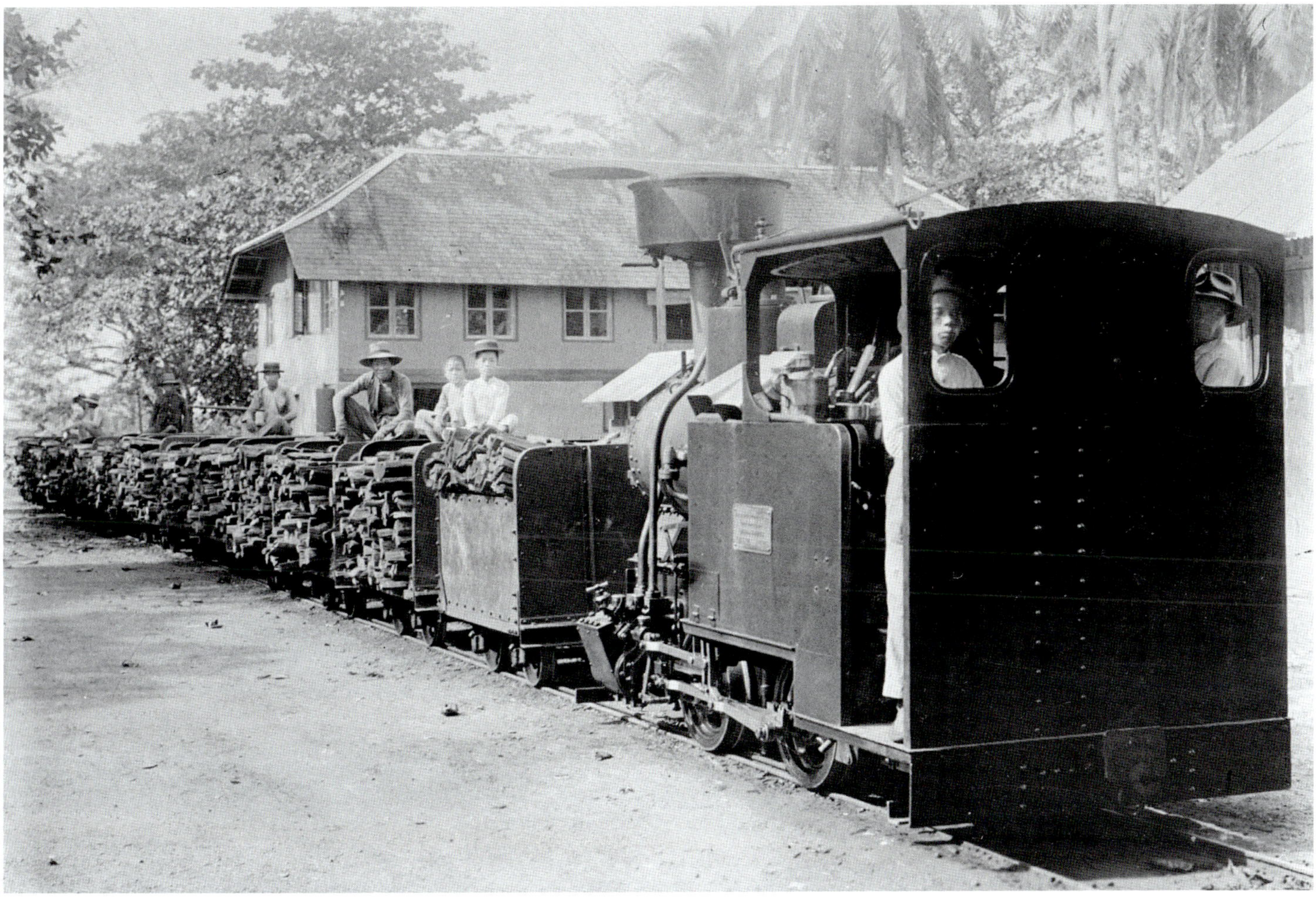

75
Transport of firewood for the exploitation of the steam tram, Billiton, South Sumatra
Glass negative
9 x 12 cm
c. 1915
10007177. Gift: Billiton Maatschappij, 1916

76
Karel Frederik Holle (1829-1896)
Willem Deninghof Stelling (1864-1931)
Oil painting
68.5 x 60 cm
c. 1894
2534-1. Gift: N.P. van den Berg, 1956

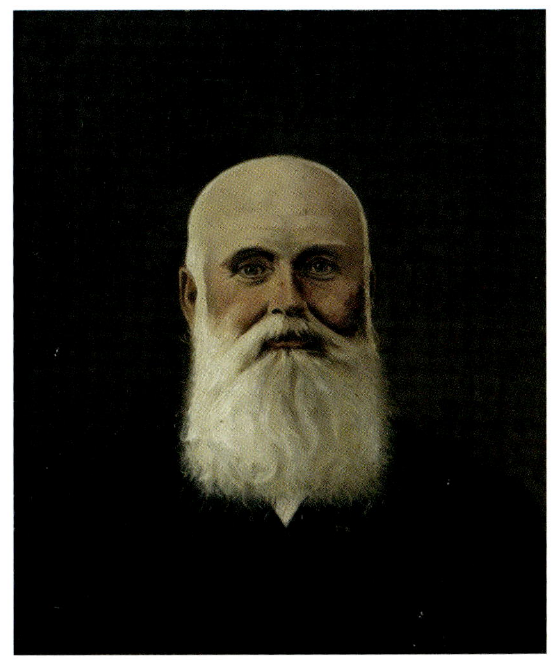

the same at the leading Dutch trading firms, in particular the renowned 'Big Five' (Borsumij, Internatio, Jacobson van den Berg, Lindeteves and Geo Wehry). Part of the conditions under which the Netherlands recognised the sovereignty of Indonesia in 1949 were guarantees for the continued operations by Dutch companies in independent Indonesia in exchange for a relatively vague promise by the companies that they would appoint Indonesians to higher positions 'as soon as possible'.[42] But the subsequent process of Indonesianisation that took place in the Dutch companies during the 1950s satisfied no one. It was introduced too quickly for the Dutch entrepreneur and too slowly for the nationalists in the Indonesian government. The process also turned out very differently in different places. The leader was the BPM, which provided technical training and replaced much of the middle management with Indonesian personnel. At Internatio, a separate category of Indonesians

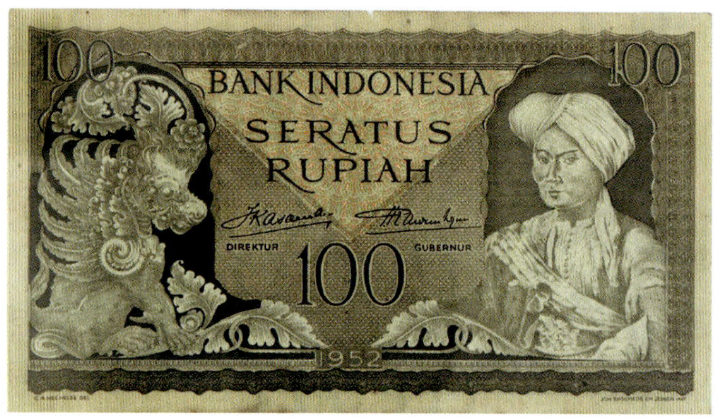

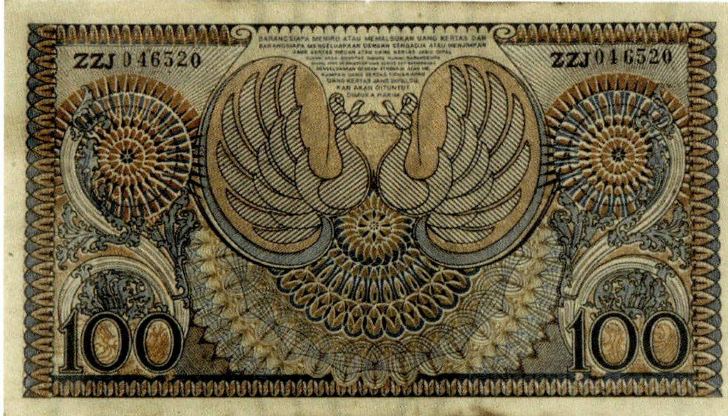

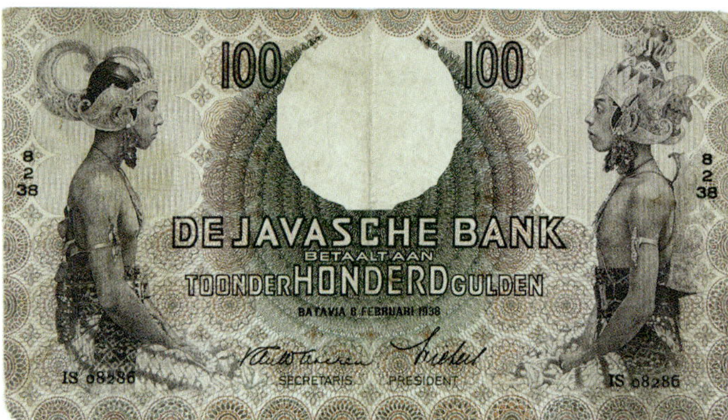

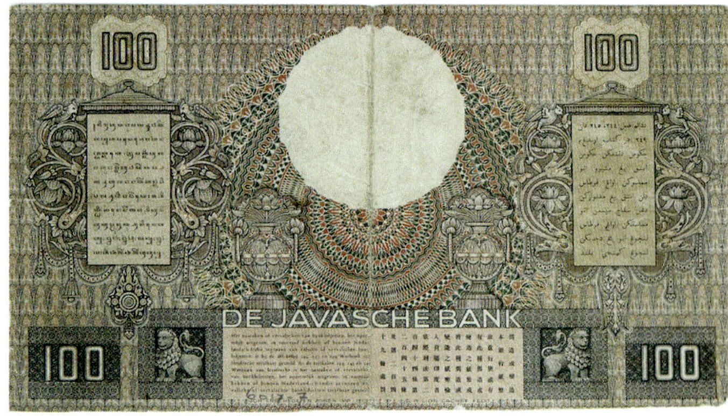

77
Banknote
One of the first bills issued by the independent Republic of Indonesia
Ink, paper
8 x 14 cm
Indonesia
c. 1949
4328-28. Purchase: 1977

78
Banknote of The Javanese Bank
C. A. Lion Cachet (1864-1945)
Paper
10 x 18 cm
Indonesia / The Netherlands
1938
6017-7. Purchase: L. van Borkulo, 2002

with a higher position was established. Yet it did not escape the attention of the Indonesian government that the majority of the promotions involved Indonesians of Chinese origin. At many plantation companies, exemplified by the situation at both Deli and in the tobacco region of Besuki (East Java), virtually no progress was booked in this respect.[43] A special situation arose at the central bank, which was bought in the early 1950s by the Indonesian state and had its name changed to Bank Indonesia. The management board and the board of supervisory directors had an Indonesian majority, while most of the departments and branch offices still had a Dutch manager. (Fig. 77, 78)

The operations at the Dutch companies in Indonesia in the 1950s were a complex matter. The times were favourable thanks to the boom on the world market, which made attractive profits a part of the forecast for exports from Indonesia. At the same time, the companies were confronted by numerous difficulties in production. In addition to the call for Indonesianisation, there were the actions of militant trade unions, occupations of land by the local people, and theft and sabotage. Most companies vacillated between two options: leaving and trying to set up elsewhere or adapting themselves and trying to make the best of things.[44] Most chose the second option in the end, but applied a short-term strategy focused on maximal profits which could ideally be transferred out of the country, and minimum investments in the modernisation or expansion of the production facilities. Such a strategy, for example, was used by the shipping company KPM (Koninklijke Paketvaart Maatschappij, Royal Packet Company), which dominated interinsular traffic and sidelined the rival set up by the Indonesian state.

The pragmatism in the Indonesian parliamentary democracy in the early and mid-1950s changed into increasing economic nationalism and increasing polarisation. The conflict between the Netherlands and Indonesia over the western part of the island of New Guinea, the only remaining Dutch colony in Southeast Asia, went from bad to worse. In December 1957, virtually all Dutch companies still operating in Indonesia were taken over within a span of a few weeks by local trade unions.[45] The

THE CLERK

For an Indonesian boy who had finished his primary school education and had attended a couple of years of secondary education, a job in an office of a company or with the local government administration was usually the highest goal attainable. Since the 1920s, private business had experienced rapid development and the apparatus of government had broadened considerably. There was an urgent need for personnel with such education under their belt in order to carry out an enormous volume of administrative work; work for which the limited number of European/Dutch senior management on hand was insufficient and too expensive. An account had to be given for everything, everything was noted down; every single pound that the harvest produced, every litre of water used to irrigate a tobacco crop, every regulation had to be written down in legible handwriting and several copies of the originals had to be made. Knowledge of the Dutch language and good handwriting were essential. Information that, up to the present day, has been lying unread in the many quarterly and annual reports maintained for various companies, as well as government documents. This model, currently depicting a clerk, is one of the three models, that have survived from the 1920s. For years he depicted a member of an ethnic group in an exhibition. JDJ

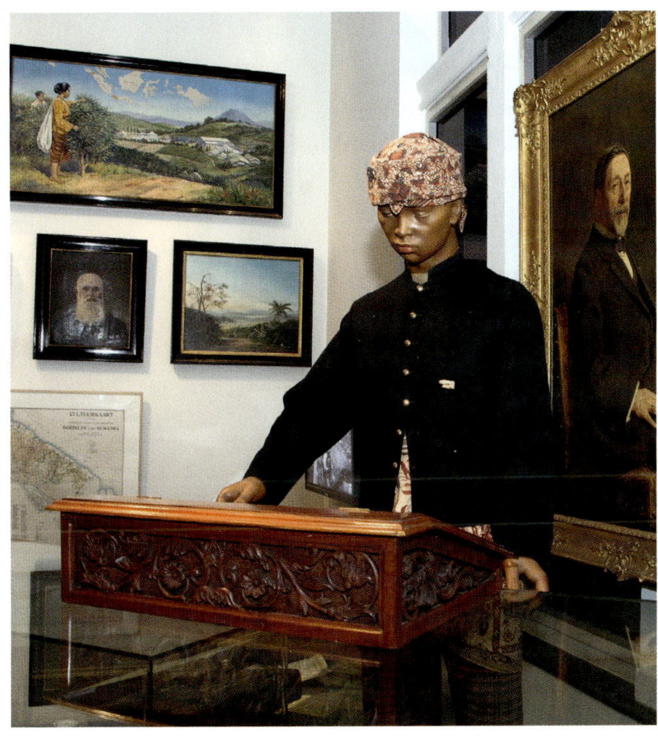

government of Soekarno hastily approved the actions after the fact but transferred the authority over the seized companies to the army in order to prevent the communists from gaining control over a significant part of the production facilities via the trade unions. Operations were taken over by Indonesians who were often employees with a long period of service – employees who on past occasions, such as during the Japanese occupation (1942-45) or the Indonesian Revolution (1945-49), had actually exercised control. The transition and adaptation to the new situation took a couple of years, but around 1960 production reached its former capacity at the plantations in Deli. In December 1958, a full year after the seizures, the Indonesian parliament decided to nationalise the Dutch companies. This nationalisation was largely implemented in the first half of 1959. In the same year, the nationalisations were sanctioned under international law through a ruling by a court in Bremen where the Deli-Maatschappij had protested against the auctioning of tobacco from its former plantations. The nationalisations were seen by the German court as a part of a wider process of decolonisation and deemed to be legal since compensation had been promised. Agreement was not reached on this last point until in 1966. Between 1973 and 2003, the Indonesian government paid damages of nearly 700 million guilders to the Dutch state, considerably less than the claimed value of the nationalised commercial holdings (2.7 billion guilders).[46] So although compensation was paid, the question remains as to whether it was sufficient. This payment was the logical completion of the colonial economic relationship between the Netherlands and Indonesia. At the same time, a new era ensued with the return of leading Dutch companies as investors in the former colony. The interest of Dutch trade and industry in Indonesia took on speed in the wake of the state visit of Queen Beatrix in 1995, but was tempered shortly thereafter by the economic crisis from which Indonesia has managed to extricate itself in the early twenty-first century.

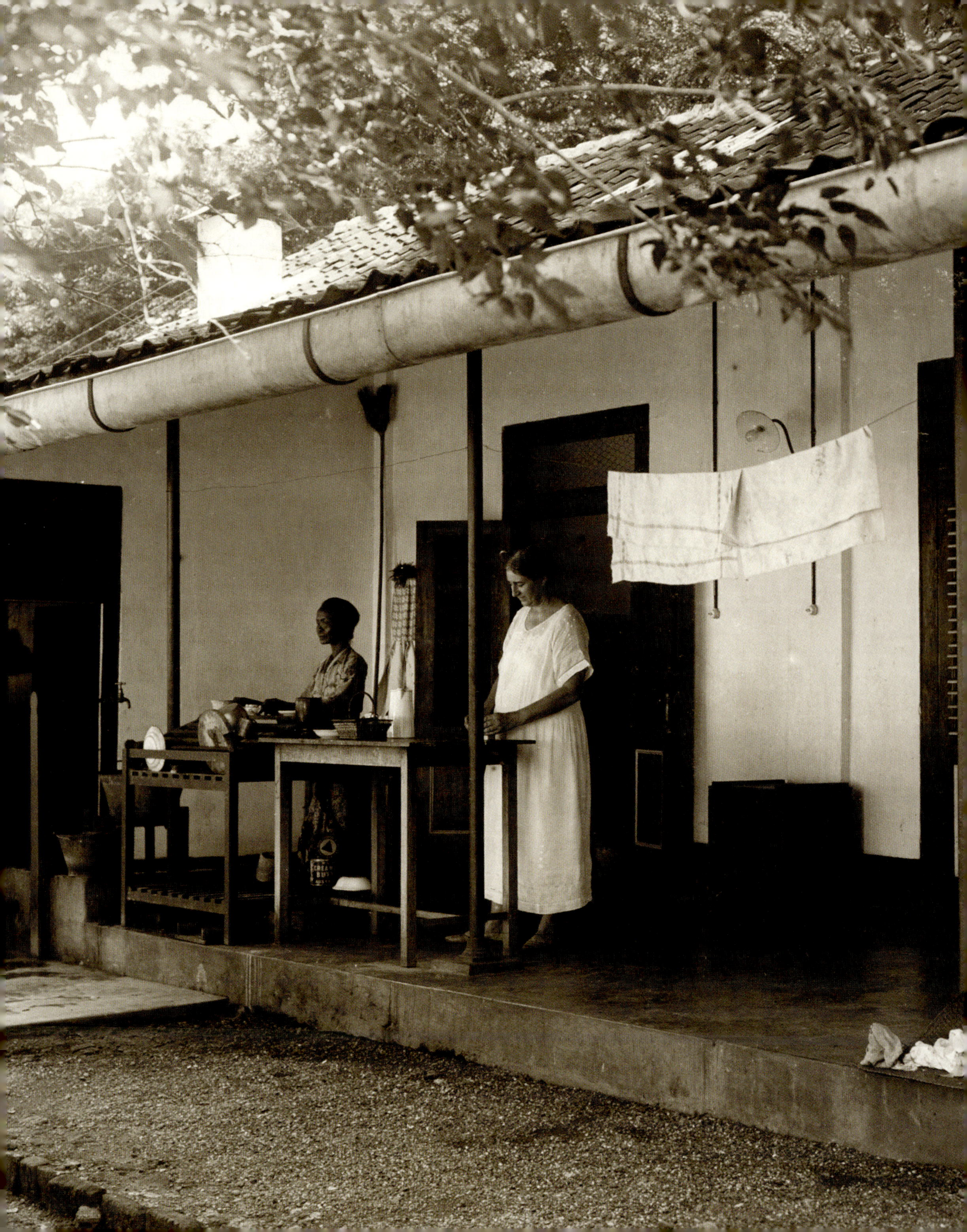

DOMESTIC SERVANTS IN COLONIAL TIMES

RATNA SAPTARI

Domestic servants as an indispensable part of the colonial household

Family photographs of colonial life in the Netherlands East Indies have become part of our visual imagery of not only how European or Dutch families lived but also of their relationships with the local population represented by those who worked directly for them in their homes. In 'freezing' certain scenes, these photographs often portray a sense of stability and certainty, showing the normality of relationships in the past. Historians and social scientists now understand that photographs are not so much historical documents that portray an objective past, but like any other historical source, are subject to particular framings, in this case by the photographer, by those who requested the photographs to be taken, or by the archivist. If we combine these visual images of the past with other historical sources, such as colonial reports, biographies, life histories, childrearing manuals, novels and historical monographs, we can have a better picture of the background of the photographs presented to us, and therefore understand these photographs better.

Europeans who were in charge of overseeing the establishment and running of plantations, mines, construction projects or had government jobs, needed not only labour to work in these various sectors but also people to do the cooking, cleaning, washing, child minding (for those with families), gardening, sewing, guarding the house and driving them from place to place. The various colonial projects which involved the reorganization of land and rural settlements, and the relocation of labourers from one place to another resulted in the loss of land and/or traditional means of income for the local population, and stimulated migration to places where work was available. Among the different jobs available, work as domestics in European households became an important occupation. According to the 1930 Population Census of the Netherlands East Indies, one fifth to one fourth of the working population in Java for instance, worked in domestic service.[47] Coming from the urban periphery or the rural areas, these men, women, boys and girls in search of work, quite often ended up in the homes of middle class or wealthy European, Chinese, Javanese or other Indonesian families in the cities, small towns or plantations, recruited by agents or through the mediation of those already employed. The presence of these servants especially in the European households, is repeatedly described in novels, books, life histories and oral interviews. *Onze Bedienden in Indië*[48] for instance shows the

79
Detail Fig. 88

MARGARETHA ENGELEN-KOETS – OFFICER'S WIFE (1870–1957)

She was the daughter of a clergyman. She attended the Academie van Beeldende Kunsten (Academy of Art) in The Hague and married Captain C.H. Engelen, who won his spurs during the pacification of Bone (1905). After a 5-year stay in a garrison town on Java, she and her husband left for South Sulawesi. He was promoted to the position of civil servant there. Both felt a strong sympathy for the Ethical Policy.
Margaretha Engelen-Koets is a fictional character; she represents the many Dutch housewives that followed their husbands to the Netherlands East Indies as 'the wife of'. JDJ

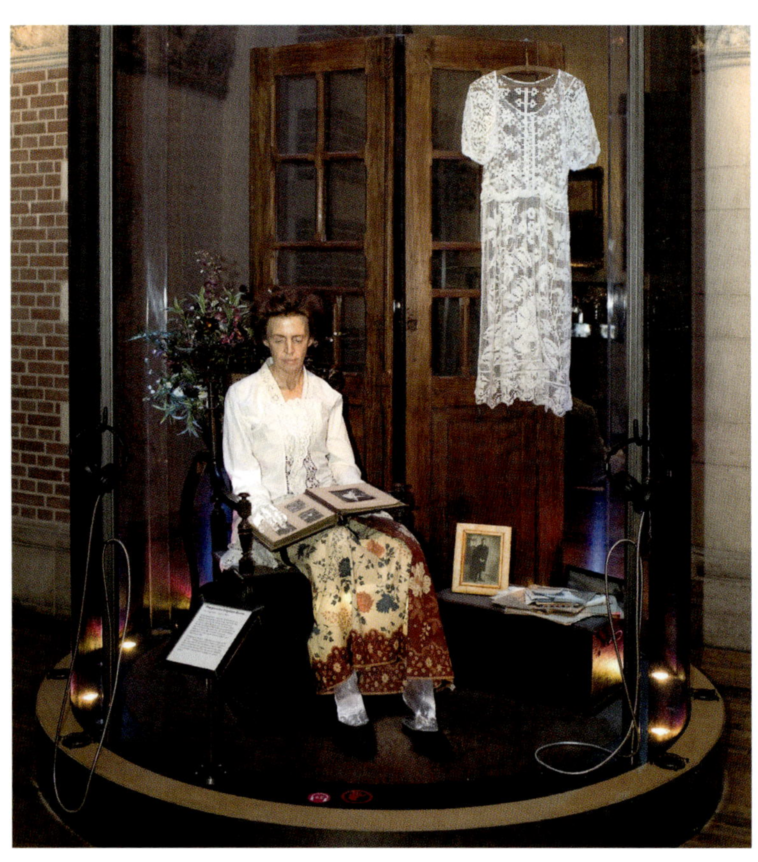

complex relationship between mistress and servant, who are separated by class and race, but share some emotional ties as women. *Uit de suiker in de tabak;*[49] *Rubber*[50] or *Heren van de thee*[51] tell the stories of Europeans and Eurasians and their struggles to establish some kind of existence in the plantations in Java or Sumatra, amidst harvest failures, market downturns, romantic entanglements, domestic tensions and the political intrigues of colonial society. Within these stories, domestics are constantly present although mostly in the shadow of the main narrative. They not only serve the needs of the employers but also become the lens through which the European colonial society views the local population. (Fig. 82, 83) Other sources about domestics are the memoirs, collected letters and oral interviews of individual family members such as those compiled and edited in works like *Brieven van de thee*[52] and *De njai.*[53]

Although stories of and by domestics in written form are difficult to find, we can still get some idea of the lives of servants through the stories told by their employers. The Koninklijk Instituut voor de Tropen (KIT) in Amsterdam has a diverse assortment of photographs which show how servants are framed in the private and social lives of the European colonizers. These photographs selected for this essay are available in the KIT collection and give us an idea of how life in the colonies was portrayed and how servants were placed in the domestic spaces of the Europeans. Since spatial and social hierarchies are not only part of the European domestic scene but very strongly also of the Indonesian elite, some other photographs are chosen to show the Indonesian domestic scenes.

European families and their domestic spaces

For European individuals and families residing in the colonies, having servants was not just about the need to have other people do all the household chores, it was also about maintaining one's status in the social hierarchy. The photographs illustrate not only that the house that one lived in, the clothing that one wore, the vehicle one used, but also that the number of servants one was allowed to or could afford to have, indicated one's ranking in the social hierarchy. Diverse historical, social and physical environments affected the nature of relations between the European or Eurasian population and the locals. Since the migration of European women was actively discouraged from the 17th until the mid-19th century, European men who came to the colonies were mainly unmarried and often took local women as their concubines.[54] The *nyai* (Indonesian concubine) usually bridged the gap between the European male and the local community, whereas the European male connected the *nyai* and the children emerging from this union, with the world of the colonial rulers.

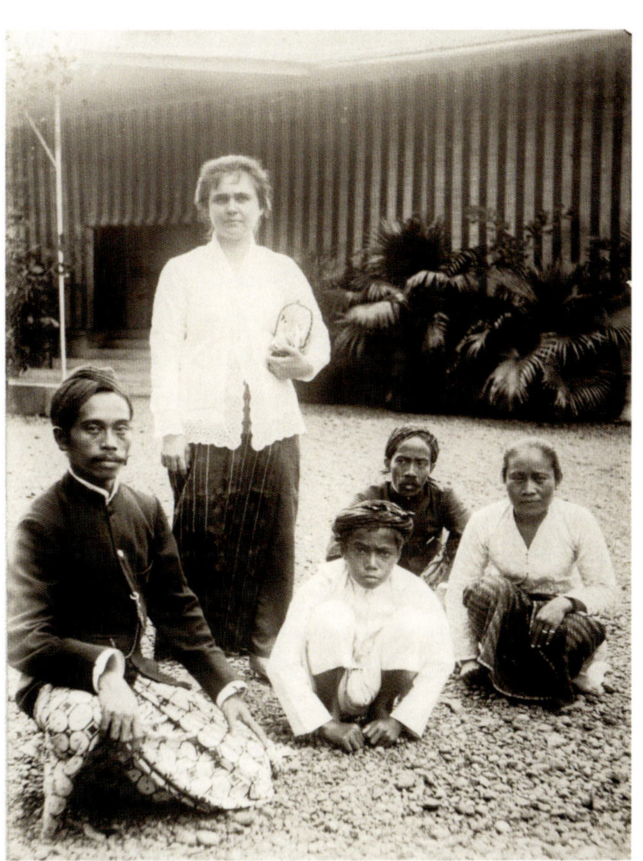

80
Mrs. L. van Breda de Haan and her servants, Buitenzorg
Photographer: Marie L. Treub (1881-1968)
Gelatin printing-out paper
11.3 x 8 cm
1904
60013590. Gift: M.L. Treub, 1970

The story of these connections and the social issues that emerged from them is a major theme in many novels.[55] The descendants of these mixed marriages took over many of the elite Javanese lifestyles and rituals. Eurasian women often wore a *kebaya* (embroidered white shirts with long sleeves) and batik sarongs; whereas men wore white shirts with batik trousers. The use of *jamu* (herbal medicine), *sirih* (chewing betel), bathing twice a day and taking afternoon naps, became habits which were taken over by the *Indo's* (Eurasians) especially in Java.[56]

Figure 80, taken in 1904, shows a European or Eurasian woman dressed in white shirt and sarong with her servants. The servants are all squatting or sitting on the ground, a common position in Java. Among the servants themselves one can also see internal hierarchical difference. The man at the forefront is sitting slightly straighter and higher than the other three. His expression is more confident and his clothes look more official.

By the early 20th century single Dutch or European women and the wives of government personnel were permitted to come to the Netherlands East Indies. There grew a gap between the Dutch who were *totok* ('pure bred') and those who were *peranakan* (descendants of mixed marriages) and thus hierarchies developed according to the degree of 'pureness'. Especially in places like Sumatra's east coast, the distinction between these two categories of Europeans became much sharper, and racial mixtures were more frowned upon than before.

Figure 84, taken around 1920, shows a *totok* European family posed to present their home life in the tropics. They are wearing European clothes, with the servant sitting on the floor watching the mother holding the baby. The caption to this photo says 'Werkkamer met Europeanen en een baboe' (work room with Europeans and a maid). Although it is not mentioned, presumably the servant is there to take care of the child but for the sake of the photo, it is the mother who is holding the child. One man is sitting behind a desk piled with paper and the other man is sitting with arms leaning against the armchair. The woman is wearing European dress and not a *kain* (hip cloth) or *sarung* (tubular skirt), and therefore shows a different profile from the woman in Fig. 80. The social distance between the employer and the servant can clearly be seen here in the body language and sitting positions.

HOUSEKEEPING BOOK

81
Housekeeping Book
Paper, ink
20.5 x 16.5 cm
Tebing Tinggi, Sumatra
1923-1930
5470-1. Gift: C. Twigt-van der Goot, 1992

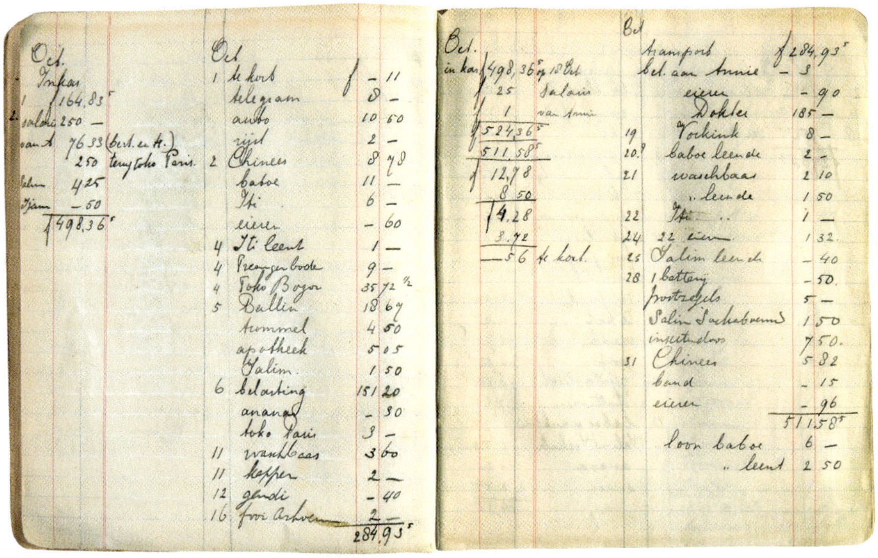

For nearly seven years, Ms Van der Goot kept a daily account of the income and, particularly, the expenditures – from June 1923 to March 1930. Her husband worked 'in rubber', most likely for the company Dolok Merangir in Tebing Tinggi on the island of Sumatra. In 1924, his salary increased from fl. 250.00 to fl. 275.00 a month. The housekeeping book provides a good picture of the life of an average family in the Netherlands East Indies. There is a baboe or *amah* (female servant) who was paid an average of fl. 10.00 a month; sometimes she borrowed more: the boy was given an occasional tip (fl. 2.50) and even the 2.5 cents that was given to a beggar is noted in the book. The subscription to the reading club cost fl. 4.50 a month in 1924. Once a month, a relatively large amount was paid to a certain toko or Chinese restaurant. As a regular customer you did not pay for each item separately. The names Iti and Salim also appear regularly in the book; perhaps they were domestic servants.
In addition to expenditures on daily living expenses – the butcher, milk, bread, vegetables – there is another repeated item: the post office at least twice a month. The dates of these expenditures coincide with the arrival of the mail boat from the Netherlands. Through letters, the family back in the home country was kept abreast of what was happening in the colony. A telegram (fl. 8.10) was an enormous expenditure, which means there must have been a special reason to send one. Although the monthly expenditures regularly exceeded the salary, there were also months in which money was deposited into a savings account with the Javanese Bank. JVD

Another scene shows how servants are also present in the recreational activities of the European employers, not as participants but as onlookers, their position still clearly demarcated as they sit on the ground watching their masters enjoy their leisure time. (Fig. 85) The caption says only that this is the Helvetia tennis court in Medan, North Sumatra. The Europeans are all wearing the white sports clothes of the period and both men and women are involved. The servant is sitting on the lawn watching them, with a child on her lap.
The circumstances in which the servants find themselves vary from place to place, often also depending on the status of their European employers in the social hierarchy. The living arrangements of domestic servants differ according to the rank of the European masters and whether the housing of the local workers was situated near the European settlements or not.

82
Female servant with a European child in a sling, Java
Postcard reproduction of a watercolour by J. van der Heijden (1865-1928)
Paper
14 x 9 cm
c. 1910
2659-2. Gift: Openbare leeszaal Groningen, 1957

83
Female servant cooking, Java
Postcard reproduction of a watercolour by J. van der Heijden (1865-1928)
Paper
14 x 9 cm
c. 1910
2659-9. Gift: Openbare leeszaal Groningen, 1957

84
Study with Europeans and an amah, Sumatra
Gelatin silver print
14.7 x 19.1 cm
c. 1920
60023174

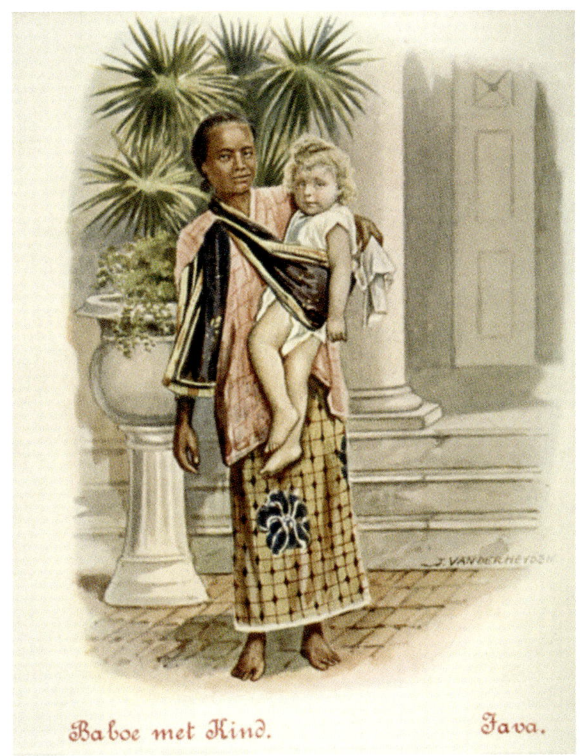

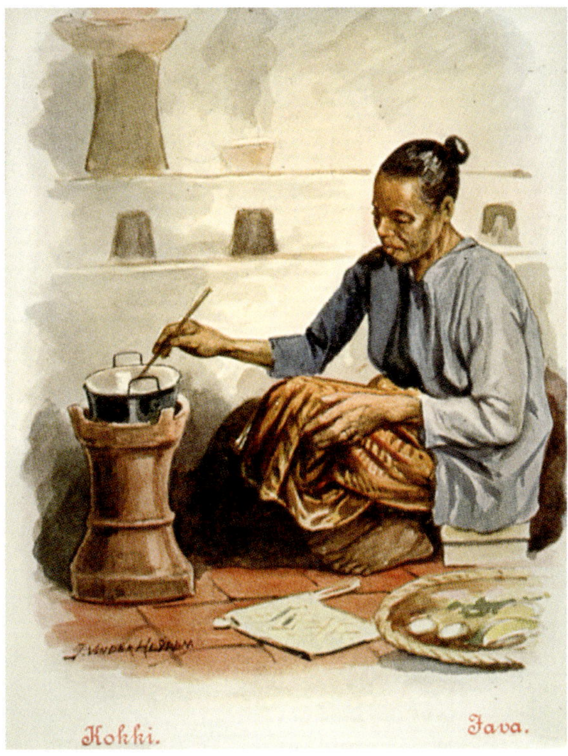

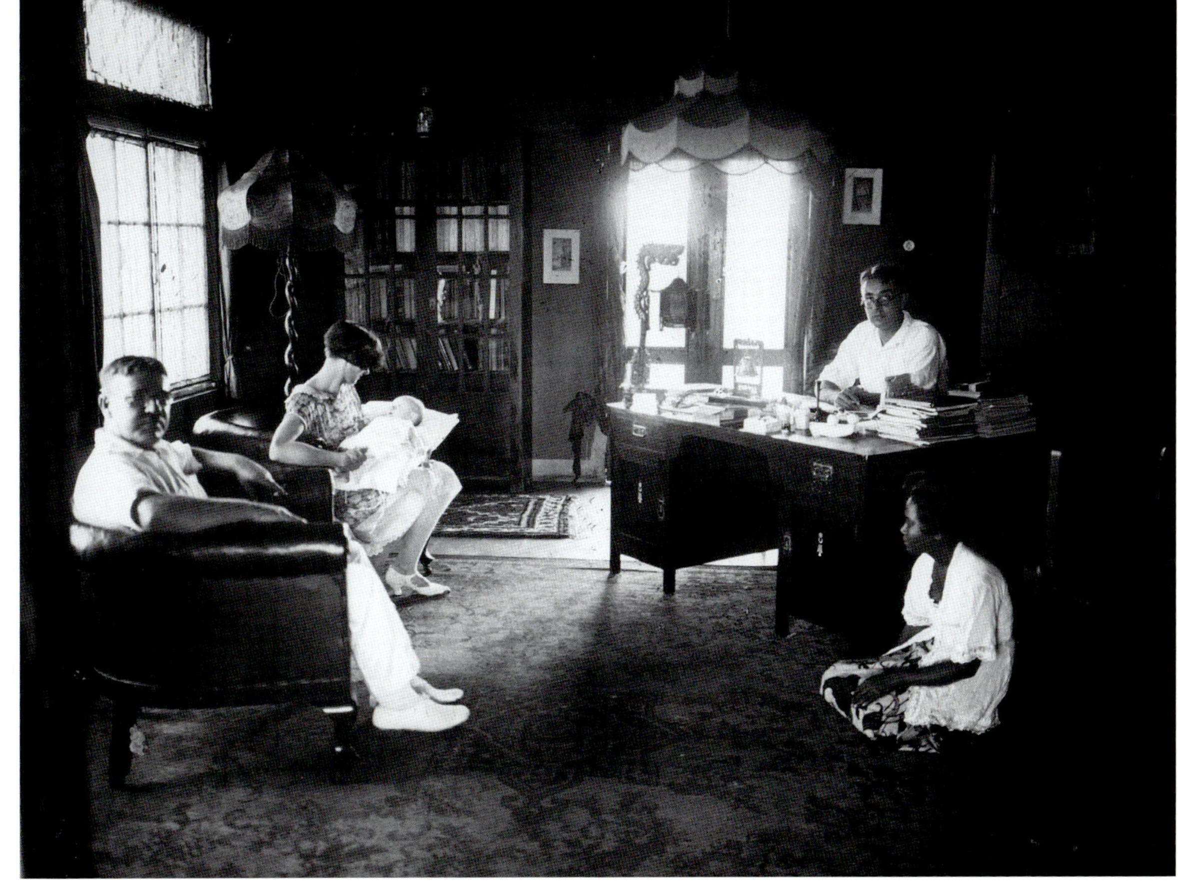

85
Tennis court of the Helvetia tobacco company, Medan
Photographer: J. Willem Schut
Gelatin silver print
12 x 16.9 cm
1890-1900
60022949

86 >
Planters and servants next to a second supervisors house at the cultural enterprise Kedongdong or Way Lima, Lampongse Districts, South Sumatra
Gelatin printing-out paper
11.8 x 16.8 cm
1897
60003125

87 >
Couple and servants in front of the new administrator's residence at the coffee company Way Lima, Sumatra
Gelatin printing-out paper
11.6 x 17 cm
1897
60013339

88 >
Mrs. Nobel with *amah* and kitchen help, Madura
Gelatin silver print
11.2 x 16.7 cm
1920-1930
60021452. Gift: B.A. Engelsman Sr., 1966

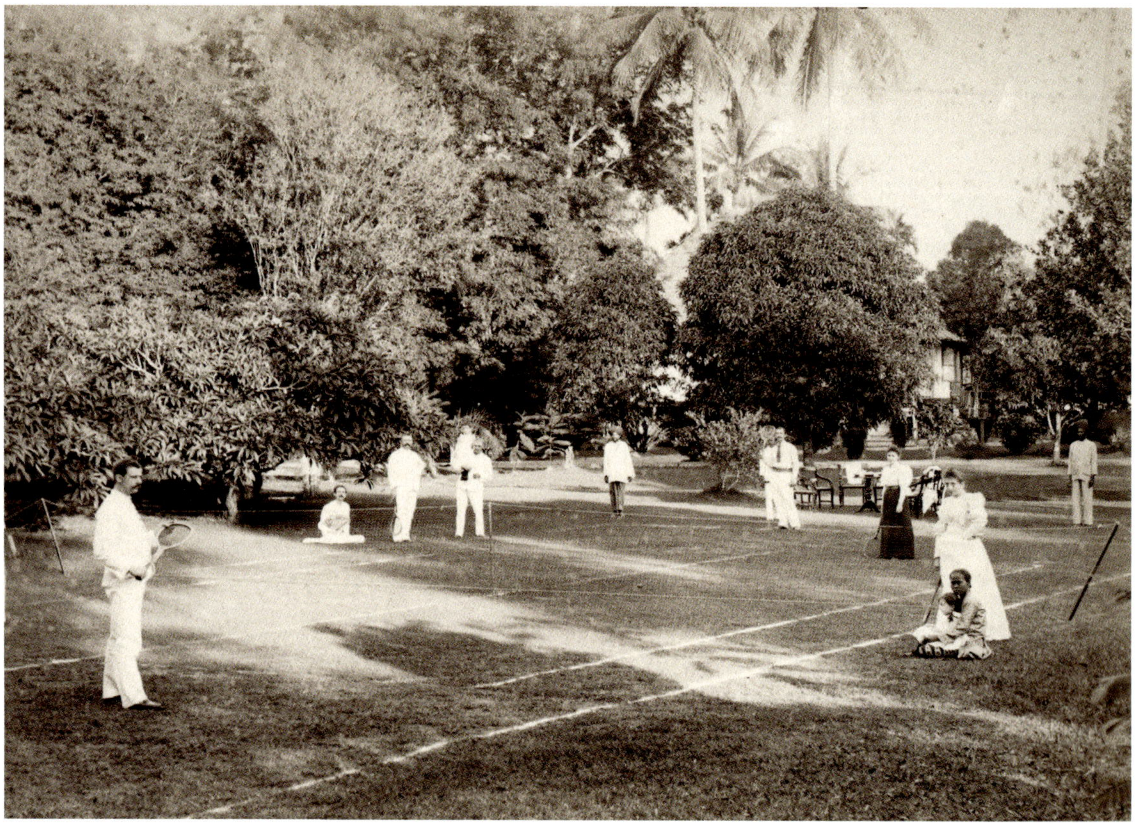

Some servants lived in rooms attached to the residential quarters of their employers, in sheds in the gardens or at the rear side of their homes. Some of the servants lived in; others came early in the morning and went home in the evening. For the latter group, this meant they could not live too far away; otherwise traveling to and fro would be too difficult. Bringing servants into the home of the colonizers always created ambivalent emotions for the employers: servants were an inseparable part of their households but their existence in private homes was also seen as a threat.[57]
The presence of servants was often associated with theft, criminality and in later years (at the end of the colonial period) with nationalist politics. On the other hand servants were also functioning as the 'eyes and ears' of their masters in times of political turbulence, particularly when moving about in public spaces was considered too unsafe.
Quite different from photos 84 and 85 above, figure 86 shows servants in front of the residence of European personnel in Lampung, South Sumatra. This photo was taken in 1897, and therefore earlier than the photos taken above.
It is mentioned that the European is the *tweede opzichter* (second supervisor) of a plantation. It is not mentioned what plantation, but because it is in Lampung, it might be a coffee plantation, since coffee was an important agricultural product of this area. His house is much smaller and there is no large yard in front; instead the house is surrounded by bushes, seemingly some of them coffee trees. He may be without family since there is no woman or child in the photo, and therefore the domestic work may involve cooking, cleaning and washing clothes only. Figure 87 is of the same area (Lampung, South Sumatra) and also the same year (1897) but shows a much larger house with a wide lawn in front; the Europeans are in their usual position sitting on chairs in front of the house. The caption mentions that this is the house of the new administrator of the Way Lima coffee plantation in Lampung. The servants are sitting on the ground next to their masters or far behind them. Interestingly there seems to be a norm that standing close to a European or a Javanese master would be considered disrespectful. This is also often found among local elite and their subordinates,

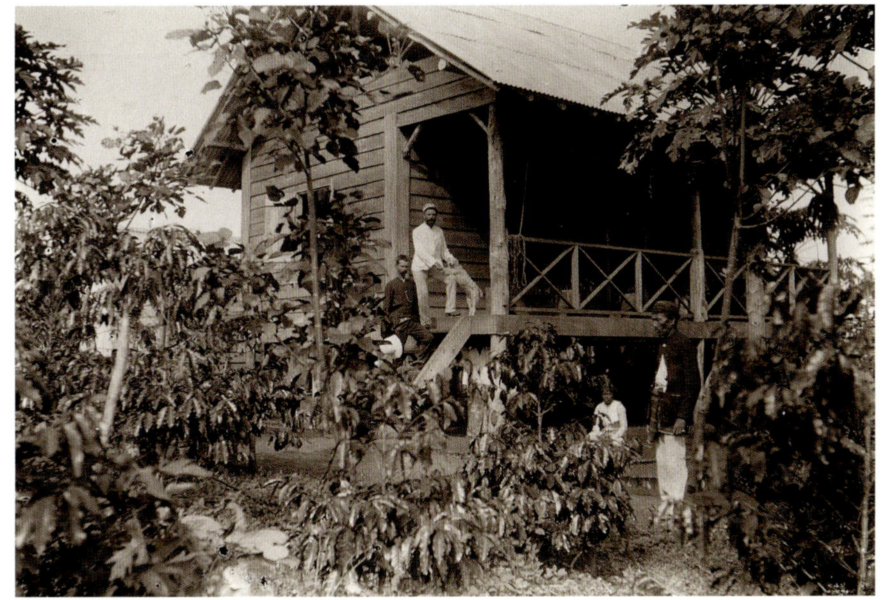

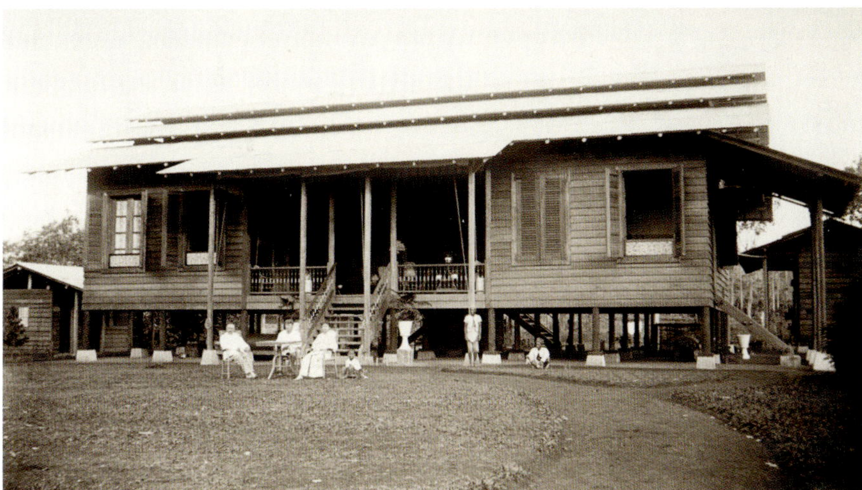

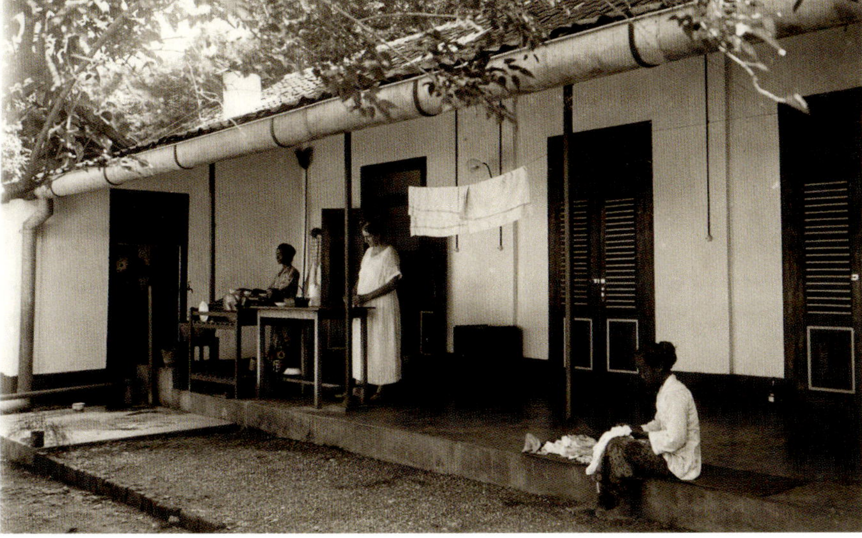

where the latter are allowed to be standing or positioned at the same level as the masters, only as long as they are at a distance.

Another source of information to get an insight into the lives of the Europeans in the Netherlands East Indies which is currently available for the public, is the oral history project conducted by the SMGI , Stichting Mondelinge Geschiedenis Indonesië (Foundation for the Oral History of Indonesia) which consists of 724 life histories of Dutch employees at the end of the colonial occupation.[58] In one interview within this project, a former employee recalls that within one company such as Shell Oil, the racial boundaries and relations among the company personnel and their relations with the local population differed between cities. In Balikpapan (Kalimantan) for instance, the boundaries were much sharper than in Surabaya (East Java).[59] Also for the wives of the employees, there was more possibility in Java to be involved in wives' associations or in developing social networks with other social groups. In Java, with a much more densely populated area and the European community having had a longer tradition of contact with the local population, servants were sometimes less isolated from the employer's family. As figure 88 shows, this European/Eurasian woman is near the *gudang* (supply room) and the kitchen, preparing something while the servants are working. The woman is dressed in casual clothing and this photo seems to be less posed than the earlier pictures we have seen, although it may also be a way to show that she is not just idly sitting at home. (Fig. 84)

Generally Dutch colonial residents in the 20th century had between four to six servants. Rich people employed more. However, in Java's cities where tap water, gas and electricity were gradually introduced after 1900, the number of servants per household declined. New city planning and residential construction produced smaller houses with modern sanitation. They provided less room for servants who traditionally used to live in the quarters to the rear of their employers' house, often together with their spouses and children. In the modern city life of the interwar years, servants might come in only during the day, while maintaining their private residence in a nearby *kampong* (village/quarter).[60]

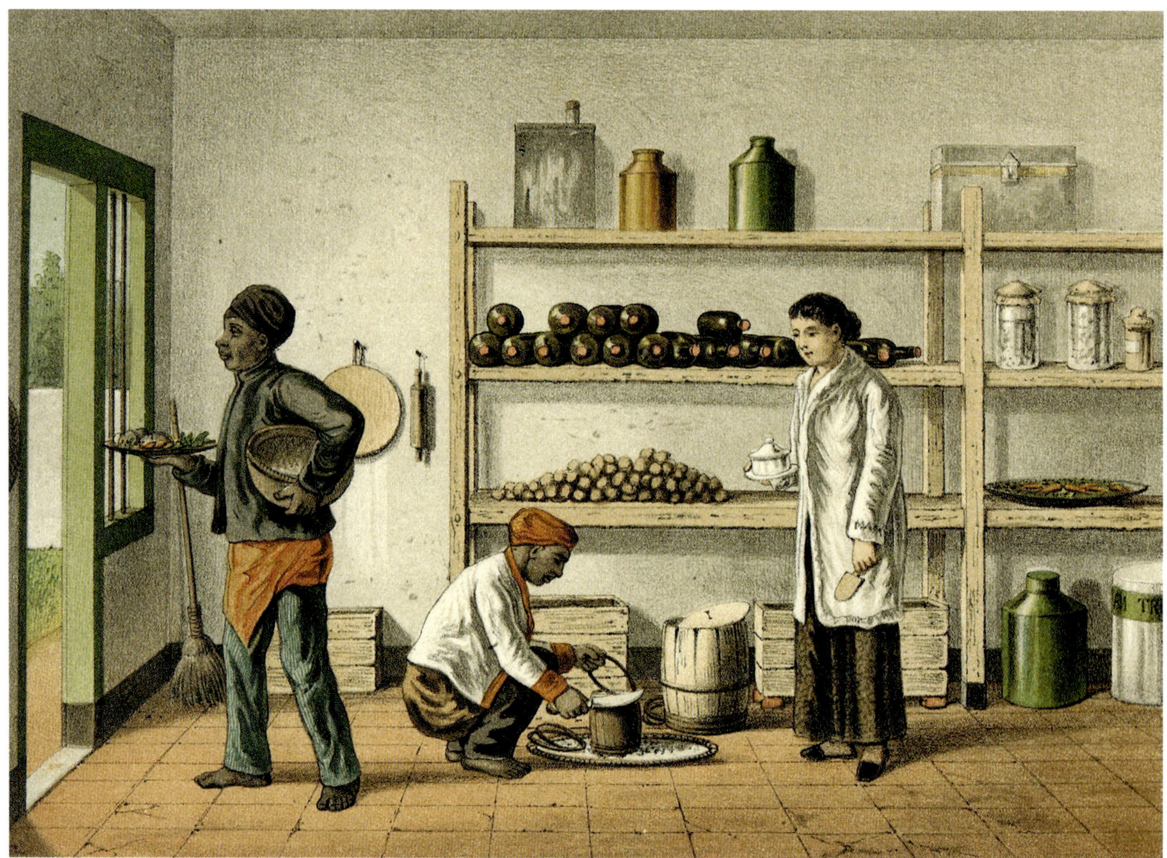

89
A pantry *gudang,* Batavia
Reproduction of watercolour by Jhr. Josias Cornelis Rappard (1824-1898)
Litho
35.4 x 42.7 cm
1881-1889
3728-790. Gift: KIT, Library, 1968

90 >
Raden Ajoe, the wife of Tjondro Negoro, regent of Kudus, with her female servants, Java
Photographer: Walter B. Woodbury (1834-1885) & James Page (1833-1864)
Albumen print
17.8 x 23.7 cm
c. 1870
60005224

91>
Prins Poeroebojo, Major-general and brother to the crown prince of Yogyakarta, with his wife Raden Ajoe Poeroebojo and servants, Java
Photo attributed to Charles & Van Es & Co (1895-1940)
Gelatin silver print
17 x 23.4 cm
c. 1920
60040201

The Indonesian elite and their servants

The social hierarchies between employer and servant, whether based on race or gender, as shown in the pictures above, are not a new phenomenon which emerged with the arrival of Europeans into the colony. These hierarchies were also an inherent part of Javanese social relations not only within the aristocratic families but also among other Javanese elite. The higher one was positioned in the social hierarchy the more numerous the servants employed. Sometimes the household staff would consist of whole families with different members doing different tasks for their masters. An example of this situation is shown by the photo, taken in 1870, of the wife of the Javanese regent of Kudus. She is propped on a chair on the stairs in front of the house, surrounded by a whole entourage of female servants, sitting on the stairs. (Fig. 90) There are more than twenty five servants in the photo. We do not see the male servants, who usually were in charge of the horses, the garden and the security of the house. According to the archival information of the KIT collection, the woman, whose name is not mentioned except for the title *Raden Ayu*, is the daughter of the sultan Mangkunegoro, of the Mangkunegaran sultanate, Solo.

Another example is the photo which shows the brother of the crown prince of the Yogyakarta sultanate and his wife in 1920, surrounded by the female household staff. All of them are dressed in traditional Javanese costume, the difference in style and sitting position shows their different statuses. (Fig. 91) The Javanese aristocrat sits with his legs set apart and arms stretched on his side. As mentioned in the caption written either by the photographer or by the archivist, the pattern of his batik sarong of *parang rusak* (broken sword) indicates his high position. The household staff are all sitting on the floor. In the picture only the female members are shown. They are of different ages, some older and some very young.

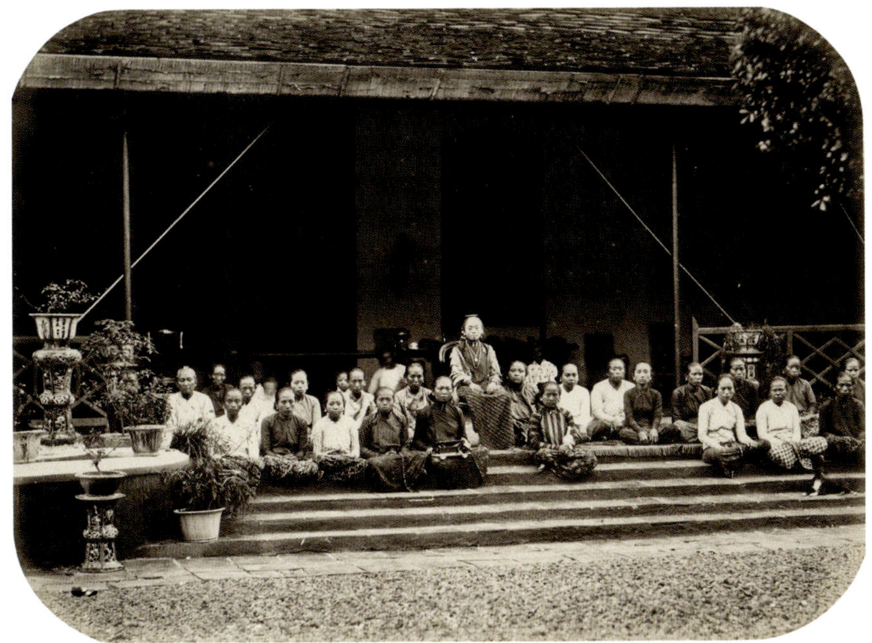

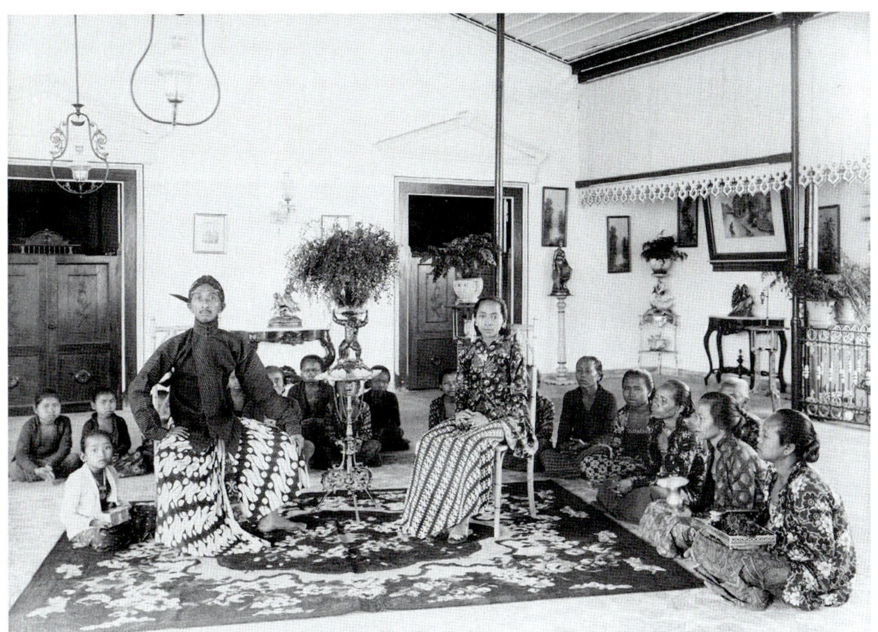

As other studies have shown, servants of royalty or the Javanese elite could be common villagers who had become servants because of debt bondage or duty obligations. In other instances, impoverished relatives could join the households of their more prosperous family members and attend to them. Relations in these households could resemble patron-client bonds and contain both elements of fear and distance and warm family feelings at the same time.[61] The work relationship was mainly built on non-written agreements and expectations. Besides their annual wages, it was normal for servants to receive food and lodging and rewards for their services when they performed well.

The work and domestic experiences of servants

We often see servants present in colonial households, captured through carefully prepared photographs, but what do we know about their lives and their working experiences *before* they entered these households? One common phenomenon among the Indonesian working population was the high rate of mobility from an early age. This could be because of family break-ups (so that the children had to be taken care of by grandparents, or other family members) or because of war or natural disasters. 'Family' was therefore not necessarily a stable unit and its composition was often fluid. Children did not automatically receive basic education or spend much time playing and learning. And paid domestic work in other families was a means for these young girls and boys to survive or to bring some income to their own families.

Indonesian cities in their development as centres of administration and trade, from the late 18th until the early 20th century were generally spatially segregated. Different ethnic communities would reside in different parts of town so that social contact amongst them was relatively limited. In Bandung in the 1940s for instance, two thirds of the Indonesians lived to the south of the railway track, which geographically and socially split the town in two. The Europeans usually lived to the north of the railway track (although some Eurasians lived to the south of it too).[62] This meant then that those who worked for the European families and lived in their own settlements had to walk or travel quite a distance to get to work every morning. In the mining towns of Balikpapan (Kalimantan) and Pangkalpinang (Sumatra) where the percentage of European personnel was much smaller than in other towns in the Netherlands East Indies, the (usually Javanese) servants were isolated from the rest of the local community.

For some, work as a domestic servant was a totally new experience and the world of the employers was

RHINOCEROS HOOVES

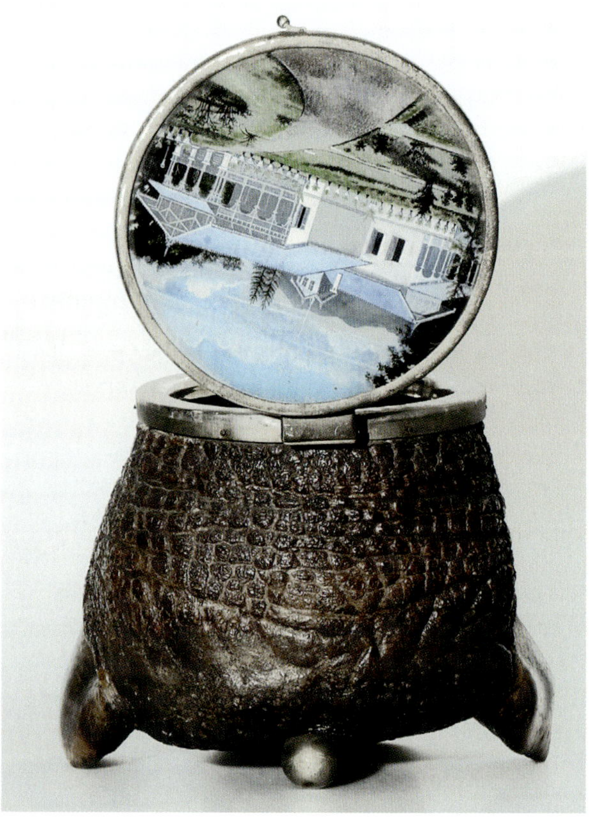

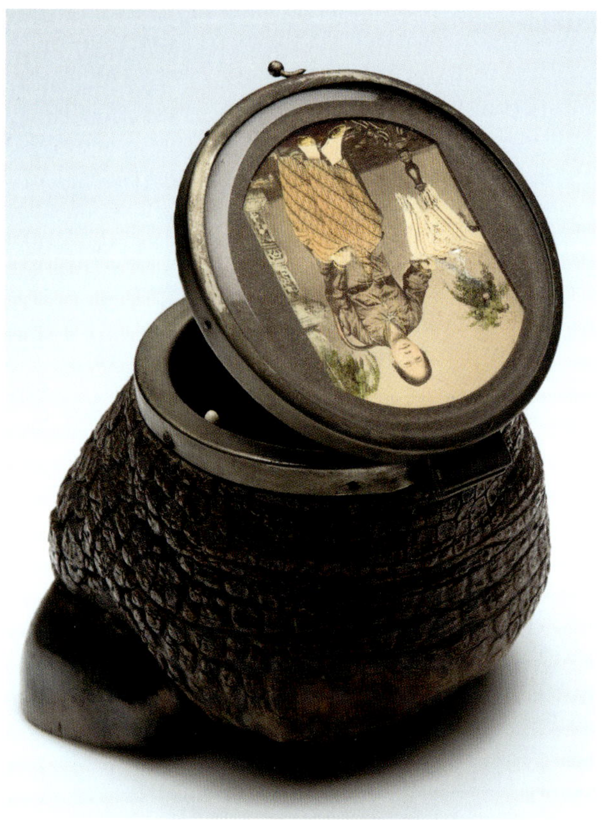

92, 93
Hoof of rhinoceros made into cigar box and sewing box
Animal materials, paint
20.5 cm
Priangan, Java
1880-1890
54-33, -34
Gift: M.S.L. van der Wijck-de Kock van Leeuwen

In 1917 the Koloniaal Museum was given a cigar box and a sewing box, each made from the hoof of a rhinoceros. They were undoubtedly hunting trophies. The sewing box contains sewing equipment made from ivory, such as a small pair of scissors, crochet hooks, a small knife, a needle case, a garn-windle and a basting pin. On the outside of the lid under glass, a coloured-in photo of Raden Ayu of Cianjur is pasted. She was the wife of the regent of Cianjur. The rhinoceros cigar box is just as large and also has a photo on the lid. This time it is not a portrait but a picture of the country house of the Governor General in Cipanas.
Both objects were probably given by Raden Adipati Ario Prawira-diredja, regent of Cianjur (Priangan, Java) and his wife the Raden Ajoe to the couple Van der Wijck-de Kock van Leeuwen. They donated these curious objects, along with the photos and many other objects, to the Koloniaal Museum in 1915 and 1917. Herman Constantijn van der Wijck (1815-89) was, among other things, a member of the Raad van Indië (Council of the Indies). He had an administrative career at various locations in the Netherlands East Indies, including Ambon, Yogyakarta and Cianjur. The husband and wife had 12 children, one of whom was Carel Herman Aart van der Wijck, who served as the Governor General of the Netherlands East Indies in the period 1893-99.
JVD

completely unknown. For others it might be an extension of the work in the plantations and mining areas, where workers' communities had been established within or adjacent to the production areas. These communities would then be a convenient source of other types of labour (often family members of the mine or plantation workers) not directly related to the work in the mines or plantations, such as domestic work, house maintenance or those who would drive the people. The ability to speak the language or not, or to follow the lifestyles and habits of their employers, affected the ability of the servants to do their duties and gain the approval of their employers. The experiences of the servants and their views regarding their masters cannot be captured by photographs, but may be obtained through their life histories.[63]

One example is the story of a Sundanese (West Javanese) girl born in 1921 who started working in an artillery factory in Bandung when she was 10 years old.[64] When the factory started to dismiss workers because of an economic downturn, her uncle found her a job as a servant for a Dutch family. He first taught her a few basic things of cleaning and dealing with Dutch employers, as he himself had working experience with a Dutch family. When she met her future employers for a first talk, she could not communicate because the person spoke Dutch, a language she did not understand. Slowly she learned to understand some basic Dutch words, but she managed, because there were other servants to help her. Every day she picked up her employers' son from school with the driver in the family car. At the same time she would do the shopping for food in the market close by. She worked seven days a week. Because her work was very heavy and it was exhausting to walk every day so far from where she lived, she eventually left her job with this family. She then worked alternately for other families whose houses were closer to her home. They were Chinese and Javanese families. Because of these different experiences, she could make comparisons between the different habits and traditions in these families. Despite the language barrier, she found working for the Dutch more predictable and clearly structured than working in the homes of the Chinese or Javanese.

94
Servants on an estate, Java
Glass negative
13 x 18 cm
1920s
10013917
Gift: J.W. Hissink, 1927

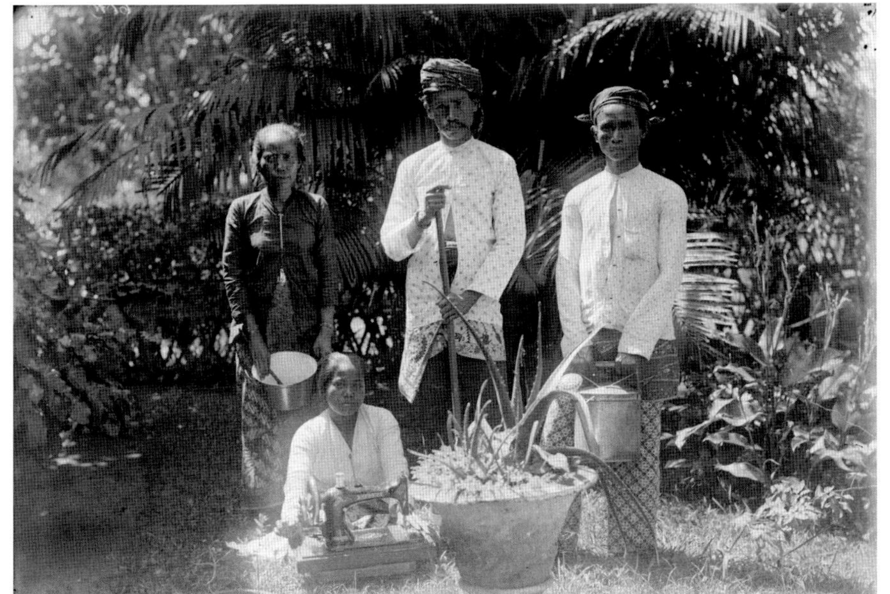

As mentioned above, the number of servants elite families had depended on their wealth and standing in society. Numerous servants, sometimes up to twenty, had to maintain the household in the European and also in the wealthier Javanese families. Since the wealthier families lived in large houses with sprawling gardens, owned house pets and horses, and had many family members or frequent house guests who needed tending to, a division of work among the servants was designed to allow the efficient running of the household. Different tasks involved also different systems of ranking among the servants themselves. The wage level of a servant depended on whether the servant was a man or a woman, whether the job was considered to involve a high degree of discretion, whether it was conducted in the house or not and how many years one had worked with an employer.

Figure 94 shows the household staff, each holding a piece of equipment which possibly indicates the kind of work they do. In comparison to some of the pictures above the people in the photo look slightly more disheveled which suggests that the picture may have been less carefully prepared. It is interesting to reflect on who was meant to see this photo, which clearly shows the division of work among the servants: the woman standing is holding a cooking pot (indicating that she is the cook), the man in the middle is holding a trough (possibly the one taking care of the animals), the man standing next to him is holding a watering can (the gardener), and the woman sitting on the ground is holding a sewing machine (probably the seamstress).

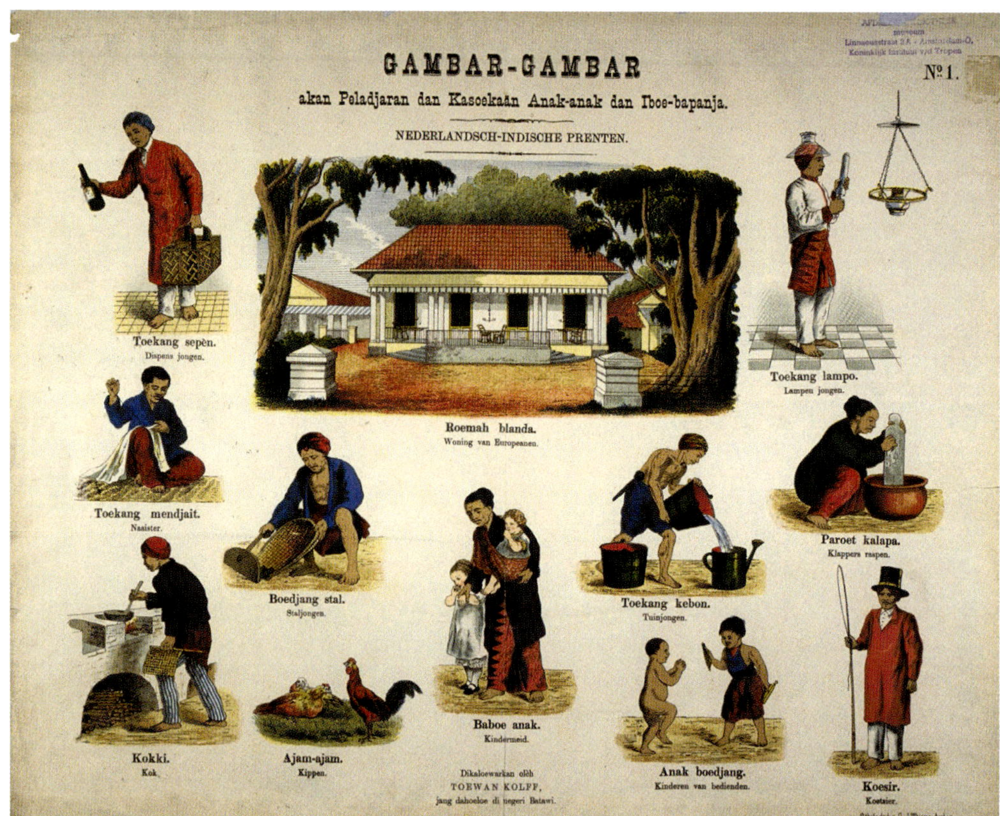

95
School poster of residence and servants
Probably reproduced from drawing by Jhr. Josias Cornelis Rappard (1824-1898)
Paper
46.3 x 39 cm
c. 1870
4370-1b. Bequest: L.M. Boerlage, 1977

Differences in wages and status sometimes led to tensions between servants, particularly when there were ethnic differences. The cook and the driver (of automobile or horse cart) usually earned the most, whereas the house cleaner and gardener earned much less. But collaboration between the servants was also common either to reduce the work load or to help ease communication with the employer. For instance if a servant had just entered employment within a European household and had not yet learned the routine of the household (as illustrated above), or was not used to the language, the other more experienced servants might help them adjust. Working in the employers' home, did not always take place in closed quarters where servants couldn't have any contact with the outside world.
In the enclave areas (or enclosed places) such as in plantations and mining areas outside Java, domestics who often came from Java were usually more isolated than in cities or towns in Java. However, quite often, especially with improved infrastructure, regular contact occurred between the rural areas or the urban fringe where the servants came from, and their places of employment. Servants usually didn't work their whole lifetime with one employer; many times they would move from one employer to the next depending on whether they felt at ease in their place of work, and whether they could fulfill their own family obligations. Sometimes employment in other people's homes would be interrupted by marriage or childbirth, or crises in their own families if a parent died or became sick.
Different from the illustrations above where the servants show their different functions in the household, figure 96 shows the private quarters of Sundanese servants in West Java. Here, what we are meant to see is not servants at work, but servants who are taking a break from work. The living quarters of the servants were usually at the rear of the main house, where they were at the beck and call of their masters. They might be related to each other as one person might also pull in other members of their family to work with the employer. This photo is different from the earlier photos in that it is less formal. There is a less clear idea of the internal hierarchy among the servants. They are all wearing their ordinary cloth-

THE SEAMSTRESS

The seamstress, the *djait*, is indispensable in a European household, says the writer of the practical book for the inexperienced Dutch housewife that is departing for the East Indies. Particularly if one lives in a remote district where there are few shops. Due to frequent washing, clothes wear out quickly. There is always repair work to do; but also children's clothing and, if the seamstress is very experienced, evening dresses in the fashions taken from magazines such as *Rijk der Vrouw* and the *Mode Oriënt* can be trusted to her.
She comes to the house – a good Singer sewing machine is one of the required items in the trousseau of a newly married woman.
This model, now depicting a seamstress, is one of three models that have survived from the 1920s. Initially, for many years, she represented a member of an ethnic group in an exhibition. JDJ

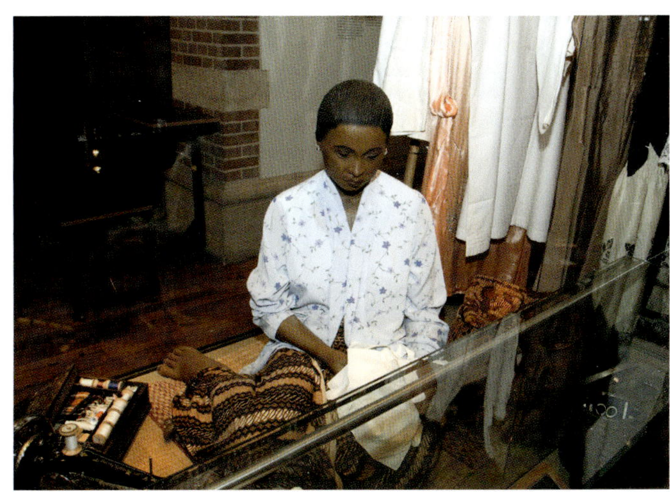

ing, there is less ceremony. The only person wearing a white jacket is the man sitting on the floor. The photograph is obviously not meant to be presented to the outside world where the European master is the centre of the public gaze. There is a suitcase lying on the floor, not put aside, which suggests that there was less planning in the composition of the objects in this photograph.

96
Sundanese servants, Java
Glass negative
13 x 18 cm
c. 1915
10013919. Gift: K. Kroitzsch, 1920

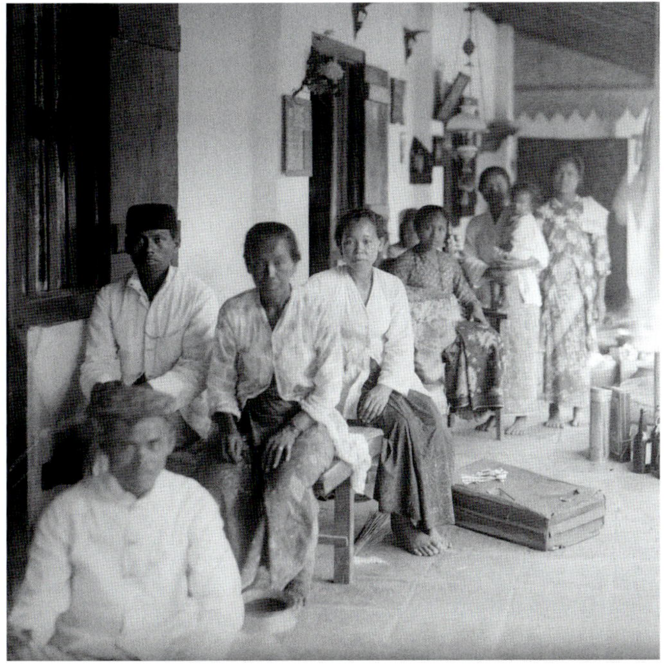

Photographs can indeed provide images of colonial life and in this case, of the relations between European employers and their servants. The different photographs above selected from the KIT collection show the various ways in which family life in colonial times was portrayed; and servants were clearly an important part of these portrayals. Particularly the photographs where the European colonial elite are the central focus of the camera, create an atmosphere of elegance, with individuals in positions of repose, where the aura of superiority of the Europeans is underlined by the presence of Indonesian servants sitting subordinately on the floor or standing at a distance. The fact that the servants are there highlights the European presence in a colony inhabited by natives. In some of the photographs, particularly those where the servants are on their own (especially in their own living quarters), the presence of the photographer is still felt by the way they all look intensely into the camera. However, their stance is less formal and the positions don't seem too contrived. Nevertheless, if we want to have a better view of the varieties of relationships between servants and their masters, of how servants remembered the past or how they are remembered, and to a certain extent what their work and life experiences were with different employers, we should search for other sources, such as life histories or correspondence, not only of the servants but also of the employers.

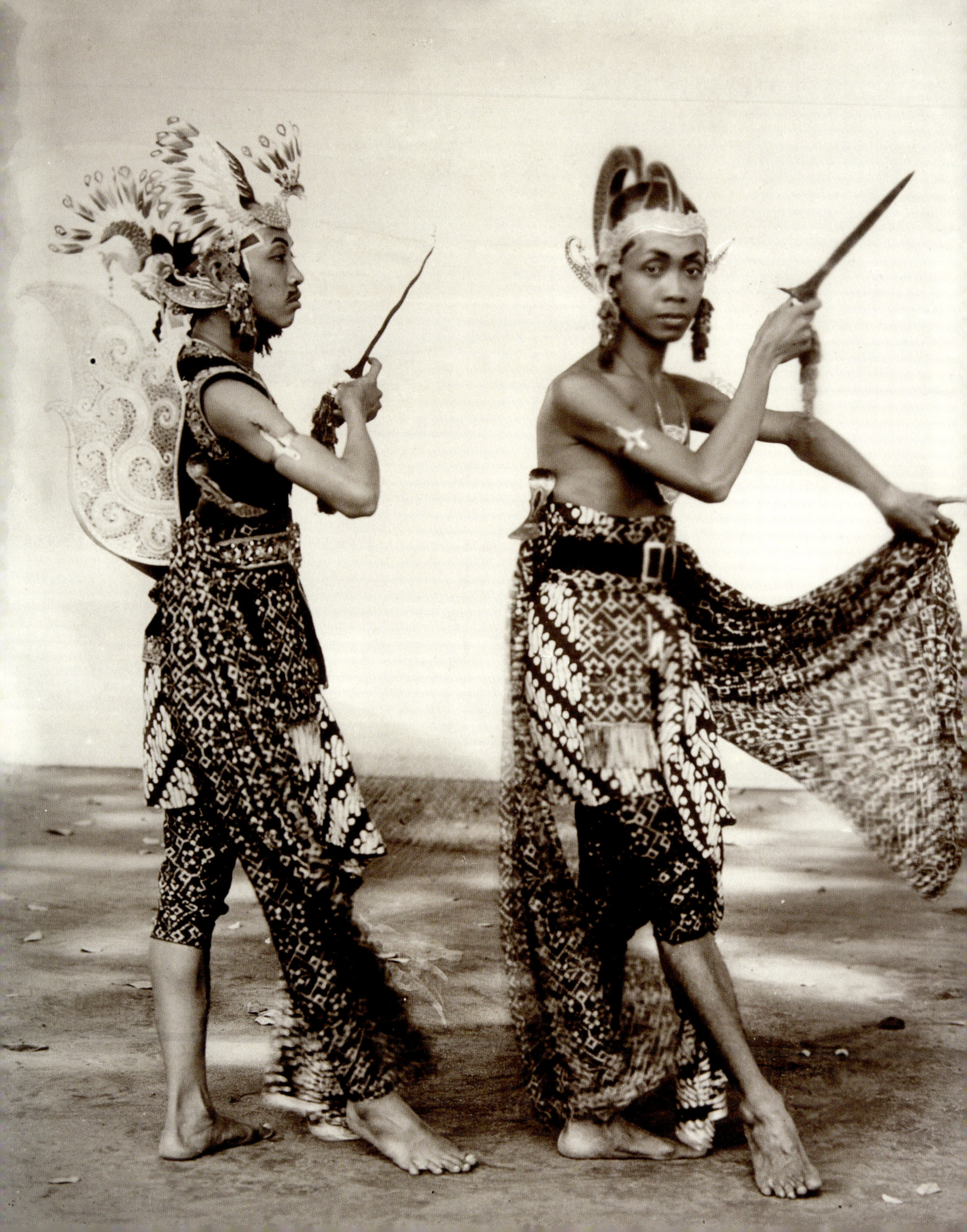

THE JAVANESE AND BALINESE DANCE THEATRE AS COMMUNITY ART

MARGARETA DORILA

97
Wayang wong performance 'Jaya Semadi and Sri Suwela'
3-6 September 1923 at the palace fort of sultan Hamengkoe Boewono VIII, Yogyakarta, Java
Gelatin silver print
28.2 x 23.1 cm
60002045

The progressive magazine *Wendingen*, a medium of the Amsterdam artists' society *Architectura et Amicitia*, devoted its March issue of the year 1919 to the theme of 'dance'. It was one year after the end of the First World War, one of the bloodiest dramas in human history. In the impassioned words of the magazine's chief editor, H. Th. Wijdeveld, the hope was expressed that a new era had dawned, an era in which the new art would play a pioneering role. 'And yet, amidst a spirit of defiance, the new art is born and this young child of the ancient tradition is once again making its way into the soul of struggling humanity. There, art will be united with the community that, like a radiant sun, shall be its source of warmth and vitality, and no other art will give more immediate expression to the community spirit than the art of dance through its independent creative urge.'[65] Wijdeveld hoped, with many like him, that following the bloody war and subsequent starvation, the world would begin the search for a new society that, through 'a single commonly held idea of beauty', would be set free from what he called 'material poverty'. Dance would play an important role in this because this ancient form of expression was a community art that appealed to all groups in society. Wijdeveld thus explicitly expressed criticism of the Western art of dance, which, in his view, had become no more than entertainment and had therefore been emptied of 'all deeper perception and experience'. To his mind, Western dance had been reduced to 'a series of earthbound movements' that attempted to escape the power of gravity; movements whose relationship to music was 'nothing more than rhythm'. Wijdeveld's hope for renewal in the art of dance was rooted in the dance traditions of Eastern peoples, but also in the avant-garde dance then thriving in the West with groups such as Serge Diaghilev's Les Ballets Russes. The dance issue of *Wendingen* therefore focused on both traditional Javanese and Balinese dance in the Dutch colonies of the time and on Les Ballets Russes. The latter, renewing dance movement was illustrated with costumes and scenes from performances that had created a furore in Europe, particularly in Paris, since 1909. Two articles were included on Javanese and Balinese dance, accompanied by photographs by the German amateur photographer Gregor Krause, among others. In this essay, I would like to show how the appreciation of Javanese and Balinese dance and theatre has evolved in the Netherlands over the centuries – evolving from unflattering descriptions to being seen as a source of renewal for the arts in Europe during the first decades of the 20th century.

The tradition of *wayang* and *topeng* theatre

Since 1596, when they first arrived in Indonesia, the Dutch have become familiar with the dance and theatre of Java. Most well-known were the traditional *wayang* performances, accompanied by gamelan music played by a *dalang* (puppeteer) with 'silhouette puppets' or stick puppets. Yet it was the performances given by actors that probably made the biggest impression. From reading a travel diary of the first expedition of the Dutch to the East Indies under the command of Cornelis de Houtman in 1595-97, it is apparent how strange the Javanese dances appeared to them. The diary states that both men and women flung their arms and legs about and twisted their bodies like dogs crawling out of their dens.

By 1915 nothing much had changed with respect to the appreciation of Javanese dance in the Netherlands. The publishers of the travel diaries of the first trading expedition thought this description 'though bluntly stated, was still a matter-of-fact observation.'[66] It took a long time 'before this matter-of-fact observation gave way to an appreciation, and still longer before this appreciation was coupled to any insight,' said N.J. Krom in the introduction to the study *De Javaansche Danskunst* by Th. B. van Lelyveld, which was published in 1931 in Amsterdam. This was the first serious study conducted into the art of dance in the Netherlands East Indies in the Netherlands. The Javanese theatre had been the subject of study in the Netherlands even earlier. G.A.J. Hazeu earned his doctorate in Leiden in 1897 with his dissertation *Bijdrage tot de Kennis van het Javaansche Tooneel.* But outside the Netherlands, attention had been given to the dance and theatre performed on Java much earlier by Sir Thomas Stamford Raffles (1781-1826). Raffles was Lieutenant Governor of Java between 1811 and 1816.[67] In his famous *History of Java* from 1817, Raffles was captivated by the Javanese national dramatic arts and dance 'as constituting, next to music and poetry, the most conspicuous and refined of their amusement'.[68] Raffles gives a detailed description of these arts in which his admiration regularly comes through. The actors are splendidly dressed after the ancient costume and perform their parts with grace, elegance, and precision; but the whole performance has more the character of a ballet than that of a regular dramatic exhibition, either of the tragic or comic kind, in which human passions, human follies or sufferings are represented in such appropriate language and just action, as to seem only a reflection of nature.[69]

The chief editor of the magazine *Wendingen*, Wijdeveld, in 1919 did not choose a Dutch author but rather two Javanese ones to make a contribution to the 'Dans' issue, the student and musician Surjoputro, and the political exile Suwardi Surjaningrat. Suwardi (1889-1959), who came from Yogyakarta from the noble house of Paku Alam, was taken to the Netherlands in 1913 against his will. Because of his anti-colonial political actions, he was forced to choose between exile within the Netherlands East Indies or departing for an unspecified period of time to the Netherlands. He ended up staying in the Netherlands until 1919. After returning to the Netherlands East Indies, he launched the Taman Siswo movement, which was focused on providing public education in the *desa* (village/countryside).[70] In the Netherlands, too, he organised his political activities in part through cultural expression. He thus founded the Javanese dance troupe Langen-Driyo. In his article 'De Dans en het Toneel der Javanen'[71] he explained that the goal of this group was 'to show, through cultural history demonstrations, that we see our people as a People that is determined to live their lives on their own terms.' He began his argument by asking what impression the national art of Java made on 'intellectuals in the Netherlands' and he described three reactions. They varied from condescending: 'nice but primitive'; to positive and proud 'because this art is native to the country where the red-white-and-blue tricolour flew for three centuries', and finally developed into a sense of shame 'when they returned to reality and noticed that they were actually a foreign people that ruled over such natural-born artists on Java'.

Like Raffles, Suwardi identifies two main types of traditional theatre: *wayang*, performed with puppets, and *topeng*, performed by masked actors. When Suwardi tries to establish how old the *wayang* tradition is, he quotes Dr. Hazeu, whom he sees as 'the best expert on Javanese theatre'. Following the example of Hazeu, he thinks that traditional *wayang* puppet theatre (*wayang kulit purwa*) 'was known long before the arrival of the Hindus on Java'. In the 11th

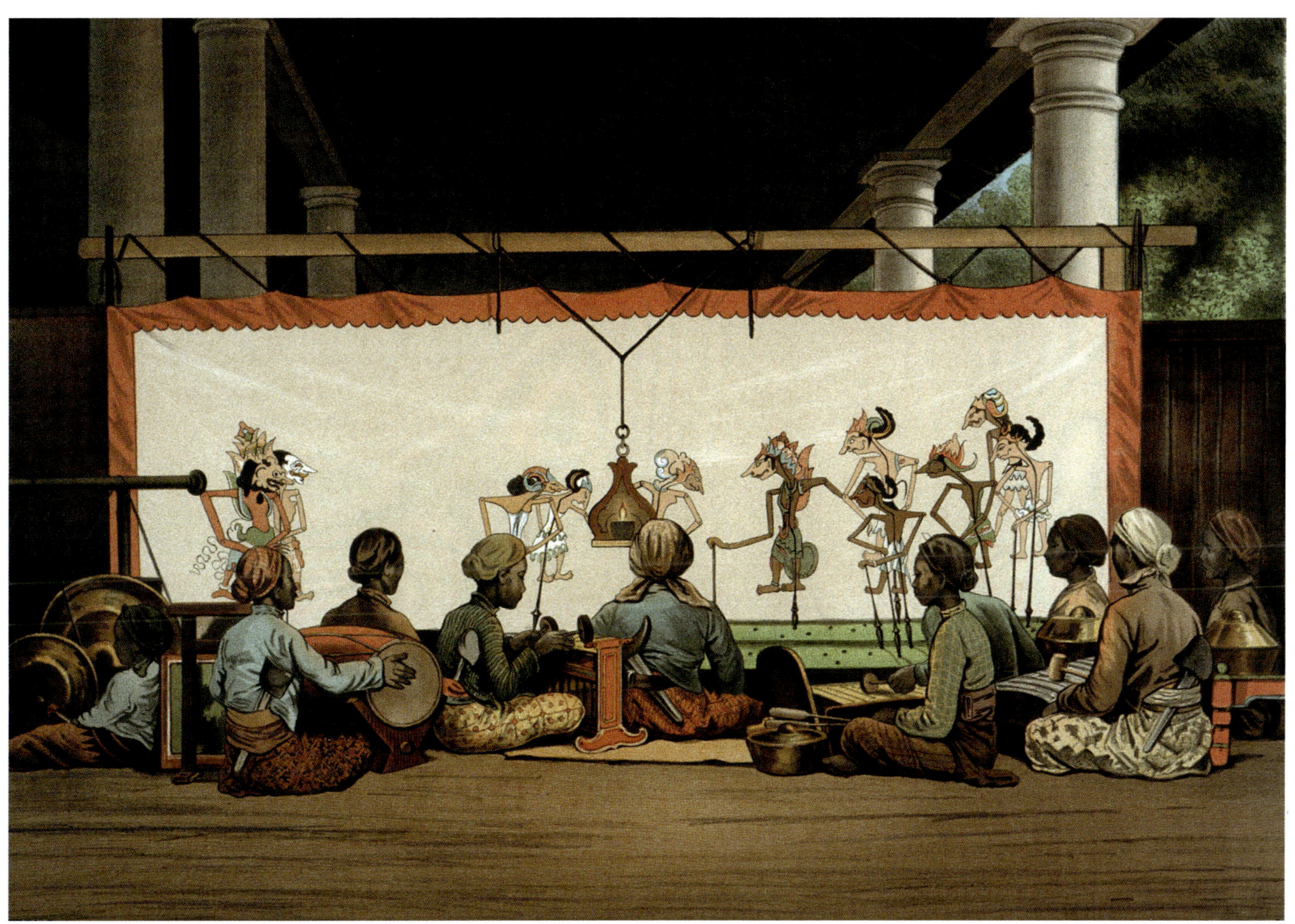

98
Wayang Kulit performance and gamelan musicians, Java
Paper
43 x 56.8 cm
1897
4442-5. Purchase: Brill Boekhandel en Drukkerij, 1978

century AD, when the renowned king Air Langga ruled on Java, *wayang* theatre was already a popular form of drama that did not differ much from the present-day form and therefore was already highly developed. The repertoire of the old *wayang* shadow (Fig. 98) (performed with flat two-dimensional puppets against a backlit white translucent screen) is derived from the two famous classical Indian stories of Mahabharata and Ramayana. Also, according to Suwardi, *wayang* belongs 'to the Javanese people as a religious-artistic drama that has continually shone beyond all thoughts of school, direction and time'. He then discusses, in addition to the shadow drama, the *wayang golek*, performed with stick puppets. *Wayang golek* borrowed its repertoire largely from the Panji cycle, an episode from the 'ancient history' of Java linked to the adventures of the popular hero Panji. Suwardi also discusses the *topeng* or the masked drama (*topeng* means mask), which is probably just as old as *wayang* theatre and in which 'the dances were particularly admired'. In the *topeng* performances, a mythical world was portrayed. Kings, princes and princesses displayed ideal behaviour, full of modesty. There were often personifications of gods. Court officials and servants were usually comical figures. Also appearing on stage were wise men, hermits that lived on mountain tops, as well as giants and demons. Dancing was an important part of another type of drama that was performed by people not wearing masks (*wayang wong*). The make-up, the costumes and the dance movements made the persons depicted identifiable for the public. (Fig. 99, 100)

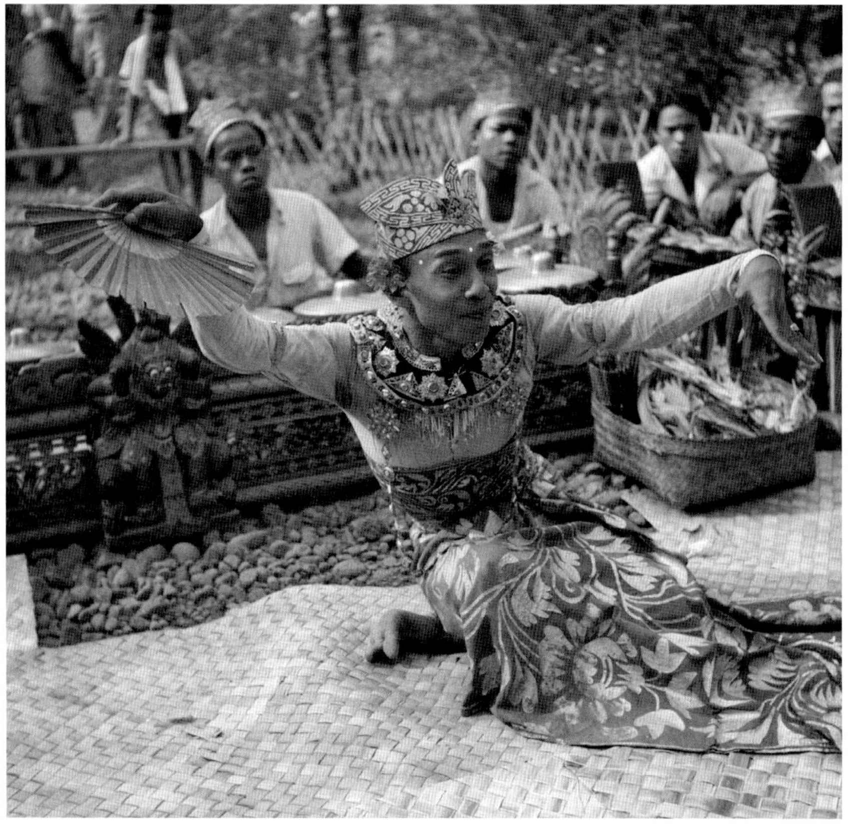

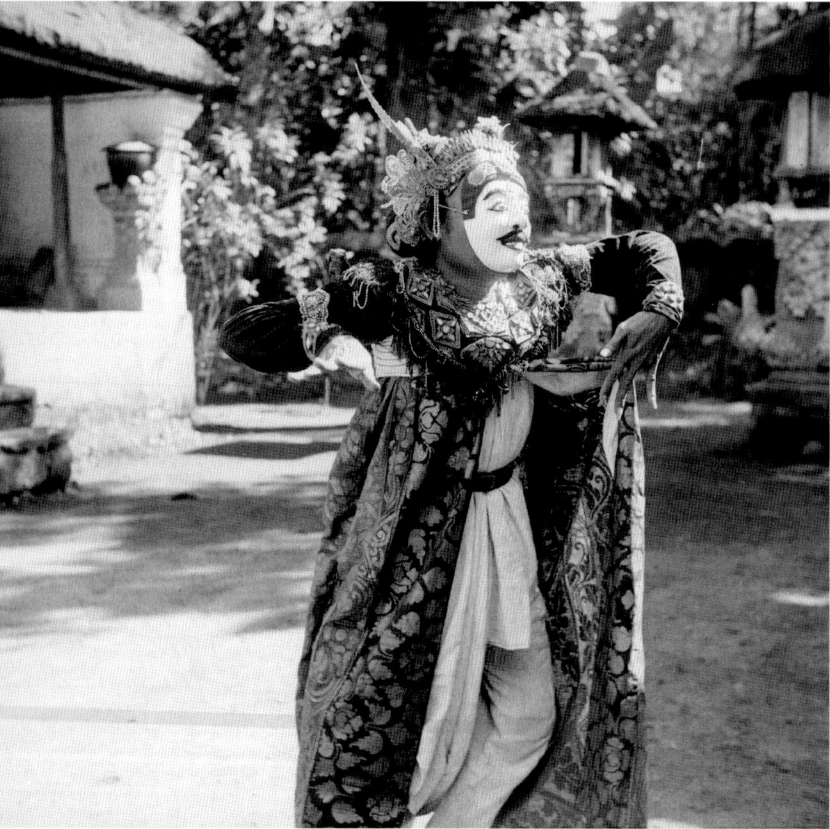

The theatre performances were organised for all the important moments in people's lives, such as a child's birth, puberty, marriage, death or to ward off disease. In addition to these parties organised by individuals, countless group parties and temple festivals were also held on religious and public occasions, such as the sowing and harvesting period of rice and the honouring of gods and ancestors. The form and length of a performance depended on the specific occasion.

'Gesamtkunst' versus separate arts

Besides being a source of inspiration and renewal, Wijdeveld probably saw another parallel between Les Ballet Russes and the Javanese and Balinese dance and theatre. Both could be seen as 'Gesamtkunst' or integrated arts. Suwardi stressed in *Wendingen* that, in the Javanese and Balinese theatre traditions, different arts such as music, dance and drama were inextricably linked. This was also the strength of Les Ballet Russes: 'It was indeed the completely new, the synthesis of different art forms in the Ballets Russes that appealed so much to the public.'[72] The German music and dance critic, Oscar Bie, wrote in a commentary about Les Ballets Russes: 'Because the Russians do not separate the arts in their performance. Between scenery, costumes, movements, the rhythms and music there is a consistently applied unity of style, and each performance is held together by an exemplary understanding of artistic cohesion.'[73]

Suwardi juxtaposed the 'Gesamtkunst' with the Western tradition, in which the arts are usually separated from one another in music concerts, opera, ballet and the theatre. 'What we possess on Java in this area is the theatre, in which, in addition to drama and music, dance also plays a prominent role. But people here do not actually envisage European opera, the music drama in which music plays a dominant role. For the Javanese, the three elements, i.e. drama, music and dance are equally important.'[74] It is up to the director, i.e. the *dalang*, to determine how these arts are combined in order to produce the required mood. As a result, the Javanese and Balinese dance theatre is a total experience – an experience that speaks to as many senses as possible at the same time.

< 99
Balinese kebyar dancer, I. Mario, accompanied by gamelan
Acetate negative
6 x 6 cm
1949
10004728. Gift: P.L. Dronkers, 1950

< 100
Balinese mask dance, performed by the famous dancer Ida Bagus Ktut
Acetate negative
6 x 6 cm
1949
10004727. Gift: P.L. Dronkers, 1950

101
Wayang wong performance 'Jaya Semadi and Sri Suwela' in the kraton of the Sultan of Yogyakarta
Gelatin silver print
23 x 29 cm
1923
60002008. Bequest: D. Fock

The difference in the experience of art that Suwardi stressed here was developed further by Van Lelyveld. In his view, the separation of the arts in the West dates from the Renaissance. Prior to that time, religious rituals were a combination of word, dance and music, just as in the East. According to Van Lelyveld, dance as a kinetic art that was linked to religious drama in the West 'was slowly but surely lost, both through the slow weakening of rhythmic characteristics in people and by the individualism promoted by the Renaissance.'[75] Many primitive societies, as well as peoples with a highly developed civilisation, such as in Egypt, Phoenicia, Greece and India, believed that dancing came from the gods. Dancing in all of these civilisations was often mimetic, that is to say: the 'emotions were expressed by gestures made to the cadence of the accompanying music'. The dances were 'not primarily performed with the legs, but using all parts of the body, as can be seen in ancient Egyptian reliefs, in the figures of ancient Greek sculpture and on ancient Greek ceramics, as well as in the dances of Japanese and Javanese drama. Often people dressed up in a certain manner, while the face was masked to ward off demonic spirits or to call on an ancestral god or hero.'[76]

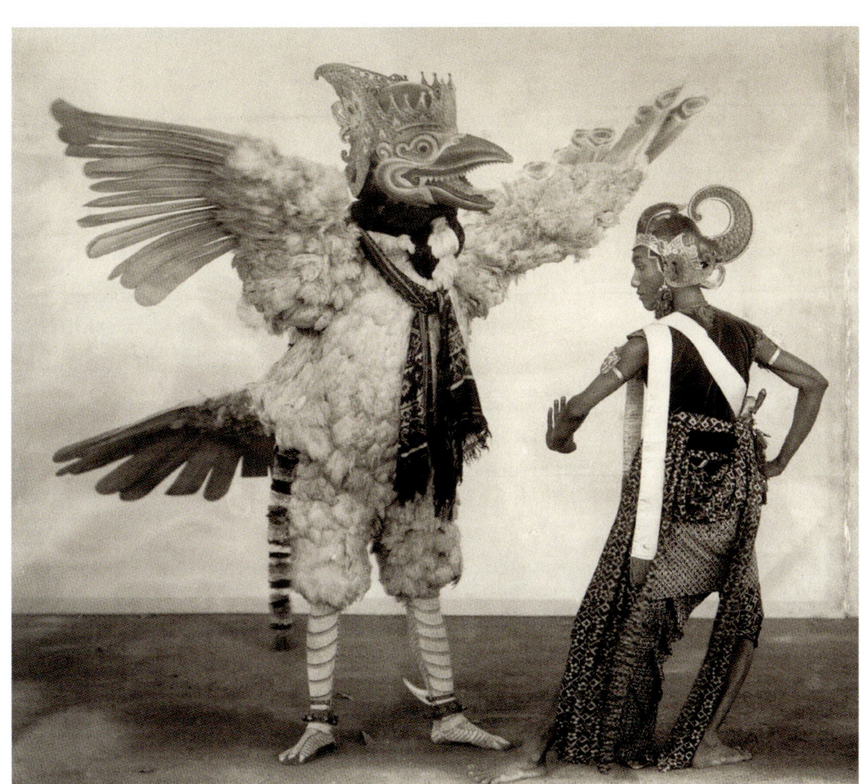

The thundering success of Les Ballets Russes could be attributed to their exoticism and authenticity, achieved through a combination of ancient symbols cast into avant-garde costumes, scenery and music. Russia has been always on the edge between the East and West. Saint Petersburg was Western-oriented and Moscow Eastern-oriented. This produced conflicts, but could also create unexpected forms of art through the melting together of these different worlds. After the first series of performances in 1909, the artistic director of Les Ballets Russes, Alexandre Benois, summed up its great success in Paris as follows: 'We showed the Parisians what theatre should be. This journey was, without a doubt, necessary in historical terms. We are the ingredient that present-day civilisation needs to avoid falling completely into decline.'[77] In 1919, when the 'Dans' issue of *Wendingen* appeared, Les Ballet Russes had long been an established and renowned avant-garde dance movement in Europe.

Dramatic arts as an expression of community feeling

We can ask ourselves: How can a dance or theatre performance express a feeling of community? This is probably most inspired by intrinsic symbols that appeals to all members of a community. Wijdeveld thought about shared religious experiences. 'Only Eastern societies have preserved the pure tradition of religious dance, and the oppressed East Indian race has, for century upon century, established wonderful dances which contain the memory of its community. There, dance is still a language that speaks to the heart and mind and gives voice to the deepest emotions. Here, modern dance, in its appearance on stage, is not yet much more than an individualistic pursuit of images from times past.'[78] In a discussion of the performances of Surjoputro, Suwardi and the Langen-Driyo group, Henri Borel also criticised the profane character of Western art in comparison with the inner maturity of Javanese art. The character of Javanese dances, in his view, contained magnificent lessons 'for Western realistic artists, who believe that the accurate depiction of an ugly reality can, in and of itself, be art'.[79]
The juxtaposition of realistic art versus symbolic art was also discussed by Van Lelyveld in the chapter

'Vroeger wanbegrip over de Javaansche danskunst'. 'It is not surprising that in the West the assessment of Eastern art – which rests on an entirely different and, in part, even conflicting foundation – has given rise to the most peculiar statements.'[80] Van Lelyveld thought that many archaeologists still assessed Eastern art from within the bounds of the realistic art of the ancient Greeks which so dominates Western thinking. 'Sometimes artists become riveted to the realistic outlook of Western art and as a result turn away from out-of-the-ordinary Eastern theories; they become blind to the synthetic-symbolic-ornamental concepts of the East. It is logical then that their appreciation of those Eastern arts whose character is more or less abstract, such as music and dance, is the most limited. This is why the magnificent art of Javanese dance has been ignored for so long.'[81] The same argument is made by the French actor, playwright and theatre critic Antonin Artaud. He praised Balinese theatre for retaining the original

BENCH

102
Bench
J.P. Strijbos (1865-1945)
and J. Bronner (1881-1972)
Commissioned by M. Greshoff
for the Koloniaal Instituut
Wood
133 x 150.5 x 63 cm
1906-1907
3401-1008

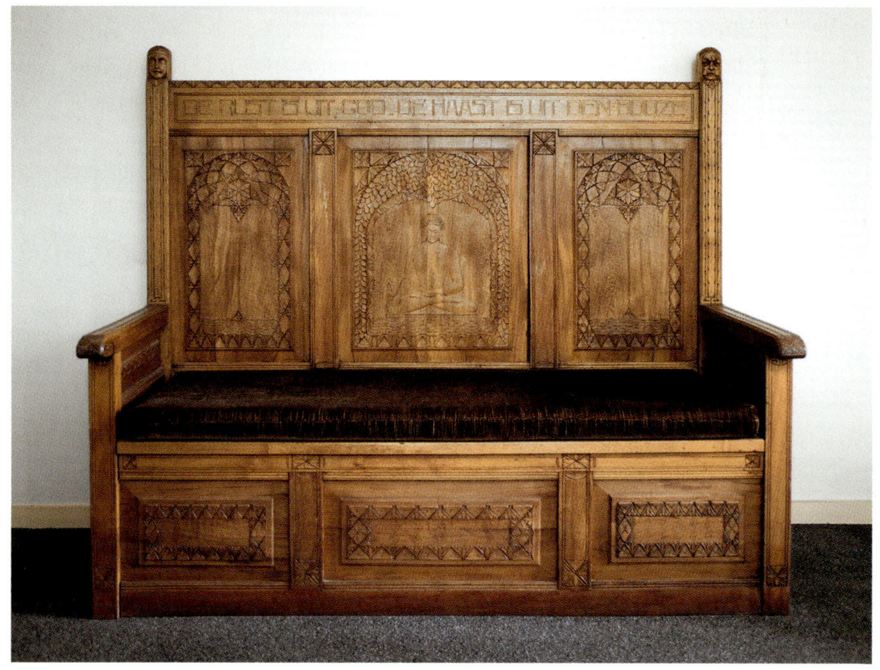

The director of the Koloniaal Instituut Haarlem, M. Greshoff, had this bench made in 1906-1907 bearing the inscription DE RUST IS UIT GOD, DE HAAST IS UIT DEN BOOZE (Relaxation comes from God, haste is the devil's work). It was given a place in the 'bamboo vestibule', a gallery that was full of bamboo, rattan and cane variations and their applications in Indonesian wickerwork. The furniture maker J.P. Strijbos and sculptor J. Bronner made it from Tembusu wood. Strijbos was a teacher at the School voor Bouwkunde, Versierende Kunsten en Kunstambachten (School of Architecture, Decorative Arts and Artistic Crafts) that was located next to the Koloniaal Museum and affiliated with it. Bronner, later the director of the Rijksacademie van Beeldende Kunsten (National Academy of Visual Arts) in Amsterdam, attended lessons there. During those years, Strijbos was an adherent of theosophy. The bench emanates a theosophical atmosphere and, as such, is an exponent of the Nieuwe Kunst (New Art), the movement of community artists in the Netherlands. The bench has three back panels. On the middle panel sits the Buddha in 'diamond position' under the sacred Bodhi tree, the tree of enlightenment, with an edge of lotus motifs that are repeated elsewhere. The tree on the seat panels is probably a contraction of the fig tree rooted in heaven and the lotus plant sprouting on the waters. The panels are flanked by two heads: 'Haste' and 'Relaxation'. The path to enlightenment requires peace and meditation. (See also Fig. 140) RC

GAMELAN ORCHESTRA

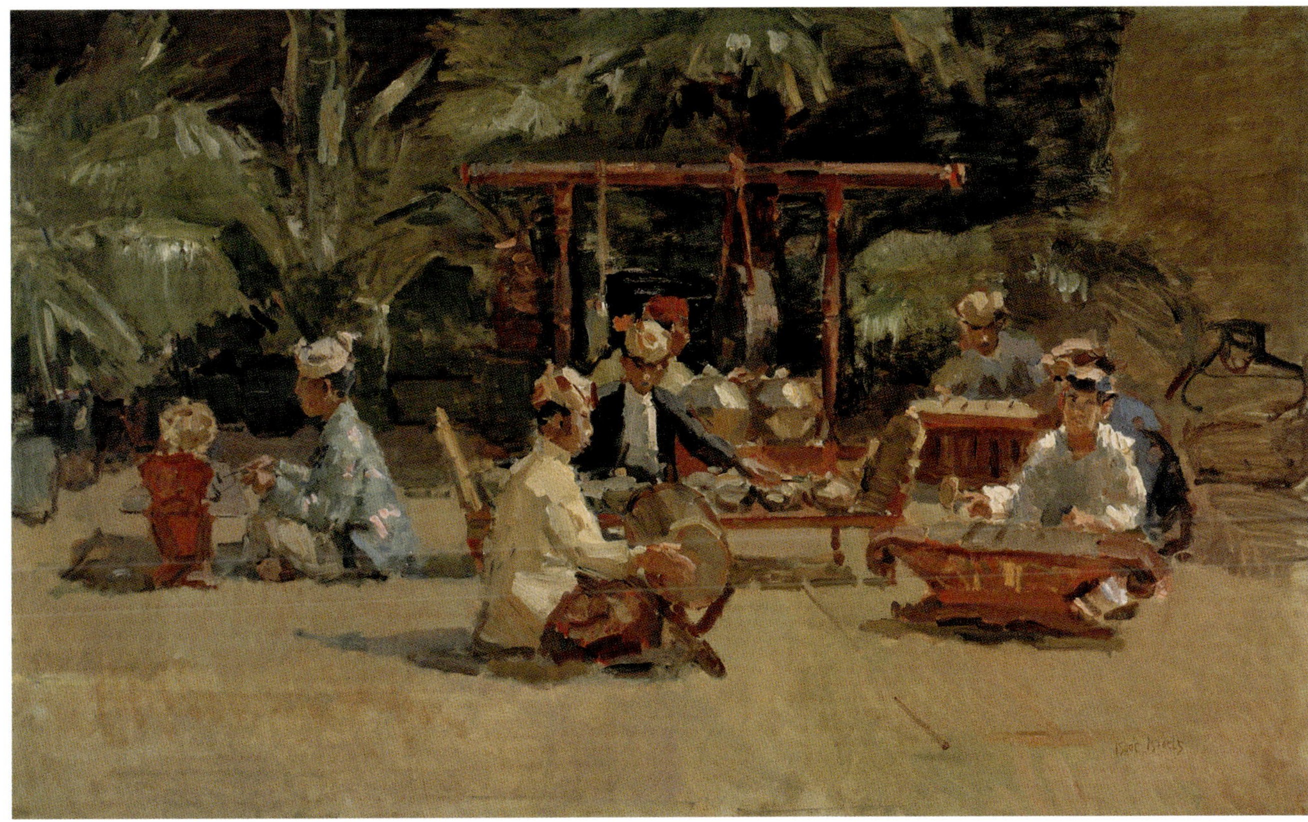

103
Gamelan orchestra
Isaac Israëls (1865-1934)
Oil painting
131 x 211 cm
c. 1916
339-1. Gift: A.M. Bourier and
C.G.M Bourier-van Gent, 1926

Isaac Israëls was one of the leading Dutch impressionists. Artists and theatre performances like the Javanese gamelan orchestra shown here were a recurring theme in his work. That is why he is referred to as a 'chronicler of the fleeting everyday life'. The Netherlands East Indies were an integral part of that cultural life and therefore also in his work. This is also true of many other artists of his generation. They became familiar with Indonesian culture through exhibitions and performances in the Netherlands or during trips to the Netherlands East Indies. In 1915 Noto Soerotoe, Soewardi Soerjaningrat and Raden Mas Jodjana gave a dance performance in the Royal Theatre in The Hague in aid of the victims of a flood on the island of Java. Israëls befriended Raden Mas Jodjana and painted his portrait several times.

In 1921-22, Israëls visited the Netherlands East Indies. Besides visiting Batavia, Bogor (former Buitenzorg), Yogyakarta and Bali, he also spent some time in Solo at the court of the Mangkunegara, where he was introduced by Raden Mas Jodjana. He was not really taken by the East Indies and therefore was glad to return to the Netherlands: 'When all is said and done, the Netherlands is a country that allows you to live the best creative existence because there is never anything to distract you, since nothing ever happens.' In answer to what impressed him most on Java he said: 'That I could endure the climate so well.'

Gamelanorkest (Gamelan Orchestra) was painted in the Netherlands, probably after 1916. It was donated in 1926 on the occasion of the official opening of the Koloniaal Instituut. SL

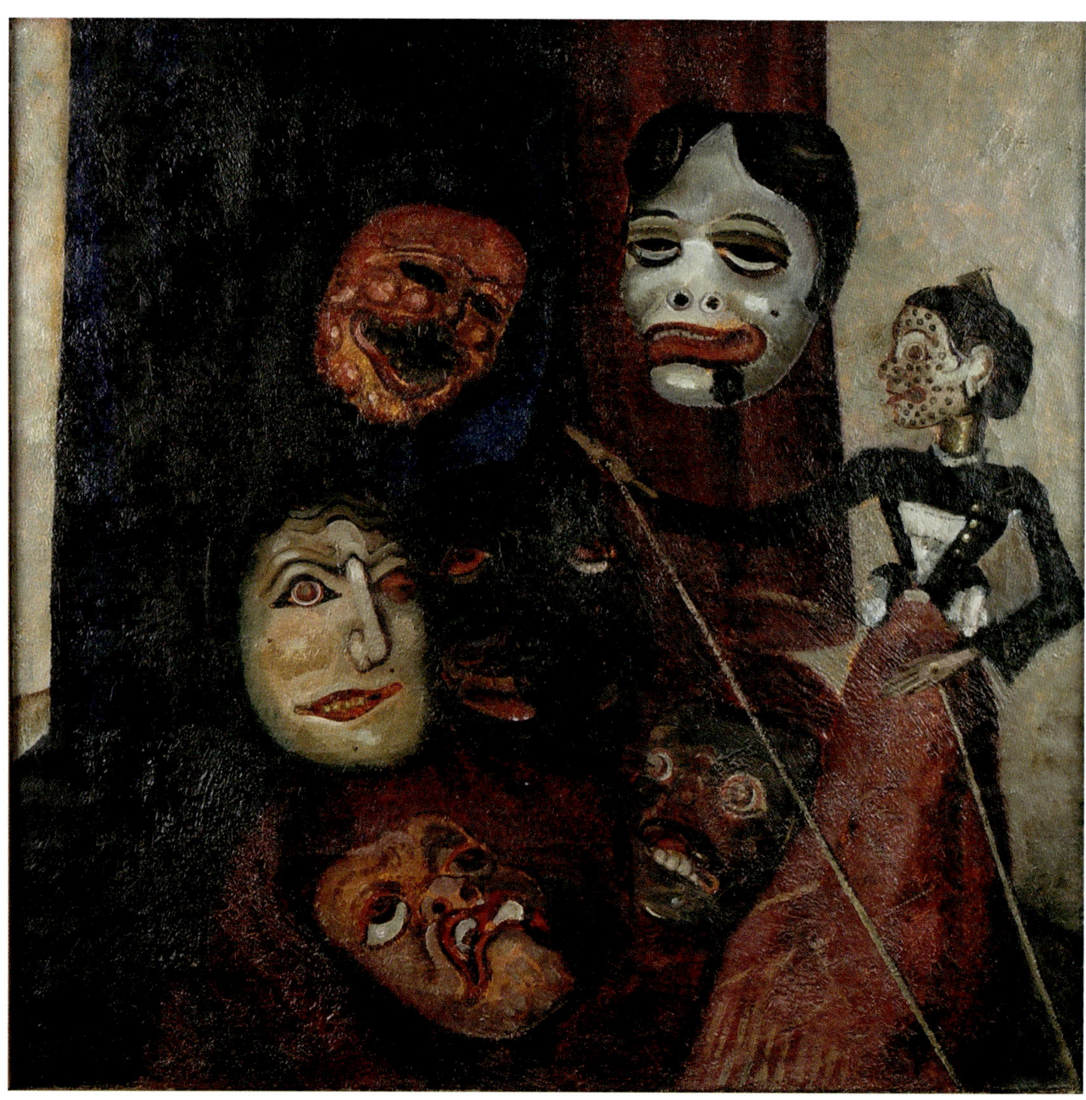

104
Still life with masks
Charles E.H. Sayers
(1901-1943)
Oil painting
95 x 95 cm
Sumatra, 1941
5998-1. Purchased: N. Vonwiller Gerhard and S. Vonwiller, Perth, 2002
Ex-collection: Ch.E.H. Sayers
With thanks to the Mondriaan Stichting and Stichting VSB Fonds

function of dance theatre and for its abstract character. In this collection of essays *The Theater and its Double,* Artaud criticises the impoverishment of Western theatre for placing emphasis on language and commonplace stories. This contrasts with the Balinese theatre, where means of expression cover a wide range and where the story is based on old myths and is therefore timeless. Commenting on this, Artaud says: 'The drama does not develop as a conflict of feelings, but rather as a conflict of spiritual states, themselves ossified and transformed into gestures-diagrams (...) The themes are vague, abstract, extremely general. They are given life only by the fertility and intricacy of all the artifices of the stage, which impose themselves upon our minds like the conception of a metaphysical state derived from a new use of gesture and voice. Through the labyrinth of their gestures, attitudes and sudden cries, through the gyrations and turns, (...) the sense of a new physical language, based upon signs and no longer upon words, is liberated.'[82]

Artaud called the themes used in the Balinese theatre performances vague, abstract and extremely general. As mentioned earlier, they were derived from the two classical Indian epics, Mahabharata and Ramayana, or from other myths, legends or folk tales. In these ancient sources, the audience sought answers to their existential questions concerning different phases of life and about death, and about their relationship to natural and cosmic powers. According to the French philosopher Emile Durkheim, myths are descriptions of a particular society expressed in symbolic, metaphysical terms. In imitation of the French cultural anthropologist Claude Levi-Strauss, different researchers see myths as a dramatic struggle in story form meant to bridge fundamental and unsolvable contradictions in a society. In his psychoanalytical approach, the Swiss psychologist Carl G. Jung brought myths into relationship with what he called the 'collective unconscious', which is present in all members of society because, just like inherited physical characteristics, it is implicitly communicated from generation to generation. According to this theory, the past lives in each of us. This implies that, when mythical symbols are alluded to in theatre performances, the allusion relies on the collective recognition of the audience.

The Romanian cultural philosopher Mircea Eliade also focused considerable attention on mythical symbols. He believed, in contrast to other theorists, that the 'archaic', 'primitive' or 'traditional' societies, which he understood to be the 'old great civilizations of Asia, Europe and America', actually had abstract thought systems. These systems were not expressed in language. Modern humans still use them. 'The symbol, the myth and the rite show us, in distinctive spheres and by their own means, a complex system of logically cohesive notions concerning the last reality of things: a system that humans may safely view as the basis for metaphysics.'[83]

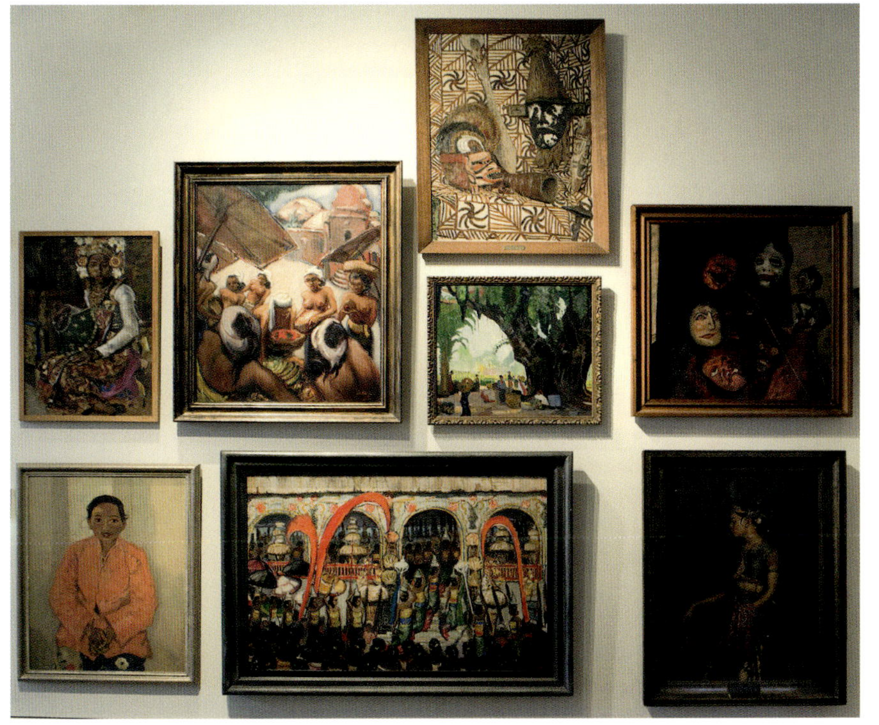

105
Display of paintings in the exhibition 'The Netherlands East Indies, a colonial history'
2010

Allusions to collective symbols that are enclosed in myths, legends and folk tales were also the driving force behind Les Ballets Russes. The performances of *L'Oiseau de Feu* (1910) and *Petrouchka* (1911) to the music of Igor Stravinsky were based on Russian folk tales; other performances were inspired by oriental legends and folk tales such as *Scheherazade* (1910, Rimski-Korsakov) and *Le Dieu Bleu* (1912, Reynaldo Hahn) or by Greek and Roman myths, such as in *Narcisse* (1911, Tcherepnin), *L'Après-midi d'un Faune* (1912, Debussy) and *Daphnis et Chloé* (1912, Ravel).

Sacred Eastern art objects in Western museum exhibits

When the exhibition 'The Netherlands East Indies, a colonial history' opened in the Tropenmuseum in 2003, the green mask of Patih Siregajapagon was chosen for the exhibition poster. The mask depicts an official that probably played a comical role in Balinese *topeng* performances. This mask[84] and other art objects that are on exhibit in the exhibition 'The Netherlands East Indies, a colonial history' were collected by Dutch people who worked on Java and Bali or had visited them in the early decades of the 20th century. (Fig. 104, 106-112)

Many of these objects were accessories used in dance and theatre performances, such as *wayang* puppets, *topeng* masks and headdresses used in *wayang wong*, such as a crown with golden quaking flowers. Even today many Dutch people keep *wayang* puppets as souvenirs from Indonesia. (Fig. 113-121)

In the museum exhibits of the exhibition 'The Netherlands East Indies, a colonial history', the objects are placed in an audiovisual presentation with real-life images of typical colonists who tell their story in their own surroundings. One of these images introduces the painter and adventurer Charles Sayers (1901-43). The organisers of this exhibition chose him in order to draw the attention of museum visitors to the arts of Java and Bali and show their influence on Dutch art at the beginning of the 20th century. (Fig. 105) Many of the art objects on exhibit at the exhibition 'The Netherlands East Indies, a colonial history' were collected by Charles Sayers on Bali and lent to the then Koloniaal Museum in

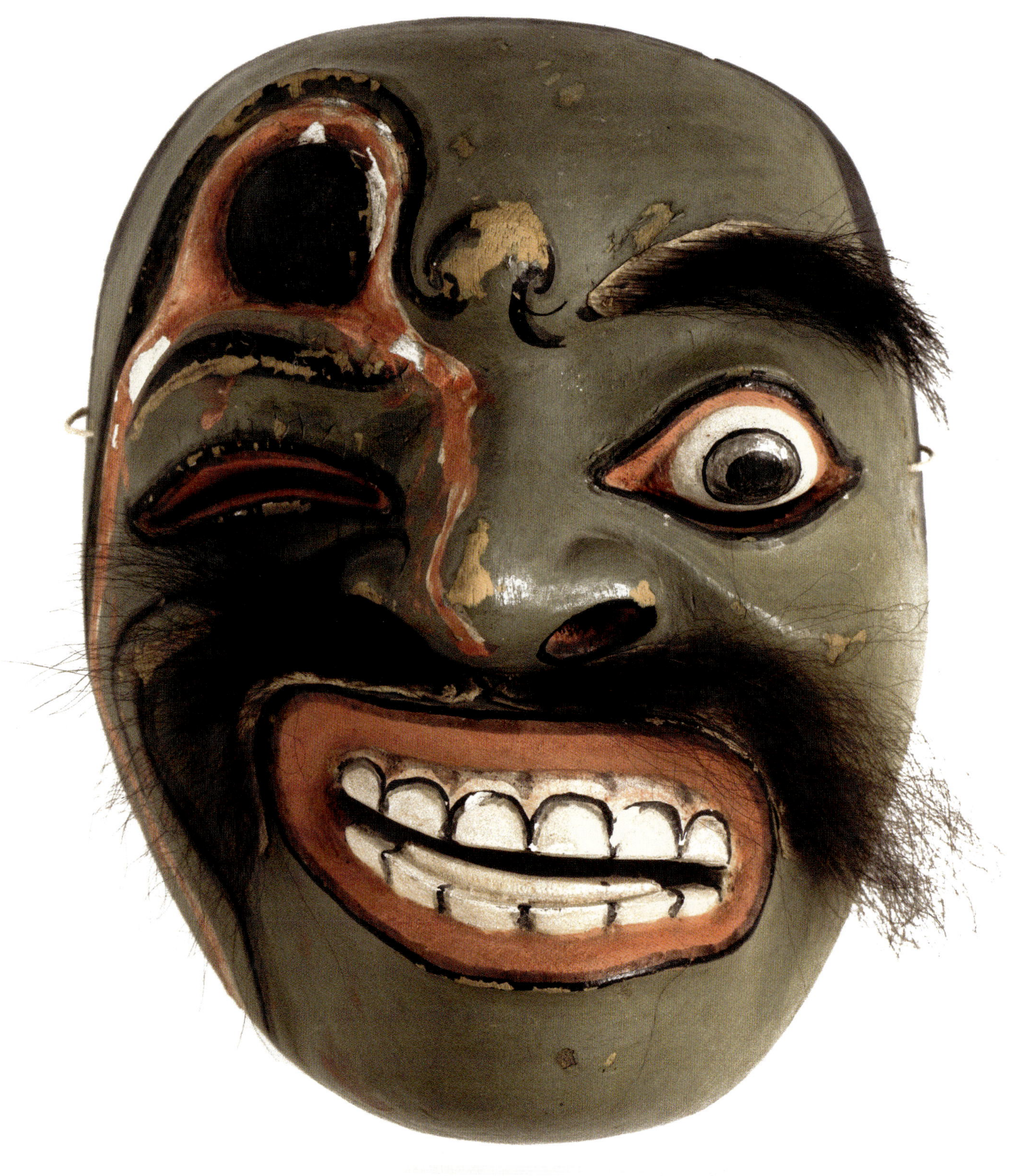

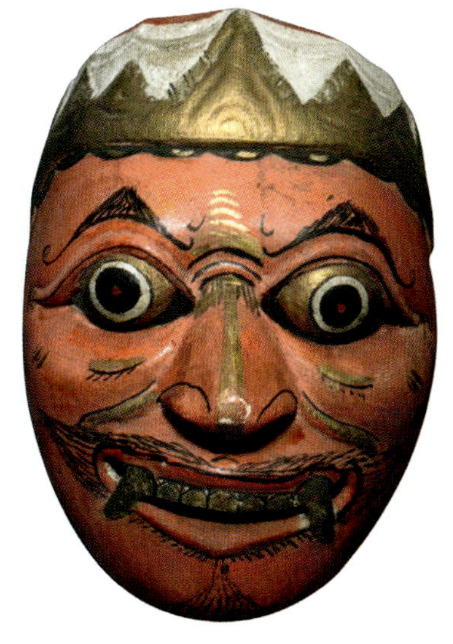

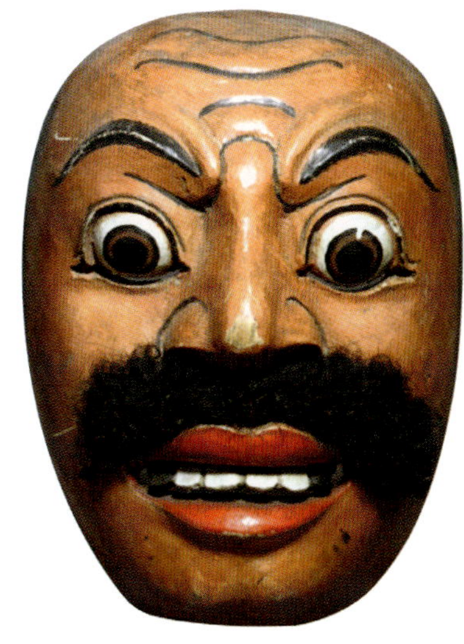

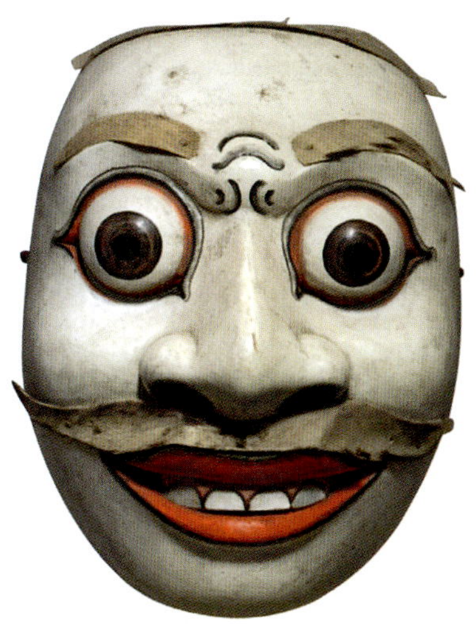

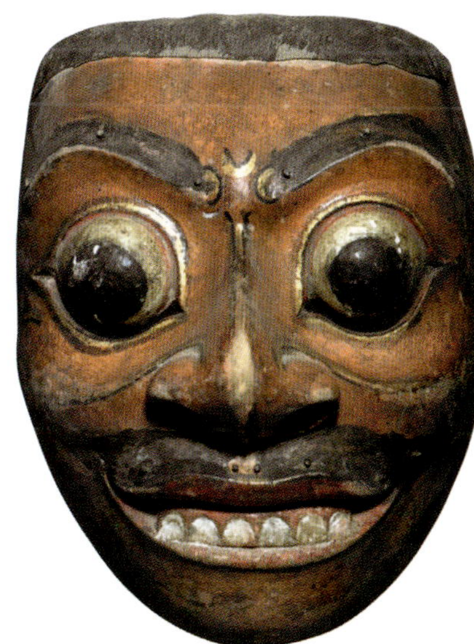

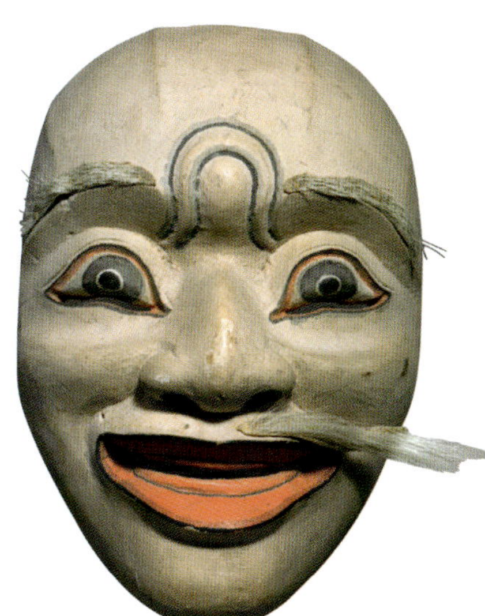

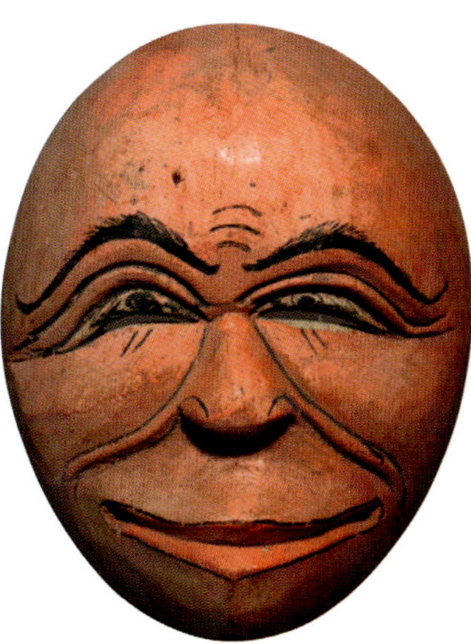

<< 106
Mask of the comic figure Patih Siregajapagon
Wood, paint
Bali
1156-28. On loan
J.A. Houbolt De St. Amand, 1937

107
Mask depicting Patih Sembora
Wood, paint
17.5 x 13 cm
Java
0-153

108
Mask depicting Kebo Sepati
Wood, paint
20.7 x 14.9 x 10 cm
Lombok
661-4. Gift: Prof. Dr. J.C. van Eerde, 1931

109
Mask depicting Jauk Manis
Wood, paint
18.5 x 13.8 cm
Bali
1112-10. Purchase:
C. Lion Cachet, 1937

110
Mask, depicting Jauk Keras
Wood, paint
16 x 13 cm
Bali
1330-13. Gift: Prof. Dr. J.P. Kleiweg de Zwaan, 1939

111
Mask depicting Topeng Tua
Wood, paint
20 x 15 x 7 cm
Bali
1335-112. Gift: J.V. Meininger 1939

112
Mask depicting Babunya Panji
Wood, paint
16.5 x 13 cm
Java
First half 20th century
0-157

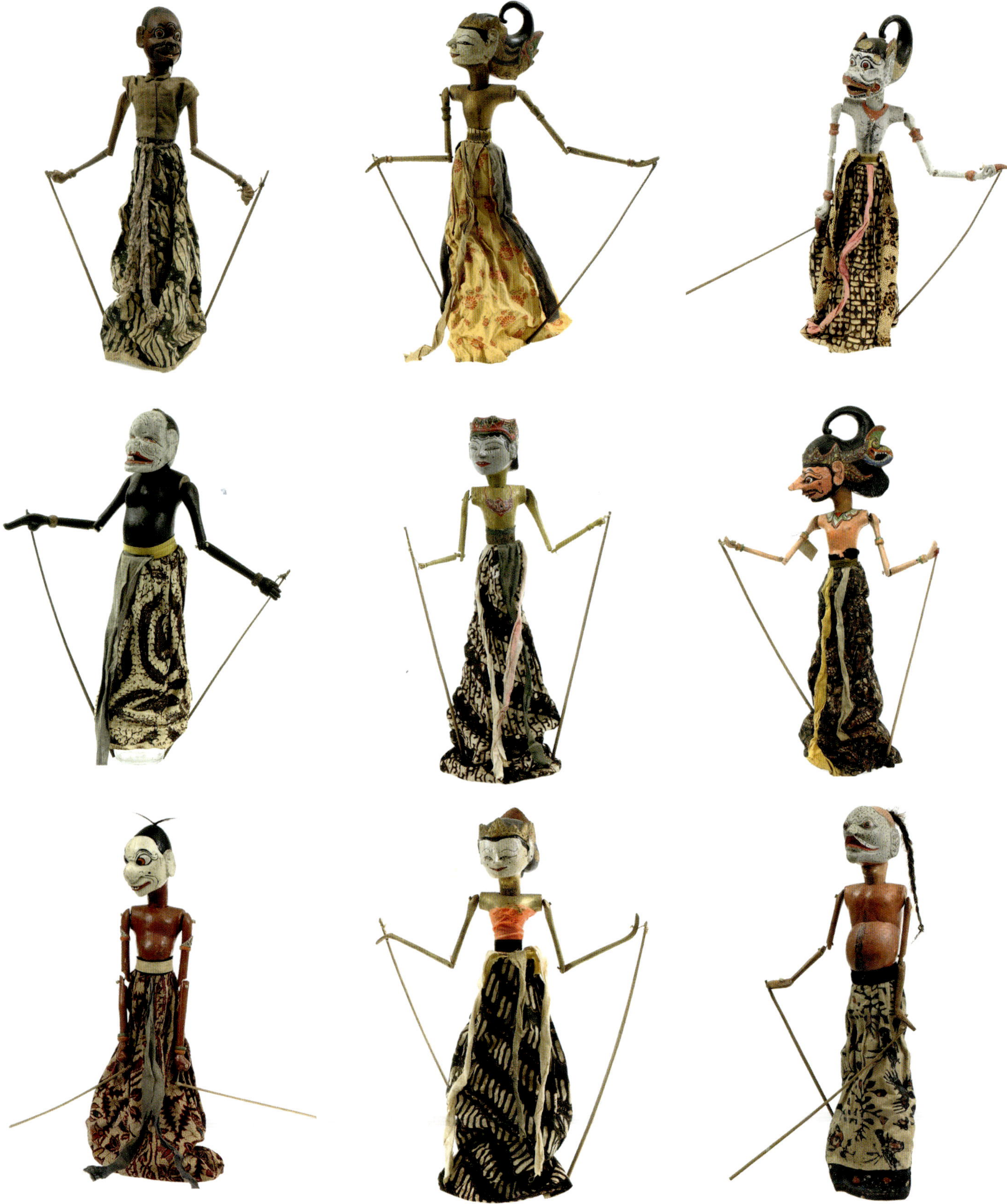

113-122
Wayang golek purwa
Wood, bamboo, cotton
Java. End 19th century
Purchase: E.S. Ali-Cohen, 1914

From left to right:

113
Wayang puppet, depicting Bagong, one of the three sons of Semar
40.3 cm
8-116

114
Wayang puppet, depicting Prabu Salya, prince of the Mandaraga kingdom
46 cm
8-105

115
Wayang puppet, depicting Hanoman, king of the apes in the kingdom of Ngamarta
52.5 cm
8-109

116
Wayang puppet, depicting Semar, the clownish servant of Arjurna
46.5 cm
8-73

117
Wayang puppet, depicting Angkawijaya, alias Abimanya, the eldest son of Arjuna
44.5 cm
8-72

118
Wayang puppet, depicting Gatut Kaca, son of Bima
54 cm
8-71

119
Wayang puppet, depicting Nala Gareng, one of the three sons of Semar
48.5cm
8-76

120
Wayang puppet, depicting Dewi Srikandi, the second wife of Arjuna
43.5 cm
8-78

121
Wayang puppet, depicting Petruk, one of the three sons of Semar
56 cm
8-84

122 >
Detail Fig. 119

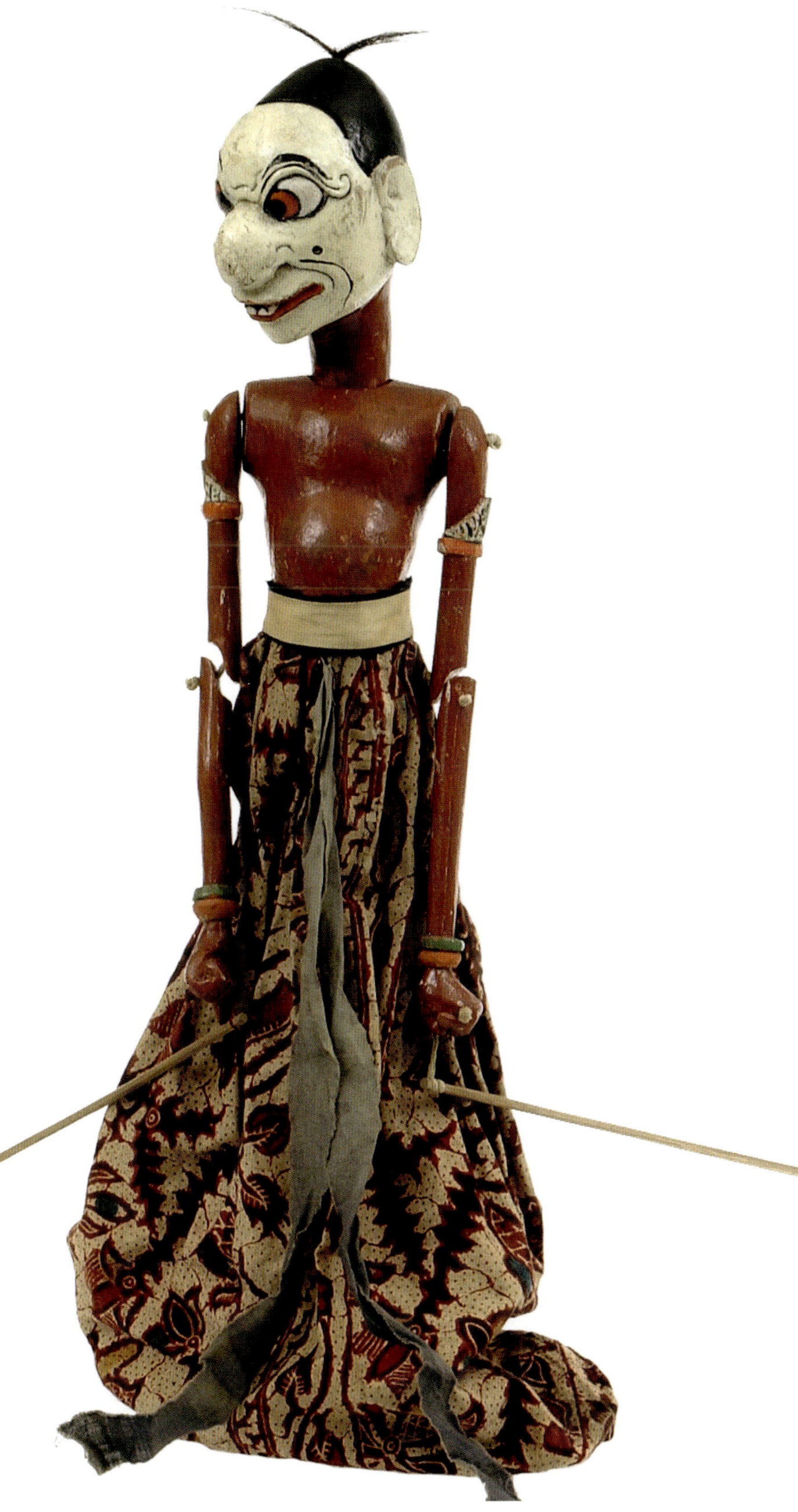

1933. In addition to implements, the exhibition also offers the opportunity to view paintings that were created by Dutch artists who recorded life on Java and Bali in the early decades of the 20th century, including Charles Sayers.

Sayers was a child of Dutch parents and lived at the sugar refinery they owned in middle Java. At the age of 11, he was sent to the Netherlands for his education. In 1920 he enrolled at the Rijksacademie voor Beeldende Kunsten in Amsterdam, attending lectures with the likes of Anton Derkinderen (1859-1935), who was a supporter of community art in the Netherlands. In 1925-26 Charles lived in Paris to continue his studies in the visual arts. After this study, he visited Egypt with his parents in 1926. In 1927-28 he returned to the Netherlands East Indies and the island of Bali. Sayers depicted his impressions of these places in paintings and drawings, which were exhibited in Paris, the Netherlands and the Netherlands East Indies. In an interview in 1932, Sayers said: 'Bali in particular drew my attention. This small, magnificent island, with an art history all its own, compelled me to take up a special study of the life of its population, their religion, their sculpture, dance and paintings.'[85]

In 1929-31, Charles was back working in Paris. During this time he exhibited work at the famous art gallery of Bernheim-Jeune, which brought the public's attention to many modern and avant-garde movements. In the same interview held in 1932, Sayers declared: 'Though I produced several good paintings of Paris that drew the public's attention at exhibitions, the most important subject for me is the tropics. Perhaps this is because of a homesickness I feel for the land of my birth. Perhaps it is the attraction to the extremely familiar, yet still foreign native people. My work is very psychological in essence. Look at those heads, that boy, that girl, the market corner, this temple festival. The mentality of the Oriental has a very strong pull on me.'

The exhibition 'The Netherlands East Indies' shows several of the most famous paintings by Sayers, such as *Balisch tempelfeest of Offerfeest te Besakih* (Bali Temple Festival or Ceremonial offering at Besakih) and *Markt in Klungkung* (Market in Klungkung). Both were painted during his stay on Bali in 1927-28.

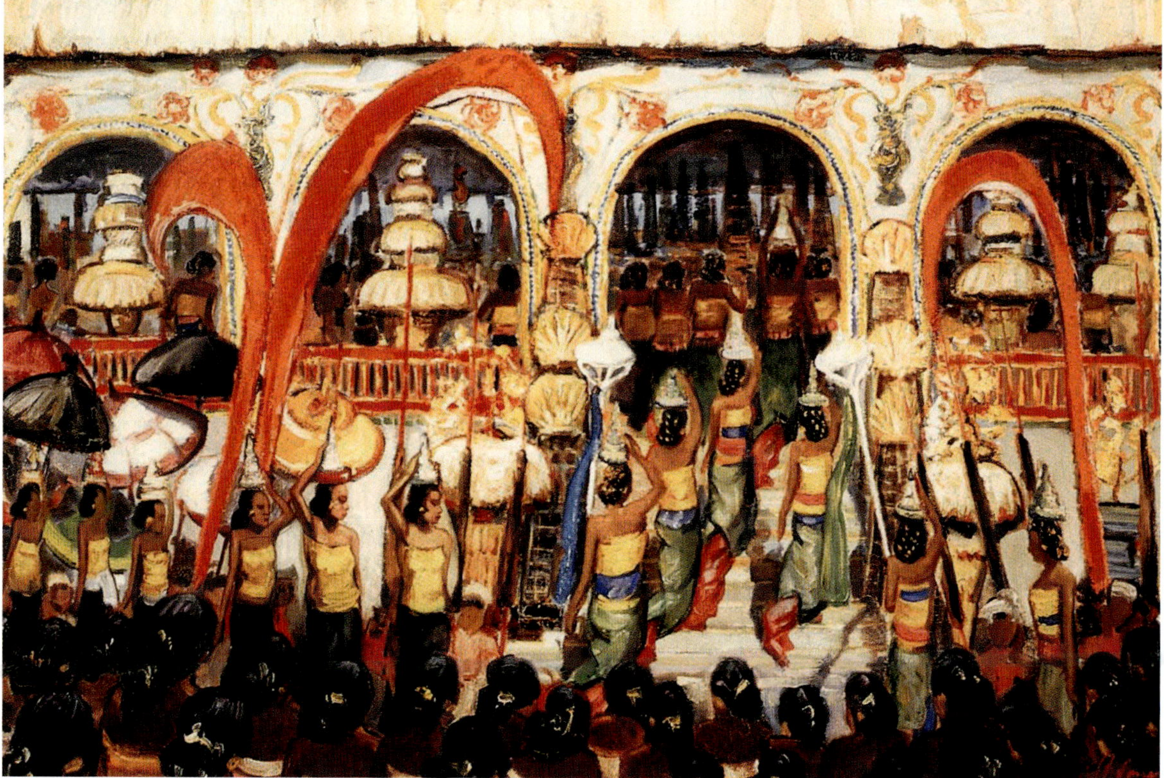

123
Ceremonial offering at Besakih, Bali
Charles E.H. Sayers
(1901-1943)
Oil painting
110 x 150 cm
1927/1928
809-204. Gift: W.E. Vonwiller-Sayers, 1993. Ex-collection: Ch. E.H. Sayers

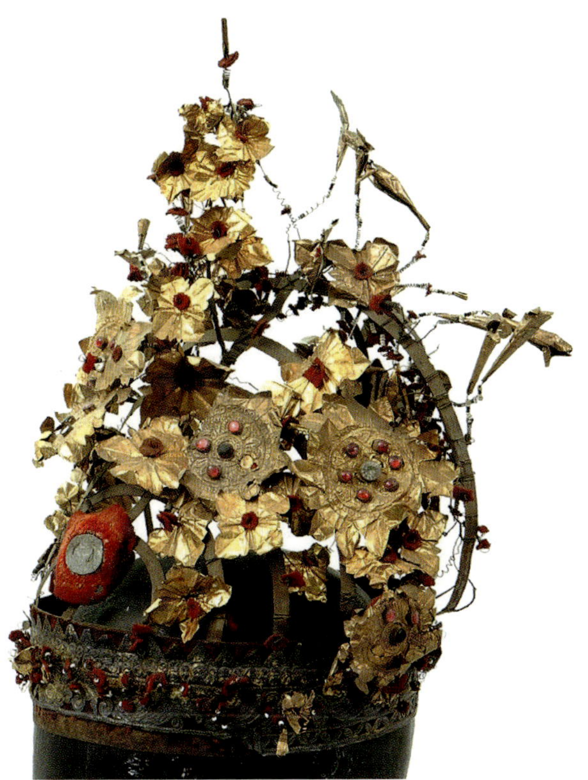

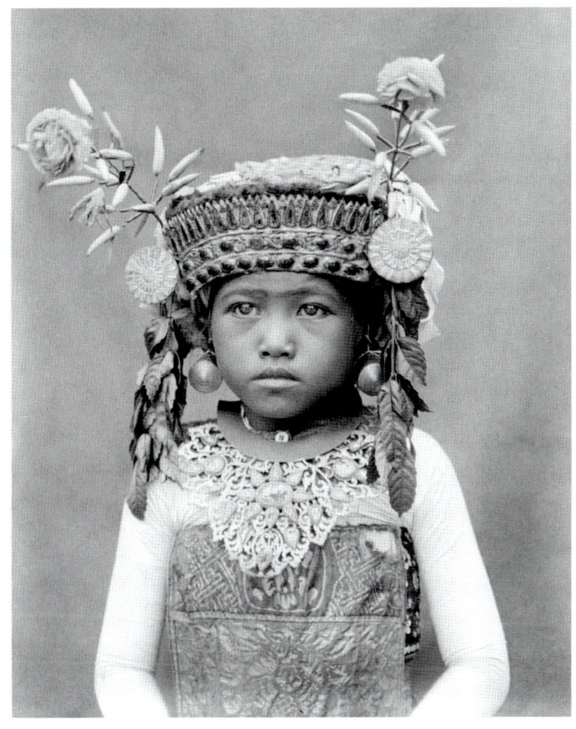

124
Dance crown with flowers and gold leaf
Metal, gold leaf
28.5 x 16.3 cm
Bali. First half 20th century
809-179. Purchase:
O. Sayers-Stern, 1950.
Ex-collection: Ch. E.H. Sayers

125 >
Balinese girl in temple costume
Glass negative
13 x 18 cm
c. 1910
10005340. Gift: Augusta de Wit, 1917

In them, he used bright colours to portray specific moments in the lives of the common people. The third painting of Sayers in the exhibition is *Stilleven met maskers en stokpop* (Still life with masks and stick puppet), 1941. In this last painting, masks are shown with faces misshapen by disease, as well as a *wayang golek* stick puppet with pimples on its face. Perhaps this puppet depicted an enchantress that performed magic rituals. (Fig. 104, 105)

As he said himself, Charles Sayers greatly admired all forms of art from Java and Bali, and therefore also the anonymous folk artists that created these works of art. He felt drawn to their outlook and the way in which they experienced their religion. Many Dutch people who worked in or visited the Netherlands East Indies at this time were fascinated by the *topeng* masks. The painter Piet Ouborg (1893-1956), who worked in the Netherlands East Indies from 1916 to 1938 as a teacher and drawing instructor, developed a passion for masks as well. He and a friend set off on journeys to paint and track down authentic masks. Just like Suwardi, Ouborg stressed the religious character of most of the art objects found on Java and Bali. Moreover, in Ouborg's view, religious art was the only real art. He was particularly impressed by the masks because of the magical powers attributed to them. 'Masks do not merely represent the spirit; in ceremonies, they become the spirit.'[86]

It was probably owing to the magical powers that the Javanese and Balinese ascribed to their ritual objects that they were opposed to them being taken out of their country. When Sayers wanted to ship his collection to the Netherlands in the early 1930s, he ran into problems because the rumour went around that the objects had been stolen. The cargo was inspected by the authorities, but they found nothing out of the ordinary in the objects. They were found to be only curiosities and their export was allowed.[87] Like the other collectors of the art objects that can be admired in the exhibition 'The Netherlands East Indies', Sayers was astounded by the metaphysical beauty that these objects radiated. On visiting this exhibition in the Tropenmuseum, I too experienced the same astonishment. It enables me to easily imagine the enthusiasm people had for the community art at the beginning of the 20th century. It just could be that what this art still gives to us is 'the belief that the creation of this art had divine origins.'[88] Although not everyone today believes in a god or spiritual power, we are all susceptible to the universal power of mythical symbols, if we take Jung or Eliade seriously.

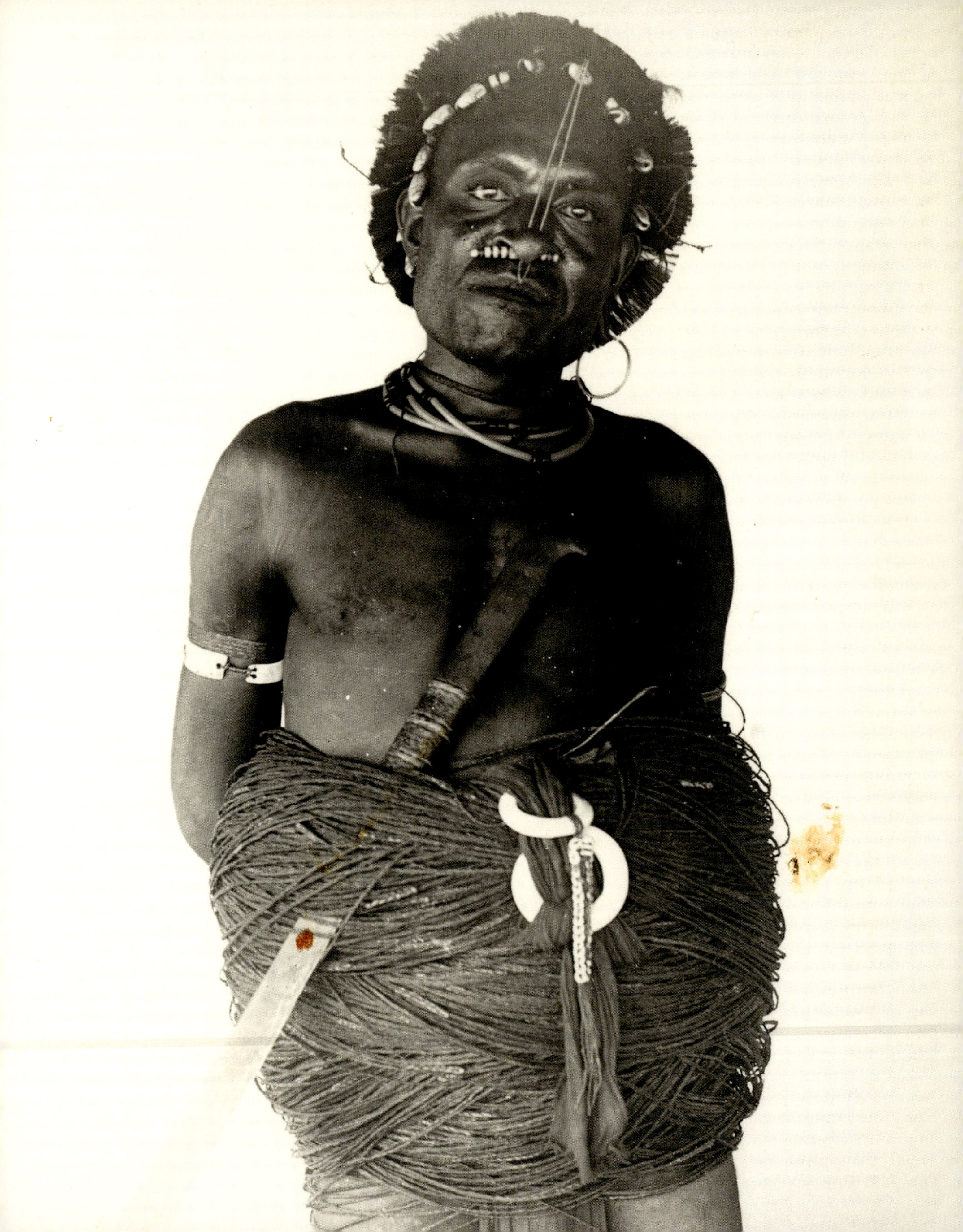

EXPEDITIONS, COLLECTION, SCIENCE
The Dutch fascination for the Papuans of New Guinea

DAVID VAN DUUREN

The Netherlands East Indies! Until the second World War it has been a very familiar name to the Dutch, eliciting a timeless image – as though the Indonesian archipelago has been in the possession of the colonial mother country since the days of Jan Pieterszoon Coen and the Verenigde Oostindische Compagnie (VOC). Nothing could be less true. Large parts of the archipelago, where the Netherlands had been present since the beginning of the 17th century – but only in a limited number of locations with trading posts and, later, a colonial administration – still had to be explored at the end of the 19th and beginning of the 20th century. And before that, they first had to be subjected to Dutch authority. Wars had to be waged with the contentious principalities of Palembang, Aceh, Banjarmasin (former Bandjermasin), Bali, Lombok, South Sulawesi (former Celebes) and other small sovereign kingdoms before they officially could be added to the Netherlands East Indies – '*ons Indië*' ('our Indies'). When Queen Wilhelmina ascended the Dutch throne in 1898, the territorial delineation of the colony of the Netherlands East Indies was reputed to be complete, though a portion of the Indonesian population continued to be defiant. After the subjection of the last rebellious princes and regions, or 'pacification', as it was generally referred to at the time, the Dutch authorities got down to the task of managing the new territories through an administrative system and bringing it under military or civilian governance. (Fig. 127)

126
Detail, Fig. 132

Scientific research, field work and expeditions

Scientific institutions and researchers were eager and excited in the meantime and were every bit as energetic in their efforts as the colonial Government. Many research projects were successfully launched at the end of the 19th and especially the first half of the 20th century. The scientific programme was multifaceted and intensive, ranging from hydrography to anthropology, from geology to plant physiology. Primary research into all these matters took considerable time and effort. The scientist had to go into the field, often with a team, sometimes alone. Expeditions crisscrossed the unexplored interiors of Kalimantan, Sumatra and Sulawesi; marine vessels set sail to map the coasts of little-known islands and conducted oceanographic measurements. The eruption of the volcano island of Krakatau in 1883 led to long-term and intensive research. Volcanoes elsewhere in the archipelago were scaled as well. Mammals and birds were mounted. Insects were pinned to maps. Archaeological sites were restored and unknown languages and cultures were documented. In 's Lands Plantentuin at Buitenzorg, the botanical garden in present day Bogor, West Java, founded in 1817 by C.G.C. Reinwardt, a range of plant species were grown and, when this was not possible, were laid out to dry in herbaria. Science flourished in the Netherlands East Indies and learned publications filled library after library. In 1929 Christiaan Eijkman was awarded the Nobel Prize for Medicine for discovering the importance of vitamin B1 on the basis of research he conducted into beriberi and other tropical diseases.

Of all Dutch possessions in the East, New Guinea was the last to be explored. The Dutch had too much on their hands in many parts of Netherlands East Indies to enable them actively to engage with this enormous, inhospitable and heavily wooded island. Though the western half of the island had been Dutch territory since the 19th century, they did not know what to do with it. Merkusoord with its fortress of Fort Du Bus, was the first Dutch settlement on the southern coast. After a couple of desperate years in which settlers were plagued by disease and attacks from Papuans, they abandoned the settlement in 1836. Thereafter a number of

ESCUTCHEON

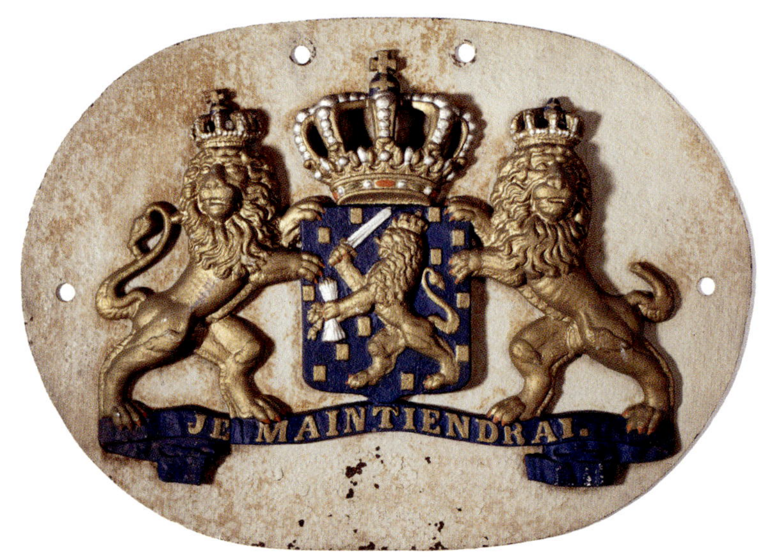

127
Escutcheon
Cast iron, paint
91 x 67 cm
Geelvink Bay, New Guinea
End of 19th century
573-63. Gift: Gewest Ternate, 1930

The Dutch administration on New Guinea was established at the end of the 19th century, in the words of the colonial administrator Jan van Eechoud: 'by nailing iron escutcheons to trees, after which boats had to be hastily found to save one's skin.' Such an escutcheon was acquired in 1929 by Prof. J.C. van Eerde from the village of Wasior on the Wandamen Bay in northern New Guinea. This is peculiar because the Dutch administration officials had never hung such an escutcheon there. Most of the locations for them can easily be found in old history books, such as the one of Colonel Haga from 1884, including the Delft earthenware plate that, due to the lack of an official escutcheon, was nailed to a pole at Lakahia. But Haga wrote only that they had hung an escutcheon in Miei in 1875, also on the coast of the Wandamen Bay. This area was apparently very restless: in 1921 an encyclopaedia still described it as being 'very uncivilised', while missionaries in the area spoke of the 'feared Wandamen'. In 1879, the inspector Van Oldenborch visited several villages on the north coast. On reaching the island of Japèn, he was told by the natives that people from Wandamen had tried to steal their escutcheon. Van Oldenborch then began to suspect 'that in the eyes of the Papuans, the escutcheons gradually came to be viewed as a suitable ornament for the *kampongs* (compounds).'
This escutcheon, for instance, was perhaps stolen by the inhabitants of Wasior from their Miei neighbours. By the time Van Eerde had acquired it, the Dutch administration was more or less established and the escutcheons had lost their function. MM

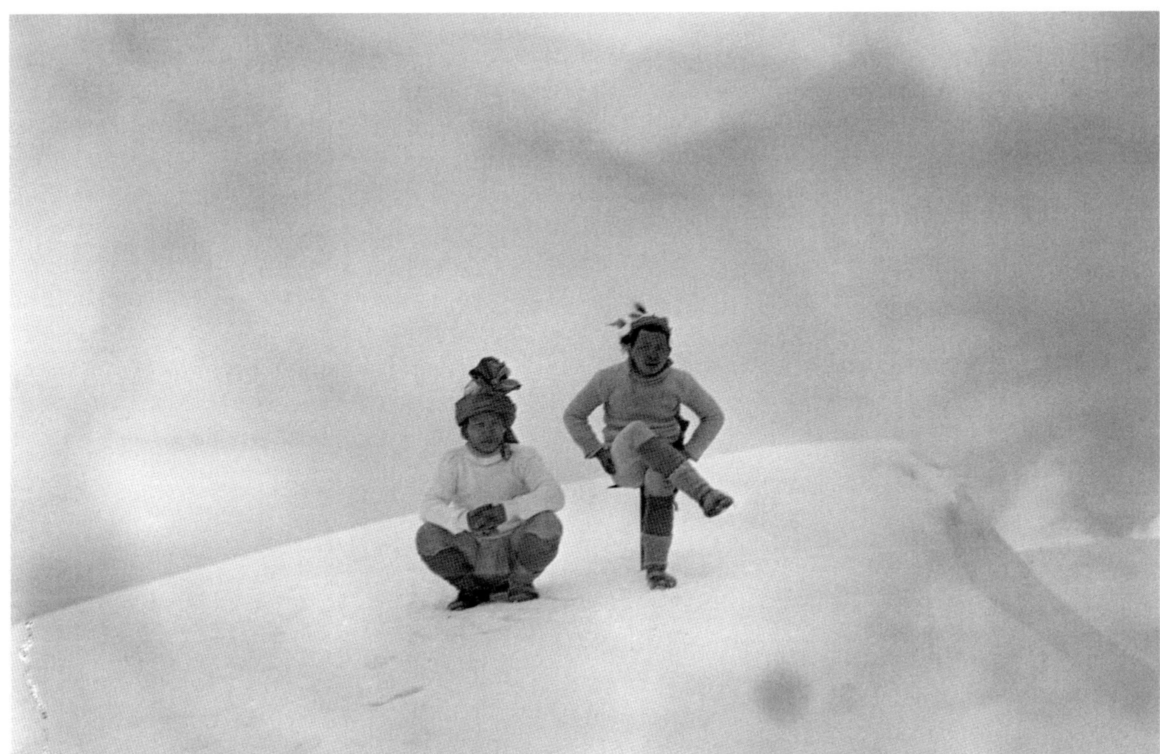

128
Two Dayaks on Wilhelmina summit, New Guinea
Photographer: Paul F. Hubrecht (1889-1929)
Glass negative
9 x 12 cm
1912-1913
10009311. Gift: A.A. Pulle, 1915

coastal regions were explored. But the deep interior of the island remained unexplored before 1900. The explorers were convinced about one thing: the tops of the mountains that could be seen from the sea in clear weather were eternally covered in snow. Chief merchant of the VOC Jan Carstensz returned home in 1623 with a story about snowy peaks he had seen while sailing past the southern coast of the intensely hot tropical island, but his findings were viewed with some scepticism in Amsterdam.

When the 20th century dawned and the time was ripe for the exploration of Dutch New Guinea, two types of expeditions were launched. Military detachments penetrated the island's interior from the south, north and west in order to put New Guinea on the topographical map, and scientific teams went in search of that everlasting snow, whose existence they were determined to confirm. To limit ourselves to the scientific expeditions, they set out from the north or south coast at short intervals of a few years, moving up the mouth and lower waters of a wide river in the direction of the central mountain ridges. These treks were difficult and not always successful. They had a fixed composition: Dutch researchers, Indonesian soldiers, Dayak odd-jobbers from Kalimantan and convict-labourers who had to bear the loads. Carstensz proved to have been telling the truth: a large snow field was trodden for the first time in 1909, while mount Wilhelmina, the peak which was always the destination of these expeditions, was ascended in 1913 and again in 1921.[89] (Fig. 128)

These expeditions provided many objects for the Dutch ethnographic collection. During the treks, contact was made with unknown Papuan groups as well. The expedition members had taken along many attractive things to trade – iron axe blades and knives, pieces of cotton cloth, mirrors, beads and tobacco. In exchange, they were able to acquire nearly all of the local cultural material available. This pertains to a limited number of different objects, because the mountain cultures were not prosperous in this regard. Yet the tools, weapons, articles of clothing and jewellery they collected came straight from newly discovered 'tribes' that lived in the 'Stone Age'. This fact spoke directly to the imagination. Every expedition returned with ethnographic objects, which were distributed among the Dutch ethnographic museums on their return. These museums were thus able to build up very extensive collections from the Mountain Papuans.

129
Auki, a Kapauko Papuan
Photo taken during the Mimika Expedition of H.J.T. Bijlmer
Gelatin silver print
17.5 x 17.5 cm
1 Jan. 1936
60011008. Gift: Prof. Dr. V.J. Koningsbergen, 1961

Yet the Mountain Papuans themselves drew much more attention than their primitive cultural objects, because stone axes and bamboo arrows were found everywhere on New Guinea. Many examples of these objects found in coastal areas had already reached the collections in the Netherlands. It was the small stature of the mountain inhabitants in particular, that captured the attention of anthropologists. In 1909, during the Second South New Guinea Expedition (1909-10) on the way to the peak of Mt. Wilhelmina, the members of the expedition came eye to eye – for the first time, high in the mountains – with a group of men who called themselves Pesegem. Compared with the stocky, pushy and sometimes aggressive coastal inhabitants they had met at the beginning of the expedition – and whom they had to confront in order to progress further – these people were remarkably small and friendly. The word 'pygmy' quickly came to mind, but the contact they had with this group was too short and too casual to be certain that this description was accurate. During the Third South New Guinea Expedition (1912-13), which largely followed the same route of the previous expedition, more time was reserved to study the Pesegem, who warmly welcomed the expedition members. They proved to be taller than 1.50 metres, the average height that anthropological science had established to classify a population group as 'pygmies'.

Yet the spectacular discovery of the short-statured Mountain Papuans did not cause much commotion outside the Dutch scientific world. One possible explanation for this is that the expedition reports were published in Dutch or German. It is more likely, however, that reports on the Pesegem were overshadowed by the discovery of a second group of small mountain inhabitants at the same time by an English expedition that had trekked inland in a more western part of Dutch New Guinea. This expedition, known since then as the British Ornithologists' Expedition (1909-11), was in New Guinea in search of unknown birds. The guides and porters, Papuans from the southern Mimika coast, returned to camp one day accompanied by two virtually naked men who were so small that they were described in the expedition reports as coming from a tribe of dwarves. The coastal inhabitants called them Tapiro. Eight months later – the expedition had long been underway – the British researchers discovered a settlement of these people where they encountered 40 male inhabitants. They were allowed by the men to photograph and film them and to exchange gifts; native artefacts for tobacco, beads and fabrics. During the three days that the British expedition set up their bivouac near the Tapiro village, the women and children remained hidden.[90]

The discovery of this pygmy population in New Guinea was announced to the world by the English in two well-written and luxuriously published expedition reports entitled *Pygmies and Papuans* and *The land of the New Guinea Pygmies*.[91] The encounter with the Tapiro was sensational world news and dominated the front pages of Western newspapers. For some anthropologists, this discovery represented proof of the existence and dissemination of an ancient 'race of pygmies' that lived in Central Africa, Southeast Asia and New Guinea. (Fig. 129) For a long time, the Tapiro were also thought to be the prototypes for the 'New Guinea pygmy'. Their photographs were reproduced many times over in scientific treatises and in books and magazines aimed at a broad public. Later expeditions would encounter more of these groups elsewhere in the high-altitude mountain valleys of Dutch New Guinea and in the Australian eastern part of the island. In the meantime, anthropologists began to ponder seriously on the problem of how these pygmy groups came to be. Were they descendants of a primitive people? Were they groups that, for whatever reason, showed signs of degeneration such as their short stature? Or were we confronted here by the processes of a physical adaptation to a specific living environment? Was their short stature the result of a combination of different environmental factors? And what could be said about the racial relationship of these dwarf Papuans with other Papuans whose height fell within the average standards?[92]

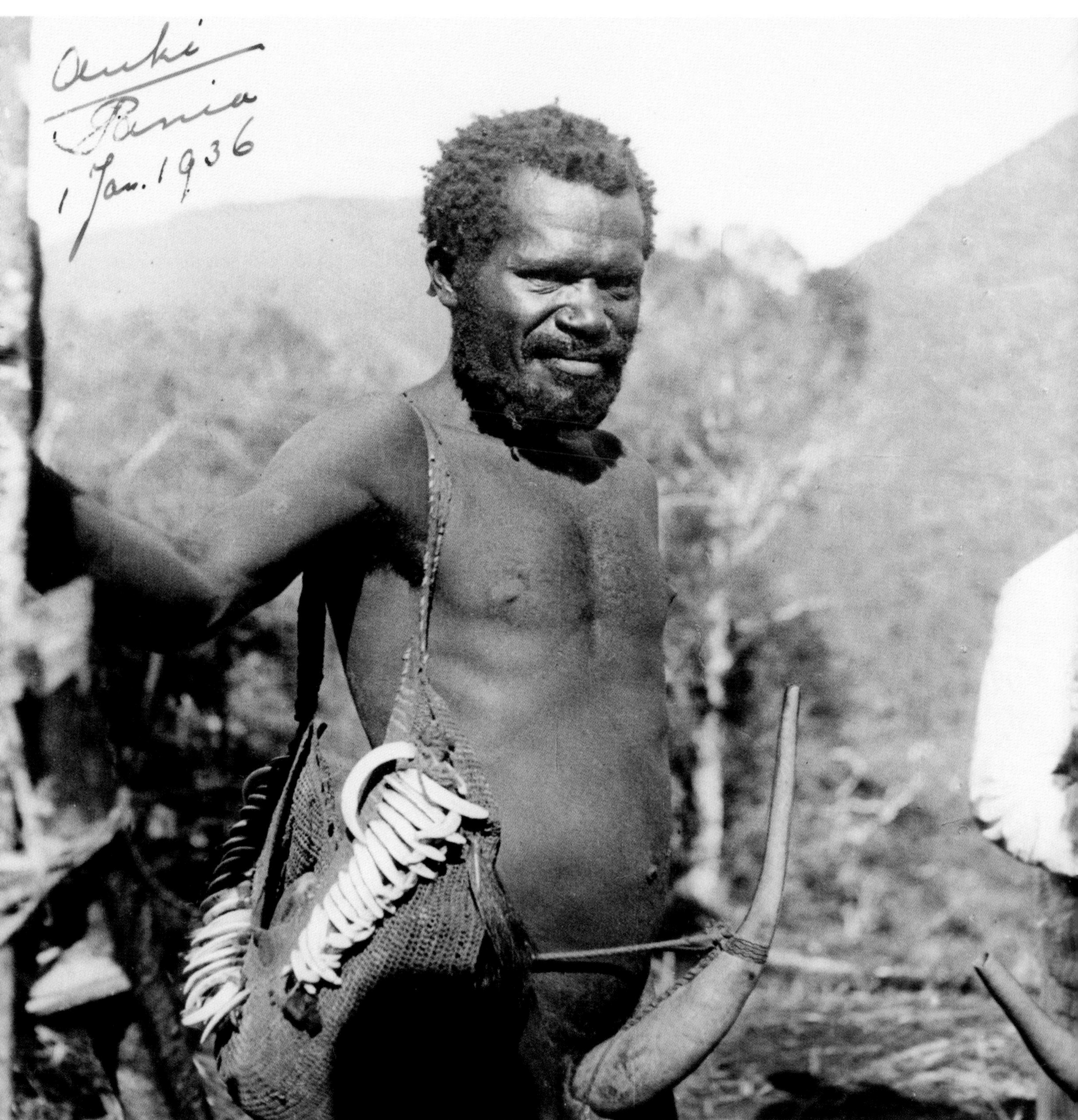
Auki
Pania
1 Jan. 1936

Anthropology and anthropologists

These questions bring us to the nature of anthropology at that time. The term 'anthropology' is derived from the Greek words *anthropos* and *logos*: the science of man. In the 19th century, this concept encompassed, side by side, the sub-disciplines that were focused on the evolution and development of humans, the fossils of their ancestors, their physical characteristics, their prehistory, their dissemination over the earth and the phases of their cultural and social development. A good example of this total approach to the prehistoric, uncivilized human species can be found in *Prehistoric Times as illustrated by Ancient Remains and the Manners and Customs of Modern Savages*, a much-studied standard work of the British Lord Avebury published in 1865, which stayed in print for half a century.[93]

130
A Papuan woman during a physical anthropological study, New Guinea
Glass negative
13 x 18 cm
10009083. Gift: Wichmann Expedition to Northern New Guinea, 1903

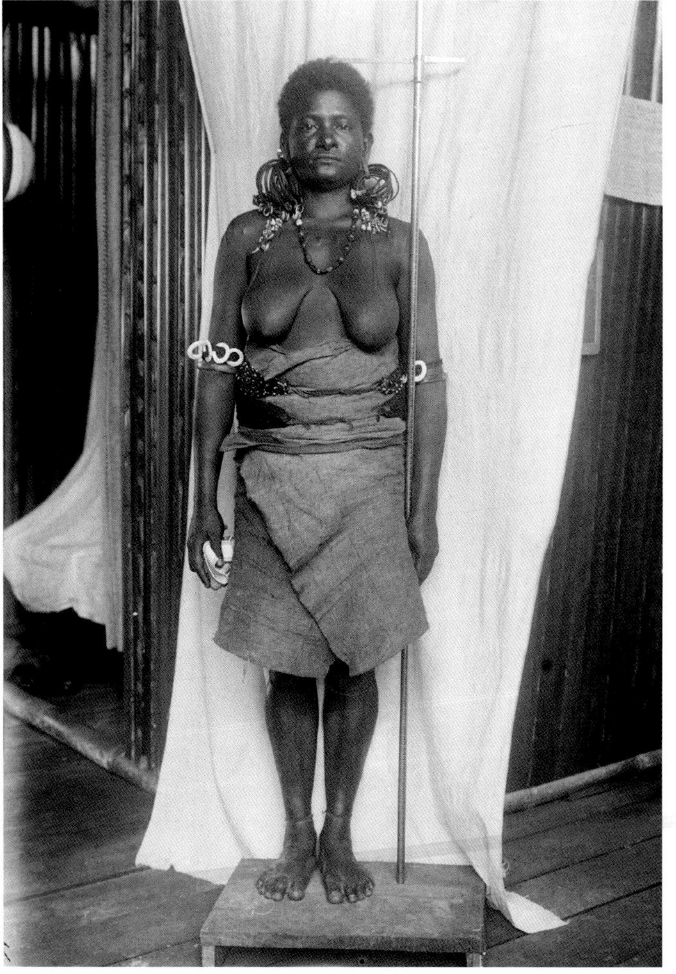

The essence of the book is that circumstances in prehistory, knowledge of which was still in its infancy at the time, could be deduced by studying the lives and behaviour of 'modern savages', including the New Zealand Maori, the Australian Aborigines, the North American Indians and the Arctic 'Esquimaux'. Avebury does not discuss the physical characteristics of the groups of 'savages' he selected, but his message is clear: 'primeval phases' or 'early phases' of culture are represented by a primitive type of people. This assumed link between the cultural development and the mental predisposition of a people then developed into a tenacious Western picture of the non-Western human that dominated anthropology until well into the 20th century.

In addition to cultural anthropology, the study of humans as bearers of culture, there was also physical anthropology, the study of humans as biological creatures and as members of the animal world. These two branches of anthropology, actually alien to one another, were nonetheless considered inseparable and were taught in conjunction with one another in order to construct a complete picture of *Homo Sapiens*. Physical anthropology was the most prestigious of the two branches at the dawn of the 20th century and was practised by people with a medical background and a thorough knowledge of the human anatomy and physiology. It was often focused on the comparative study of variations in human constitution, i.e. determining hereditary similarities and differences between 'natural groups' in order to draw conclusions, by means of the 'racial characteristics' found, concerning the origin, dissemination and cross-breeding of human populations. This is why the expeditions to the unknown island of New Guinea – with its isolated, small Papuan societies and their untouched cultures – offered such exciting prospects. As mentioned before, explorers collected what they could and this included data on the physical characteristics of the Papuans. They were measured with instruments specially developed for the purpose and photographed from the front and the side. (Fig. 130, 132-136) If possible, skulls and bones taken from old graveyards were collected. (Fig. 131) The human remains were studied in detail back home. The measurements taken, which were expressed as indices and recorded in tables and charts, filled in the presumed gaps in the knowledge of the recently discovered

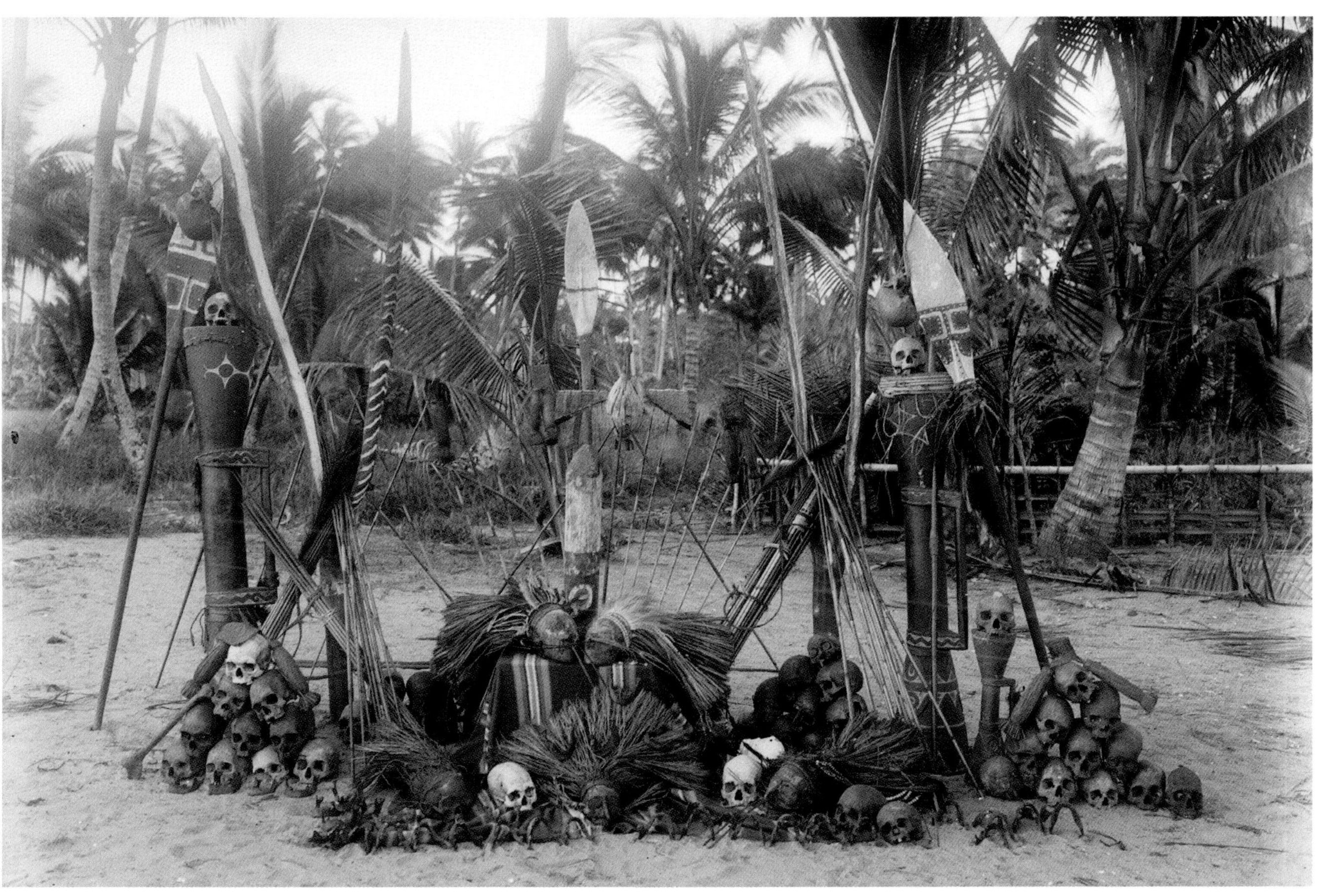

131
Collection of objects, decapitated heads and skulls of the Marind Anim in Sanggasé in South-East New Guinea
Glass negative
13 x18 cm
Early 20th century
10008181. Gift: L.M.F. Plate, 1916

people. They also served as material for comparing the physical development of Western groups. In the Netherlands, for example, this pertained to the populations of small islands such as Urk and Marken which, due to their isolated location, were considered as possible descendants of the original inhabitants of the delta area.

Some of the human remains that were taken from New Guinea by the expeditions are housed at the Koninklijk Instituut voor de Tropen (KIT). The rest are in other museum collections in the Netherlands. The KIT, still known as the Koloniaal Instituut at the time, was prepared to house them: the existence of a department of cultural and physical anthropology – the name (in Dutch: Afdeeling Culturele en Physische Anthropologie) still appears above one of the service entrances of the building – implied that the institute had someone on staff who was an expert on human biology. The expert in question was Dr. J. P. Kleiweg de Zwaan (1875-1971), a physician who in 1907 had participated in a German exploratory expedition in Central Sumatra, where he conducted a physical anthropological research among the people of the Minangkabau. In 1908, he took his doctor's degree in Amsterdam *cum laude*. Dr. Kleiweg de Zwaan was a private teacher in medical cultural history at the University of Amsterdam when, in 1915, he was asked by Prof. van Eerde at the Koloniaal Instituut to join the staff there in order, firstly, to determine the content of the planned 'Sub-department of Physical Anthropology' and then to develop it. Dr. Kleiweg de Zwaan consented to the proposal and remained on the staff until 1927 as a paid employee. But as an 'honorary anthropologist', he actually headed the sub-department until 1948. With the backing of the Koloniaal Instituut, he became a professor occupying an endowed chair in anthropology and the medicine of the native population of the Netherlands East Indies in 1919. In 1924 he also became Extraordinary Professor and in 1932 Professor of Anthropology and Prehistory, a post he held until his retirement in 1939.[94] (Fig. 137)

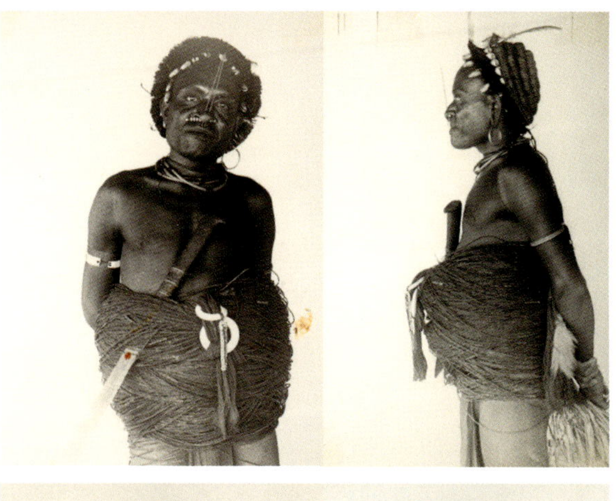
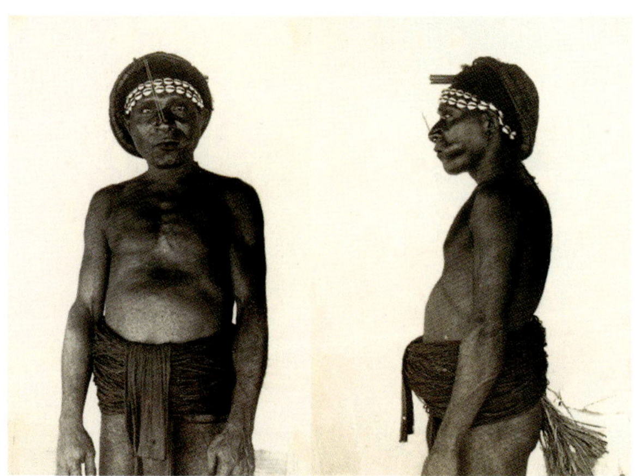
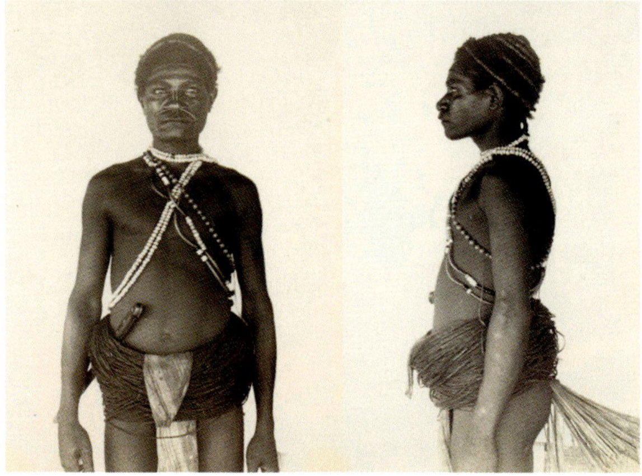
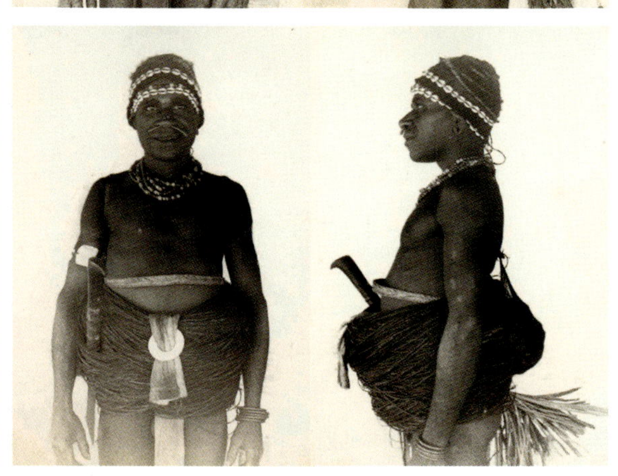
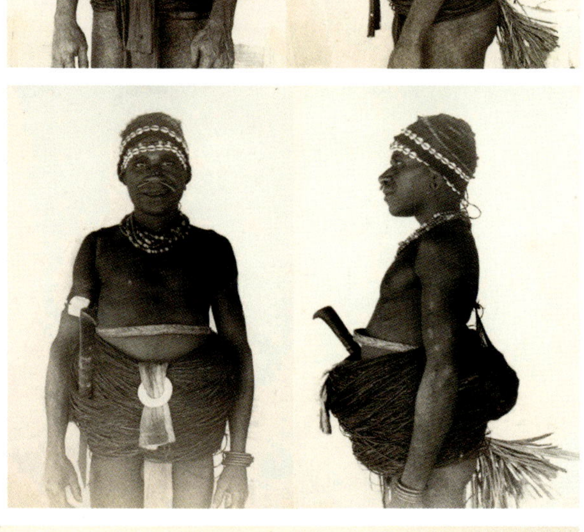
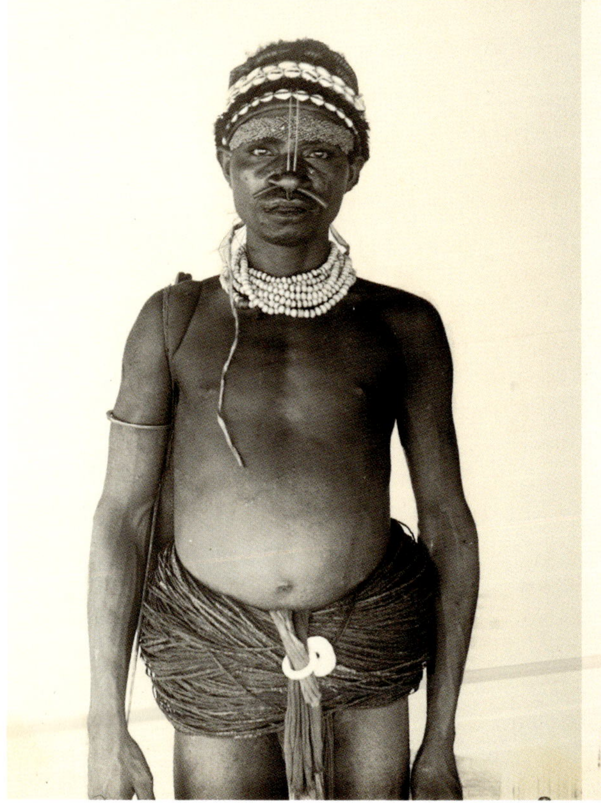
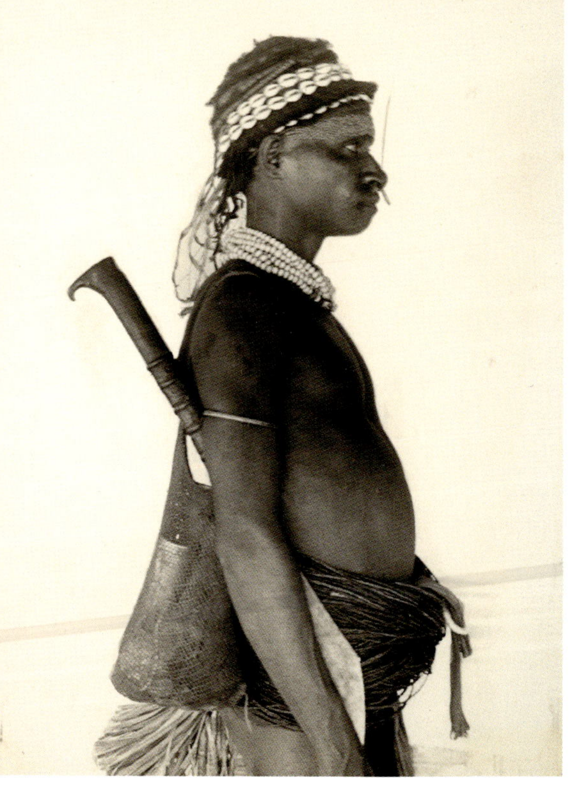

132-136
Kauwerawet Papuans during physical anthropological research, New Guinea
Photographer: C.C.F.M Le Roux (1885-1947)
Gelatin silver print
14 x 9.3 cm
1926
Gift: Koninklijk Nederlandsch Aardrijkskundige Genootschap, 1927
132: Ediso. 60050877, -78
133: Isaja. 60050879, -80
134: Komaha. 60050885, -86
135: Jakob. 60050881, -82
136: Kwisa. 60050883, -84

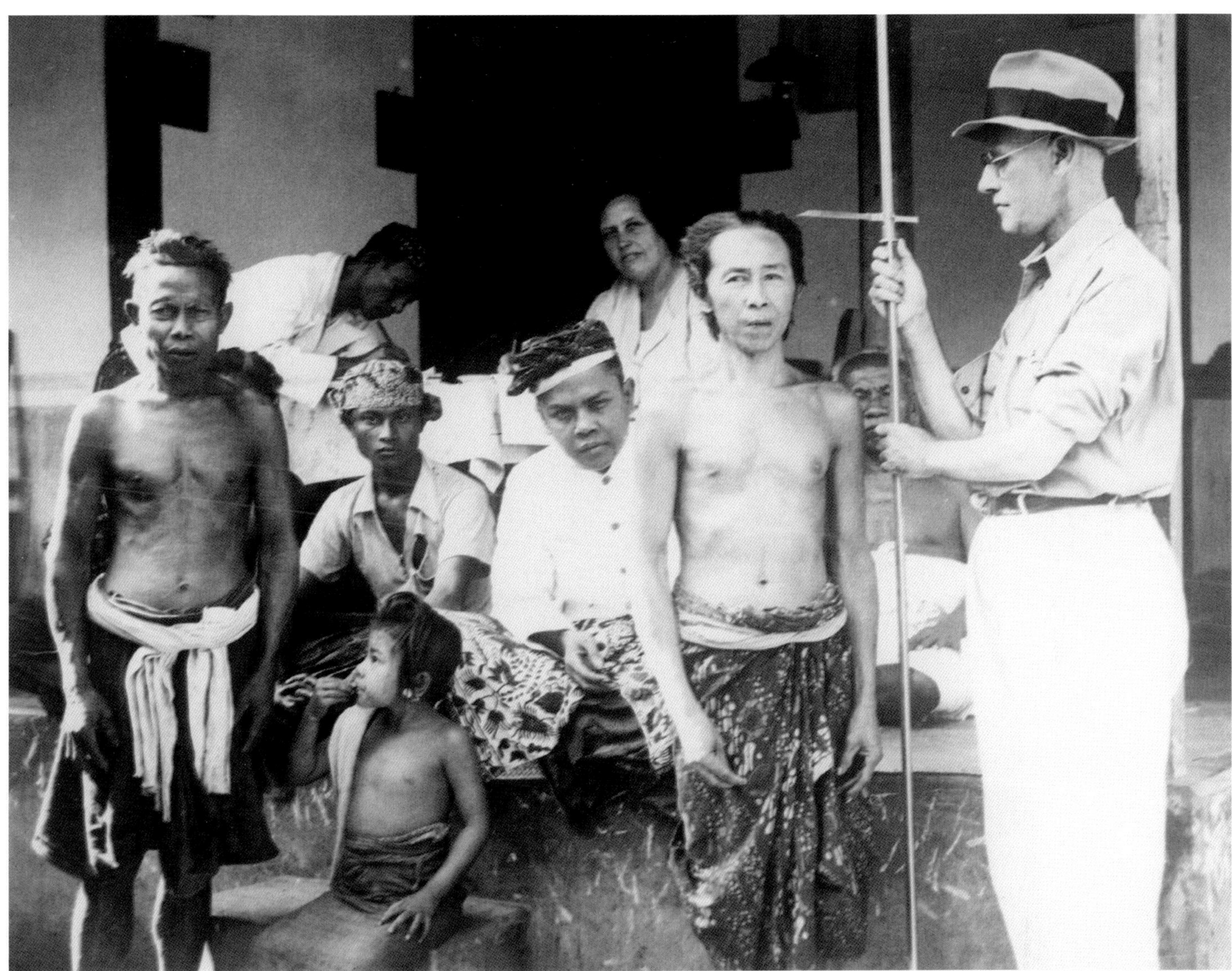

137
Professor Dr. J.P. Kleiweg de Zwaan takes physical-anthropological measurements in Tenganan, Bali
Glass negative
9 x 12 cm
1938
10004939. Gift: Prof. Dr. J.P. Kleiweg de Zwaan, 1939

Collections

Under the leadership of Kleiweg de Zwaan, a collection was built up that consisted of skeletal remains, plaster casts of the faces of members of a particular community, and photographs. The people who were the subject of study posed in the photos, often with a measuring staff in hand and sometimes against the background of a grid in order to better highlight the proportions of their bodies. Such measurements were also filmed and sketched. These collections were intended for research. In the Koloniaal Museum they found a counterpart on public display in the form of wax mannequins and drawings, and in pictures taken of different types of indigenous people. Their appearance, posture and features were composed in such a way that the Dutch public formed a mental image of ethnic diversity in the archipelago. This image was actually ethnic stereotyping and classification which, within the colonial context, reinforced the position of different population groups with respect to the colonial establishment. (See for instance Fig. 21)
This entire aggregate of discovery, collection and classification linked to the Dutch exploration of New Guinea in the first half of the 20th century is brought to life in the exhibition at the modern-day Tropenmuseum by an installation in which the figure of

138
Expedition member C.C.F.M. Le Roux photographs a proa with a group of Papuans with his Eastman Kodak panorama camera at Albatrosbivak during the American-Dutch Central New Guinea Expedition in 1926
Photographer: W.M. Docters van Leeuwen (1880-1960)
Nitrate negative
9 x 12 cm
10008109. Gift: W.M. Docters van Leeuwen, 1930

Charles C.F.M Le Roux plays the key role. He is an archetypal anthropologist shown surrounded by expedition essentials and discoveries, scientific instruments, a fully loaded proa and a collage of fragments from an old expedition film. In line with the past museum practice of exhibiting people, his image has been made with the aid of 'lifecasting', making a cast of a human form using the body of a real person. Le Roux (1885-1947) played an important role in the history of the island's exploration. He left for the East Indies in 1908 as a 2nd lieutenant, but later entered the employ of Burgerlijke Openbare Werken (Department of Civil Public Works) in the Netherlands East Indies. During his stay on Flores, where he was responsible for road building, he became interested in ethnology. He developed this interest to a professional level. As a result, when he returned to Batavia (present day Jakarta), he became adjunct curator at the Museum van het Bataviaasch Genootschap van Kunsten en Wetenschap (Museum of the Batavian Society of Arts and Sciences). In 1926 he was a member of the American-Dutch expedition to the interior of New Guinea, also called the 'Stirling Expedition' after its leader, Matthew Stirling. Le Roux returned to the Netherlands in 1934, where he became first curator of the Koloniaal Museum and thereafter the curator and director of the Rijksmuseum voor Volkenkunde (National Museum of Ethnology) in Leiden. In 1939, he became leader of a large expedition organised by the Koninklijk Nederlands Aardrijkskundig Genootschap (Royal Dutch Geographical Society) to the inhabitants of a broad area surrounding the recently discovered Wisselmeren in the central west highlands. He wrote his opus magnum, *De Bergpapoea's van Nieuw-Guinea en hun woongebied* (two volumes and a collection of prints) that was published posthumously between 1948 and 1950.[95] Hundreds of artefacts collected and photographs taken by Le Roux are present in the Netherlands ethnographic collections, including those at the Tropenmuseum.

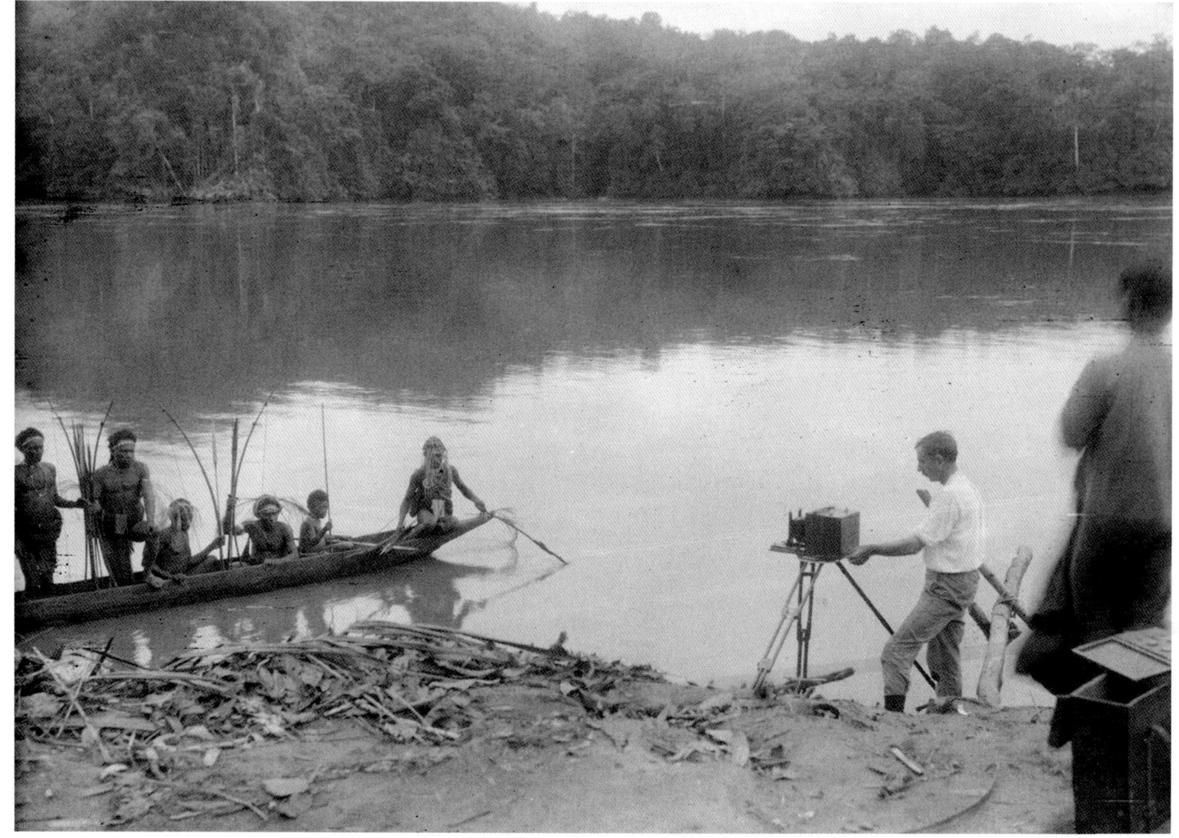

CHARLES CONSTANT FRANÇOIS MARIE LE ROUX – ANTHROPOLOGIST (1885-1947)

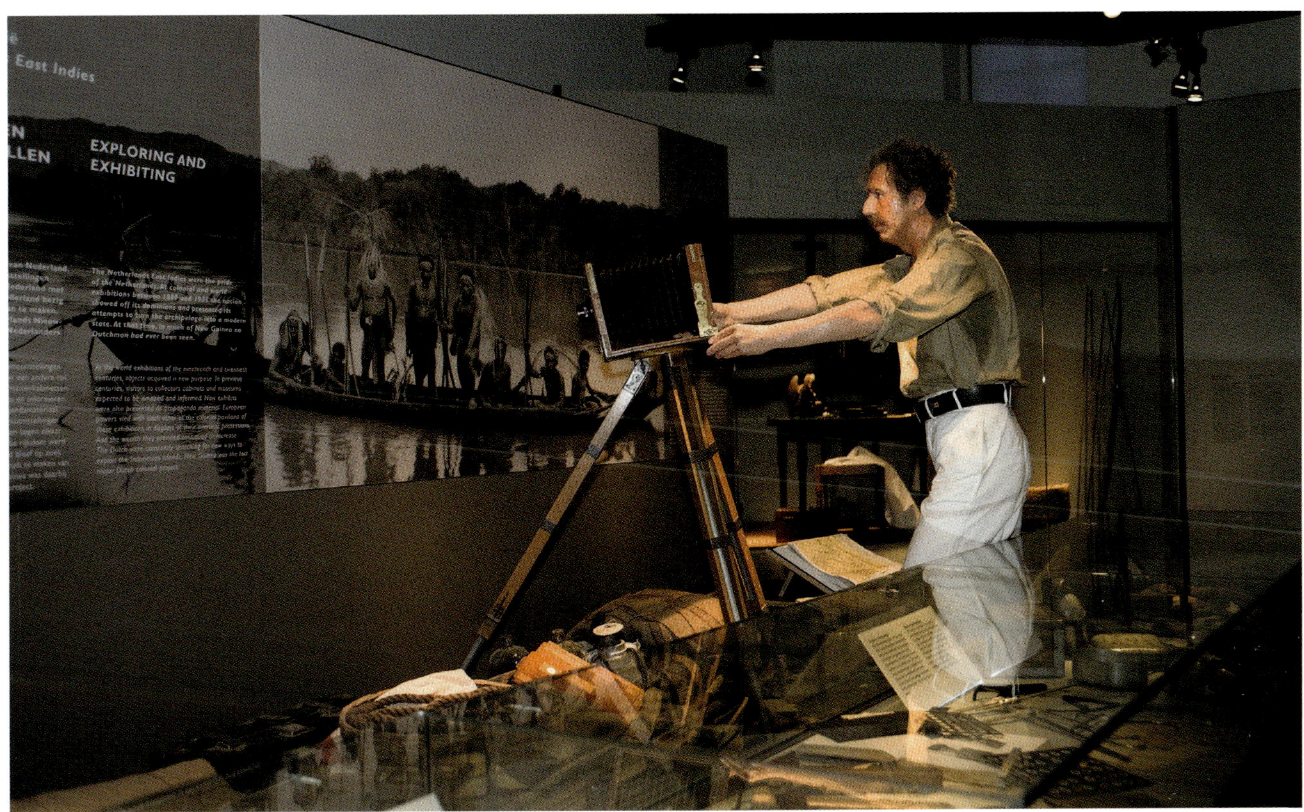

In 1907 he departed for the Netherlands East Indies as a 2nd lieutenant of the KNIL and – as explained elsewhere on this page – over the years he increasingly combined his own cultural anthropological field work with an active role in the musealization of the peoples of the Indonesian archipelago. In Batavia, after 1920, he took on an intermediate role between extending colonial control and improving cultural knowledge in the context of the Stirling Expedition to New Guinea, for instance, and as a deputy curator for the Bataviaasch Genootschap van Kunsten en Wetenschap (Batavian Society of Arts and Sciences). In the Netherlands, after 1927, he applied his knowledge both at the Koloniaal Instituut in Amsterdam and the Rijksmuseum voor Volkenkunde in Leiden.

Today Charles le Roux himself is on display in the Tropenmuseum as well. He has been typecast in his role as the leader of the Scientific Expedition around the Wissel Lakes during his last visit to New Guinea in 1939. With his camera at ready, the anthropologist represents the very moment a photograph is made. Another member of the expedition took a photograph of this scene and thus documented the documenting of culture as such. Le Roux's photograph is not a snap shot. The Papuans were ready to pose for the anthropologist, just as they were ready to share their knowledge and serve as guides for the expedition members. Most people in the Netherlands at the time who saw the photograph of Papuans standing crosswise in a row inside their boat probably did not think about the photographer. He was invisible. They saw the image as imparting information about the Papuans. Now it is regarded as visual information on the many types of encounter that can happen at the same time. SV/SL

Current significance of human remains

Kleiweg de Zwaan was a respected scholar with an international reputation, but the majority of his research and extensive work is now very outdated and probably only of interest for scientific historiography. Physical anthropology, now more often called human biology or anthropobiology, has changed radically and is no longer focused on classifying races and racial characteristics, at least not in the manner common in the days of Kleiweg de Zwaan. The term 'race' is now avoided or used only with extreme caution. Collections of human remains can be found throughout the Netherlands, but they are now studied for other reasons. Especially since the discovery of DNA, a range of new research perspectives have opened.

139
Display case with skulls in the museum of the Koloniaal Instituut, Amsterdam
Gelatin silver print
13 x 11.6 cm
1923-1940
60054941

The Tropenmuseum still has the collection of human remains from the sub-department of physical anthropology, which was discontinued in 1964 after the retirement of Kleiweg de Zwaan's successor, Prof. A. Bergman. It was discontinued because, according to the *Zeitgeist* of the time, a museum that kept up with a rapidly changing world no longer needed a collection of human skeletal remains that were once seen as being primitive or exotic – a collection that conveyed messages focused on 'races' or 'native peoples' which now were no longer thought appropriate. (Fig. 139) In 2003 however, the entire collection of human remains, the majority of which came from the former Dutch colonies, was again inventoried and organised. Packed in custom-made boxes, they are now ready for a new destiny, either inside or outside the Tropenmuseum. The option of 'de-accessing the collection' was consciously considered. Another option is to keep the collection, principally as one that is closely linked with the history of the museum, and as the remnant of a branch of science which was practised for a half century under the roof of the KIT. But the museum preferred to join the current, worldwide discussion about the possession and exhibition of human remains in museums, about the legitimacy of possessing such remains and about the willingness of anthropological museums to repatriate these remains if the representatives of ethnic groups – whose ancestors' mortal remains have ended up in the collection – submit a request for their return. Considering to submit such a request to the Tropenmuseum for the return of human remains is facilitated by the recent publication of a book – based on the initial research report on the remains – which tells the history of physical anthropology in the Tropenmuseum.[96] On the one hand, this book and the inventory of the remains, the history of their acquisition and the list of donors it contains, substitute the physical presence of the human remains as a part of the museum's historical collection. On the other hand, the book is a testimony of a proactive policy that provides an open account about what is, for a modern museum, a contested possession (the human remains) and it opens the possibility of a return of the remains to the so-called source societies. For this reason, the entire text can also be downloaded in digital form on the website of the KIT.
Because the exact origin of many of the human remains, including those from New Guinea, is not always known, nor is it known from which ethnic group they came, repatriation will not be an option in many cases. Besides source societies possibly have no interest in the return of what, in some cases, are hundred-year-old, completely anonymous human remains. In such cases, the relocation of the remains to an institute that is equipped to conduct modern research on human bones might be an option. The current Eijkman Institute for Molecular Biology in Jakarta, for instance, is conducting research into pathogenic DNA. Should this lead to new research on the existing collections of human remains, it is certain that new research on the remains will be done in accordance with national and international museum regulations and agreements that focus on the ethical aspects of possessing, exhibiting, relocating and studying human remains.

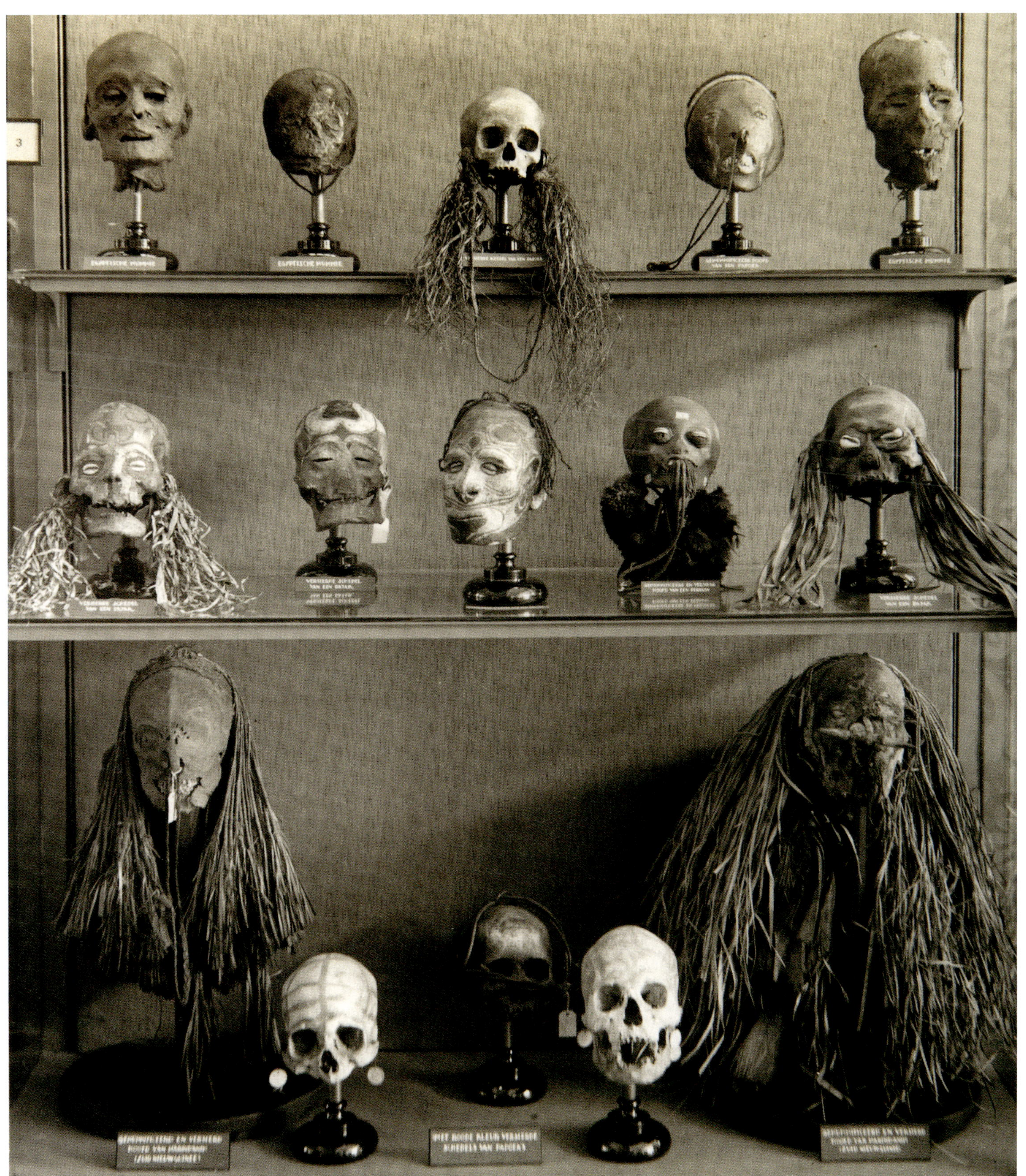

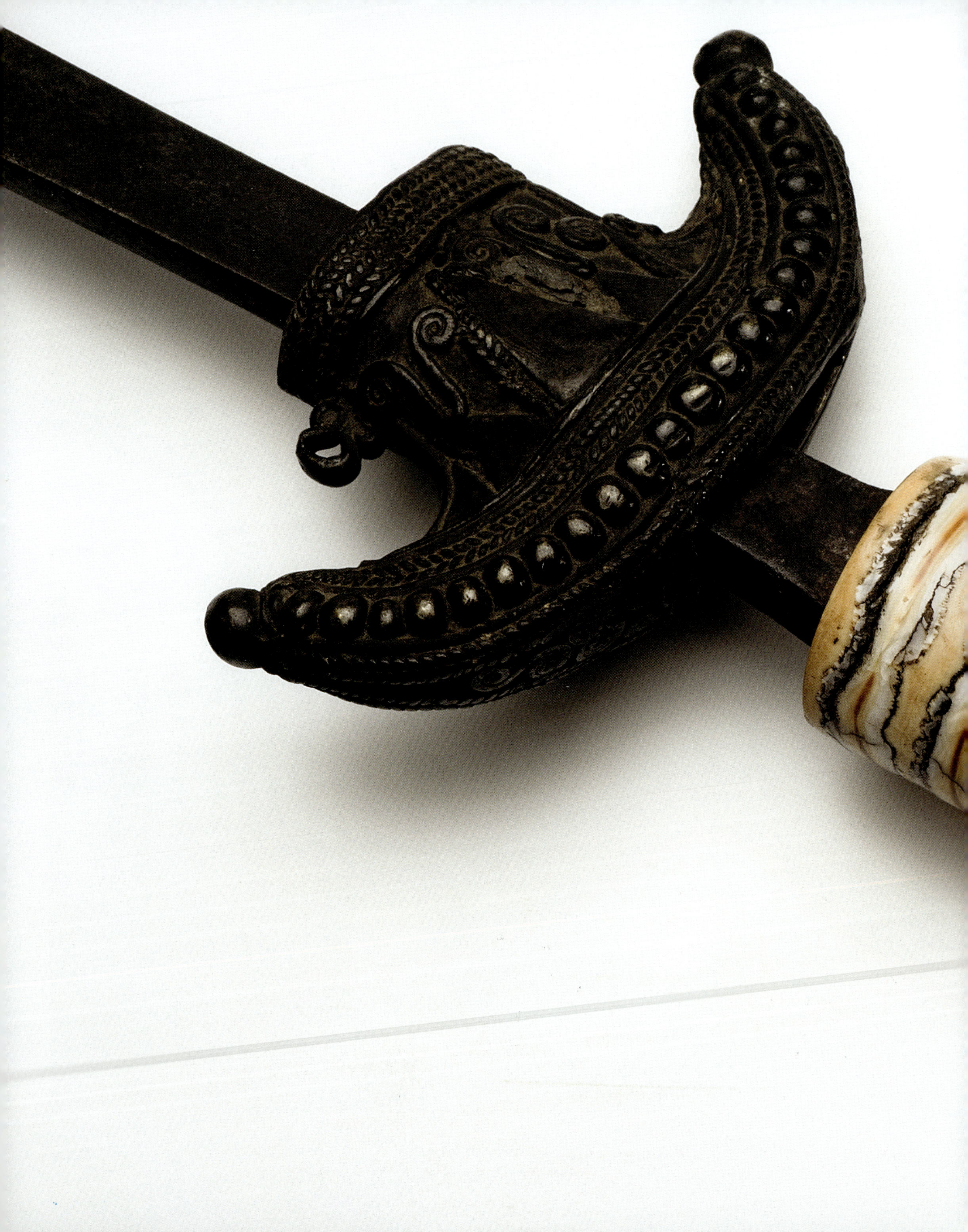

COLONIAL COLLECTIONS AT THE TROPENMUSEUM

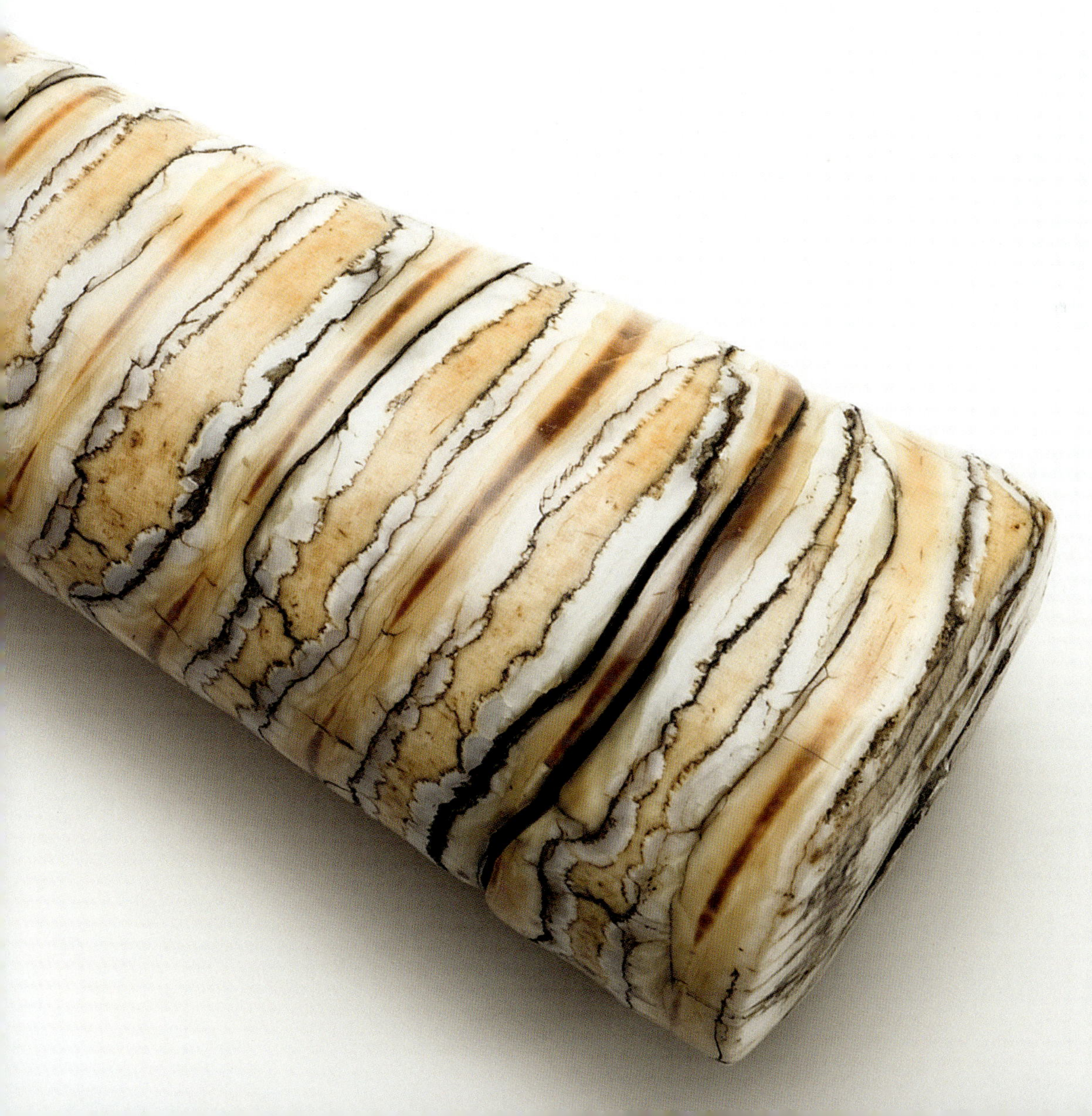

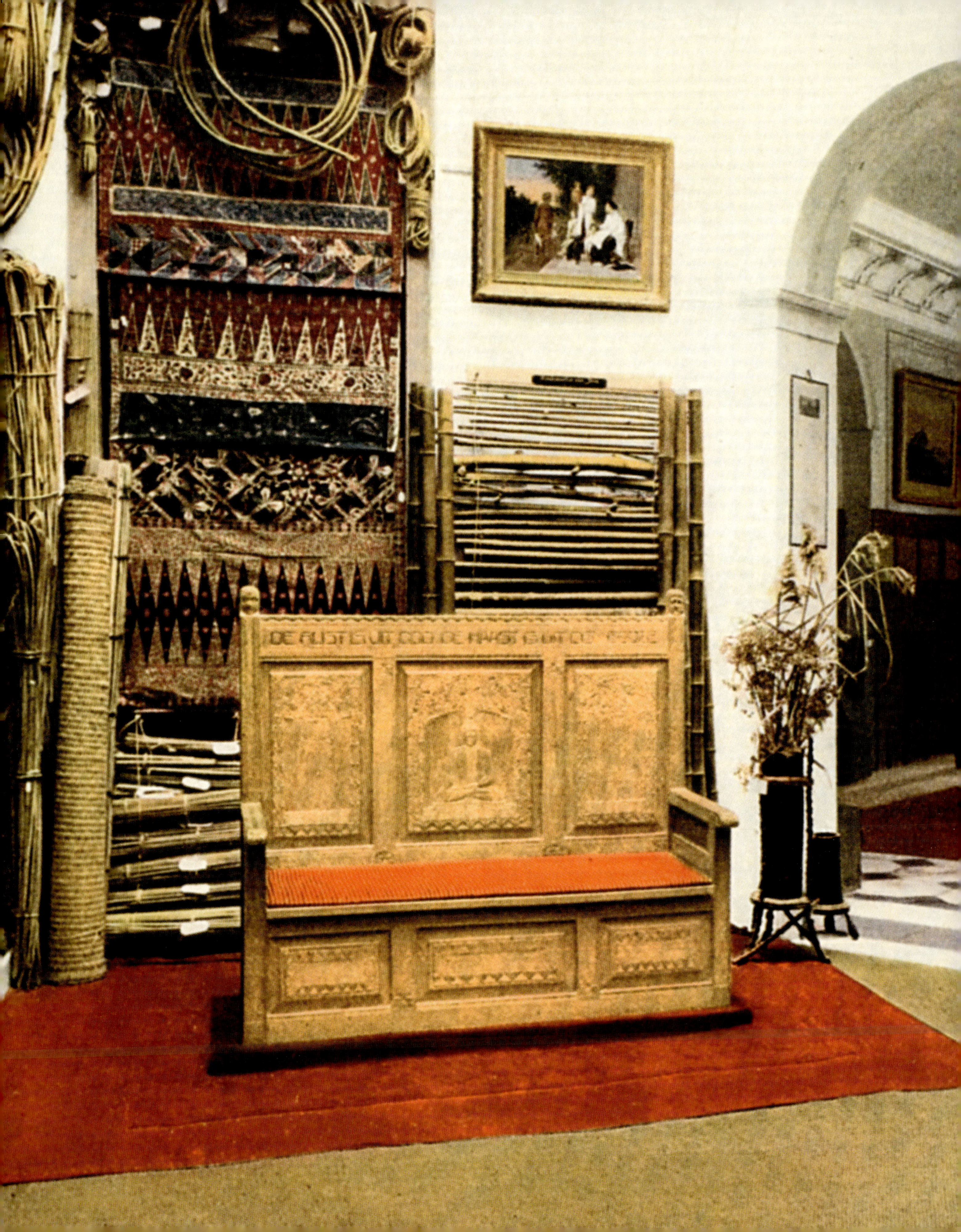

TEN COLLECTORS, TEN COLLECTIONS

SUSAN LEGÊNE AND JANNEKE VAN DIJK

The canon of ethnography

The historical essays in the previous chapters of this book provide a framework from which the collections at the Tropenmuseum can be interpreted, embedded as they are in just as many collecting histories attached to specific objects. Both overseas and in the Netherlands, thousands of people were involved with the Netherlands East Indies in one way or another. Hundreds of them have contributed both to the composition and interpretation of the current collections in the Tropenmuseum. The previous essays zoomed in on a wide range of interactions within the colonial society from which the collections were taken: i.e. military, educational, economic, cultural and scientific. Objects were literally collected during the military contact between the Dutch commander Christoffel and Si Singamangaraja. Other collections are connected to the education movement led by nationalists such as Soewarsih Djojopoespito, in opposition to colonial authorities. Or they are linked to the economic success story of major entrepreneurs such as Jacob Theodoor Cremer, who cannot be imagined without his plantation workers. They are also connected to the colonial housewife and her servants, to the inspiration that Dutch artists found in Javanese art around 1900, or to the scientific research conducted in the Netherlands that was able to follow new lines of enquiry thanks to the colonies. It is just such military, ethical, economic, social, cultural and scientific relationships that form the basis for the collections at the Tropenmuseum. This second part focuses on the collections and the collectors themselves. Museums continually conduct research into the objects in their collections and the very process of collection formation as such is increasingly the subject of study as well. For instance, the famous Pitt Rivers Museum in Oxford, which is specialised in anthropology and global archaeology, studied the acquisition history of all the objects in its collection. The collector was identified for each object. In this way the museum, which was founded around 1884, shed light on the role objects played within a network set up between collectors and the communities from which the collections came. These collections were once an expression of colonial cultural relationships within the British Empire. Today, they provide points of departure for modern-day meetings between the parties concerned in the areas of origin and the museum.[97]In an earlier research, the Australian anthropologist Nicholas Thomas showed, on the basis of collections taken from Oceania (Fiji, Marquesas and the Solomon Islands), that the collecting of objects and formation of collec-

140
View into the bamboo gallery of the Koloniaal Museum, Haarlem
From: Bulletin Colonial Museum, 1907
(See also Fig. 102)

tions were certainly not unilateral actions taken by the (colonial) collectors, leading to the inclusion of the objects collected in museum collections.[98]
It might be that the collector initially prided himself in the fact that he (or she) recognised and selected the interesting objects in communities that were themselves unaware of the artistic value or trading value attached to their authentic culture. And, of course, ethnographic museums subsequently presented these objects as the timeless witnesses of static communities that could not speak for themselves. Yet today we understand that those who collected the objects had a definite influence on the story that the museum subsequently told about these objects. In one situation, the initiative was taken by the community of origin, whose own members decided for themselves to make, trade, sell or relinquish certain objects. In other situations, the initiative came from the side of the colonists and the objects were captured, stolen or ordered and, at their request, made or reproduced in series. In all cases, the collection of objects was a process that had social impact, both in the community of origin and in the society in which these objects were later exhibited in museums.
With their arrival in a museum, the objects continued to play a double role – which was to stress the significance of the relationships between the community of origin and the country of their final destination. Some pieces were designated as masterworks. Similar objects were brought together within genres with specific characteristics. And, gradually, regional and thematic specialisms arose within museums which in themselves contributed to the image formed of the specific communities of origin. Studies were continually conducted into the choice of material, the function, the use and the significance of ethnographic objects. Collecting objects was a dynamic process. Not only was the cohesion within collections reformulated with each new acquisition and each subsequent innovative exhibition plan, but this process also influenced how developments in the areas from which the object originated were interpreted.

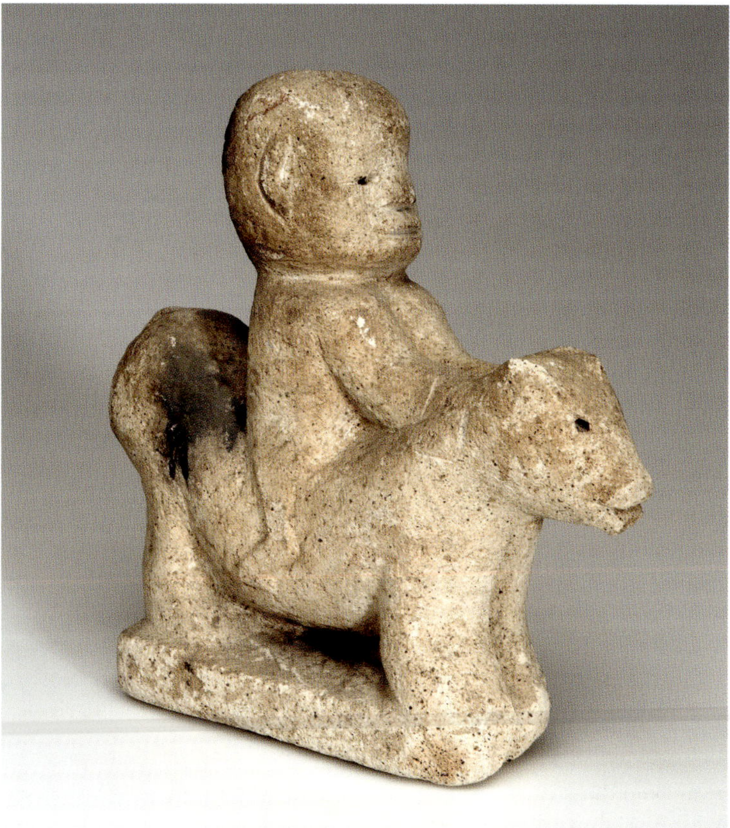

141
Figure of horseman taken from a gravestone
Stone
27 x 8.5 x 28 cm
Karo Batak (culture). Sumatra
18th/19th century
1772-34. Gift: Dr. W.G. Tillman 1994. Former collection: G. Tillmann/ C.M.A. Groenevelt/ van Voorst van Zijp

The objects within the collections of the Tropenmuseum had (and still have) this double role. We will give two examples of this that involve major pieces: the first is a stone horseman from Sumatra (Fig. 141), acquired by a collector who had no personal connection to the community of origin; the second concerns the *kris* (Indonesian dagger) of Knaud (Fig. 142), an heirloom that was passed down from father to son and finally came to the museum. The stone horseman was acquired by the German-Jewish banker Georg Tillmann (1882-1941) in the 1930s via the art trade. The art dealer told him that, according to the accompanying documentation, the first collector, a certain Voorst van Zyp, had 'personally taken it from a gravestone'.[99] Tillmann was a passionate collector who was familiar with the colonial society only from his perspective in the Netherlands. He had never had the opportunity to travel to the Netherlands East Indies and he obtained his precious collection via the art trade. When he escaped to the United States in 1940 from the Netherlands just prior to the German invasion of the country, he placed this collection with the Tropenmuseum on a loan basis to guarantee its safety. More than fifty years later, in 1994, the majority of the objects was donated to the museum by his son.[100]

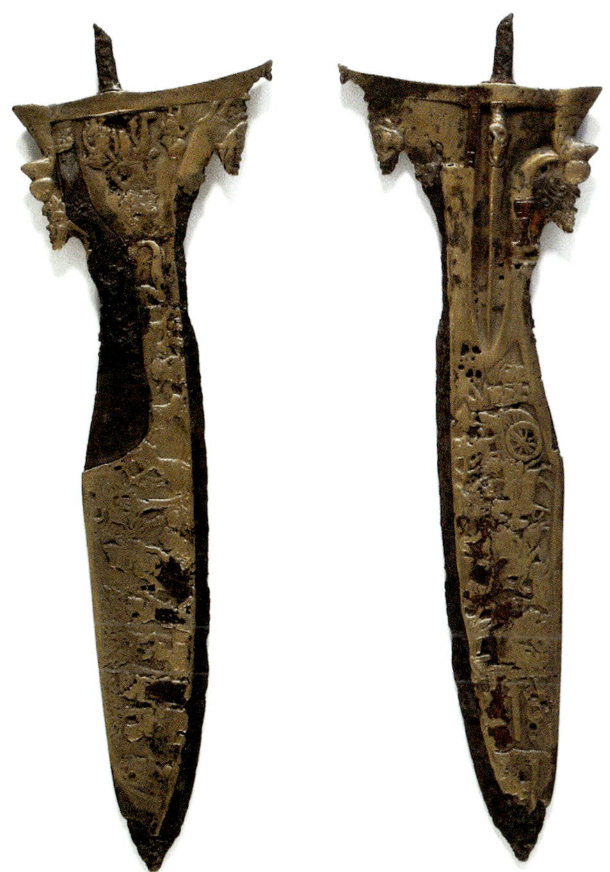

142
Blade of a kris
The kris is known
as the kris of Knaud
Iron alloy, copper
27.8 x 8.5 x 1.2 cm
Indo-Javanese culture. Java
1342
6046-1. On loan: R.V. Knaud

This story of an anonymous stone horseman that once graced someone's grave contains points of contact for countless histories about Indonesia and the Netherlands. So does the *kris* of Knaud, the oldest *kris* dated, which according to an inscription was made in the year 1342. This *kris* was given by Paku Alam V to Charles Knaud at the end of the 19th century as a sign of appreciation for the miraculous cure of his son by Knaud, who had been trained in local medicine. Knaud made sure that the *kris* was soon featured in a publication. It was a prominent historical source of information with respect to the Indo-Javanese prehistory of the modern *kris*. Yet during the years of the Japanese occupation, the *kris* disappeared from view for a long time. In 2002 it reappeared, still in the possession of the family. Since then it has been on loan to the Tropenmuseum. These are two, almost diametrically opposing examples of the many forms of transfer and appropriation that occurred in colonial society, and forms of mystification that often surrounded these objects: theft and trade, versus a gift of appreciation. At the same time, they are acquisition histories that need not detract from the intrinsic significance of the objects in question. They remain first-rate objects that can establish new relationships with the society in which they function. And as with these two examples, thousands of stories can be told that contain historical relationships, with just as many ties to the colonial history.

The colonial history of acquisition and the ups and downs of the objects after their acquisition is not the only story to be told. Museums also attach great importance to the intrinsic significance of the objects and the story that they tell about the art and culture of the community from which they came. But for this story too, we need to know the acquisition history. What was collected and what was not? What developments remain out of sight when, in the pursuit of a cultural history, we limit our focus to the collections that were collected over the course of time? Ethnologists came up with their own subjects of study. Their categories, the formation of series, the subdivision into types and the naming of styles, style differences and quality all led to a certain stereotyping of cultures and cultural difference.[101]
In the collections of museums, cultures, religions, ethnic communities or peoples were made discernable in a comparative framework based on several essential characteristics. In exhibitions they were often tied to objects. Consider the wax human figures around the empty throne of Queen Wilhelmina with which the introduction of this publication ended. (Fig. 21) The clothing, objects and even the postures of the figures express something that could be recognised and identified by the public in the Netherlands. They learned how to recognise a *Niasser* by his warlike pose, his large shield and *mandau* (sword), as well as his ornamented helmet as a headdress. The fact that this represented the typical appearance of a man from the island of Nias off the coast of Sumatra was confirmed by the series of similar headdresses, lances, swords and shields from Nias in the depot. And anyone that later travelled to Nias recognised the sword and shield and perhaps even brought examples back as souvenirs. Travellers, scientists, museums, the art trade, collectors, soldiers: all of them collectively gave shape to and confirmed a canon of ethnography. (Fig. 145, 146)
Ethnographic museums such as the Tropenmuseum have to jump over their own shadow, as it were, to extricate the objects from the ethnographic canon.

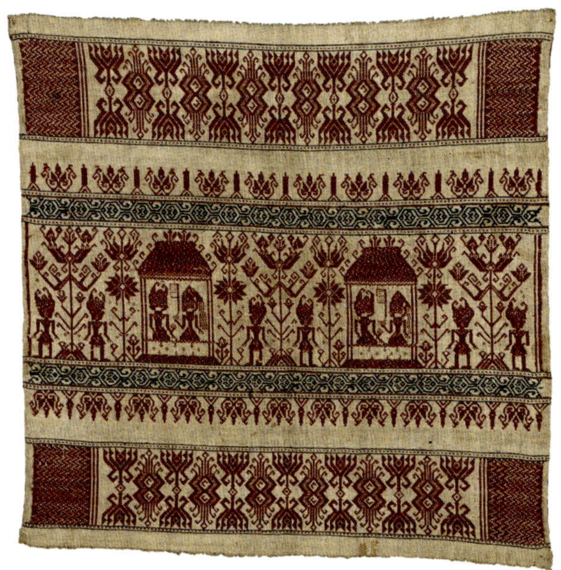

143
Ceremonial cloth *tampan,* with picture of two houses and human figures in wayang style
Cotton, dye
76 x 76 cm
South Lampung, Sumatra
Early 20th century
1772-1277. Gift: Dr. W.G. Tillmann 1994. Former collection: G. Tillmann/ C.M.A. Groenevelt/ Van Voorst van Zijp

To this end, it is important to make the knowledge that exists about the collection historically specific: to approach each piece as unique and to think anew about its origin, material, function, use and significance. To achieve this, the Tropenmuseum has followed three strategies that we shall briefly explain. In the first strategy, the ways in which collections are organised are abandoned, by expressly looking for other connections between objects. For example: the former Koloniaal Museum collected Indonesian textiles, including ship cloths from Sumatra, and published articles on the symbolism in the fabrics. The ship cloths from the collection of Tillmann were a part of the series of ship cloths on which this research was based. But when we study the ship cloths of Tillmann within the context of his entire collection of singular, first-rate pieces spread over

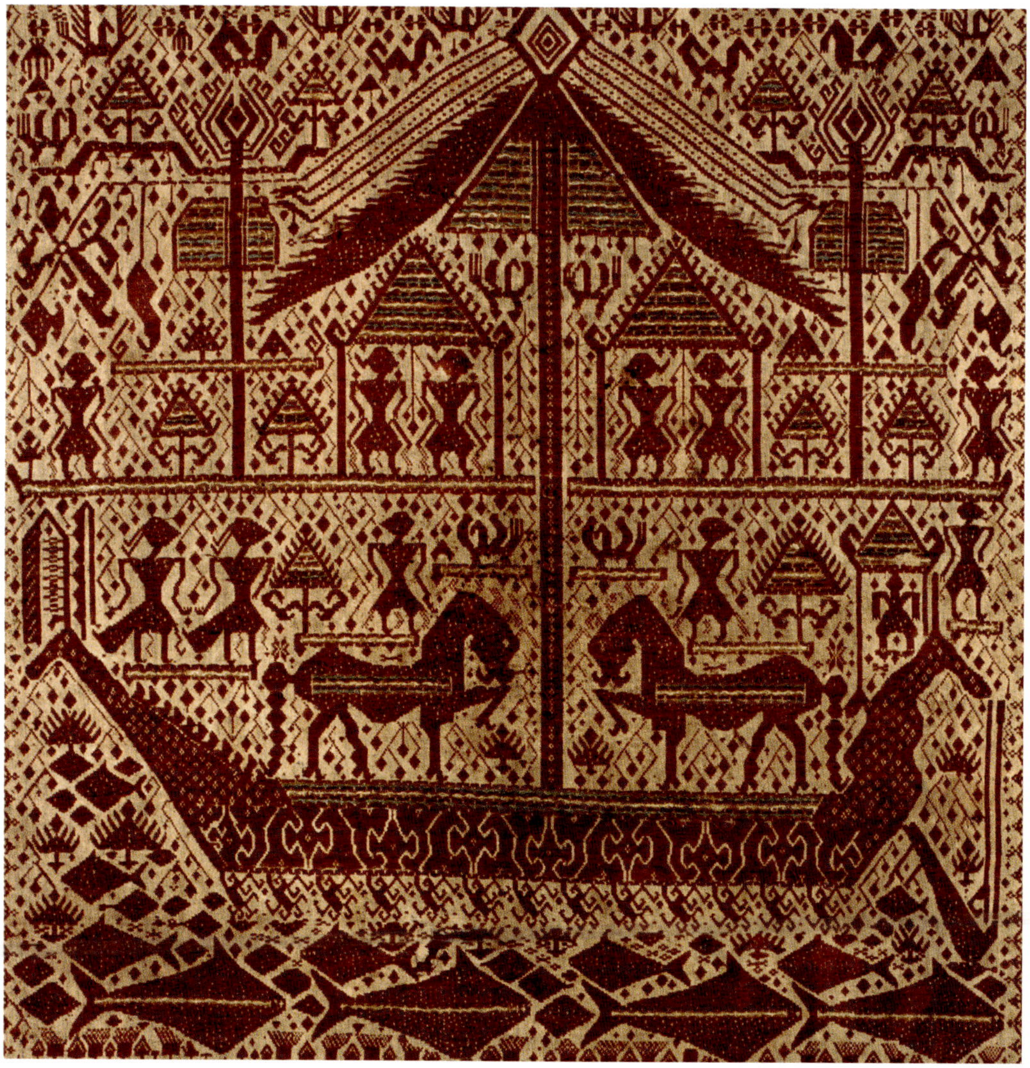

144
Ceremonial cloth *tampan* pengantar (detail)
So-called boat canvas symbolizes the transition from one life phase to the other: from birth, marriage to death.
Cotton, dye
92 x 68 cm
Kampong Karang (South Bengkulu), Southwest Sumatra
1772-1278. Gift: W.G. Tillman, 1994. Former collection: G. Tillmann/ C.M.A. Groenevelt/Van Voorst van Zijp

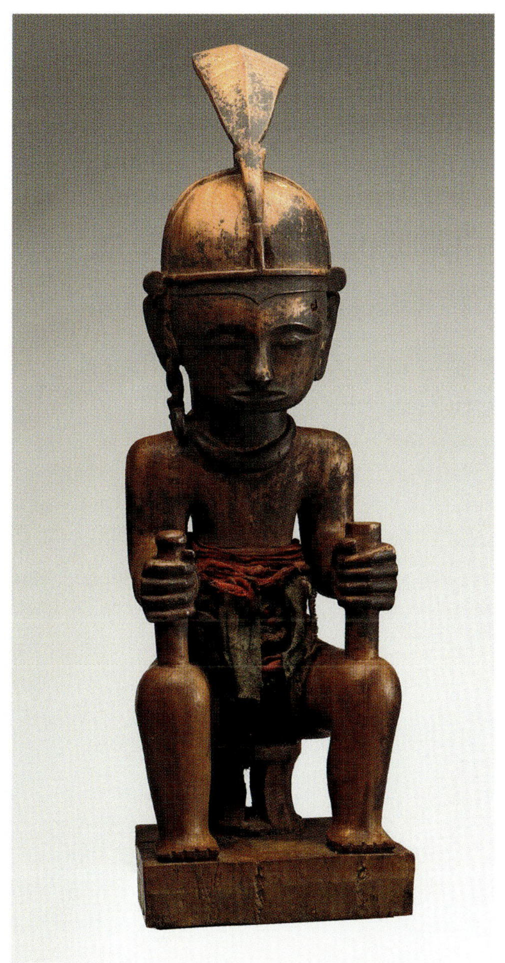

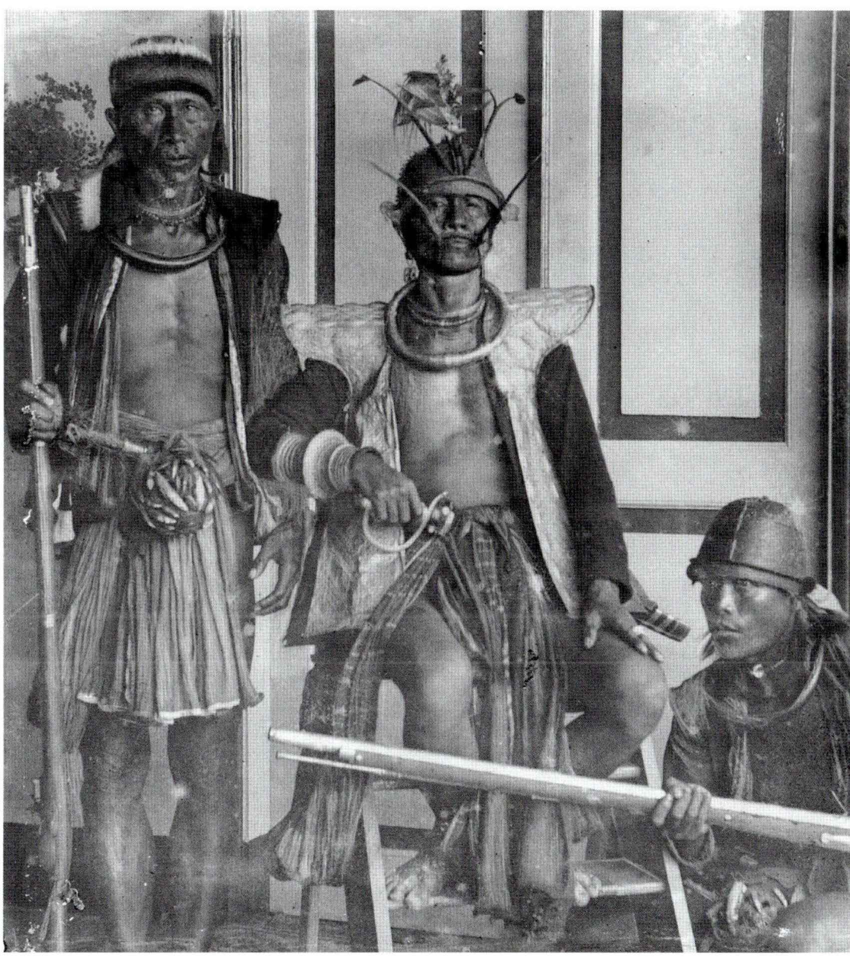

145
Man's ancestor figure
Wood
52 cm
South Nias. 19th century
1772-111. Gift: W.G. Tillman, 1994 Former collection: G. Tillmann/C.M.A. Groenevelt/Van Voorst van Zijp

146
A village chief from Nias after his submission in Balohalo
Glass negative
9 x 12 cm
1910-1920
10001506. Gift: J.K. Koops Dekker, 1935

a wide range of genres, then we begin to see how such cloths also have a more canonical significance as classic art within the history of Indonesian art that encompasses the archipelago. (Fig. 143, 144) The second strategy for breaking out of the existing genre classification in search of new significance for objects takes the usual collection arrangement as its point of departure, yet studies one and the same genre of objects within different museum traditions. So, for instance, the ancestral figures of Nias were a cherished collectors item. They can be found in many places in the world in different types of museums; ethnographic, art history, natural history. Each type of museum has another type of story attached to the same type of figure. The Tropenmuseum possesses no fewer than 94 ancestral figures, twelve of which are on exhibit. (Fig. 145) Because of its nature, each ancestral figure is unique, it refers in each case to specific ancestors, yet we no longer know to whom an individual figure refers or to which family it belongs. They have become a genre in the museum, a 'type' whose unique story is almost never recorded, not to mention the relationship between the people that acquired the figure and the families in question. In ethnographic museums such as the Tropenmuseum, the figures provide general information through which a connection is made between ancestor cultus and headhunting on Nias.[102] But because the figures' specific artistic style makes them stand out, they have also made their way into the art trade as first-rate ethnographic pieces.
It was for their esthetic value that Georg Tillmann obtained five of these figures which, like his ship cloths, subsequently ended up in the ethnographic context of the Tropenmuseum. Other figures actually made it into art museums, as in the case of the ancestral figure from Nias that has been exhibited in the Louvre in Paris since 2000.[103] It came from

the French surrealist André Breton, for whom these and other ethnographic objects were an important source of information. The story told by the Louvre through the figure focuses primarily on its aesthetics and on its reception in European art history.[104] Research into the difference between the meaning of an object in an ethnographic museum or in an art museum could also help to pry open the ethnographic canon.

The third strategy to achieve this goal is based on the designation of entirely new collection categories. Thus the Tropenmuseum, working on its own history and the role of the museum in the formation of the ethnographic canons, constructed the category of 'colonial collections'.[105] The designation of this category had a twofold effect. On the one hand, new connections were made between separate genres. As a part of the category of colonial collections, photographs, sound recordings and objects suddenly were tied together much more closely than they had been. Moreover, a wide range of 'orphaned' objects were given greater significance in the collection because they could be tied to cultural developments in the Netherlands, instead of development in the Netherlands East Indies. An example of this is the design pewter tea pot with milk jug and sugar pot (Fig. 147) of Royal Begeer Factory from Batavia. Among these objects were many that up to then had always been considered as props. Now they were given collection status as a part of the colonial collections. This is true, for instance, for a model of a tobacco shed, an imitation tobacco plant, packaging material for colonial merchandise, for the wax puppets that once stood in the museum, and for many documents of the museum itself. The category of colonial collections appeared to form the cement that linked large parts of the collection together. Below we provide a general outline of the construction of this category.

147
Tea Service
Pewter, wood
10 x 17.8 x 12.2 cm
Jakarta. 1948
3401-489a/f. Gift: KIT
Tropische Producten, 1964

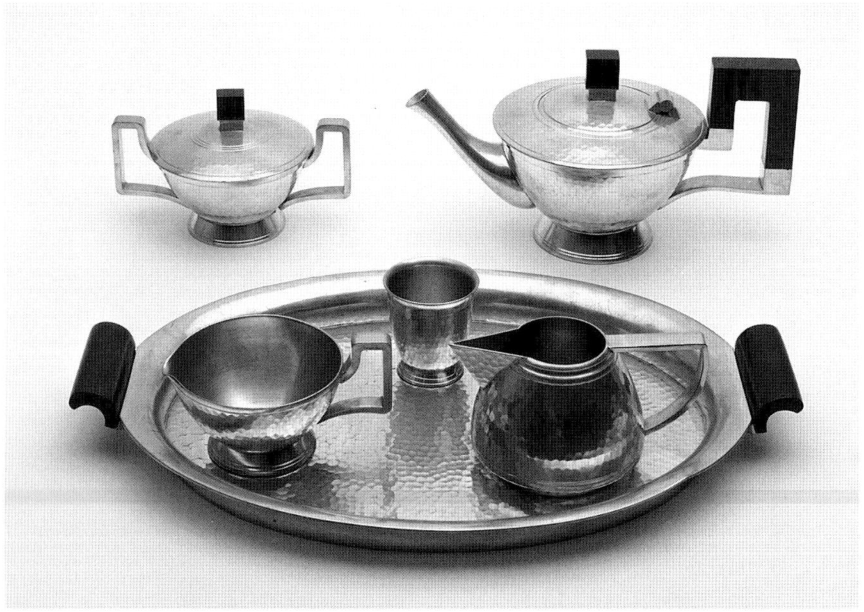

Colonial collections

The Tropenmuseum now designates three main forms of colonial collections: (1) the material culture of those who, overseas in the colonial society, held the status of Europeans and those seen as equal to Europeans; (2) the material reflection of the colonial relations at home in Dutch (European) society; (3) the visual representation of the colonies and of colonialism.

Colonial culture overseas

The material culture of those in colonial society who had the status of a 'European and those deemed equal to Europeans' primarily pertains to white Europeans and Indo-Dutch people – the (East Indies) mixed population that was strongly oriented to the Dutch language and culture and to Christianity. Elsbeth Locher-Scholten described this European community in the colony, which had a European orientation, as an ethnic group. A description is also given of how much the acute awareness of racial boundaries within colonial society ruled the personal lives of the Europeans.[106] Many people of one of the other population categories at the time also obtained the legal status of 'equal to Europeans'. This was true, for example, of the traditional rulers of the Javanese royal households or Chinese people for whom the title Foreign Oriental was no longer seen as appropriate since they were successful businessmen. As early as 1900, even the supporters of this legal division of the population primarily along the lines of race and ethnicity had to admit that it was highly arbitrary and, with respect to Foreign Orientals and *Inlanders* (natives), was often based on the external status someone carried and on religion. A change in status was, for example, easier to achieve for a Christian than it was for a Moslem.

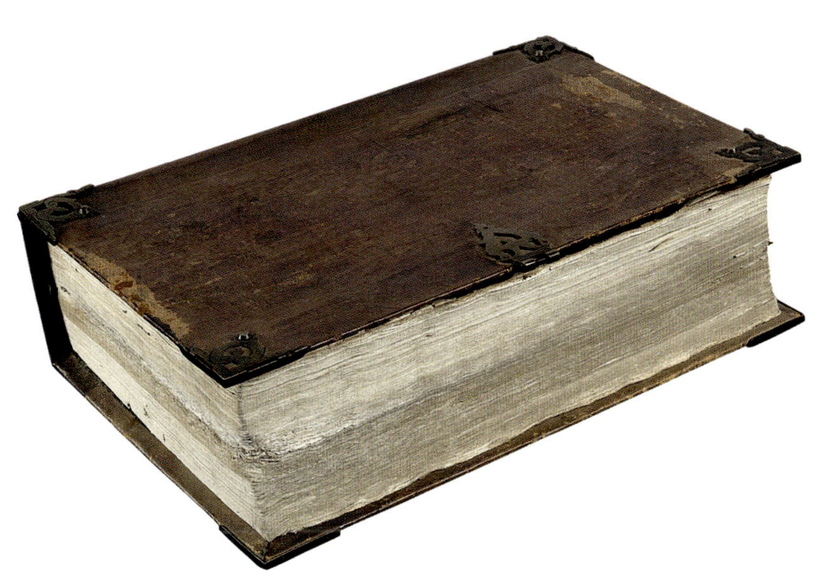

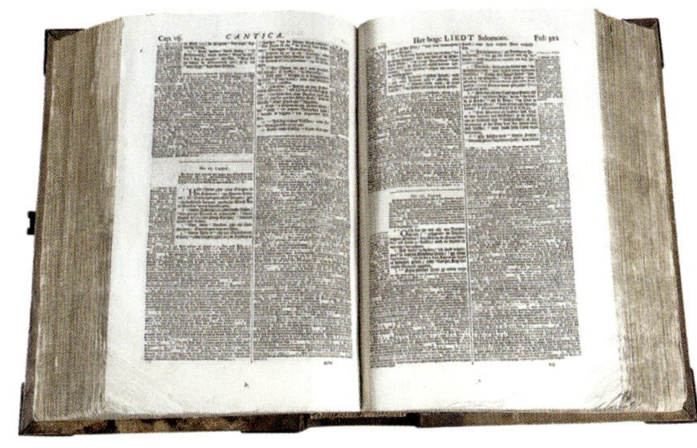

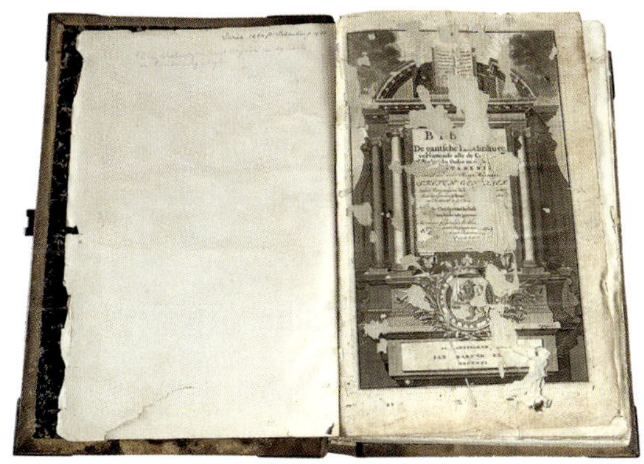

148
Dutch Authorised Version of the Bible
Paper, leather
43 x 27.5 cm
Buitenzorg, Java. 1791
1260-1. Gift: C.G. de Wilde Schaap, 1938

Many objects were collected from this primarily European group in the colony. Very old pieces are a part of this collection, such as 17th-century Verenigde Oostindische Compagnie (VOC) furniture, as well as modern material, such as a complete set of stationery, telegram paper, Morse code paper, envelopes and postage stamps from the 1930s. Important collection categories pertain to clothing, furniture, household objects, personal objects (e.g. embroidery or cut-outs), documents, bank notes and securities, objects from Japanese internment camps, objects related to the army, or related to Christian missions, European education and travel. From a museum perspective, the objects that were produced in the colony itself were the most interesting. But Dutch objects with a colonial history, such as the Dutch Authorised Version of the Bible that lay on the pulpit in the church in Bogor (former Buitenzorg), (Fig. 148) between 1815 and 1949, or the last Dutch flag that was lowered in 1949 at the port authorities office of Tanjung Priok, belong in the collection because of their history.

A strict delineation cannot be made for this category; the point at which the crossover to Indonesian objects occurs is often fuzzy. The Tropenmuseum, for instance, owns a figure of the archangel Gabriel in *wayang* (shadow puppet) style from the 1920s (Fig. 149). Many of them were made at the time. The copy at the Tropenmuseum was from the collection of the priest Petrus Vertenten and therefore tells the story of a missionary in New Guinea. It illustrates the fact that Indonesian artisans and artists also worked for European clients. Other examples of such points of crossover can be found in the sound collections of the Tropenmuseum. The recordings of Indonesian, Arabic and European music are full of examples of mutual influence in the use of instruments or musical ideas.

From this category we will discuss colonial clothing, weapons and Yogya silver later on in the second part of this chapter.

Colonial relations at home

Written sources, objects used in scientific research and Dutch design inspired by influences from the colonies are the clearest examples of *Dutch* colonial collections in the Tropenmuseum. The archives and the sources for the collection documentation are also

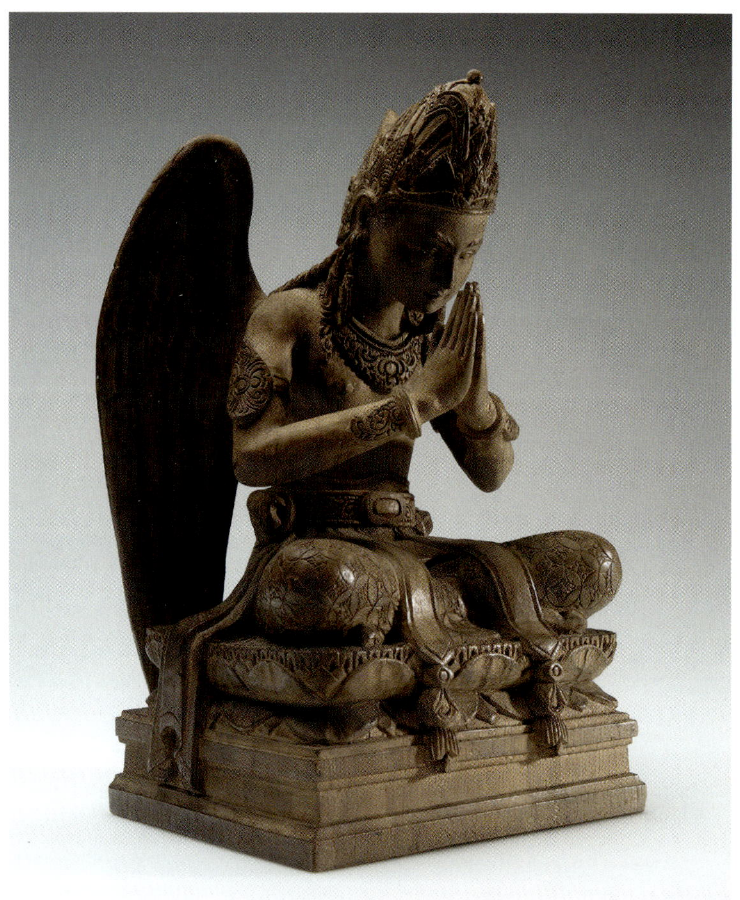

149
Archangel depicted as a Javanese wayang prince
Wood
28 x 17 x 16 cm
Bogor, Java. 1925
5969-66b
Purchase: Missionaries of the Sacred Heart Borgerhout, 2002

a part of this. Many of them are not in the museum depot, but in the library or at the offices of the museum's staff. It is an open archive in development that is used to the present day and continues to take on new significance. Consider scientific publications (and the notes and models for these), or cards and atlases, or the 'settels', i.e. the documentation cards for the objects. Also relevant in this context are all objects mentioned earlier that originate from the history of the museum itself, such as the wax figures, the plaster models that ornament the building, portrait busts of founders and other renowned people, the school collection for educational activities in the Netherlands and the dried examples of tropical products.

And then there are the (art) objects made in the laboratory of the Koloniaal Instituut, where Dutch artists experimented with Indonesian techniques such as batik and with dyes such as indigo. For fabric and furniture designs and for a very large number of book covers, the artists of the Dutch Arts and Crafts movement from around 1900 sought a way to apply Indonesian design and decoration principles. The chairs of the luxury passenger ship *Johan van Oldenbarnevelt*, designed by C.A. Lion Cachet, are an example of this. Many book covers in the collection of the library of the KIT also reflect this trend. From this category, we will discuss the wood collection, the map collection and the library collection in the second part of this chapter.

The image of the colony

Visual images of the colony and of colonialism constitute the largest category of objects from the colonial collection. The Tropenmuseum possesses a unique collection of paintings, drawings, prints, illustrated books, historical photographs and films whose individual parts together produce a multifaceted picture of the processes of representation and self-presentation in a colonial context. The many models and dioramas of houses, bridges, plantations, means of transport and agricultural equipment that were produced in Indonesia and meant for exhibitions in Europe also fall into this category. Here, too, boundaries cannot be strictly drawn; paintings that illustrate how the colonised people viewed the colonisers could also be included in this group. Examples of this are the painting depicting the murder of captain Tak (Fig. 150), the Wayang Revolusi shadow puppets that act out the stories about colonial history, or the large painted narrative canvas of Sitisiwan (1865-1948) from Gegesik, North Java showing countless scenes from the colonial era. (Fig. 225) From this category we will discuss family photo albums, films, paintings and models in part two of this chapter.

The collectors

In itself, the category of colonial collections does not produce a cohesive picture of colonial society, any more than the 'Javanese' collection produces a cohesive picture of Javanese society. Only in combination with people can a fabric be created that makes the historical contours of this society visible. In the first essays of this book, the different forms of contact were discussed: military, educational, economic, social, cultural and scientific. Here, we discuss

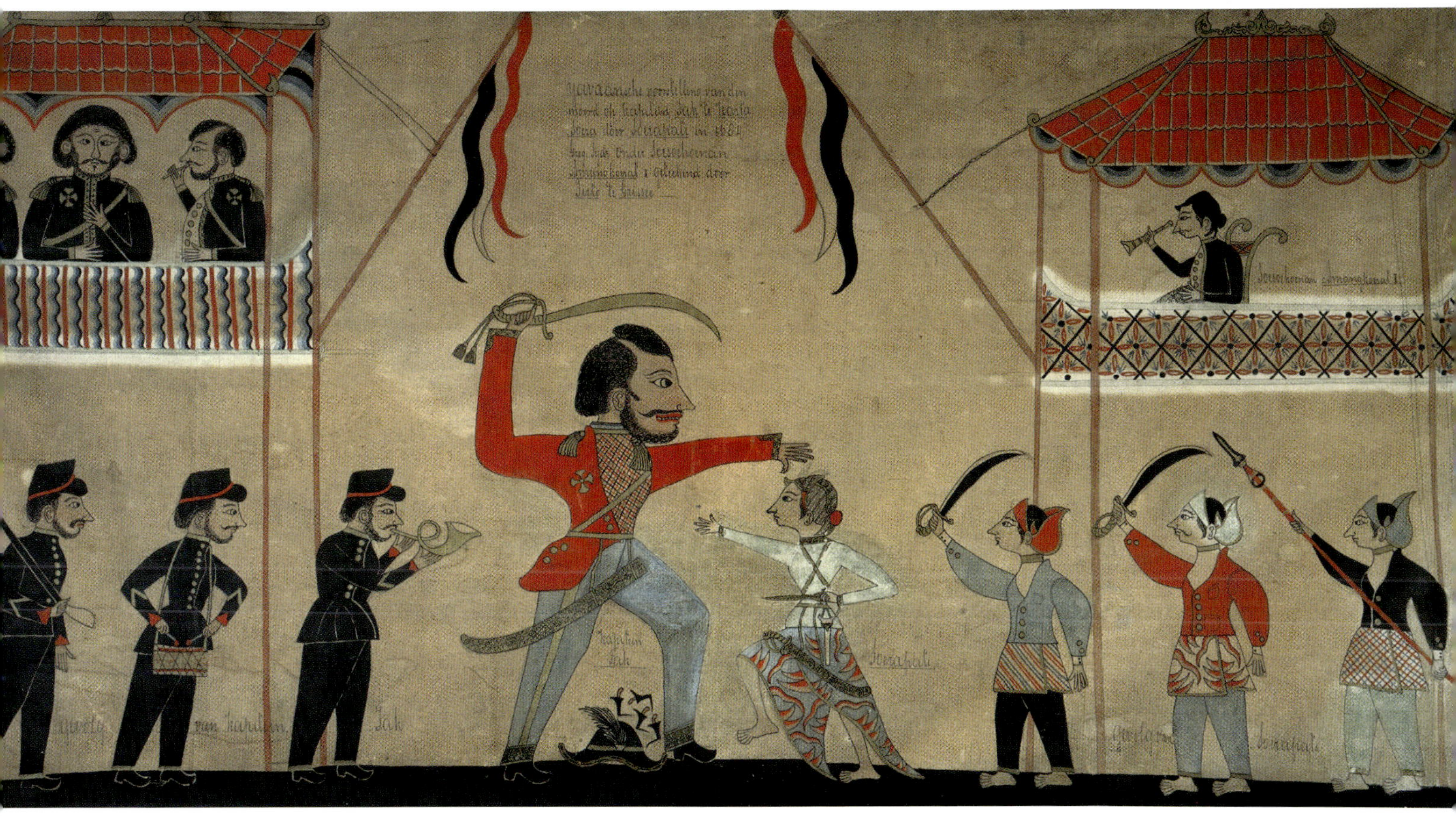

150
Painting depicting the murder of Captain Tack in Kartasura in 1686
Tirto
Paint, linen
67 x 123 cm
Gresik, East Jawa. 1890-1900
H-796. Koloniaal Museum Haarlem, 1910.

a number of collectors that fulfilled different functions in colonial society as a colonial civil servant, businessman, missionary, artist, housewife, photographer, scientist, wife of a soldier, museum director, music collector. The people that here represent such a role can, in the best ethnographic traditions, also represent other, similar collectors. Unlike the past stereotypes of individuals in the ethnographic population around which the collections were organised, such as the wax Nias warrior with his helmet, shield and sword, the people here were chosen instead as historical archetypes. They played a specific role in certain circumstances. Their role is not timeless, nor does it transverse all eras. And each individual person involved made considerations that did not necessarily, or often did not, apply to the entire group.
The persons highlighted in this article all have in common that they all, in different areas, have collected ethnographic objects from Indonesia. They have transferred these objects, with their story attached, to the Koloniaal Museum. At the same time, each of them also 'collected' colonial collections from one of the three aforementioned subcategories. After all, people furnished their houses overseas, they dressed for the tropical climate, according to local style and they studied the society in which they lived and maintained contact with the Indonesian population.
People took photographs and wrote letters, conversed with one another and maintained contact with their family and friends in Europe and usually they returned to the Netherlands at a given moment. These roles, of course, are not by any means sufficient to sketch a complete picture of the colonial society. But they do give an impression of the many historical ties that are woven into the fabric of ethnographic collections via the collectors. The exposition of this fabric, in our view, is an important condition for allowing both the Indonesian and colonial collections to fully play their historical roles within both Indonesian and Dutch history.

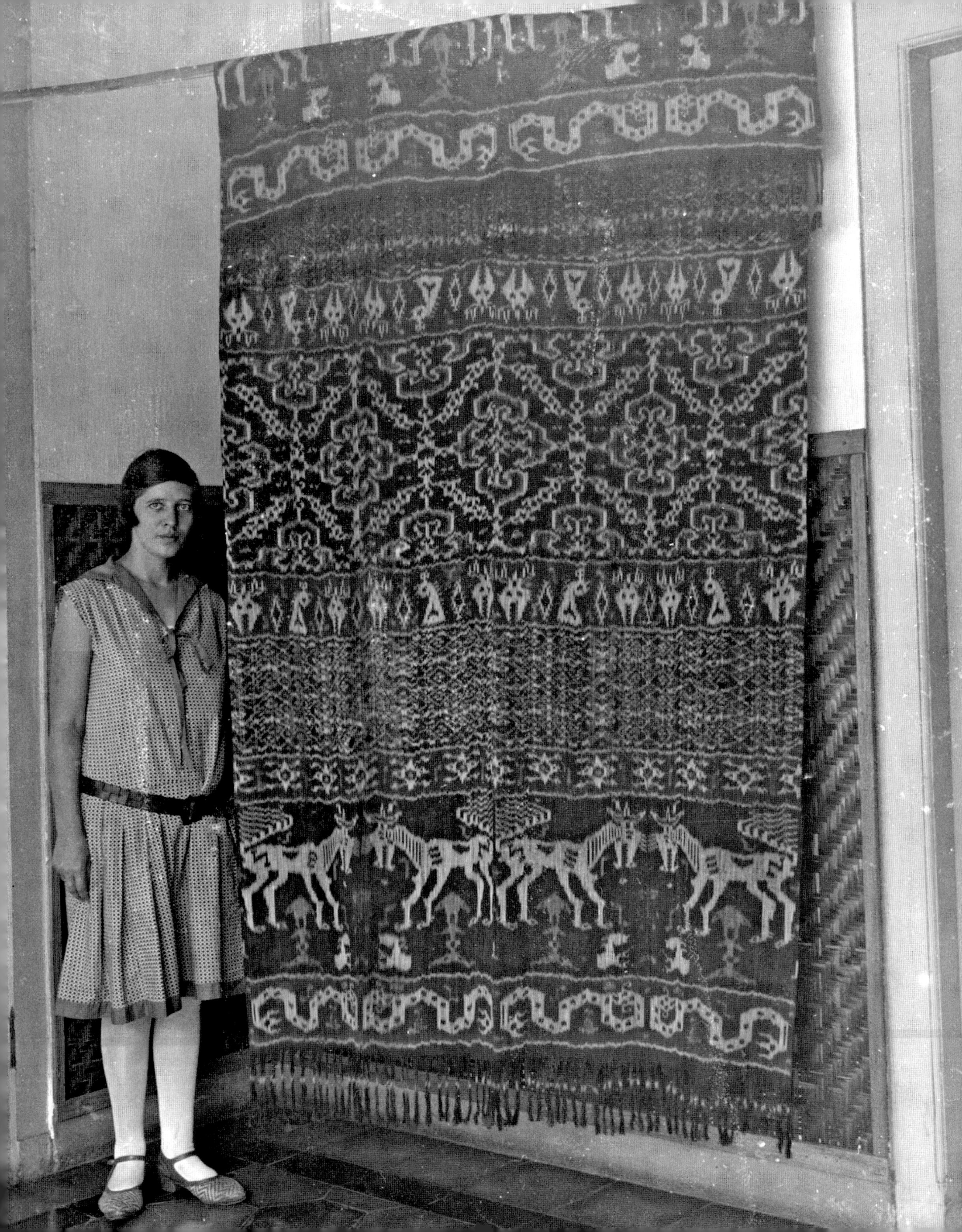

TEN COLLECTORS

The colonial civil servant: Johan Ernst Jasper (Surabaya 1874 – Tjimahi 1945)

Johan Ernst Jasper was born in Surabaya into a family of mixed Indo-Dutch descent. He attended school in Surabaya and Batavia and became a civil servant in the colonial administration in 1895. His career took him from the rank of *controleur* (official in the government of het Netherlands East Indies) in 1902 to Commissioner of Yogyakarta in 1928. Towards the end of the Second World War in 1945, he died in a Japanese internment camp.

Jasper was a man with many talents and broad cultural interests. He wrote novels, published cultural articles in *Tijdschrift voor het Binnenlandsch bestuur*, and was chief editor of the newspaper *Java-Bode.*

He worked during a period in which the Ethical Policy dominated Dutch colonialism. He was eager to develop an educational system and to stimulate economic activities in order to raise the standard of living of Indonesians. In this context, he was especially interested in indigenous arts and crafts, due to their economic importance.

In 1906 the colonial government gave him an assignment to investigate the technical and artistic aspects of the applied arts. Together with the Javanese artist Mas Pirngadie (1875-1936), Jasper studied the crafts, collected objects, took photographs and made sketches. It resulted in five volumes on indigenous crafts, *De Inlandsche Kunstnijverheid in Nederlandsch Indie*: braid work, weaving, batik, brass and silver work. This research introduced an economic

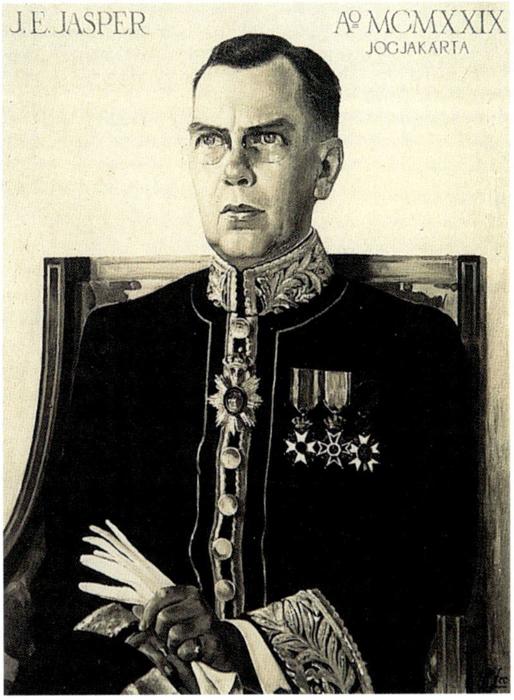

151
Mrs. Bergman beside a cloth from Sumba, Java
Photographer: R.A.M. Bergman (1899-1967)
Glass negative
9 x 12 cm
5 December 1929
10027138

152
J.E. Jasper by Hendrik Paulides, 1929
In: Peter E.M. Hamman, *Hendrik Paulides, schilder en verteller, Utrecht 1892-1967*, Amsterdam, Haarlem, 1997

J.E. JASPER A° MCMXXIX JOGJAKARTA

153
Man's ceremonial shoulder cloth
Cotton
228 x 116 cm
Sumba
48-45. Purchase: J.E. Jasper, 1916. From Brussels Exhibition 1910

> 154
Anak Agung Madé Karang Asem
Artist unknown
He was the illegitimate son of the last Prince of Lombok
Oil painting
53 x 37.5 cm
Lombok
c. 1890
82-1. Gift: T.F.A. Delprat, 1919

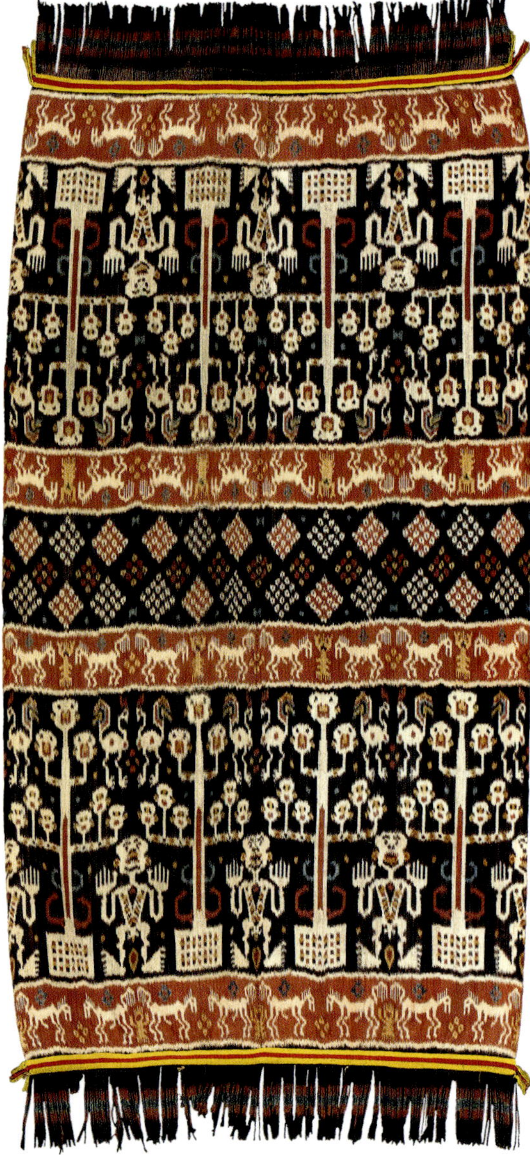

approach to crafts. The products should serve not only the local markets, but foreign trade as well. Jasper knew that knowledge of techniques was crucial to stimulating new developments and preventing the crafts from disappearing. He also acknowledged that to improve the economic situation, craftsmen had to look for innovations, both in the modes of production and the materials used. He encouraged the crafts with annual fairs and issued awards for the best objects.

Many of Jasper's collections, after being exhibited at annual fairs or in the Dutch pavilions at international and world exhibitions, were transferred to Dutch museums. For the Brussels World Fair of 1910, Jasper acquired a collection from the fair of 1909 in Surabaya. This collection of textiles went to the Koloniaal Museum in Haarlem in 1912. In 1916 Jasper's acquisitions became part of the collection of the Koloniaal Instituut. The Tropenmuseum now owns a collection of 553 textiles collected by Johan Ernst Jasper. (Fig. 151-153) IVH

The entrepreneur: Théodore F.A. Delprat (Breda 1851 – Amsterdam 1932)

Théodore Delprat, born in Breda into a prominent family, was a civil engineer. He had his first 'colonial' experience during a six-year stay in Scotland (1872-78). While he was working there on the construction of a large railway bridge, he met a certain Mr Knott: a large, sturdy man, covered with tattoos, who had followed Livingstone through darkest Africa. According to Delprat, Knott was: 'so covered in tattoos that when he undressed, he was still dressed'. Impulsively, Delprat decided in the spring of 1878 to walk into the Ministerie van Koloniën (Ministry of Colonies) in The Hague to ask whether perhaps railways were being built in the Netherlands East Indies. The same year, Delprat headed for the East as a deputy engineer 1st class in order to build railways on Java. Life in the East Indies for him was not easy in the beginning. For the first few months he had to put up with vindictive bosses, vermin, misunderstandings with his staff and looted suitcases. His career did progress quickly, however. In 1884 he met J.W. IJzerman (1851-1932), who was also a railway engineer. IJzerman had become fascinated by the Hindu-Javanese antiquities. He seems to have inspired Delprat to become enthusiastic about the cultures in the Netherlands East Indies.
Delprat began to build a large, very diverse ethnographic collection. Gifts from local authorities he befriended, such as the head of Sungai Puar, the region inhabited by the Minangkabau (Sumatra), contributed to the collection. Delprat also liked to take photographs: not only of the dozens of roads, bridges, harbours and railway lines that he built on Java and Sumatra, but also of people and animals. Some of the glass negatives that have been preserved are fairly large: 24x30 cm. Gradually, he donated

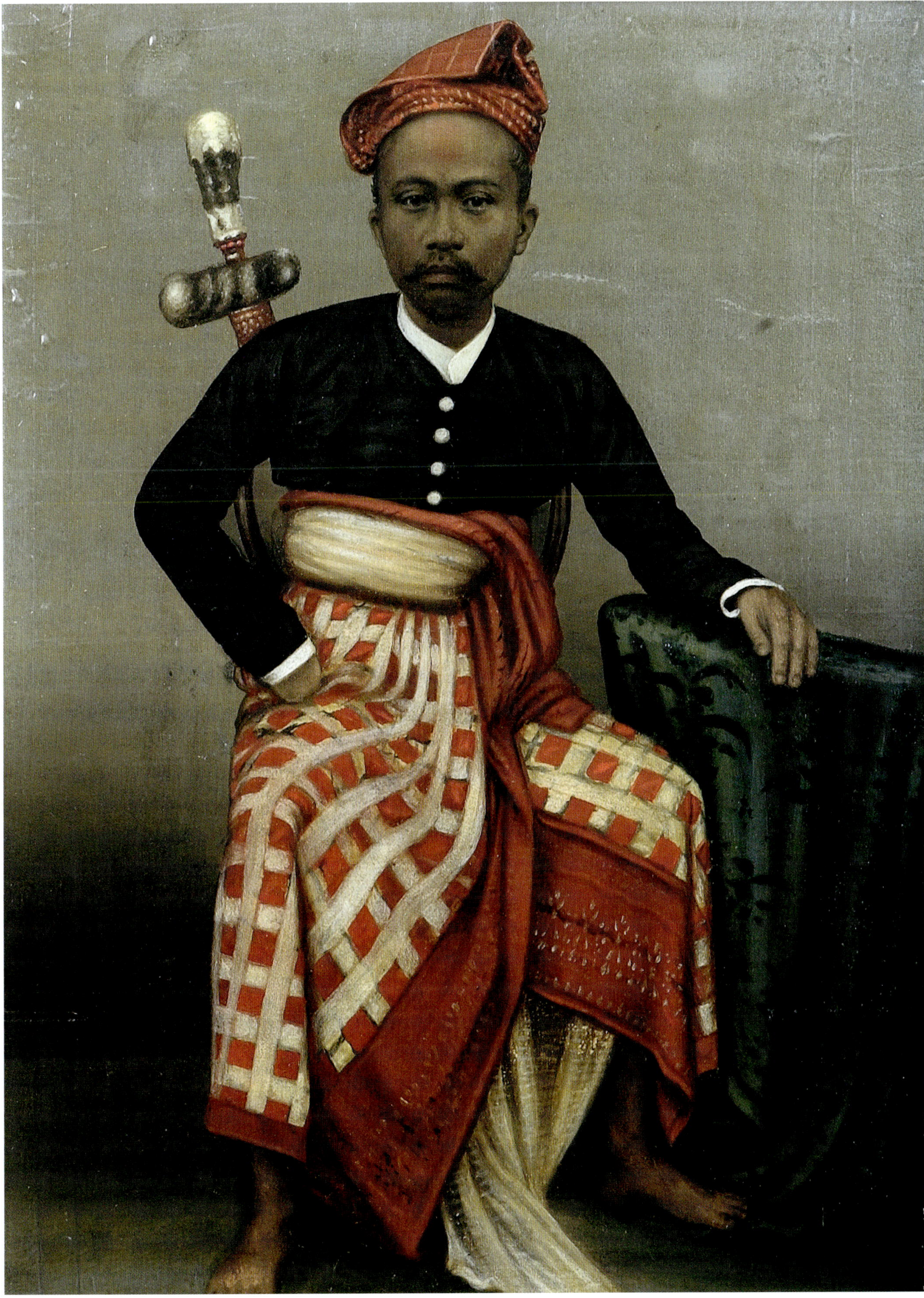

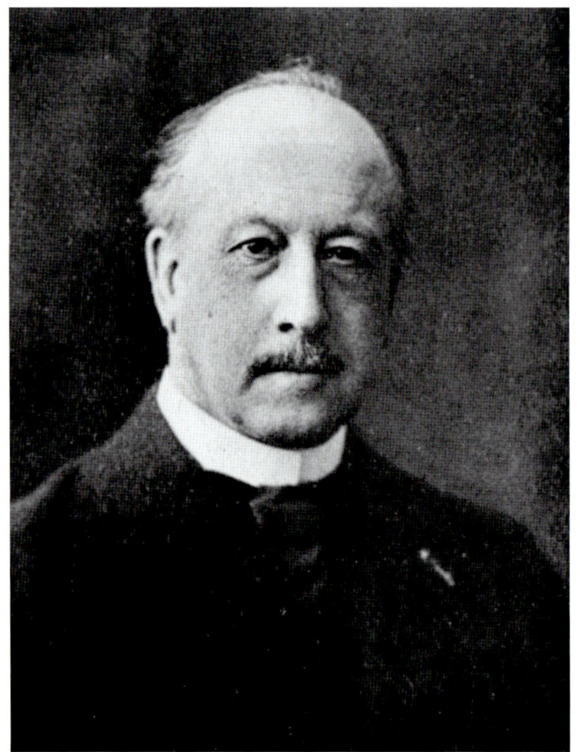

155
Ir. T.F.A. Delprat
Gelatin silver print
8.7 x 6.2 cm
1910-1930
60052314

156
Priest P. Vertenten with the Marind man Kariem
Photo
108 x 77.5 x 3.5 cm
1910-1925
5969-65. Purchase: Missionaries of the Sacred Heart Borgerhout, 2002

> 157
Marind youth from the age group of the Ewati
P. Vertenten (1884-1946)
Oil painting
53 x 45 cm
1914
5969-2. Purchase: Missionaries of the Sacred Heart Borgerhout, 2002

objects to the ethnographic museum in the Artis Zoo. The entire collection of Artis was transferred to the Koloniaal Museum in 1911.
After he returned to the Netherlands in 1902 he did return occassionally to the Netherlands East Indies for his work as the Director of the Petroleum company Moeara-Enim. In addition to his work as an alderman in Amsterdam, he was also Chairman of the Koninklijk Nederlands Aardrijkskundig Genootschap (KNAG) and he gave lectures using so-called 'lantern slides' about the Netherlands East Indies. From 1912 to 1931, he was a member of the Koloniaal Instituut's Board of Directors, initially as a representative of the Amsterdam city council and finally even as the secretary of the Institute, the actual director. During these years, bit by bit he donated the remainder of his private collection of objects and photo archive to the Koloniaal Instituut and he continued to have a personal involvement with the content of exhibitions. Under his directorship, the Koloniaal Instituut was officially opened in 1926 by Queen Wilhelmina. (Fig. 154-155) CD

The missionary: Petrus Vertenten (Hamme 1884 – Borgerhout 1946)

In 1902, on the south coast of New Guinea, the Dutch administrative post of Merauke was established. Shortly thereafter, in 1905, the Missionaries of the Sacred Heart established themselves in and around the new post. Of all the missionaries that lived there, the Flemish priest Petrus Vertenten continues to be the most well-known. Due to his great empathy with the local Marind culture, which was considered to be very wild at the time, and his great social commitment, he became the leading pioneer in the outposts of New Guinea. When, not long after his arrival in 1910, 'his people' were in danger of being exterminated by imported, severe venereal diseases, Vertenten successfully mobilised Batavia for a large-scale, effective medical operation on site. As a result, he went down in history as the 'saviour of the Kaja-Kajas', an older name for the Marind people. Vertenten was a multi-faceted man. He studied the local language and culture intensively and published many books and articles about it. Moreover, he was a talented amateur painter and draughtsman. He primarily produced portraits in

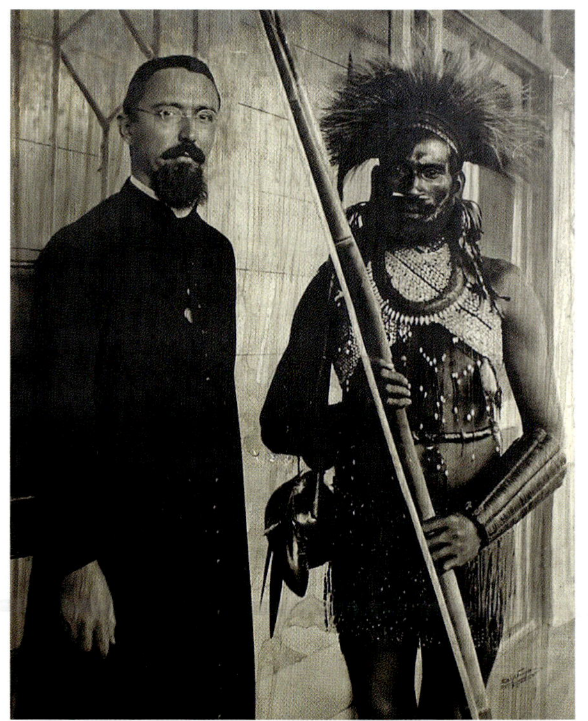

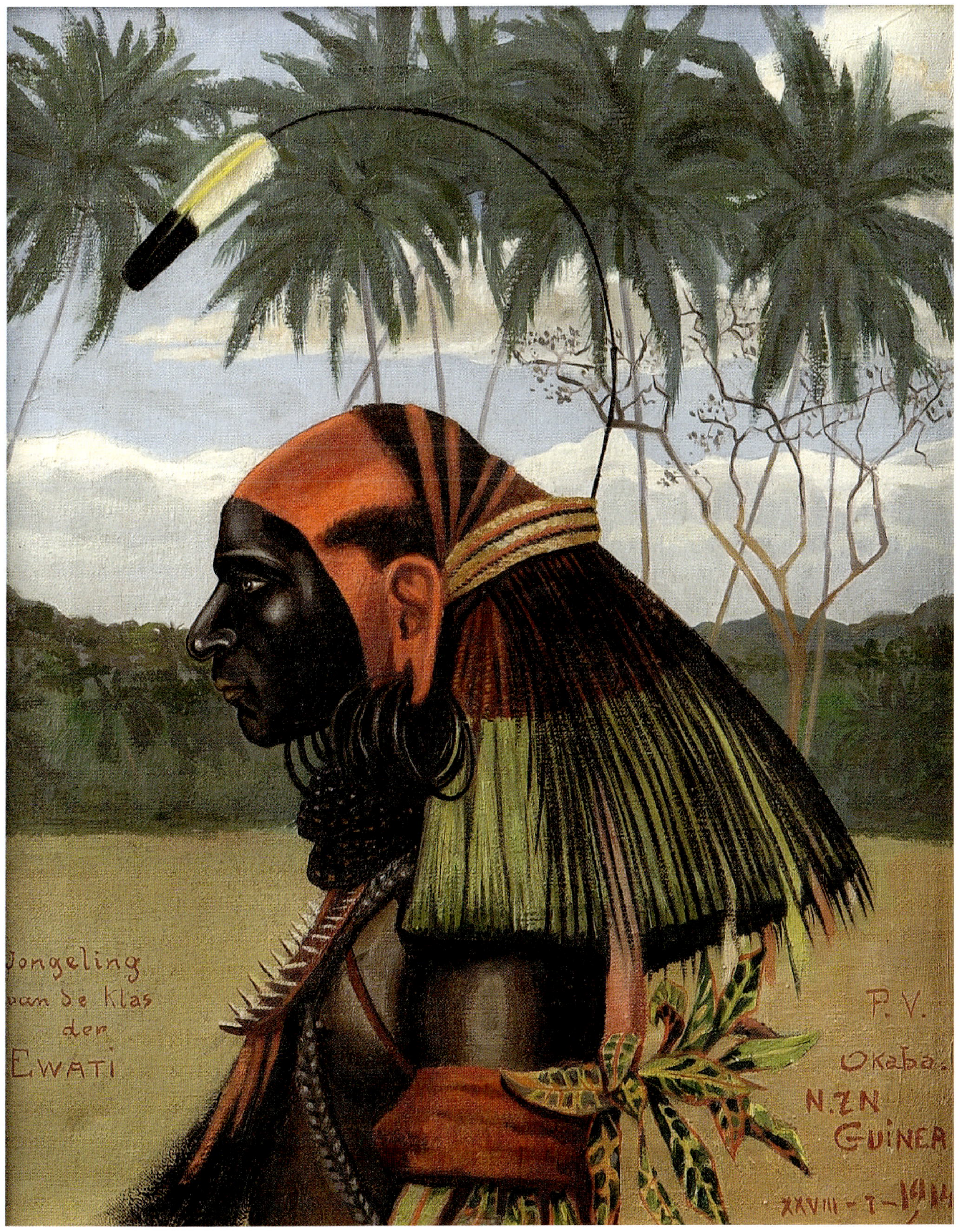
Jongeling
van de Klas
der
EWATI
P. V.
Okaba.
N.ZN
GUINEA

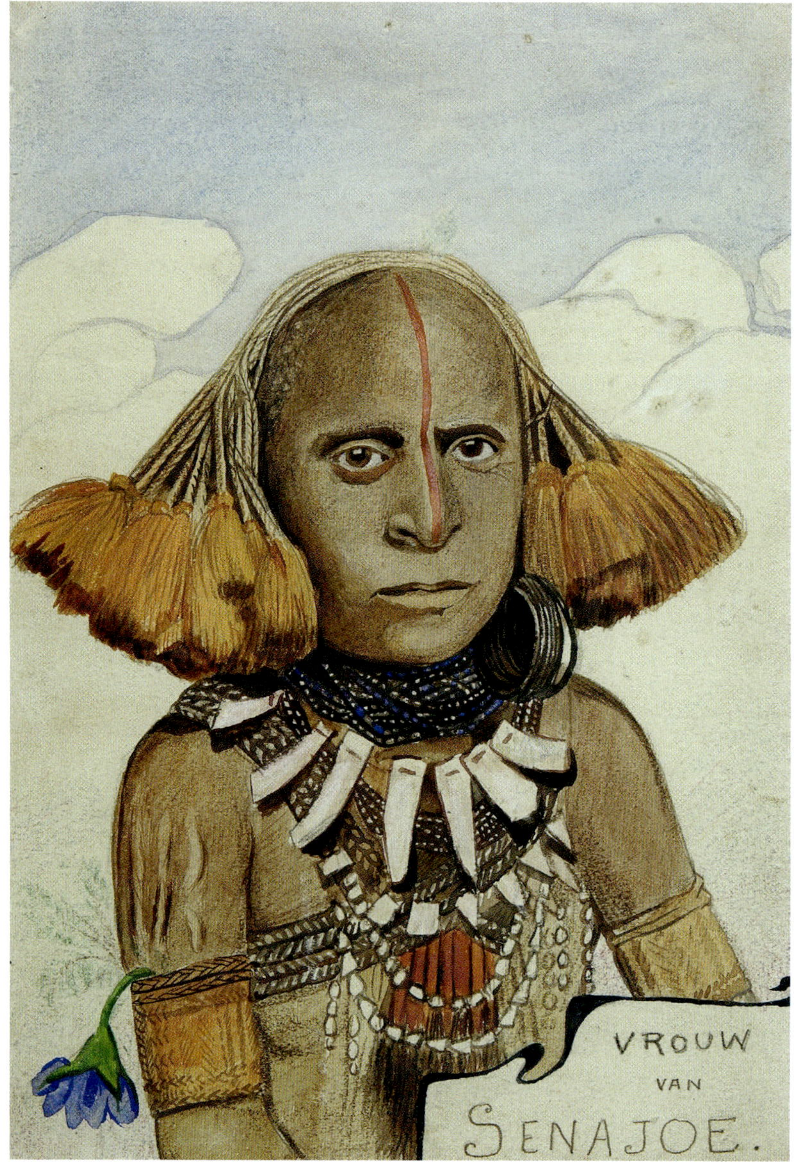

158
A young Marind woman from Senajoe
P. Vertenten (1884-1946)
Drawing on paper
20 x 14 cm
1910-1925
5969-42. Purchase: Missionaries of the Sacred Heart Borgerhout, 2002

oil and watercolour, working from both live models and photographs. According to a Marind warrior who was posing for him and on the occasion watched his own portrait slowly take shape on paper, the priest had 'a wonder in his fist'. Vertenten left a considerable number of paintings, finished pencil drawings and books full of sketches. He was the first person in this period to record, on black-and-white photographs, the body paintings and ceremonial dress of the old Marind culture in their full and marvellous wealth of colours.
In 2002, the Tropenmuseum came into contact with the missionary house of the fathers of the Sacred Heart in Borgerhout, where the legacy of Vertenten had been preserved and archived. Thanks to the mediation of the Tilburg priest Arie Vriens, the Tropenmuseum now possesses a unique collection of paintings and drawings. These are irreplaceable documents of a Papuan culture that has since changed beyond recognition. For this reason, at the exhibition 'The Netherlands East Indies, a colonial history', ample attention has been given to the person and artistic creations of this legendary pioneer. (Fig. 156-158) DVD

The artist: Hendrik Paulides (Utrecht 1892 – Amsterdam 1967)

After being educated at the Rijksacademie voor Beeldende Kunsten in Amsterdam – where he was taught by Prof. Derkinderen among others – and obtaining his secondary school teaching certificate in freehand drawing and linear drawing, Hendrik Paulides left for Java in the spring of 1922 for a long stay. From a young age, he had nurtured a love for the Netherlands East Indies. He was very interested in the mythology, the daily life and the traditional arts and applied arts of Java. During his first trip, he produced a large number of sketches and aquarelles. One of his first East Indies paintings was the painting *Java*, which he submitted for the exhibition organised for the coronation jubilee of Queen Wilhelmina in the Koloniaal Instituut in 1923. Van Eerde, the then director of the department of Cultural Anthropology at the Koloniaal Museum, praised Paulides' style as a landscape painter and in him recognized a highly developed intuition for capturing the inner spirit of the Indonesian people. His style was far superior to that of so many other 'oriental painters', said Van Eerde. With a folder full of letters of recommendations under his arm, Paulides left for the Netherlands East Indies in March 1929 for the second time and also visited Bali. On commission, he produced a portrait of the departing Governor General, De Graeff, and the Commissioner of Yogyakarta, J.E. Jasper, who was also very knowledgeable about indigenous trade and industry. (Fig. 152)
The bond between Paulides and the Koloniaal Instituut was strong. The museum purchased work from him and gave him commissions to paint murals at different locations in the building. Paulides also

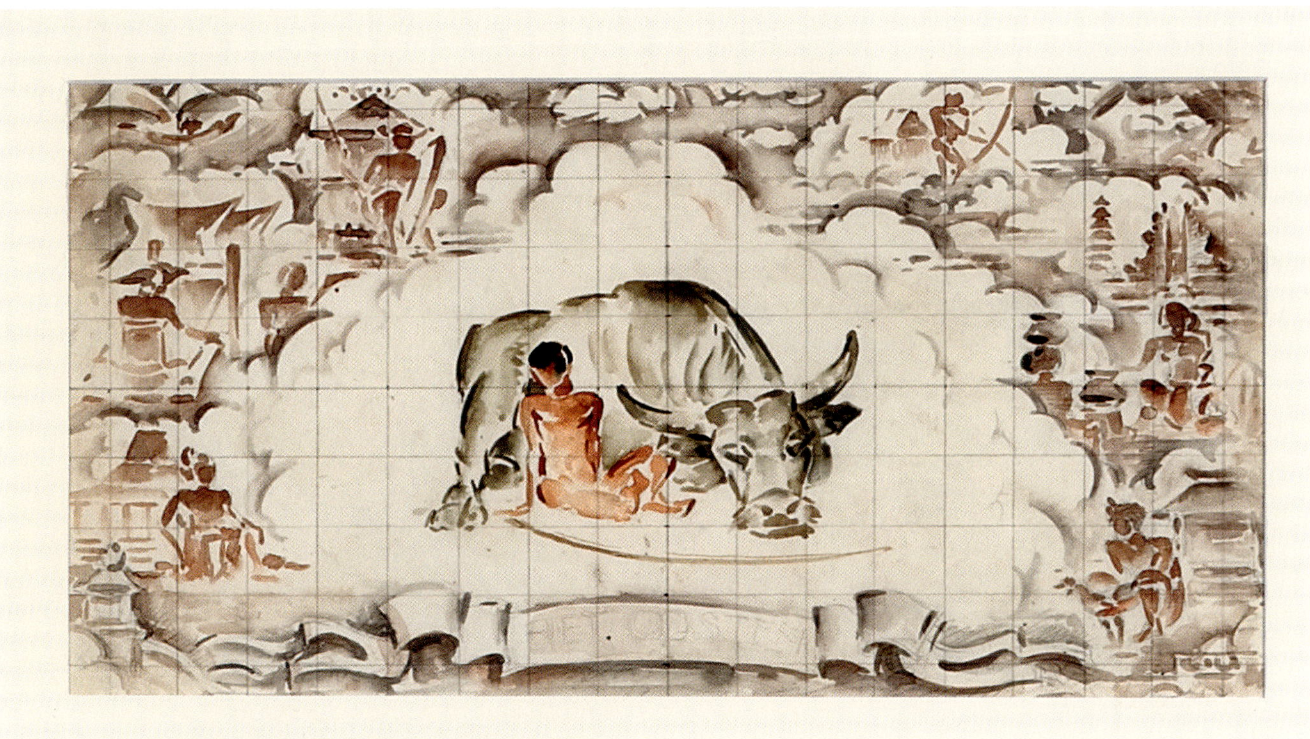

159
Design for the mural, Het Oosten
Hendrik Paulides (1892-1967)
Paper, paint
32.2 x 122.1 cm
1938
6190-6. Purchase: R. Colauto, 2004

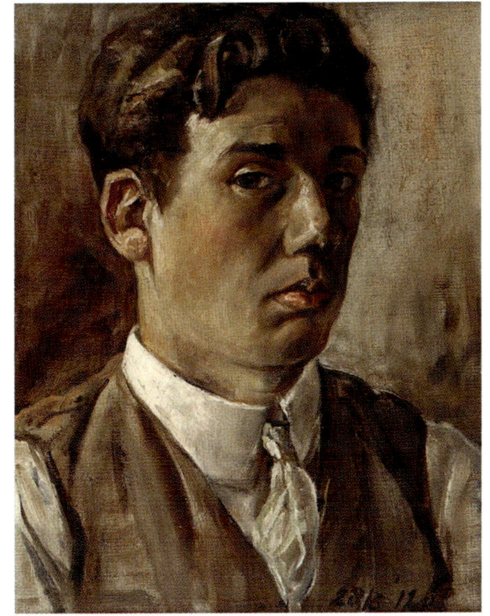

160
Self-portrait of Hendrik Paulides
Oil painting
40.4 x 31.8 cm
1912
6191-1. Gift: R. Colauto, 2004

received the commission to produce murals for different World Fairs: Paris 1931, Paris 1937 and New York 1939. For this last World Fair he made two exceptionally large works: one that was 27 metres long entitled *Het kunstleven der Javanen* (The Arts of the Javanese), and another work that was 22 metres long whose subject was *Vrouwen brengen offers na een ritueel bad* (Women bringing offerings after a ritual bath).

In a letter written to the Koloniaal Instituut (9 February 1936), Paulides expressed his motives: 'I have sacrificed everything to achieve what I have set as the goal of my life: to give expression to the beauty of the East Indies in the monumental visual arts.' (Fig. 159-160 and Fig. 5-7)[107] JVD

The artists couple: Mr and Mrs Quirien A.A. Krijnen and Petronella Maria Helena (Nellie) Krijnen-Surie (The Hague 1883 – Ambarawa 1945 and Rotterdam 1887 – Scheveningen 1965)

Shortly after their marriage in 1915, the young couple Quirien A.A. Krijnen and Nellie Krijnen-Surie, both artists, left for the Netherlands East Indies. They settled in Batavia. Quirien Krijnen had graduated from the Art Academy in The Hague. After graduation, he started a technical bureau and studio called Emulation in 1911, which organised lectures on decorative arts. Many students at Emulation were of 'Indo Dutch' descent. In 1912, Nellie Surie enrolled as a student.

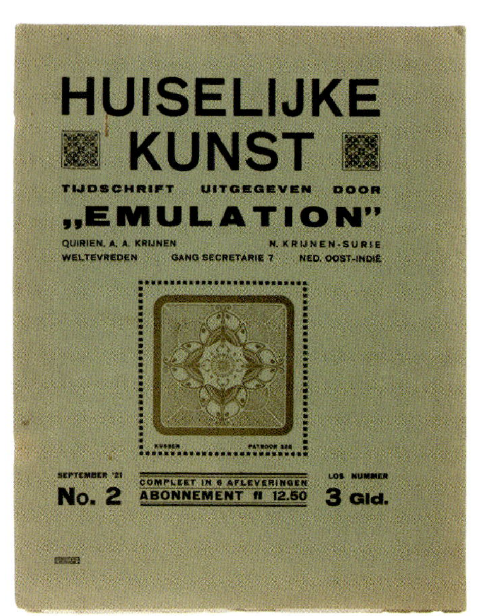

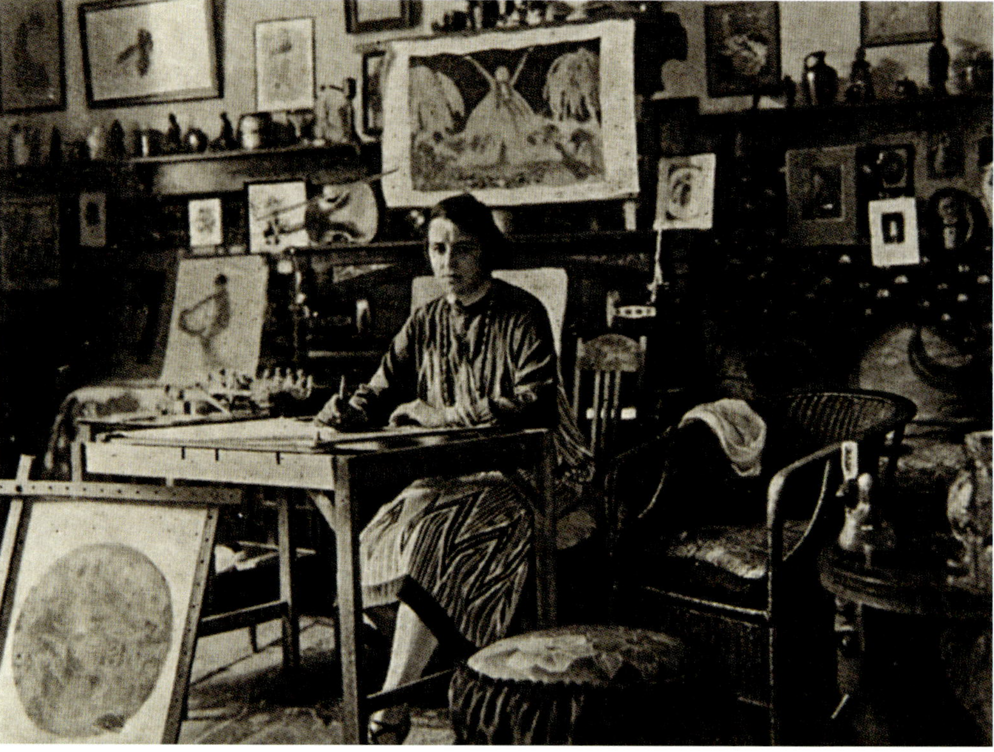

161
Cover magazine Huiselijke Kunst
Published by Emulation, Weltevreden september 1921

162
Mrs. Nellie Krijnen-Surie in her office
Photo: Gamelan magazine

163
Batik pattern with two birds and floral motifs
Nellie Krijnen-Surie (1887-1965)
Paper
26 x 38 cm
Netherlands East Indies.
c. 1910
62731e. Purchased from H. C. Veldhuisen, 2006

Batik was one of the arts presented at Emulation. In those days, Art Nouveau was the prevalent style in art. The batik technique – the wax-resist dyeing textile decoration technique from Java – influenced the Art Nouveau, as European artists were fascinated by the East Indies and Javanese art. Since the end of the 19th century, the Koloniaal Museum in Haarlem had been executing technical batik research. Quirien Krijnen developed his own technique: 'batik on silk'. Once in Batavia, he started to work for the State Railway, while Nellie Krijnen opened an Emulation studio in 1917. Its mission was 'to increase homely happiness by encouraging handicrafts'. This was motivated by the philosophy of the Arts and Crafts Movement, which aimed to provide 'applied arts for everybody in everyday life'. The studio proved to be successful and Quirien soon quit the railways. Among its products, Emulation developed 'ready-made batik on silk' packets, which were sent to customers all over the world. At the zenith of its success, Emulation operated through seventeen agencies throughout the archipelago. In 1920, the Krijnens launched the magazine *Huiselijke Kunst* (Homely Arts), dealing with applied arts and giving instructions on 'Krijnen's batik technique', later followed

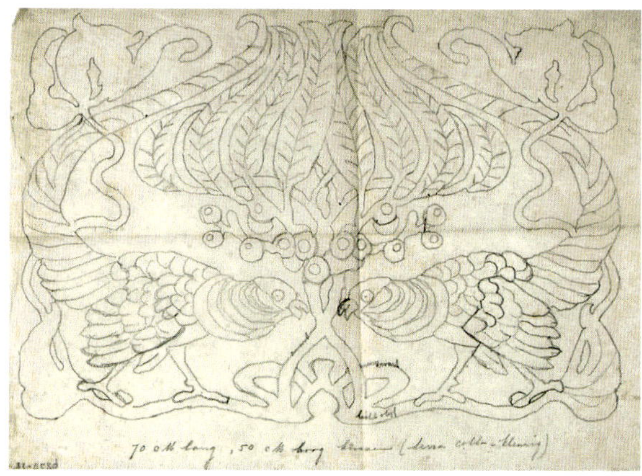

by *Emulation – Guide to Promote Homely Arts and Crafts* published in Dutch, Malay, English, French and Italian. Nellie Krijnen organised exhibitions of the work of customers in Australia, South Africa, the Netherlands and several other European countries. After the 1929 Wall Street crash, Quirien and Nelly Krijnen opened a vendue house in Batavia and published *Krijnen's Maandblad*, a magazine on indigenous crafts, ethnography, antiques, collections and home-interior decorative arts. The Second World War made it impossible to continue their enterprise.

The Krijnens were imprisoned by the Japanese and Quirien died in 1945. In 1948, Nellie returned to The Hague, where she passed away in 1965. From Indonesia she brought some examples of their 'batik on silk' application. The designs on the cloths represent both traditional Javanese iconography and Art Nouveau inspired images. Through their design, this precious and modest collection expresses the creative energy of the couple. The Tropenmuseum is grateful that Mrs Wabeke-Krijnen, the couple's granddaughter, donated this collection to the Tropenmuseum in 2009. She also provided most of the information for this article. (Fig. 161-163) IVH

The photographer: Margaretha Mathilde ('Thilly') Weissenborn (Kediri 1889 – Baarn 1964)

Thilly Weissenborn was, as far as is known, the first female professional photographer in the Netherlands East Indies. She learned the profession at the renowned Kurkdjian studio in Surabaya. In 1917, she moved to Garut on West Java. D.G. Mulder, the founder of the NV Garoetsche Apotheek en Handelsonderneming (Garut Pharmacy and Business Enterprise) and himself a passionate amateur photographer, entrusted Thilly Weissenborn with the

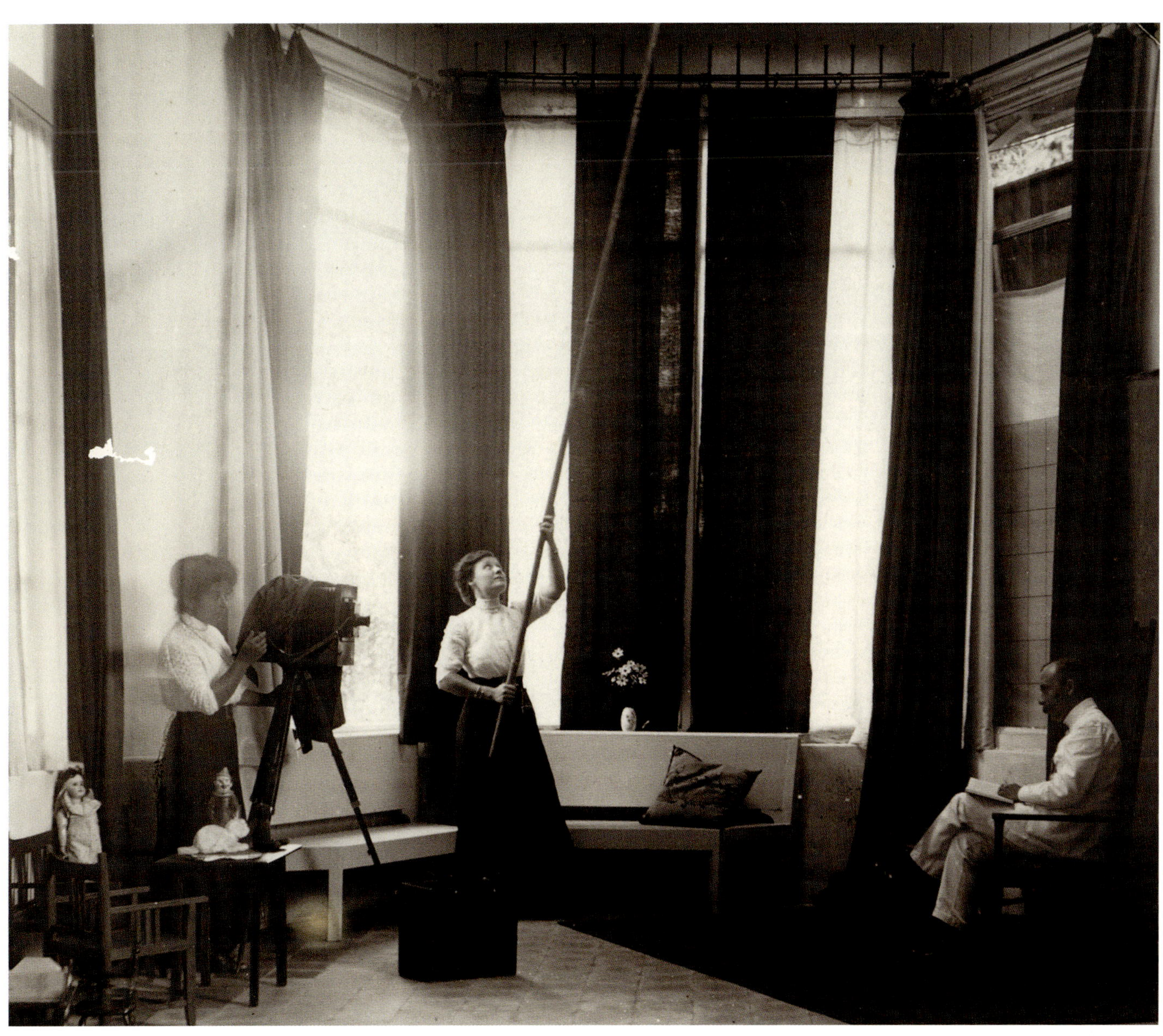

164
Thilly Weissenborn left while photographing her brother Theo, Java
Gelatin silver print
7.5 x 8.4 cm
1910-1930
60054003. Gift: H.E. Eilerts de Haan

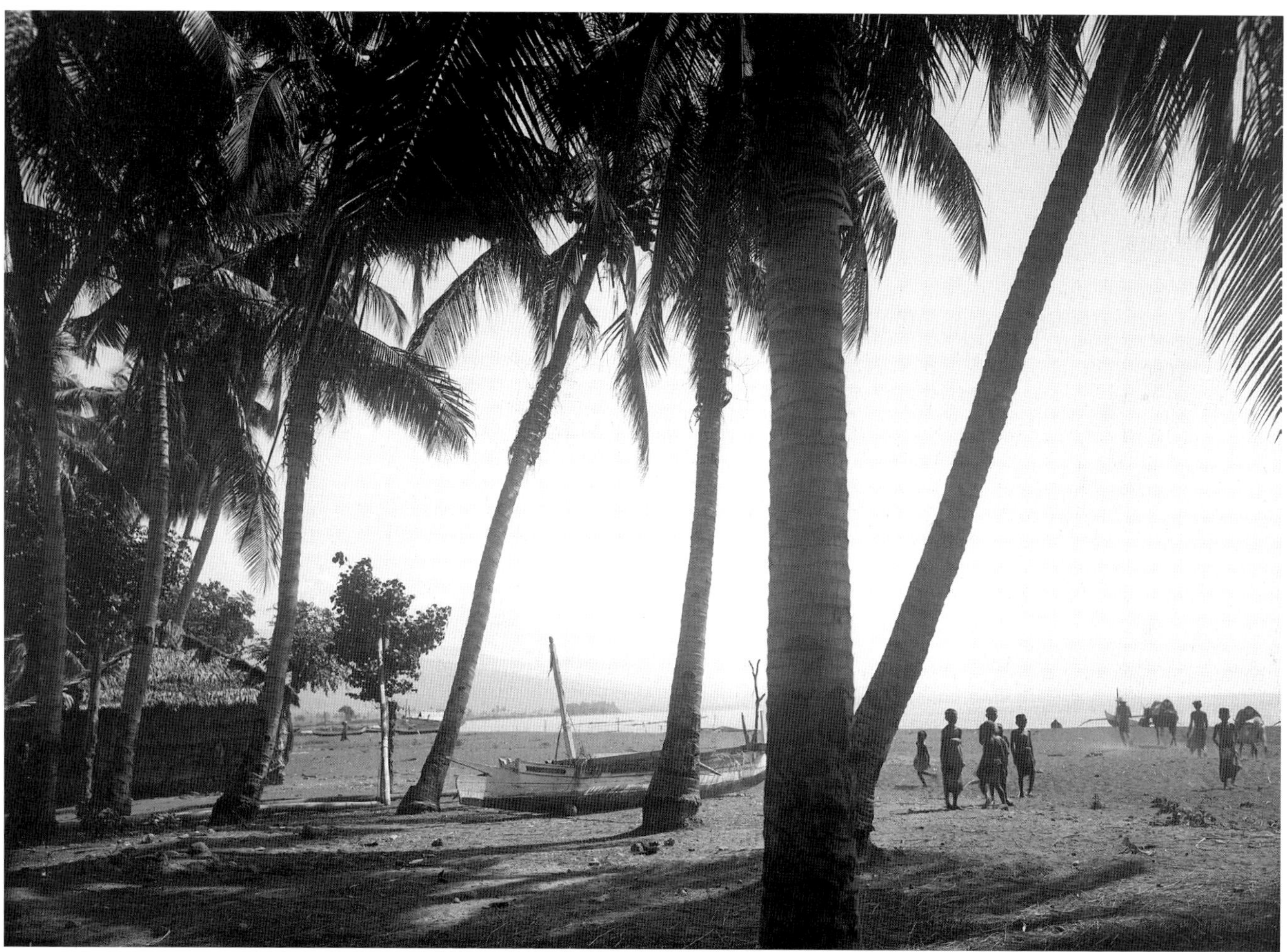

165
Beach scene with palm trees, Bali
Photographer: Thilly Weissenborn (1889-1964)
Glass negative
18 x 24 cm
c. 1925
10026496. Gift: W. Viallé, 2004

166
Goesti Bagoes Djilantik, vice regent of Karangasem, with two of his wives, Bali
Photographer: Lux Foto Studio Garut
Glass negative
9 x 12 cm
1915-1925
10018716. Gift: C.C.F.M. Le Roux, 1927

management of GAH Foto-atelier Lux, a photo studio. In 1920, she acquired ownership of the studio and named the business Foto Lux. She managed the studio for twenty years. In 1943 she was imprisoned in a Japanese internment camp in Bandung. Following the war, Garut was largely destroyed by fire. During the first police action in 1947, Weissenborn's studio in the Sociëteitstraat was completely destroyed. In the same year, she married Nico Wijnmalen and moved to Bandung. The couple was forced to leave Java in 1956 and departed for Holland. Thilly Weissenborn made both portraits and technically perfect photographs of buildings and interiors. Her photographs of landscapes and staged scenes quickly garnered attention due to their idyllic *'Mooi-Indië'* ('Beautiful East Indies') character. The Tropenmuseum possesses more than 370 of her photographs. One album apparently served as a 'pattern album'. From it, clients could order photographs. All prints in this album were produced using the daylight gelatin silver print procedure and, in most cases, bore the label: *"Foto Lux" Garoet.* Another striking collection consists of forty-eight glass negatives (dimensions 13x18 and 18x24 cm) that were picked from the rubble by a soldier/amateur photographer named Viallé, during the first police action in Garut in July 1947. Fascinated and feeling great admiration for the quality of the photo shots, he saved the material for years without knowing who had produced them. In 2004, Mr Viallé donated them to the Tropenmuseum.
In the initial decades of the 20th century, many of Weissenborn's photographs were used in publications; most of her photographs of Java and Bali appeared in Couperus' book *Oostwaarts.* [108] (Figs. 164-166 and Fig. 11) JVD

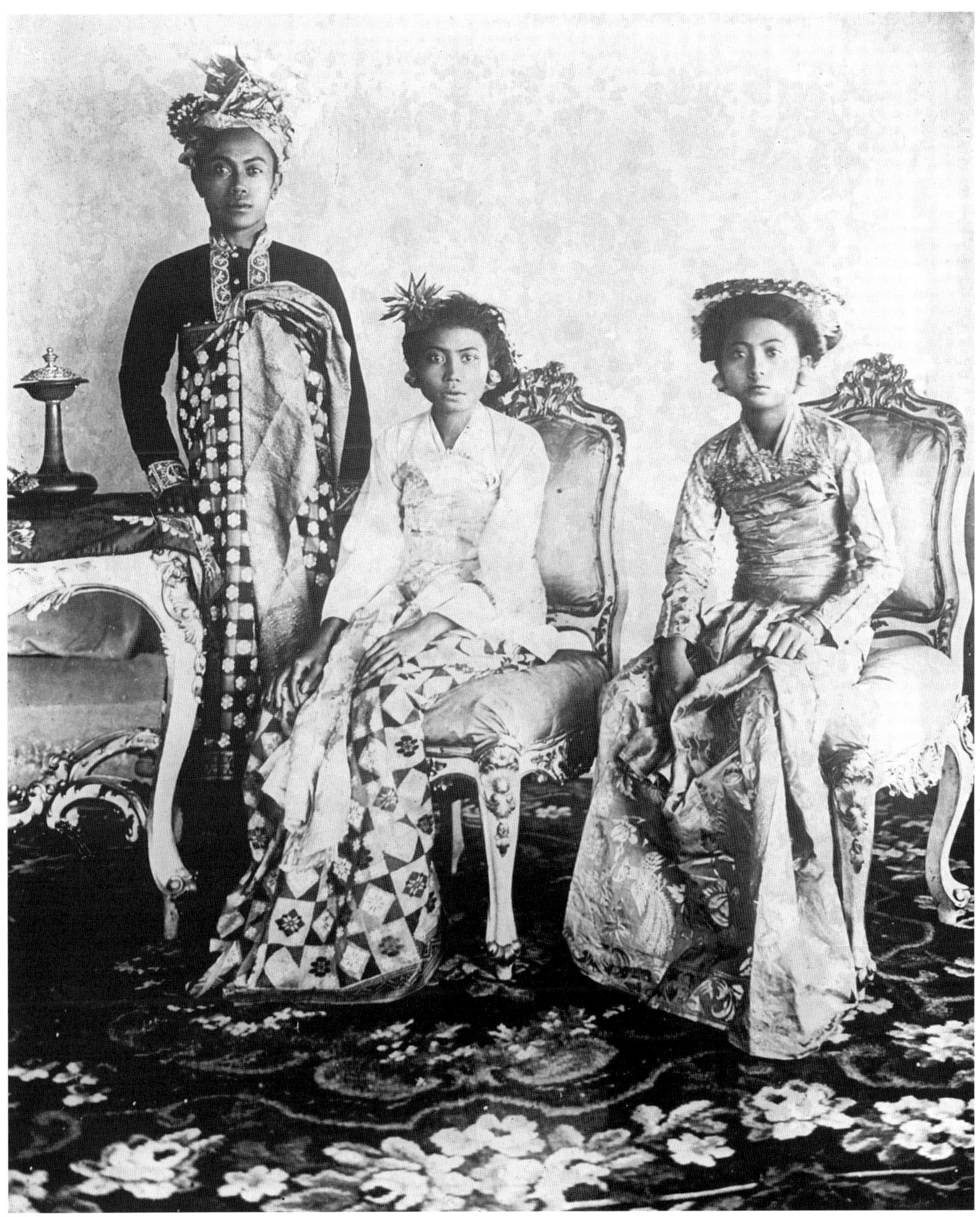

The scientist / museum director: Johan Christiaan van Eerde (Workum 1871 – Amsterdam 1936)

In 1913, the Indologist Johan Christiaan van Eerde was appointed as the Director of the Cultural Anthropology Department of the Koloniaal Instituut. He had eleven years of civil service for the Internal Administration of the Netherlands East Indies under his belt, during which he had profiled himself as a decisive man who possessed a great organisational talent.

Van Eerde's directorship of the Cultural Anthropology Department also meant that he was the first director of the Koloniaal Museum. In the year of his appointment, the new building of the Koloniaal Instituut, (founded in 1910), on Amsterdam's Mauritskade was far from complete. It would take until September 1923 before the first exhibition could be opened; an exhibition organised to celebrate the 25th jubilee of the coronation of Queen Wilhelmina (3 September - 31 October 1923). Van Eerde therefore occupied a special position – he could determine how the layout of his future museum was to look like down to the smallest detail. To meet the challenge, he made an orientation trip to a number of European ethnographic museums. But his primary source of inspiration and driving force was the ideology of the Ethical Policy of the day.

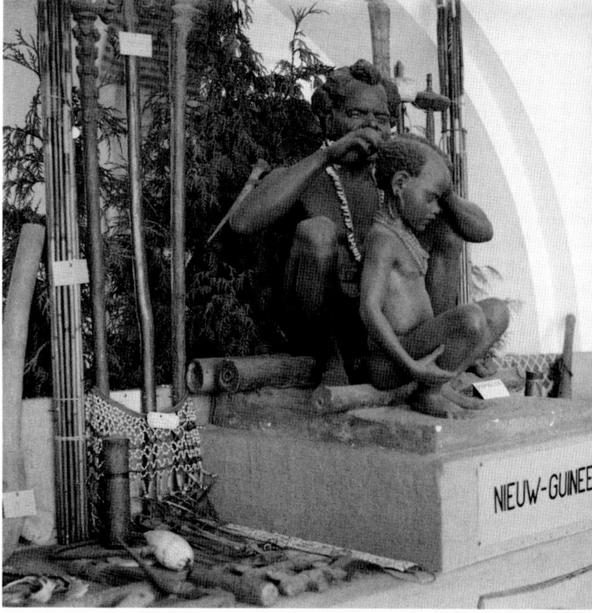

> 167
Papua man and child at the Jubilee Exhibition in the Koloniaal Museum, Amsterdam
Glass negative
13 x 18 cm
1923
10000395

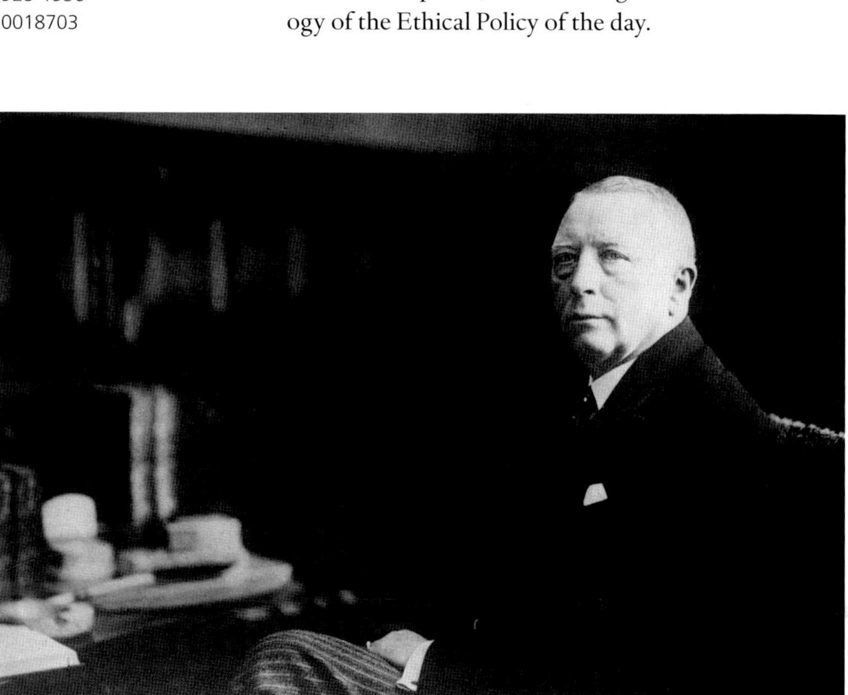

168
Prof. J.C. van Eerde
Glass negative
9 x 12 cm
1925-1936
10018703

In the museum, this focus on the Ethical Policy led to balanced exhibitions that elicited understanding and sympathy for the people and cultures of the Dutch overseas territories. Not only objects set up in display cases, but also reproduced scenes and life-sized wax figures that were usually modelled on (field) photographs taken on site in the Netherlands East Indies were meant to depict the daily lives of the colonial subjects. The cultural anthropology galleries of the museum, with their high educational quality and their positive image with respect to what was seen as the benevolent and edifying presence of the Netherlands in the colonies were, in the thriving initial years of the museum, almost exclusively created by the enlightened colonial Van Eerde.

Van Eerde worked as a scientist as well. He had published his ideas in the then much consulted manual *Koloniale Volkenkunde* (first edition 1914, fifth edition 1928). In 1917, through the Koloniaal Instituut, he was appointed a professor holding an endowed chair at the University of Amsterdam in Colonial Geography and Ethnology, and also held several other endowed professorships.

Van Eerde remained a highly committed director of the Koloniaal Museum until 1936, the year of his retirement. Several weeks later, he died. Over the years he donated and acquired more than 450 objects for the then Koloniaal Museum, including many textiles, and 250 photographs.[109] (Fig. 167-168) DVD

The soldier and his wife: Henri N.A. Swart and Victorina M.G. Stadlmair (Citibung 1863 – The Hague 1946 and Sumatra's west coast 1877 – The Hague 1945)

In 1901, Victorina Stadlmair married Henri Swart. He was born in 1863 in Cibitung, West Java. He was in the Netherlands at the time for his military training. Together they returned to the Netherlands East Indies, where the couple lived on Kalimantan, Timor and Sulawesi, respectively, before Swart was transferred to Aceh in 1909. A guerrilla war had been raging there since 1873 against the introduction of the Dutch administration. As a soldier, Swart made a name for himself and in 1909 he succeeded General G. C. E. van Daalen as the Governor of Aceh. He held this office for ten years and ended his career as Vice President of the Council of the East Indies between 1918 and 1921.

Like her husband, Victorina Swart-Stadlmair was a supporter of the Ethical Policy of the time, be it, as he called it, as 'practical ethics'. Their motto

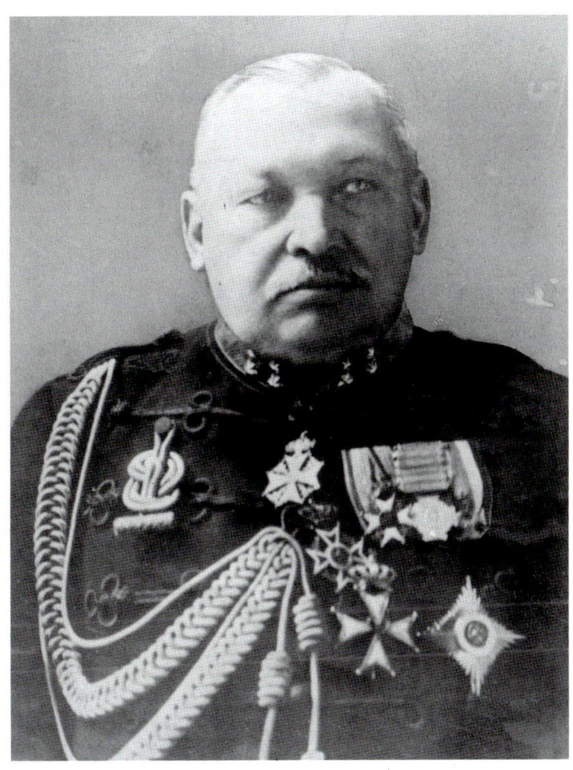

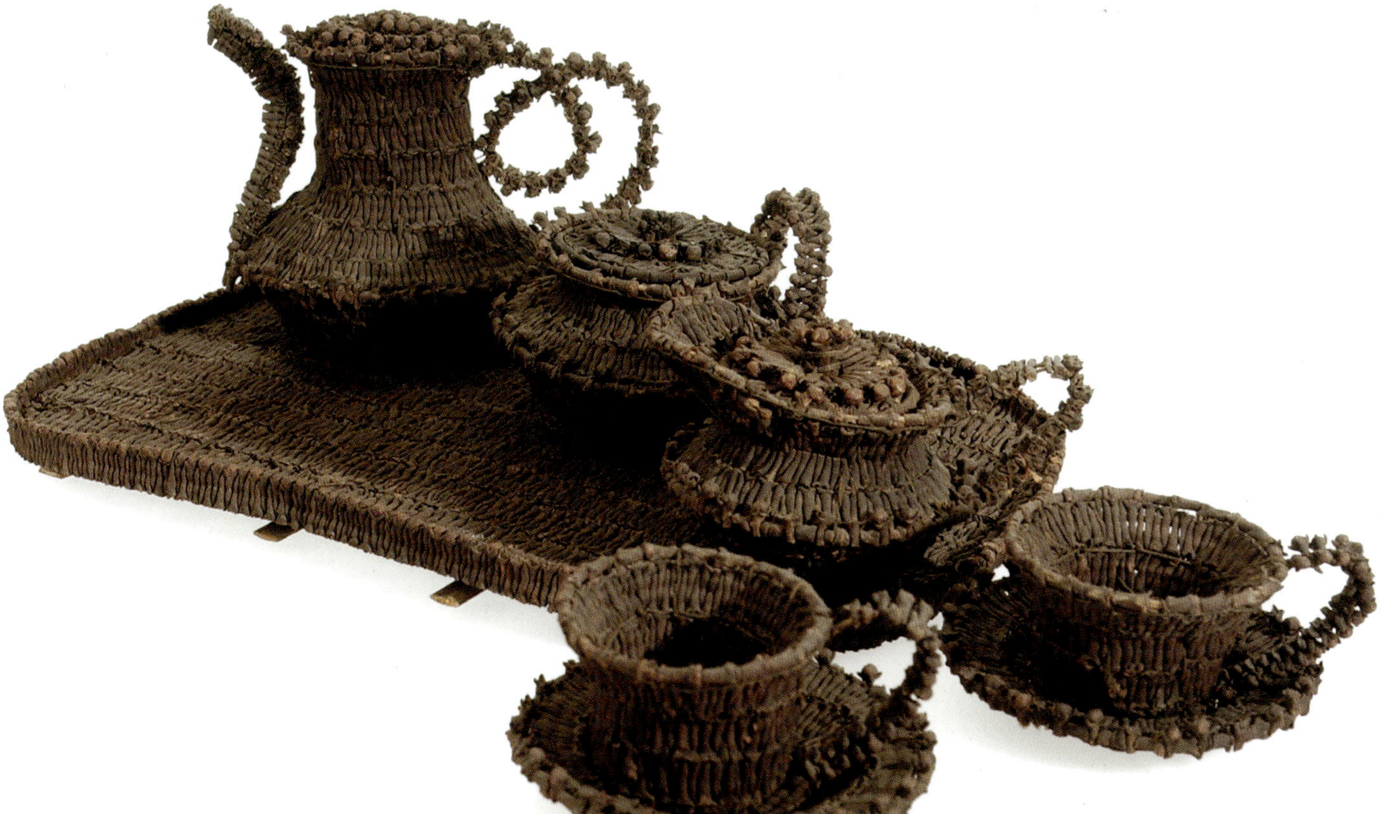

> 169
Lieutenant General H.N.A. Swart
Glass negative
9 x 12 cm
1900-1920
10018811. On loan: H.J. Schmidt 1944

170
Tea Service
Clove
Ambon
239-32. Gift: V.M.G. Swart Stadlmair, 1925

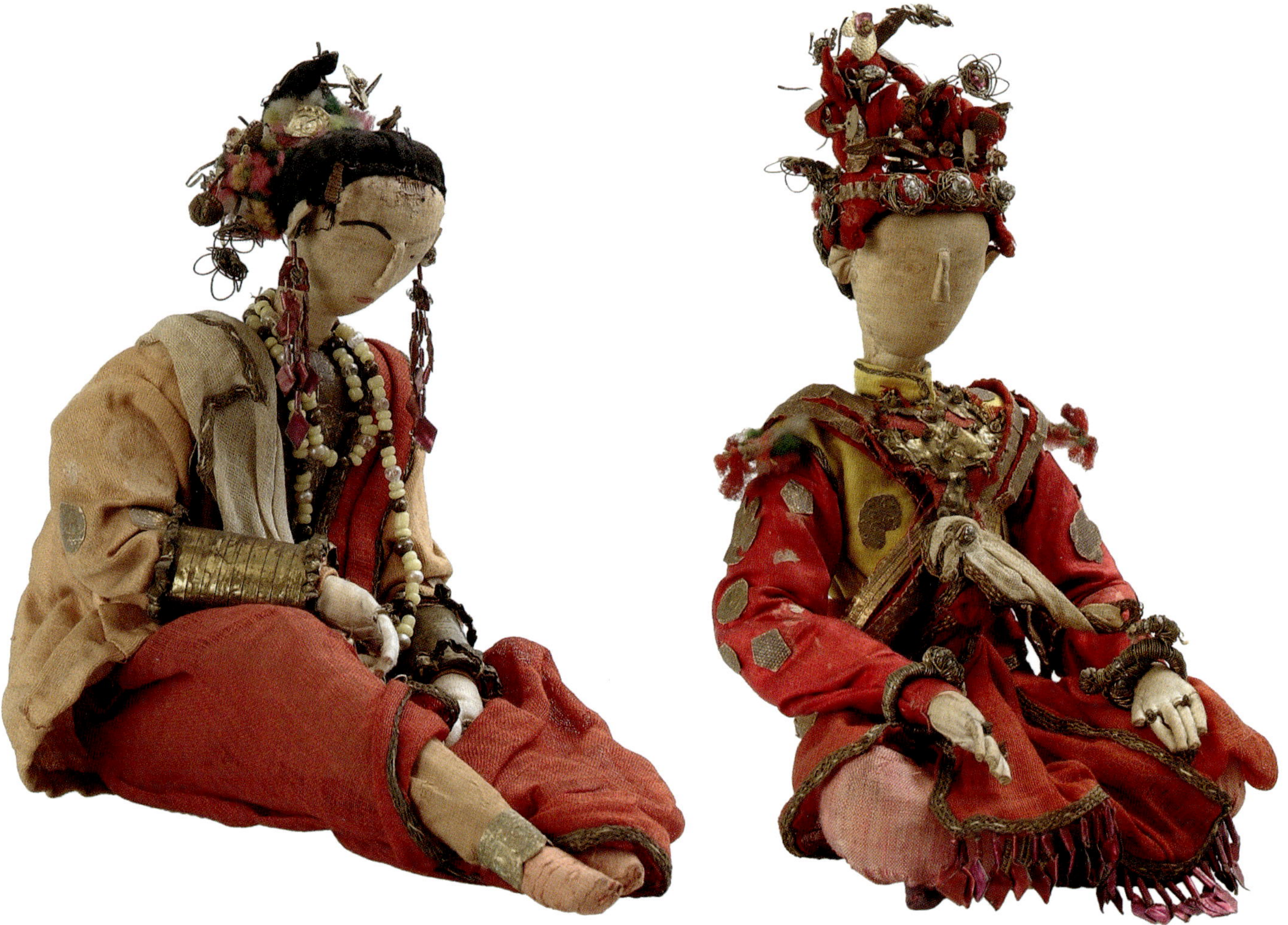

171
Doll, a bride from Makassar
Cotton
17 x 10 cm
South Sulawesi
239-20. Gift: V.M.G. Swart Stadlmair, 1925

172
Doll, a groom from Makassar
Cotton. 19 x 11 cm
South Sulawesi
239-19. Gift: V.M.G. Swart Stadlmair, 1925

was: 'Show the inlander that you trust him, but at the same time make sure he understands that you have the power and the strength to impose your will on him, so that he obeys you.'
The collection of Victorina Swart-Stadlmair not only reflects her nomadic life in the archipelago, the some sixty objects that she donated to the Tropenmuseum can also be called typical 'feminine' objects. In addition to photographs, she donated puppets, wickerwork, clothes and textiles to the Koloniaal Museum. The puppets had been made of wood and some came from Aceh. In 1914 they had been displayed at the Colonial Exhibition in Semarang in the pavilion of Aceh, where they were awarded two gold medals. After the exhibition, her husband had this pavilion, which was built in the form of an Aceh house, dismantled and later re-erected in Aceh to serve as a museum there.

The Aceh museum in Koetaradja (present-day Banda Aceh) was given a strong 'ethical' slant: emphasis was put on the development of the peoples and the Dutch attempts to bring progress in the area. As an extension of this effort, the Dutch for the first time had an interest in the (arts and) crafts of the Netherlands East Indies. Preserving 'authenticity' became important. Swart's collection in the museum primarily consisted of objects that were related to the local method of weaving. He spent a lot of money on his collection, paying ten guilders for a cover over a fly cap (*seubah*); a covered Aceh seat cushion cost 12.50 guilders. Victorina Swart devoted herself to the 'elevation of the indigenous woman', such as during the emancipatory exhibition 'The Woman 1813-1913' in Amsterdam.
In the East Indies, she promoted education for girls. In 1925, she donated her collection to the Koloniaal Museum, with her husband following suit in 1928. (Fig. 169-172) CD

The founder of the Koloniaal Museum: Frederik Willem van Eeden (Haarlem 1829 – Haarlem 1901)

The founder of the Koloniaal Museum in Haarlem, Frederik Willem van Eeden is of course a very important figure in the history of the Tropenmuseum's collection. As the General Secretary of the Nederlandsche Maatschappij ter bevordering van Nijverheid, in 1864 Van Eeden was given the assignment to build a permanent collection of colonial products. Convinced of the 'moral and material importance' of the colonies, he energetically assembled a collection. After only a year, this collection had to be transferred from his own attic room to the government building Paviljoen Welgelegen in Haarlem. In 1871, the Koloniaal Museum opened its doors there to the public at large.

Van Eeden himself was a botanist. He wrote a substantial amount on Dutch flora, and his interest in colonial products was an extension of this. With little means, but considerable enthusiasm and persuasive powers, he assembled in a short period a large collection of natural products, ordered by minerals, products of export cultivation, plant products and wood types. The applications of natural materials, such as medicines, pigments or examples of the so-called *inlandsche volksvlijt* (industry of the indigenous people), such as wickerwork, woven fabrics, batik, wood and brass work, were also collected. Organisations such as the Nederlandsche Handel-Maatschap-

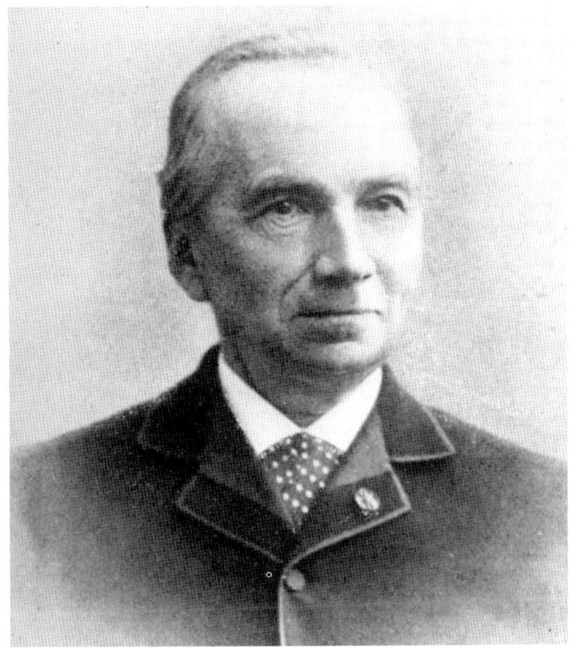

> 173
Frederik Willem van Eeden
Gelatin silver print
20.8 x 16 cm
c. 1880
60036545

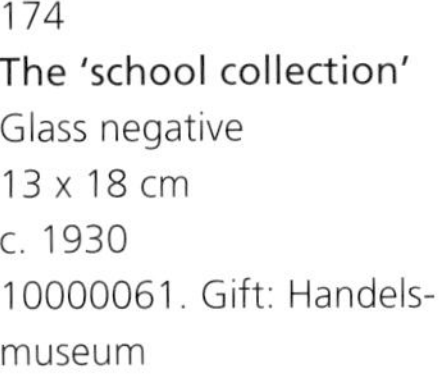

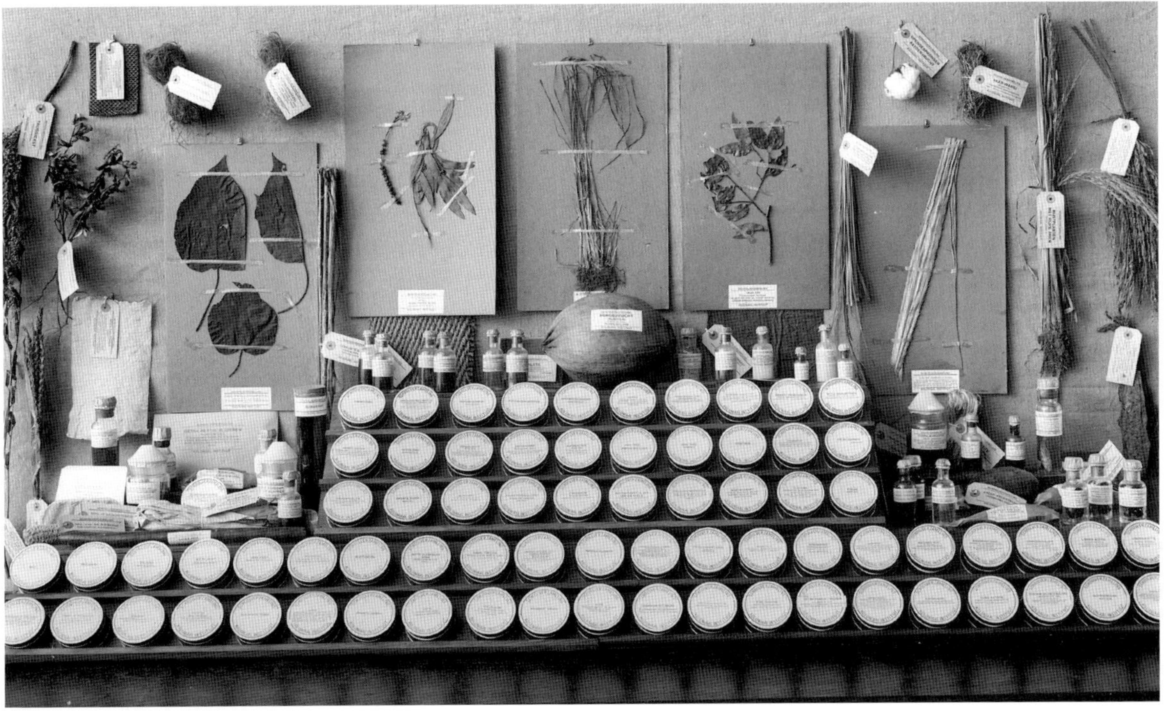

174
The 'school collection'
Glass negative
13 x 18 cm
c. 1930
10000061. Gift: Handelsmuseum

pij (NHM) and authorities/administrators such as the Governor General of the Netherlands East Indies and the Governor of Suriname supported the acquisition policy.
From this orientation on both traditional skills and design, a Museum van Kunstnijverheid (Museum of Applied Arts) was established in 1877 on the twelve-and-a-half year anniversary of the Koloniaal Museum's founding. This museum too was placed under the management of Van Eeden. In 1898, the Koloniaal Museum was also expanded with a research laboratory in order to strengthen its role in the further exploitation and development of the colonies. The Koloniaal Museum was seen as Europe's best museum for tropical products.
At his own admission, he wanted to use the Koloniaal Museum 'to prick the interest of young Dutch people to devote their efforts to the immense job given to us in our Colonies.' He saw the collection of products meant for teaching and a study for colonial civil servants as an important means for achieving this goal. Van Eeden is described in different texts as a lively, hard-working man, who was meticulous and enthusiastic. A man whose writings 'sparkled with humour and proved the enormous knowledge, the power of observation and the ingenuity of the writer, who sometimes poured out his heart in facetious poems'.[110] (Fig. 173-174) DVDa

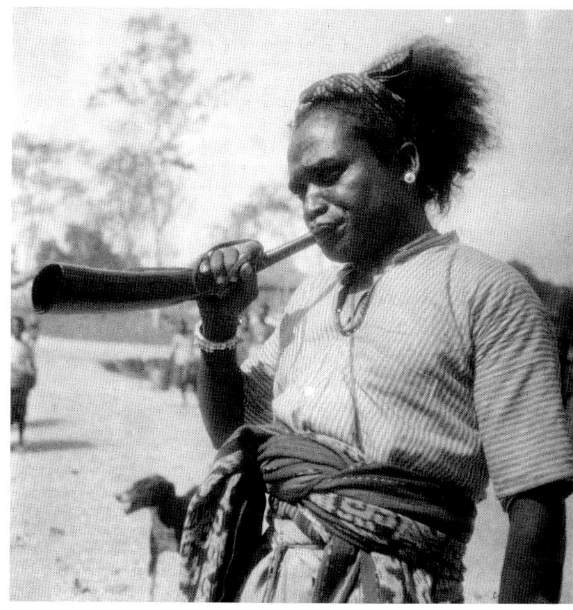

175
Atoni van Soë blowing on a buffalo horn, Timor
Glass negative
9 x 12 cm
1936
10005960. Through the mediation of J. Kunst

The music collector: Jaap Kunst (Groningen 1891 – Amsterdam 1960)

Jaap Kunst is one of the finding fathers of ethnomusicology, the study that focuses on the exploration of folk music. In the case of Jaap Kunst, this initially concerned the music of the Dutch island of Terschelling, then the music of the Indonesian archipelago, and later all non-Western music. His strongest desire was to record and document indigenous music that was in danger of disappearing through Western 'infection', which, among other things, included the influence of Christianity. Beginning in 1942, Kunst taught comparative musicology at the University of Amsterdam. In 1958, he became a member of the Koninklijke Nederlandse Academie van Wetenschappen (Royal Netherlands Academy of Sciences).
Jaap Kunst was born into a family of musicians and began playing violin at the age of five. He once said that he learnt to read notes before he knew to read script. After his law study, in 1919 he persuaded two fellow-musicians to accompany him to the Netherlands East Indies in order to play in clubs and art or other societies. The trio's repertoire consisted of folk songs, chamber music and music with lantern slides for which Kunst very artfully imitated animal noises. It was in Yogyakarta that he heard gamelan music for the first time at the court of Paku Alam VII. This experience so impressed him that he decided not to return to the Netherlands and to start studying Javanese music. In close consultation with the Director of the Berliner Phonogramm Archiv, Prof. E. M. von Hornborstel, Kunst began collecting sound recordings on wax rolls and descriptions, photographs and films of music. He also collected musical instruments. Kunst published his findings and gave many lectures.
While on leave in Europe in 1927, Kunst persuaded the Dutch Minister of Colonies, Prof. J. C. Koningsberger, that research into native music was a task of the government. From 1930 to 1932, he fulfilled a unique function as 'official for systematic musicological research in the Netherlands East Indies Archipelago', i.e. government musicologist, at the Department of Education and Religion, over which Prof. B. Schrieke held sway. He was able to carry out his work with ample financial resources and considerable passion until the financial crisis hit the Netherlands East Indies in 1932. Prof. Schrieke travelled through

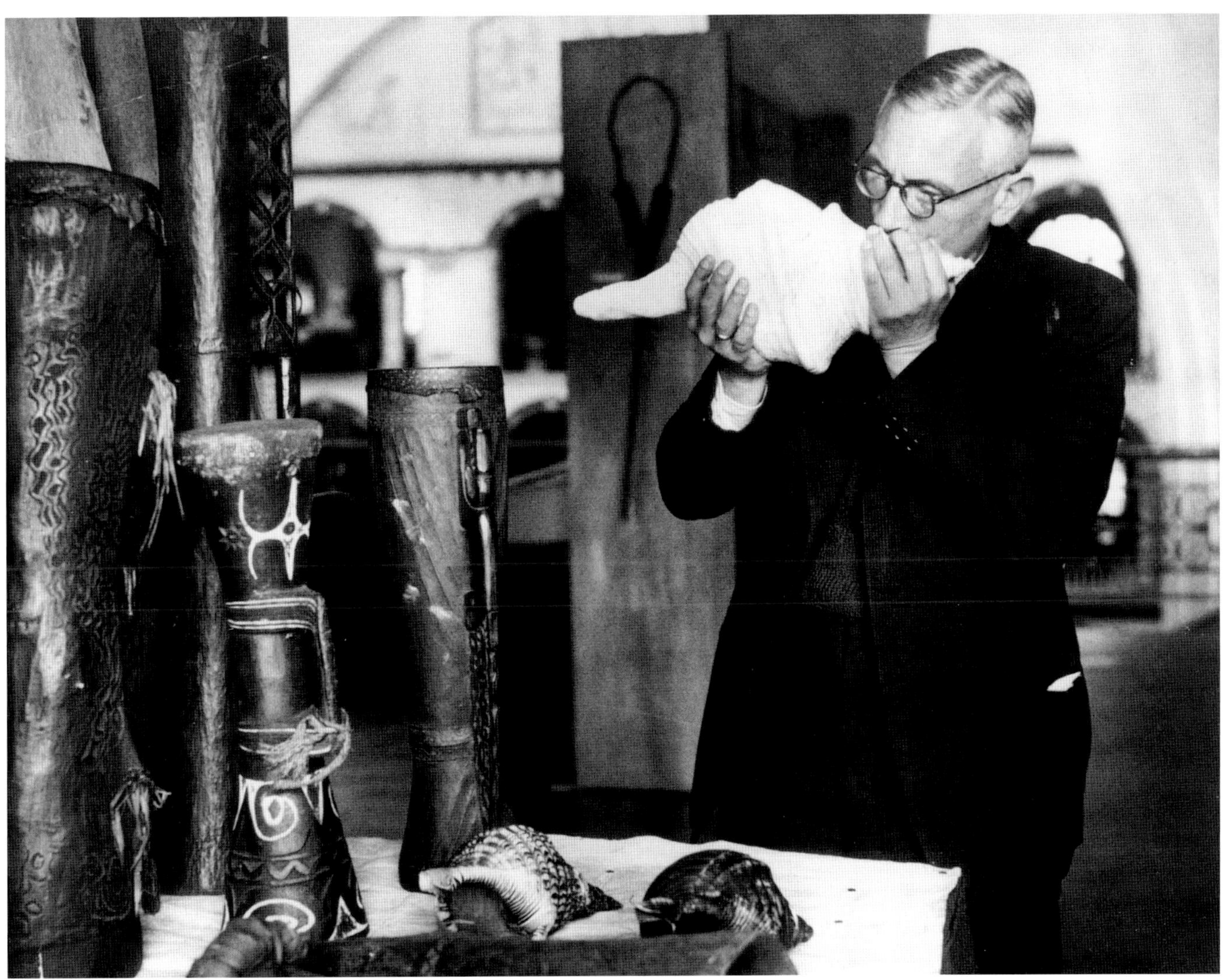

176
Jaap Kunst demonstrates how to blow a of conch shell
Gelatin silver print
13 x 18cm
1940-1960
60006844. Gift: University of Amsterdam

the archipelago to explain the cutbacks in education on site locally. He made Kunst his 'travel secretary', which took him to New Guinea, Sulawesi, Flores and Timor, among other places. In the morning, he would take minutes of meetings, in the afternoon and evening, he focused on the local music around him. But at the end of 1932, the travelling came to an end. His collection, a large archive and more than 1,150 musical instruments, was handed over to the Museum van het Bataviaasch Genootschap in Batavia. He became the curator.

When Kunst again went to the Netherlands on leave in 1934, he decided to stay, in part because of the school career of his children. Two years later, he retired (at 45) and became the curator of the Cultural Anthropology Department at the Koloniaal Instituut, a postition that, in his own words, 'was tailor made'. In his view the music collection of the Koloniaal Museum did not amount to much at that time. He energetically set himself writing to all of his contacts in the Netherlands East Indies asking them to collect instruments. Just before the outbreak of the Second World War, 'the treasure came in' – more than 420 objects were added to the museum.

The biggest legacy of Jaap Kunst is that he built a bridge between various forms of traditional music from outside Europe and the field of study of Western composers and researchers. He was a pioneer in the research into relationships between music and the social-cultural context, and put ethnomusicology on the world map. (Fig. 175-176)[111] JVD

sprinckhaan uijt Amboina:
24: julij 1699. twijffliu

TEN COLLECTIONS

Wood

During its long existence, the Tropenmuseum has not only collected knowledge and objects, it has also 'de-accessioned': that is to say it has disposed of collections, exchanged them or placed them with other institutions. This happened because the collections no longer fit within their policies, or because people were no longer interested in them, or because the expertise had been lost or was being combined with something else. This was what happened to the collection of tropical wood.
The first director of the Koloniaal Museum in Haarlem, Frederik Willem van Eeden, was a botanist. He had a penchant for wood, particularly tropical wood, and was interested in the economic application of wood in industry. In the report of his visit to the Colonial and East Indies exhibition in London (1886), he proudly stated that the wood collection of the Koloniaal Museum was not surpassed by what he had seen in London. The collection consisted of samples made up of wood planks that were sent on his request by civil servants and forest rangers from the Netherlands East Indies and Suriname. In 1872 he produced the first catalogue of the types of wood then present. It described 1,367 different types of wood in scientific terms with their generic name, local name, place of origin, quality, fibre structure, resistance to moisture and insects, and the applications they were or could be used for. Thus one type of wood is more amenable to being nailed into, another type is 'burned clean and suitable for Euro-

177
Illustration from Hendrik d'Acquet, *Insecta et animalia coloribus ad vivum picta*, 1708
KIT Library

178
Wood sample *keroewing*
Former collection: KIT Tropical Products, 1964

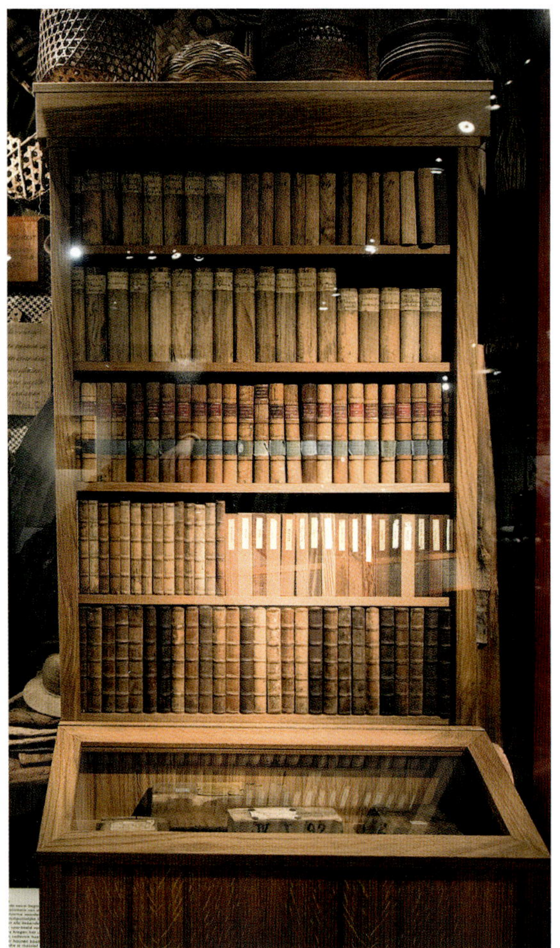

179
Detail showcase with wood samples in the exhibition 'The Netherlands East Indies, a colonial history'
Former collection: KIT Tropical Products, 1964

> 180
Detail from map of the northern part of the east coast of Sumatra; scale 1:400.000
Ed. by J.H. de Bussy, Amsterdam, 1914
The numbers on the map stand for different plantations

> 181
Employees of the topographical service in Salatiga, Java
Photographer: Jonson & Co
Gelatin silver print
22.5 x 28.6 cm
c. 1920
60045063

pean furniture' and a third species produces 'fruit that can be eaten or a bark that contains a type of pigment'. Additions to the collection arrived and in 1903 the third augmented edition of the catalogue was published, assembled by J. Duyfjes, who had continued the work of Van Eeden after he died.
The goal of the collection was to promote knowledge of one of the most important products produced by the Netherlands East Indies and to bring about an effective use of it. How this was interpreted was expressed by Van Eeden back in 1872: '...that the most durable and noblest trees of the forest would be protected against reckless extermination and that they would be multiplied as much as possible through planting efforts.'
When the Koloniaal Instituut was founded in Amsterdam in 1910 and the Koloniaal Museum was given a new building there, a special space was set up for the wood collection, the so-called Wood Gallery.
The wood collection of the KIT/Tropenmuseum was transferred in 2004 to the herbarium collection of the University of Leiden.
A very small part of the collection that had no scientific value was not transferred and is used to give the Wood Gallery of yore an atmosphere that reminds people of the original situation. Another part of the collection is being stored and managed by the museum. They are separate wood blocks in the shape of a book and planks the size of a man in which the name of the tree and the shape of the leaf have been carved by the sculptor J. Bronner.
With the transfer of the wood collection, the knowledge of this material has also left the building. But the collection has been given a new existence in a new scientific context. (Fig. 178, 179) JVD

Maps

Sea and land maps, contour maps, street maps, thematic maps and atlases made the large colonial empire visible. Borders, overgrowth, buildings, the course of rivers, the presence of volcanoes – in short, the territory was visualised to scale. With the map in hand, an enemy border incursion could be fought off, land taxes could be levied, the size and the ownership of plantations could be determined and new city districts could be planned; precisely drawn maps were always necessary. Maps are a confirmation and proof of presence, a legitimation of the self-appropriation of an area. The development of cartography in the Netherlands East Indies kept pace with the economic development and the advancing knowledge of survey technology. First Java and Madura were surveyed, followed by the Outer Regions.
The production of maps was the work of three services: the Topografische Dienst (Topographical Service) of the army, founded in 1874, the Dienst voor het Boschwezen (Forest Service), founded around 1860, which focused on the exploitation of primeval forests, the mapping of where the expensive teak trees grow and the planning of new trees to prevent erosion, and finally the Land Register.
The basis for the collection of cartographic documents was laid by the Koloniaal Museum in Haarlem around 1865. The collection is now part of the KIT-library and consists of some 11,500 map pages; 80 percent of which pertain to the Netherlands East

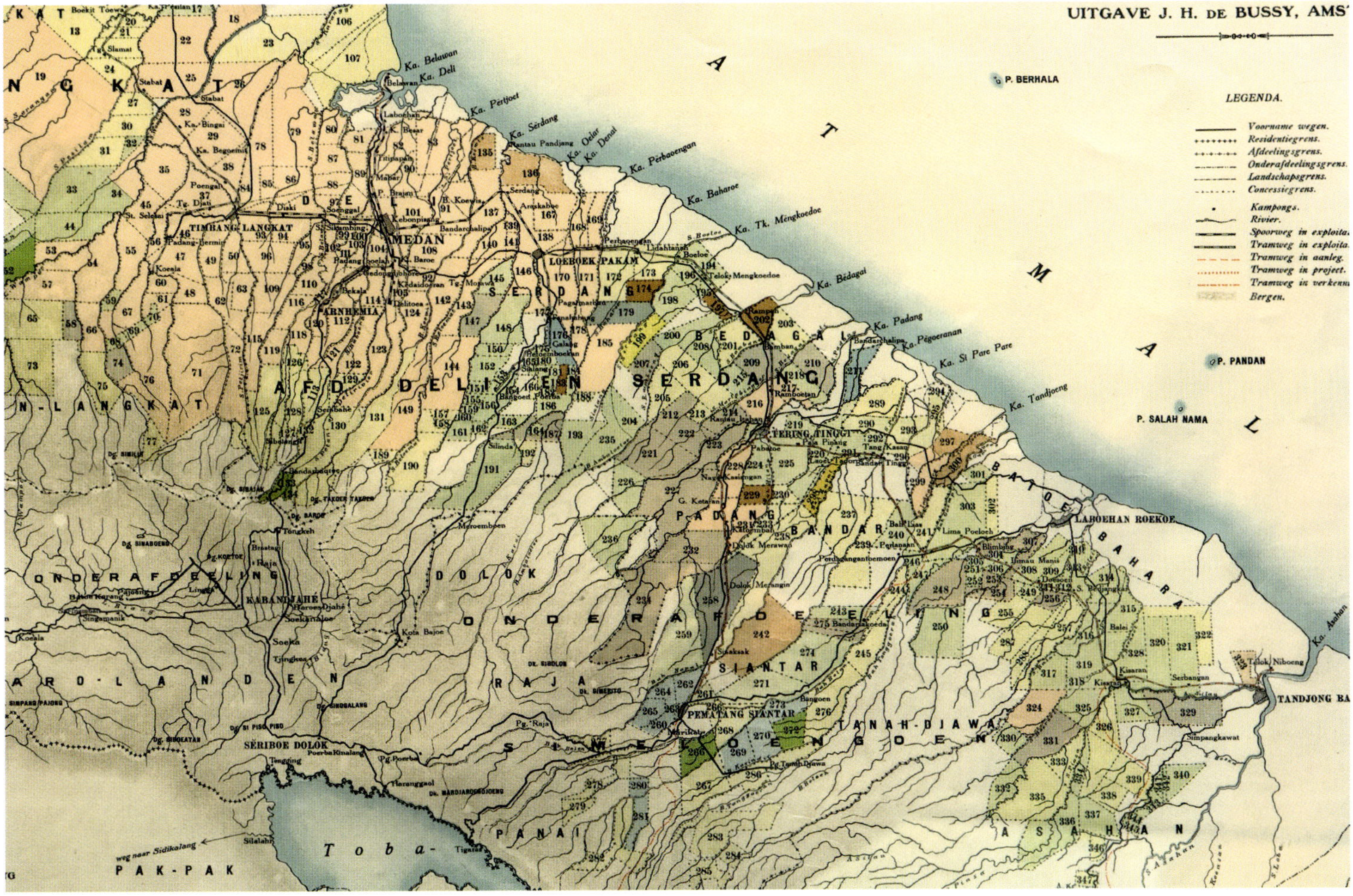

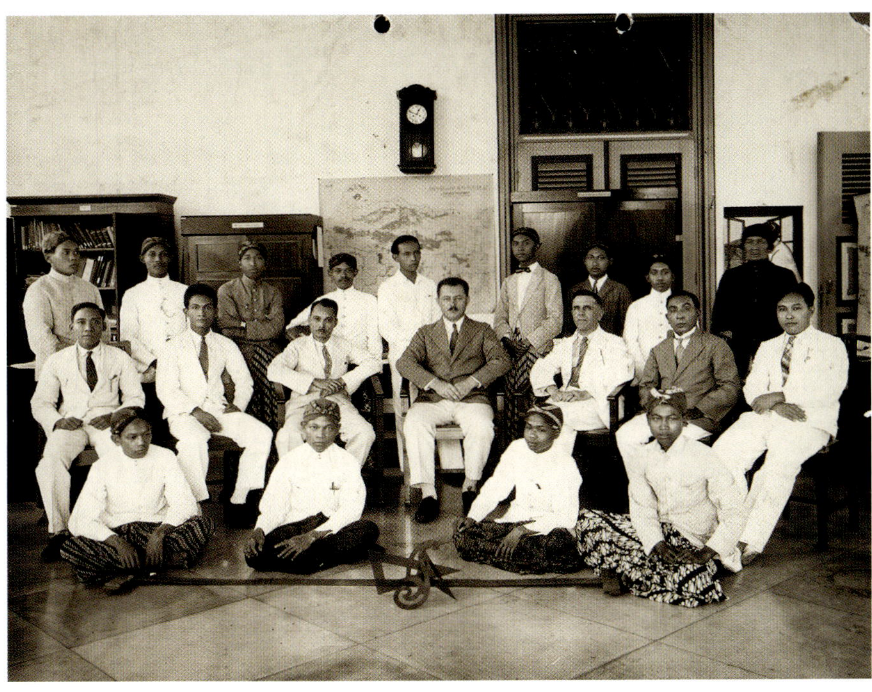

Indies. In 1927 the collection of the time nearly doubled in size through a gift from the Topografische Dienst in Batavia of more than 2,600 map pages. Another large gift came in 1947. On the instruction of the then Governor General, Van Mook, 1,543 new and revised topographical maps and 13 maps of *Terrain Studies* were donated. The *Terrain Studies* were produced between 1942 and 1945 by the allied forces fighting the Japanese and consist of very detailed maps and topographical descriptions.
In the early 1990s, all the maps were re-catalogued. The emergence of the computer and standard rules for the descriptions of map material made this necessary. All maps, including the oldest map from around 1680 showing the coastline of the island of Kalimantan, can now be accessed online via the KIT website and can be linked to other geographical sources. (Fig. 180-181) JVD

Family photographs

Some of the more than 2,000 albums in the photographic collection of the Tropenmuseum are registered as the Hillerström collection. This collection was placed under the management of the museum in the 1970s.

The 1948 annual report of the Koninklijke Vereniging Indisch Instituut (Royal Indies Institute) – the current KIT – stated under the heading of 'social work': 'On request, we received some 30 boxes of private photographic material from Indonesia, followed later by a box from Deli. This photographic material was found by our soldiers during the first police action inside houses abandoned by Europeans on Java and the east coast of Sumatra. This collection was put on view by the parties concerned in our Institute and then in The Hague (fa. Gerzon) and Leeuwarden (office of Ver. Oost en West). Also 466 albums and 1,319 single photographs could be returned to visitors.'

One year later, another two shipments arrived containing photographic material that was found in abandoned Japanese army depots. Once again viewing days were organised: in Amsterdam, Utrecht, Arnhem, Den Bosch and The Hague they attracted nearly ten thousand people. Although many of them found their lost family photographs, some 365 albums remain unclaimed. In the 1960s, Mrs M.J. Hillerström, sympathetic to the destiny of unidentified photographs, tried to find the owners over a course of years. In the end, she placed the remaining photographs and albums in the photography department of the Tropenmuseum.

The photographs provide a glimpse into family life in the Netherlands East Indies in the 1920s and '30s, lovingly recorded and pasted in albums. A life that suddenly ended with the Japanese invasion in 1942. The photographs also served to give the home front in the Netherlands an impression of the living conditions and the social status that people had acquired. Seldom were these images meant to be seen outside the confines of the family. Now, included in the col-

182
Hillerström Photo Collection open for viewing at the Indisch Instituut, Amsterdam
Gelatin silver print
12 x 18.1 cm
1949
60043952

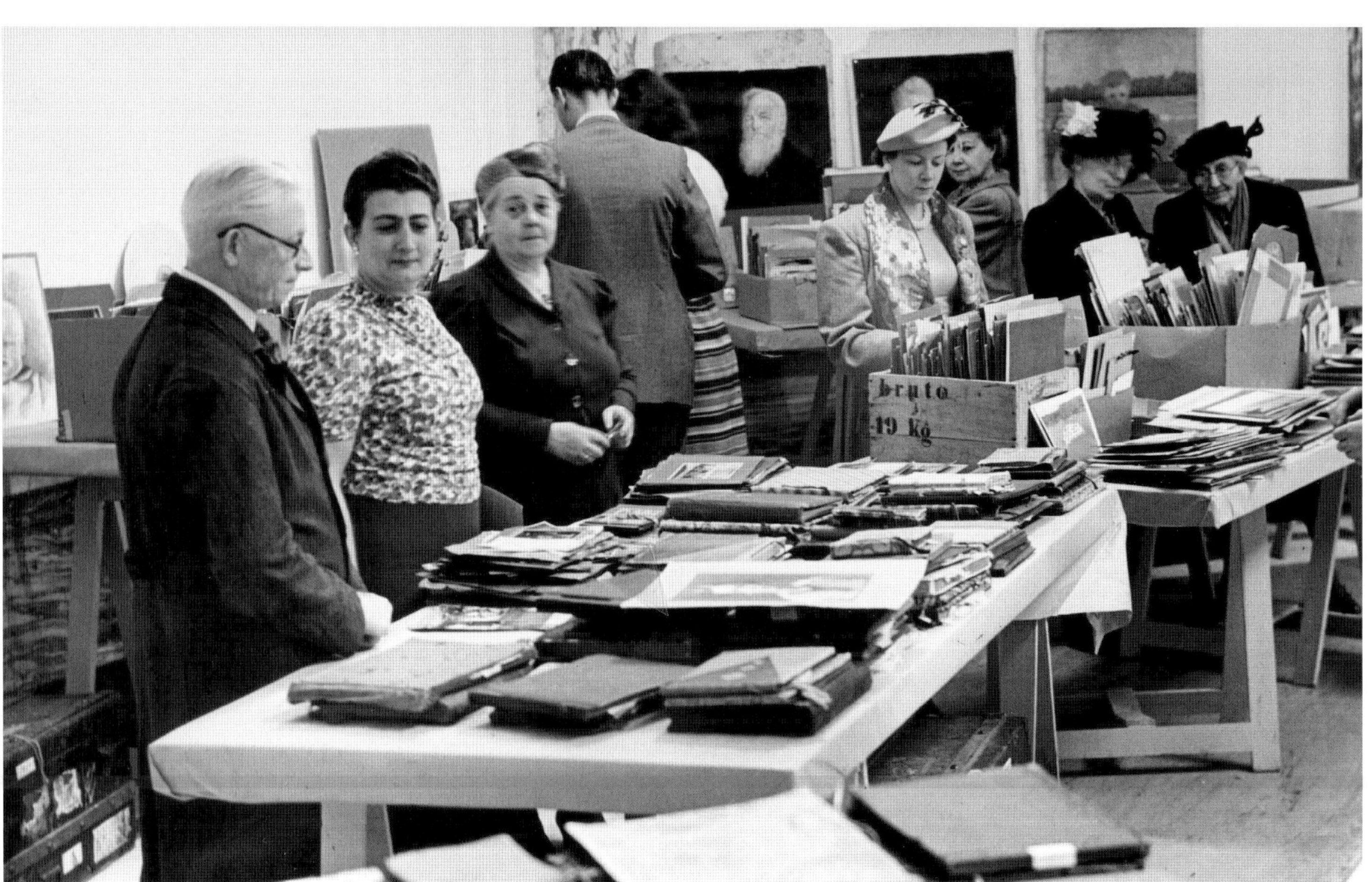

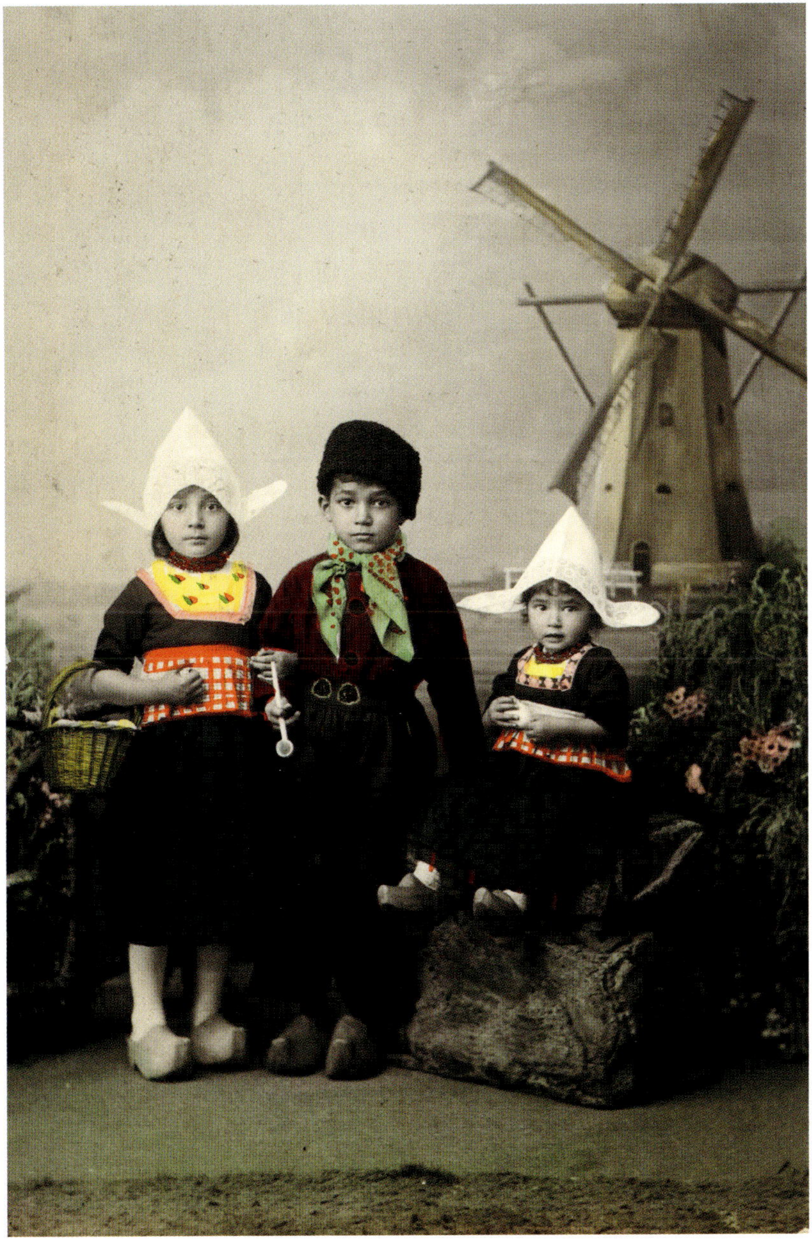

183
Children of the Van Lingen family in traditional Dutch costume
Hand-coloured gelatin silver print
13.8 x 8.8 cm
c. 1925
60013169. Through mediation of M.J. Hillerström, 1970s

lection of the Tropenmuseum, they are a part of the public domain. The collection of East Indies family photographs was expanded in 2008 with the donation of approximately 500 albums by the Indisch Wetenschappelijk Instituut (Indies Scientific Institute). They provide a revealing picture of life in a colony at the micro level and complement the arranged 'official' photographs or those taken on commission. (Fig. 182-183) JVD

Films

Soon after the founding of the Koloniaal Instituut in 1910, an important role was assigned to visual sources in service of the institute's objective to expand the knowledge of the colonies in the mother country.
The then common lantern slides (precursors of modern slides) were insufficient; they did not show movement and had to be supplemented with 'cinematographic pictures'. But who could make these images on location?
It should be someone who possesses a certain prestige in the eyes of Europeans and inlanders, who is used to moving around in both European and indigenous societies and can cope with the climate and the fatigue of a life on the road.
Former Governor General, J.B. van Heutsz, a friend of Chairman Jacob Theodoor Cremer of the Koloniaal Instituut, drew his attention to a captain working at the Topografische Dienst of the Koninklijk Nederlandsch-Indisch Leger (KNIL). During his period of leave in the Netherlands, this Captain Johann Lamster (1872-1952) received the request from the Koloniaal Instituut for filming in the East Indies. As a topographer and soldier, Lamster knew a lot about the East Indies, but nothing about the new medium of film. At the expense of the Dutch Ministry of Colonies – it involved the general interest of the country, after all – Lamster travelled to Paris and, at the studios of Pathé-Frères, learned the technique of working with the 35-mm film camera. In 1912, he departed for the East Indies in the company of a camera-operator because constant turning of the handle of the film transport required a skill that Lamster did not yet master. After three months, the camera operator Collet returned to Paris and Lamster continued by himself. His films, recorded in 1912-13 on Java and Bali, are among the first moving pictures of the Netherlands East Indies taken. He meticulously recorded the lives and work of both Indonesians and Europeans.
The Lamster collection originally consisted of 53 short films. In 1919, new – anonymous – Pathé material was purchased and a new montage of the entire collection was made. The total collection now consisted of 76 titles.
Up to the late 1920s, the Lamster films were used intensively. They were lent to third parties for a small

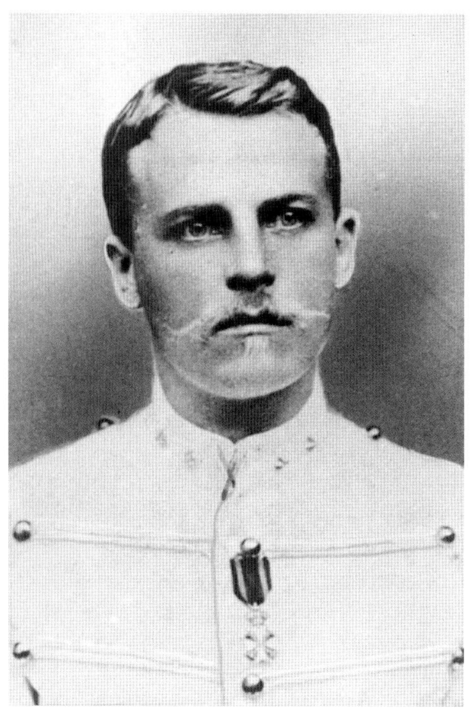

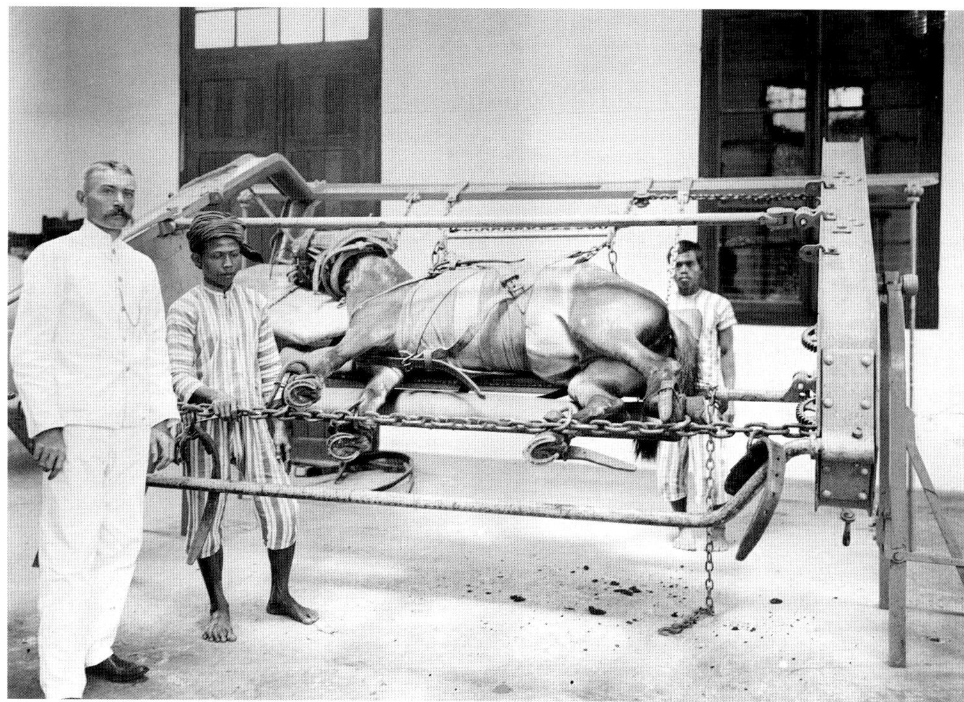

184
1st Lieutenant J.C. Lamster
Glass negative
9 x 12 cm
1895-1910
10018749. On loan:
Mr. H.J. Schmidt, 1944

185
Horse on scales
Veterinary medicine laboratory in Buitenzorg. One of the film Lamster made was on this subject
Glass negative
9 x 12 cm
Buitenzorg, Java, 1912-1913
10013160. Through mediation of J.C. Lamster 1913

> 186
Cotton tube skirt
Sarung Prankemon
C.J. von Franquemont
The motifs are derived from the nutmeg tree
Cotton, dye
110 x 107 cm
Semarang. Java. 1840-1867
1585-4. Gift: P.H.Q. Bouman 1942

fee (1 cent per metre and per showing). Cinema shows were absolutely forbidden by the institute. The films were to be used for educational purposes only, not to entertain the public.

After Lamster, other filmmakers came to the Netherlands East Indies. In the 1920s and '30s, L.Ph. Cosquino de Bussy, Isidore Ochse, Tassilo Adam, Willy Mullens and Mannus Franken were active in the archipelago. Apart from L.Ph. Cosquino de Bussy (director of the Handelsmuseum (Trade Museum), a part of the Koloniaal Instituut), they did not film exclusively for the Koloniaal Instituut. Yet much of their material ended up there over the course of time, as valuable cultural history documents.

The 16-mm material dates from a later time. This new format made films accessible to non-professionals. Within many businesses, the employees started to film their own company and work activities, the company's entire production process was recorded on film with a sense of pride. The collection of family films also dates from this period. They show remarkably many similarities, with pictures of the house and garden, pictures of personnel and day trips to cool mountain retreats. Yet the local population seldom appeared on film.

In the 1970s, the Tropenmuseum considered getting rid of this film collection; all those rusty cans containing flammable nitrate did not fit into the focus of a scientific institution that had put behind its colonial past and was now looking ahead to development cooperation with countries in the global south. This did not happen in the end; the historical film collection has now been placed with the EYE Filminstituut Nederland, where it has been preserved and digitalised. In the current Tropenmuseum the moving images provide a valuable source for the visualization of colonial society, as they did in the past. (Fig. 184-185) JDJ/JVD

Clothes

As from the start, textiles have been given an important place in the collection policy of the Tropenmuseum. This primarily pertains to artisanal traditions of weaving and ornamentation and the local cultural significance of clothing and images. Textiles also played a role in colonial relationships. The Dutch colonial presence influenced the outward appearance of Indonesians and the colonists were influenced by Indonesian clothing. But this exchange was not on

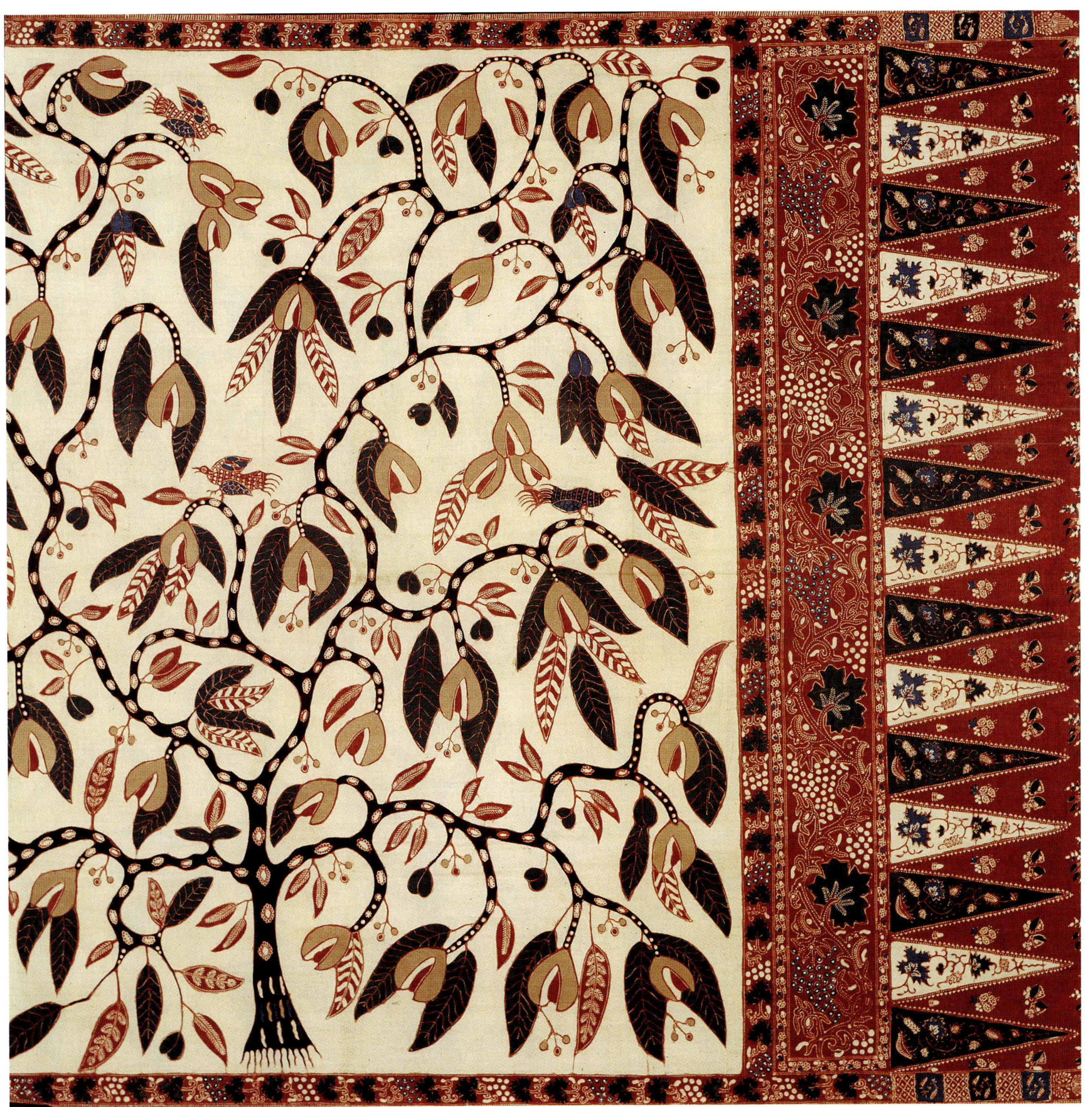

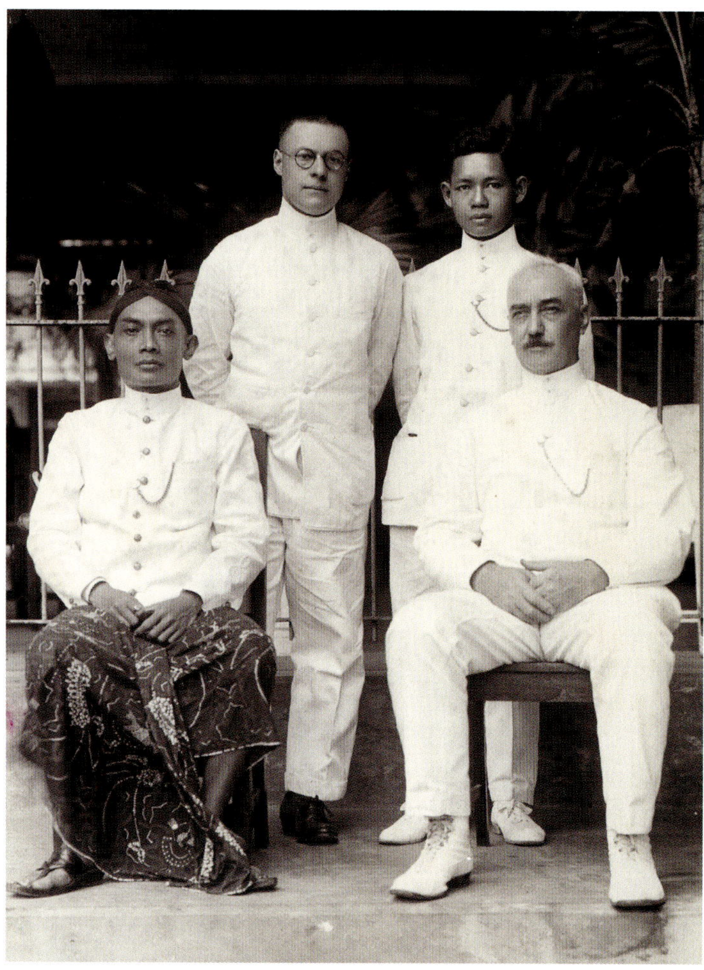

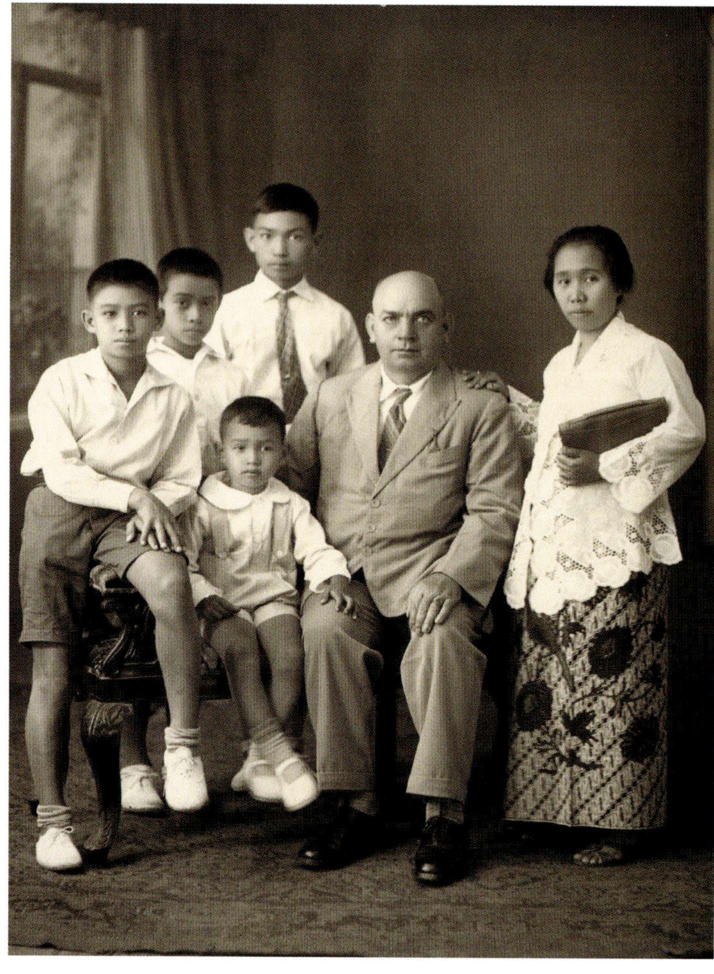

187
Regent of Bentool: Dirdjokoesomo (left) and the government doctors: Reich, Slamat Djojoesodo and Donk, Java
Gelatin silver print
14.8 x 10.2 cm
c. 1920
60017277. Gift: Mr. Lonkhuyzen

188
Studio portrait of an Indische family
Gelatin printing-out paper
17.6 x 12.7 cm
1920-1935
60029839. Through mediation of M.J. Hillerström, 1970s

equal terms. Dress conventions and regulations made social relationships explicit. We see this reflected when the photo collection of the Tropenmuseum is used in the study of the textile collection.
By the end of the 19th century, the Dutch colonial government no longer maintained the dress regulations enacted in the context of VOC rule, with its clear dress distinctions between European and indigenous people. A growing number of Indonesian people (mainly young urban men) adopted Western dress and manners of social interaction. Adopting Western dress and life style was part of the process of inclusion and exclusion in a society organised along ethnic/racial lines of division. Although racism was inherent in colonial society, Western-style Indonesians experienced being treated in a more polite manner. Not all Indonesians approved of the adoption of Western dress, however. Anti-colonialists said that adopting Western dress led to a loss of identity and a slavish adherence to the coloniser's lifestyle.
It comes as no surprise that the Tropenmuseum rarely collected such Western dress, except for some daily wear for civil servants in the colonial administration. Such costumes consisted of white trousers and, depending on the rank, an open jacket with shirt and neck-tie or a *jas tutup*, a closed high-collared white jacket. For formal occasions, white or black trousers were combined with richly gold-embroidered jackets. At gatherings where the Javanese and European cultures interacted, dress and deportment evolved into a mixture of the two, comprising a Western-style jacket, white shirts with a bow-tie or a neck-tie combined with trousers or, for the Javanese men, with a batik *kain* (hip cloth) and a batik head cloth, socks and shoes or mules. The photographs of official occasions, in particular, show these dress conventions.

Meanwhile, women's clothing developed in a different way. Not many Indonesian or Chinese women chose to wear Western dress. Instead, well into the 19th century, European and Eurasian women wore the Indonesian *sarong kebaya* combination (tubular batik skirt with long-sleeved blouse) at home as well as in public. From 1870, women newly arrived from the Netherlands also dressed in *sarong kebaya*, but only in the domestic sphere and in the early morning hours. Many chose a sarong in *batik belanda* style, made in the workshops of Eurasian entrepreneurs on the northern coast of Java in a new style with new colours and new motifs, such as the flower bouquet. By 1890, the *sarong kebaya* gradually was replaced by Western dress and, from the 1920s onwards, the fashions of Paris were followed. Yet the batiks were retained. They were and still are highly valued. As such, many found their way into the collection of the Tropenmuseum. (Fig. 186-188) IVH

Paintings

The collection of Netherlands East Indies paintings and drawings at the Tropenmuseum consists of more than two hundred oil paintings and approximately two thousand drawings and prints. They provide a good style overview of the colonial art of painting, covering a wide range of themes. Some were produced in the style of the so-called *Mooi-Indië-kunst* (Beautiful East Indies art): landscapes, portraits, plantations, festivals and rituals. The subject matter of these paintings are of a conservative nature and were painted in a strongly realistic style with a colourful palette. Some of these *Mooi-Indië-kunst* painters were born and raised in the Netherlands East Indies. Starting in the 1920s, many European and American artists visited the East Indies. As an exotic and untouched archipelago, it exerted a strong attraction, particularly the island of Bali. A certain interaction

189
Rudolf Bonnet at work in his studio on the painting *Aankleden voor de voorstelling*, Ubud, Bali
Photographer: Paul Spies (1904-1963)
Acetate negative.
6 x 6 cm
1950-1958
60030475. Gift: Dr. H. de Roever-Bonnet 1970s

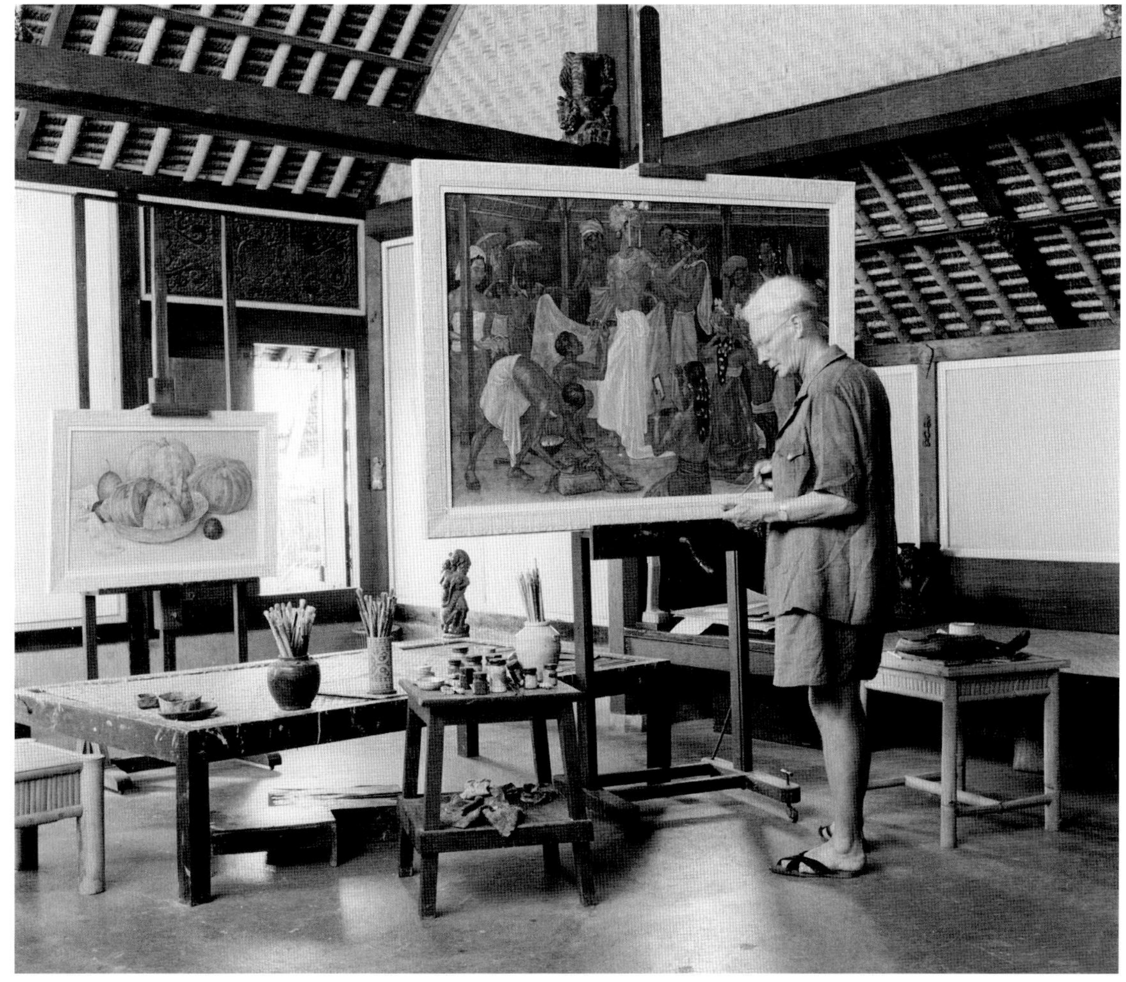

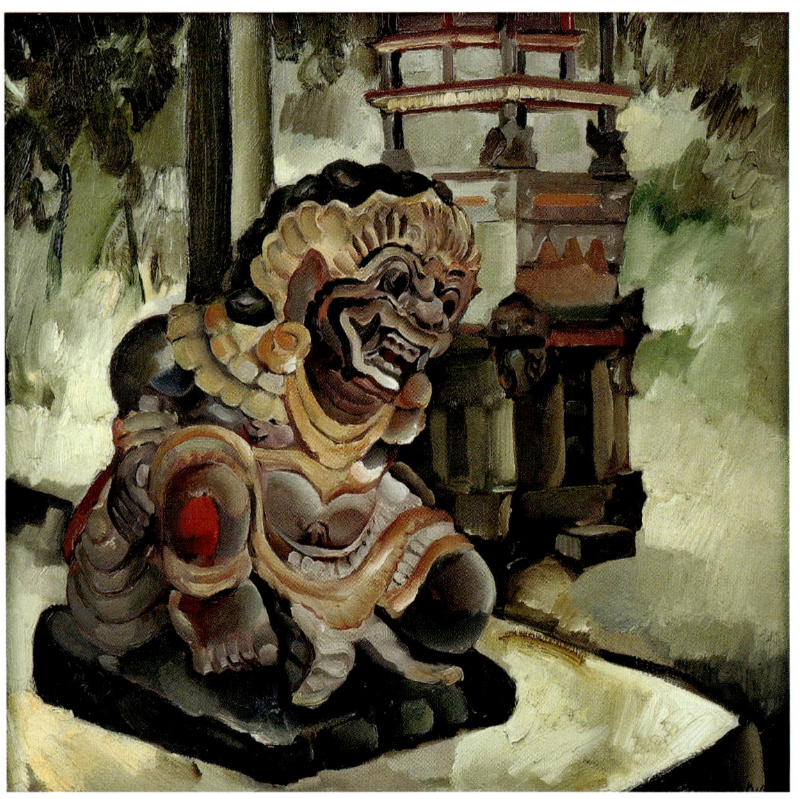

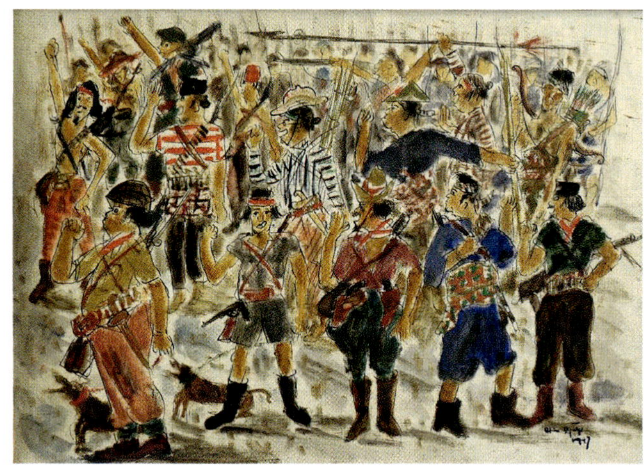

190
A stone temple guard on Bali
A. Breetvelt (1892-1975)
Oil painting
72.5 x 72.5 cm
c. 1930
942-1. Gift: A. Breetvelt, 1935

191
Revolusi
Otto Djaya (1916-2002)
Oil painting
49.2 x 65.7 x 4.1 cm
1947
6230-1. Gift: Stichting Beeldende Kunst, 2005

also arose between the Netherlands and the Netherlands East Indies with respect to themes in the visual arts (such as Javanese dance), technique (batik) and design and architecture. In 1921, the famous Dutch painter Isaac Israëls visited the East Indies and, during a study trip in 1923, the architect H.P. Berlage researched the convergence between the traditional architecture of the Netherlands East Indies (Fig. 103) and contemporary Western architecture.
Next to the painters working in the *Mooi-Indië-kunst* style, a group of East Indies painters, among whom Pieter Ouborg and Dolf Breetvelt, incorporated influences from developments in the art of painting in Europe, although their work continued to be dominated by the romantic image of colonial society. A modern Indonesian art of painting was also born. When one of its founders, S. Sudjojono, called on others at the end of the 1930s to focus greater attention on themes such as working conditions on sugar plantations or the living conditions of farmers, he was virtually ignored by both Indonesian and Indo-Dutch painters.
In the collection of paintings at the Tropenmuseum, the various styles of Indo-Dutch painting are represented, but the emphasis lies on *Mooi-Indië-kunst* paintings. Indonesian painters are represented by five works of the 19th century painter Raden Saleh and by the 20th century work of Agus and Otto Djaya, Abdullah, Affandi, and others. The museum does not possess any works from the 18th century and only one work from the 17th century: the masterly *Gezicht op Batavia (De markt van Batavia)* [View of Batavia (The Market of Batavia)] by Andries Beeckman from around 1656. (Fig. 216) The East Indies paintings of the 19th century are well represented by the work of A. Salm, among others. But the largest part of the collection dates from the 20th century, with work by P. Ouborg, Ch. Sayers, A. Breetvelt, W. Dooyewaard, Cz. Mystkowski and many others. Some of the East Indies paintings were produced by painters that only visited the East Indies, such as J. Poortenaar and I. Israëls, or they were largely produced in the Netherlands, such as the works by L.J. Eland and H. Paulides.
Until recently, the museum considered the paintings as merely a visual source depicting the colonial society and landscape in all its diversity. Today, this art is appreciated in both Indonesia and the Netherlands as a cultural heritage beyond the colonial context. Many works possess a vitality and quality that transcends this context. The Tropenmuseum intends to reinforce this aspect by linking the collection to contemporary developments in the areas of art and design. This will give this historical collection a new frame of reference.[112] (Fig. 189-191) KVB

The library collection

The collection of the KIT library contains a special work. It is a portfolio with gouache paintings of insects and reptiles primarily from Asia. These paintings were once a part of the gallery of the Delft mayor and physician Hendrik d'Acquet (1632-1706). Following D'Acquet's death, his collection was auctioned. In 1931 one of the bindings with paintings was purchased for the 'book collection' of the Koloniaal Instituut. The money for this purchase came in part from Greshoff's Rumphiusfonds.[113]
This is not surprising, since a number of D'Acquet's paintings were used in 1705 for Rumphius' posthumously published *D'Amboinsche Rariteitkamer*. The chemist and botanist Maurits Greshoff (1862-1909) was director of the Koloniaal Museum in Haarlem from 1901 to 1909; he was a great admirer of Rumphius. Greshoff, who died young, left his book collection to the Koloniaal Museum.
Opened in Haarlem in 1871, the museum had a respectable library from the very beginning. It was a library that was primarily focused on the applied natural sciences: raw materials, natural products, agricultural and industrial products – called 'colonial products'. At this early date it was already adding a broad field of subjects to its collection, as can be seen from the printed *Catalogus der boekverzameling* (Catalogue of the Book Collection) from 1908. In this catalogue there is a listing of books on medicine, history and ethnography. And there is a section on 'Travel Stories', for which 'Africa' is one

192
Illustration from Hendrik d'Acquet's *Insecta et animalia coloribus ad vivum picta*, 1708
KIT Library

193
Illustration from Hendrik d'Acquet's *Insecta et animalia coloribus ad vivum picta*, 1708
KIT Library

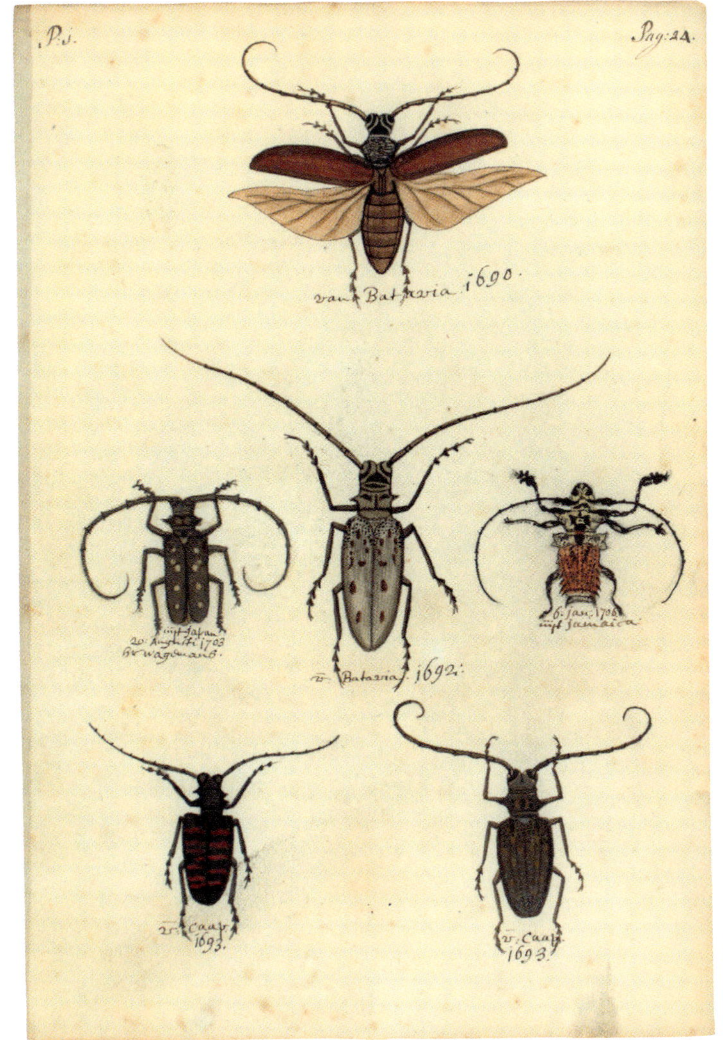

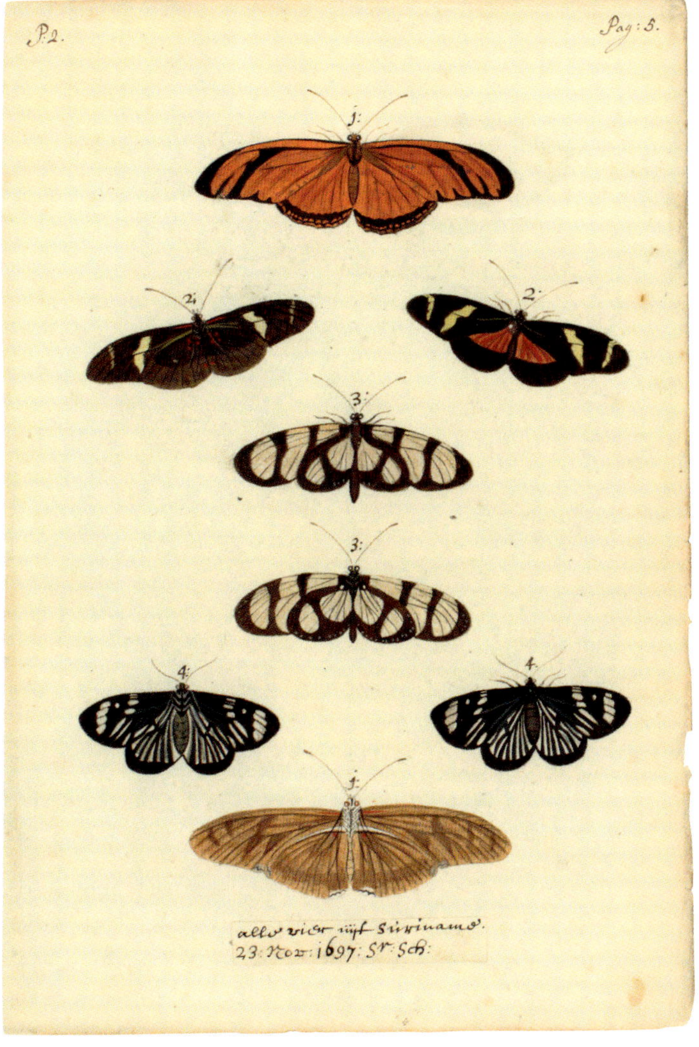

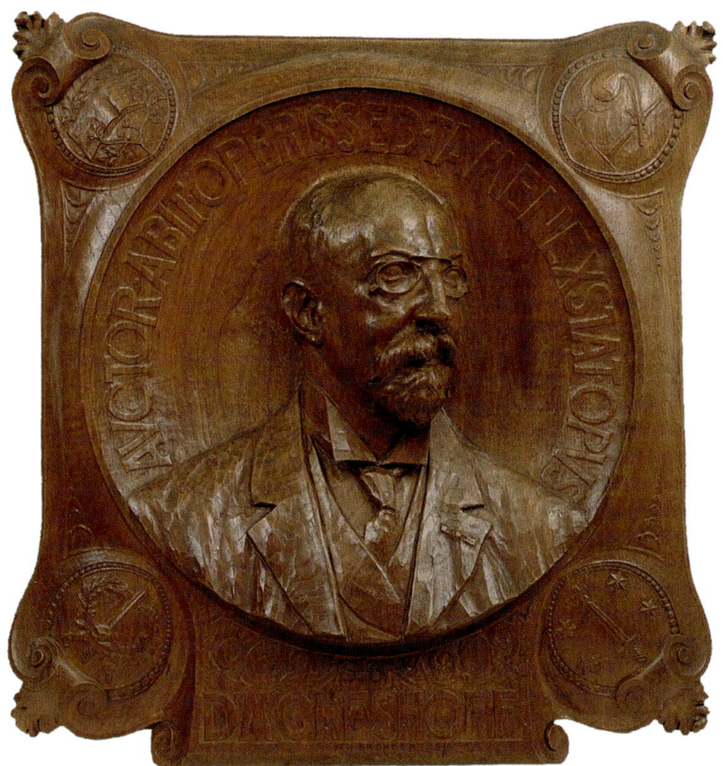

194
Carved relief depicting Dr. M. Greshoff
Jan Bronner
(1881-1972)
Wood
76 x 80 x 17 cm
1911
3401-1646. Gift: KIT Tropische Producten, 1964

of the subsections. When the collection was transferred from Haarlem to Amsterdam in 1917 the endeavour was made to make the library a 'reliable and complete encyclopaedia' in the colonial realm. The library received many publications through donations and exchange, although purchases were also made. At the end of 1923, the collection was transferred from Plantage Middenlaan 15 to the Koloniaal Instituut. Today, the library still endeavours to be an encyclopaedia; its orientation to 'edification' and cooperation has remained intact, although today the library collection pertains to the entire tropics and subtropics and the emphasis has shifted to the social sciences.(Fig. 192, 193, 94) EVD

Weapons

Indonesia was the leading country for *armes blanches* or weapons made of cold steel. Swords, sabres, knives and daggers were found in impressive numbers and varieties. Each population group or region, from Aceh in the far north of Sumatra to the smallest islands of the eastern Moluccas, had its own characteristic weapons.

Although many bloody conflicts were settled by their use, *armes blanches* were not only combat equipment but also prominent symbols of masculinity that underlined the social status of the bearer: the higher the status, the more expensive and extravagant the weapon. In many regions of Indonesia, the weapon and its owner were an inseparable unit and sometimes this unit was protected by amulets or, in Islamic areas, by a proverb from the Koran engraved in the blade of the weapon. The most notorious Indonesian weapon is the *kris* (dagger). By virtue of its design and construction, it not only told something about its owner, it also possessed magical powers that had been introduced by the blacksmith, an artisan who had a nearly sacred status.

The Tropenmuseum has a large collection of Indonesian weapons that, interestingly enough, can seldom be connected with historical persons known by name. One exception is a ceremonial sabre from Sumatra in a brass sheath with a cylindrical handle made from polished, fossilised elephant tusk. This *podang raja*, 'king's sabre' was once owned by Si Singamangaraja XII, the divine king of the Batak people around Lake Toba who was gifted with secret, amazing talents. As discussed before, in 1917 he was shot by a KNIL military policeman after a long

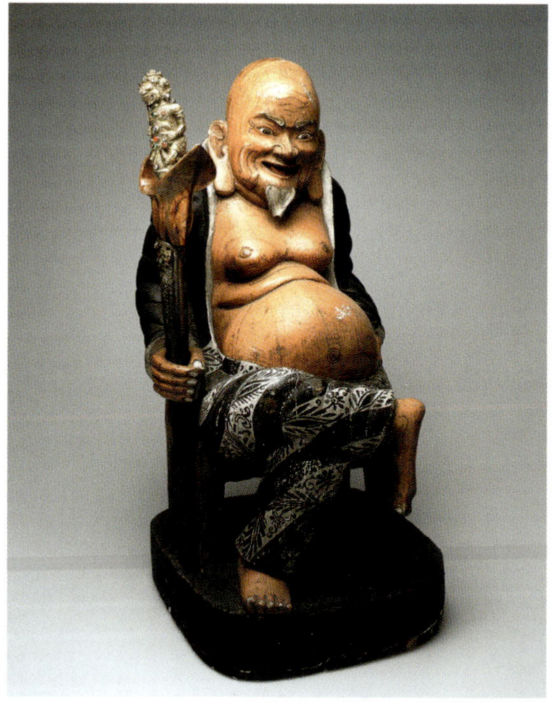

195
Kris holder, depicting a Chinese man
Paint, wood
56 x 25 cm
Lombok.
739-1. Gift: Prof. Dr. J.C. van Eerde, 1932

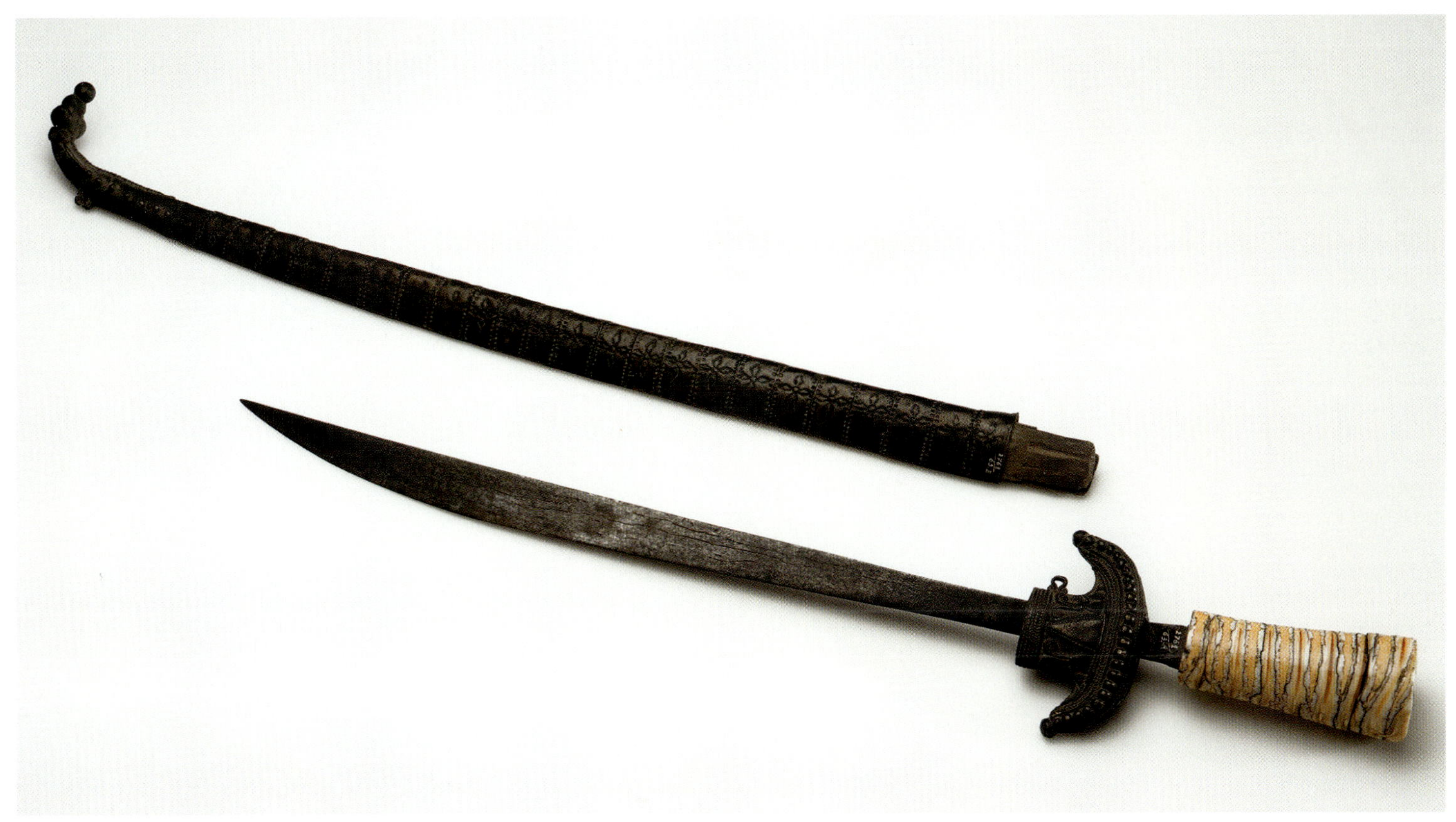

196
Sabre with ivory hilt
podang
Iron, ivory, silver alloy
62 x 5.5 x 5.5 cm
Toba. Tapanuli. North Sumatra
2761-62a. Gift: Vrije
Evangelische Gemeente, 1959

chase in connection with him being at the centre of an armed resistance movement against the Dutch authorities.
The *podang raja* was a gift from Si Singamangaraja to one of his male family members, a minor *raja* (prince) who later had himself baptised by a brother of the Evangelical Congregation. The sabre came into the possession of this missionary community, which donated its collection to the Tropenmuseum in 1959. (Fig. 195-196) [114] DVD

Yogya silver

At the beginning of the 20th century, Dutch attention to Indonesian arts and crafts, which were in danger of disappearing due to the import of inexpensive Western products or due to other forms of Dutch interference, grew as a result of the Ethical Policy. Mrs Mary Agnes van Gesseler Verschuir-Pownall (1882-1968), the wife of the Governor of Yogyakarta, devoted herself to preserving the Yogyakarta arts and crafts during her husband's term as governor (1929-32). She focused primarily on the local silversmith arts and sought new sources of inspiration and new designs for new markets. She had Javanese employees of the Archaeological Department make drawings of Javanese temple reliefs and mosque ornamentation, and also had motifs copied from books of traditional crafts or from traditional Sumatran brass objects.
At her request: the silversmiths of Kota Gede, south-east of Yogyakarta, applied these new motifs – such as foliage and lotus flowers – to European luxury articles: plates, cake boxes, smoking materials and toilet accessories. A large number of these objects she bought for herself. Some of them were sold in the shop of the foundation Pakarjan Ngajogjakarta (Arts and Crafts of Yogyakarta). The foundation was the result of Javanese and European cooperation to stimulate the local applied arts.
After the departure of the Van Gesseler Verschuirs, the art of silversmithing, which was focused on the European market, developed further. The silver-smiths also used other motifs, such as the double peacock and *wayang* (shadow puppet) figures. Europeans were able to afford the relatively inexpensive

197
Dish
Silver alloy
12 x 19.4 x 19.1 cm
Yogyakarta, Java. 1929-1932
6326-1. Purchase: E.W.S. James van Gesseler Verschuir, 2008, with thanks to the BankGiro Loterij 2008, among others

198
P.R.W. van Gesseler Verschuir, his spouse M.A. van Gesseler Verschuir Pownall and their daughter, Bandung
Photographer: Krueger & Austermühle
Gelatin silver print
17.7 x 22.7 cm
1928
60054181
Gift: E.W.S. James van Gesseler Verschuir 2008

199
Design for a dish or basket
Produced for M.A. van Gesseler Verschuir-Pownall
Paper
25 x 24.1 x 0.1 cm
Java. 1929-1932
6316-7
Gift: E.W.S. James van Gesseler Verschuir, 2008

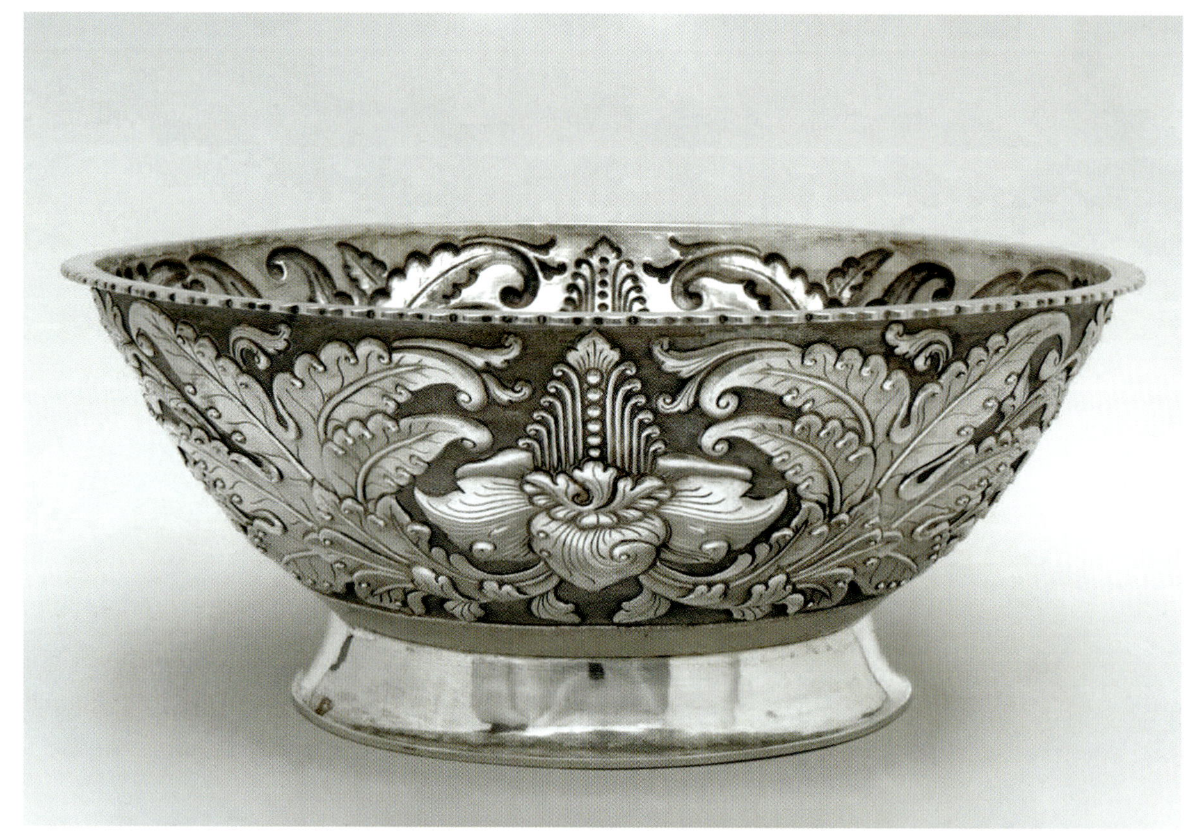

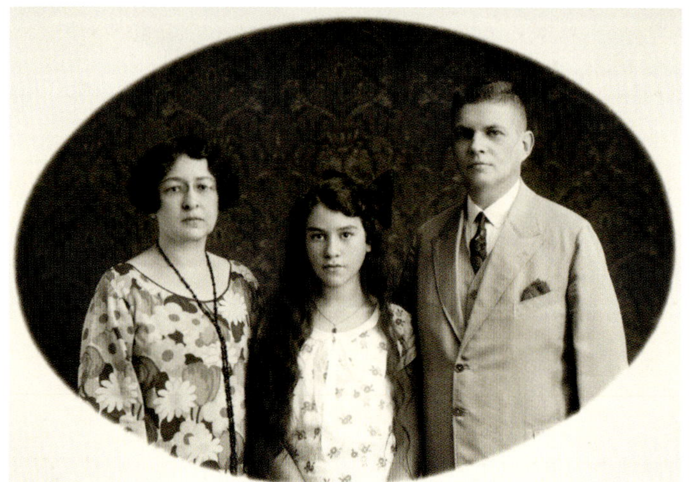

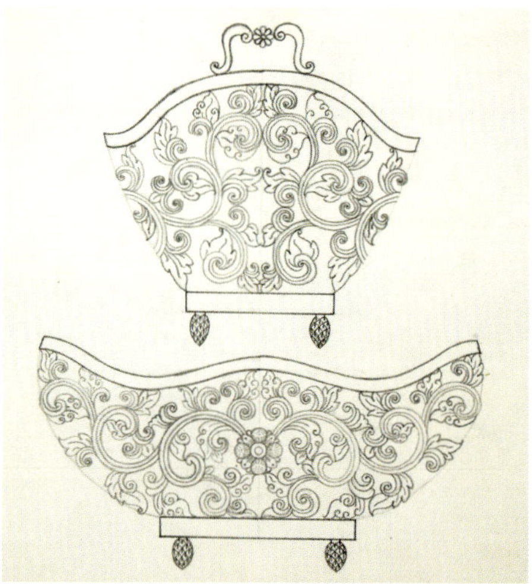

silver and the demand for luxury articles rose sharply. This popular silverware was given the name Yogya silver. It is usually marked with 800 or 900 for the silver content and sometimes with the initials of the silversmith or the workshop. This boom lasted up to the end of the 1950s. In 2008, the daughter of Mrs Van Gesseler Verschuir gave the Tropenmuseum the original photographs and drawings that her mother had made. By way of purchases, twenty objects from her private collection have been obtained. This supplements the existing Yogya silver collection from the period after 1932. So the Tropenmuseum now possesses one of the most significant public collections of Yogya silver in the world. (Fig. 197-199) PW

Models and miniatures

The Netherlands East Indies was far away, large and culturally diverse. One of the ways to make this complex society understandable to a larger public in the mother country was to organise exhibitions. Models and miniatures were an important means of exhibition. These objects, made to scale, depicted recognisable scenes from daily life. It were primarily Indonesian artisans who were commissioned by the coloniser to depict their fellow Indonesians for an overseas public they did not know. Traditional costumes, social and political authorities, festivals and rituals, as well as proas, houses and household effects, mosques, bridges and railways – everything was meticulously copied. The artisans thus contributed to the proud self-image of the Netherlands as a great power and progressive coloniser. At the same time, the models created an often static picture of the native society, presented in a clearly directed and regulated manner. This manner of presentation and visualisation was common and popular in the period between 1860 and 1940.
The collection of models and miniatures at the Tropenmuseum consists of more than a thousand objects. The oldest date from the Internationale Koloniale en Uitvoerhandeltentoonstelling (International Colonial and Export Trade Exhibition) that was held in 1883 on the now Museum Square in Amsterdam. There the public was able to obtain an impression of the overseas part of the kingdom by means of this illustrative and educational material. At subsequent world fairs in which the Koloniaal Instituut cooperated, such as the Paris World Fairs of 1900 and 1931, and at the exhibitions in the museum, full use was made of the models and miniatures. Following decolonisation and the reorientation of the Tropenmuseum in the 1950s, the fragile colonial models and miniatures lost their value as exhibits. Little if any significance was attributed to them. At best cases, they ended up in the depots. At worst, they were de-accessioned altogether.
At the beginning of the 21st century, after sixty years, they were taken out of obscurity. With the passing of time, attention for the collection and presentation history grew and the old models and miniatures took on new significance as former points of contact for the colonisers with Indonesian artisans. At the exhibition 'The Netherlands East Indies, a colonial history' they have become storytellers again. They tell a tale about the inter-play between presentation and self-presentation. (Fig. 200-07) JVD

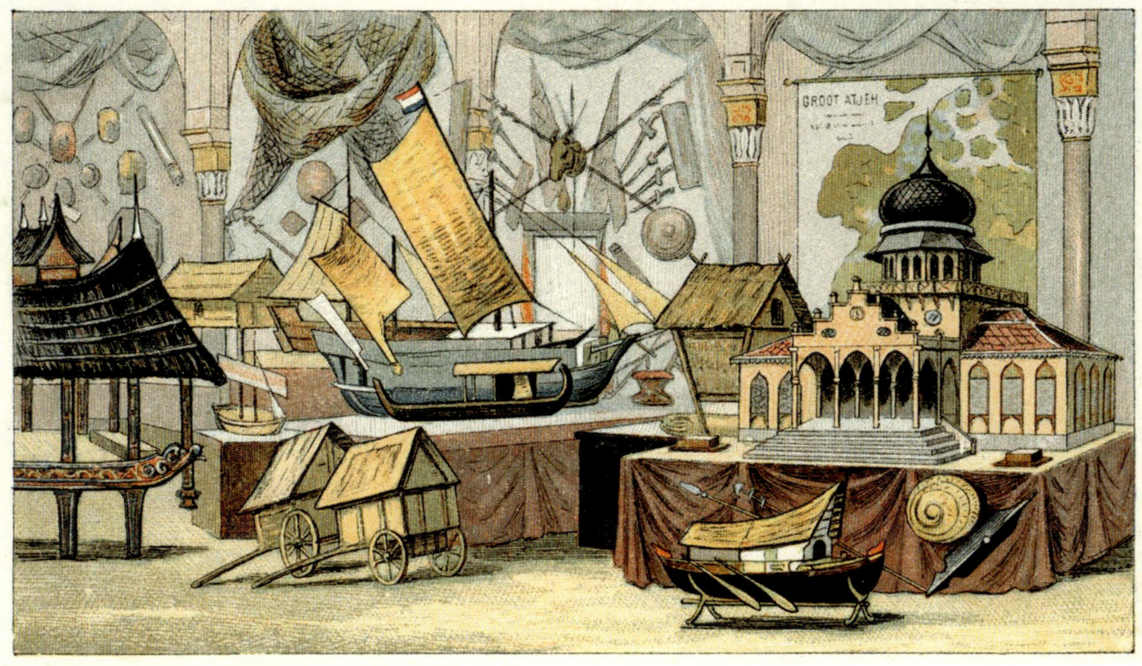

200
Models from the Dutch colonies at the International, Colonial and Export Trade Exhibition, Amsterdam
Litho
11.7 x 18.2 cm
1883
60050478. Gift: N. Kaastra, 2006

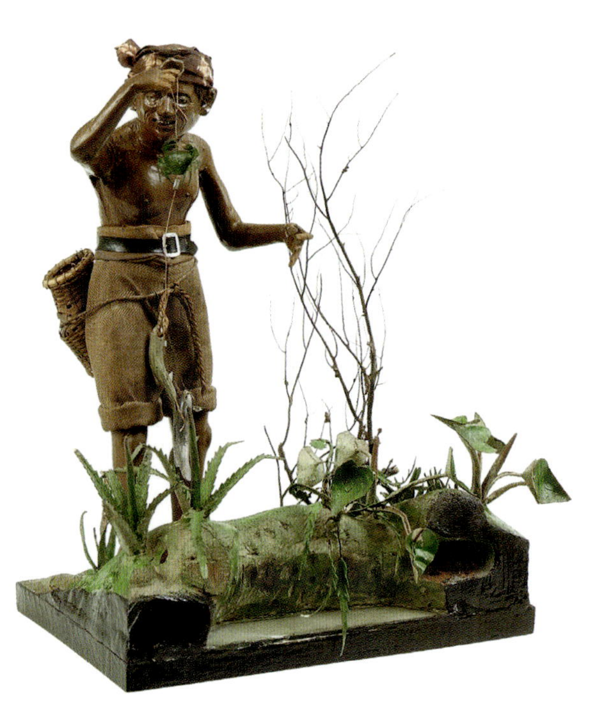

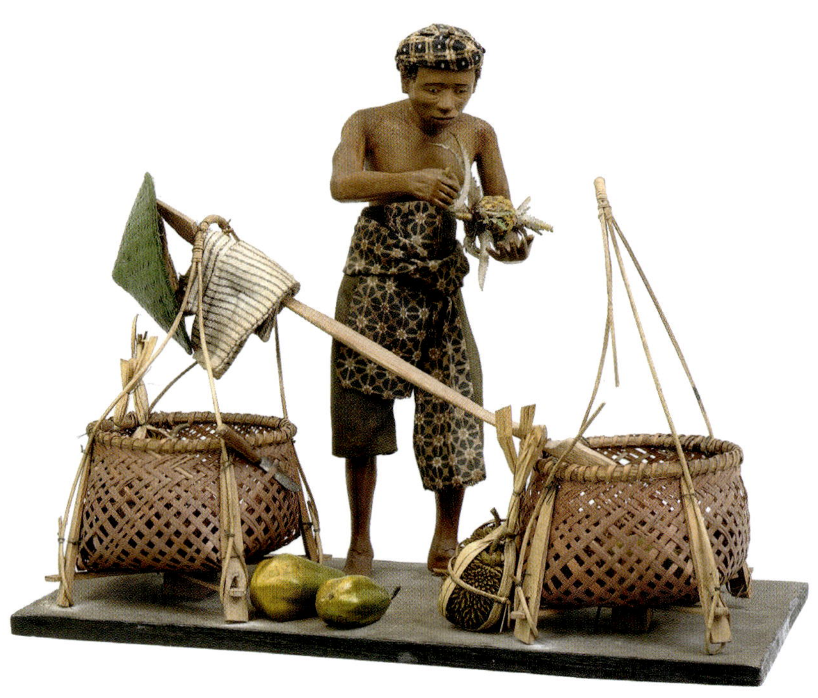

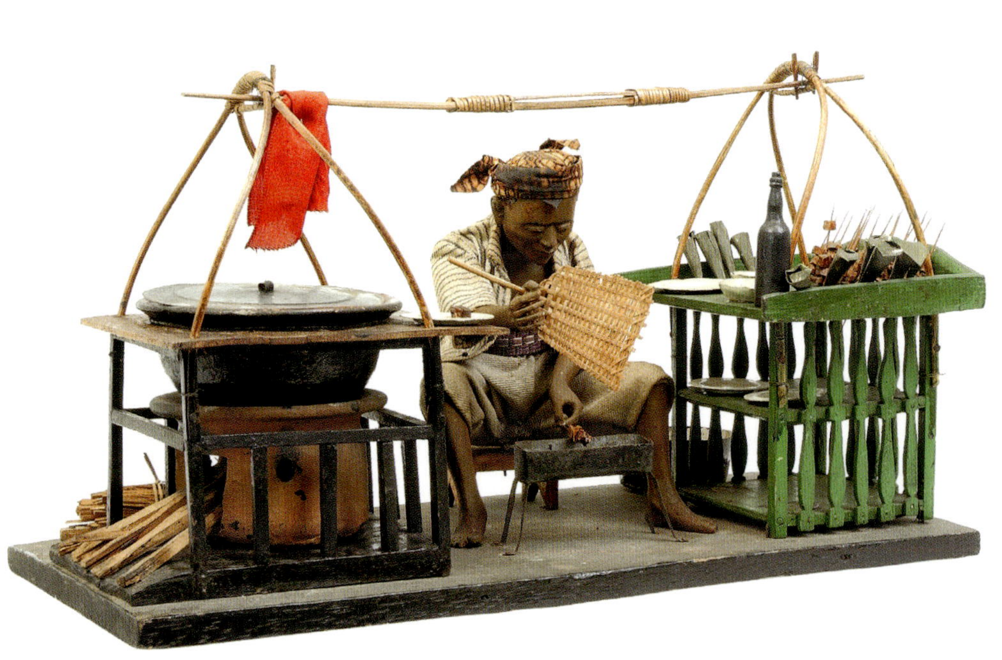

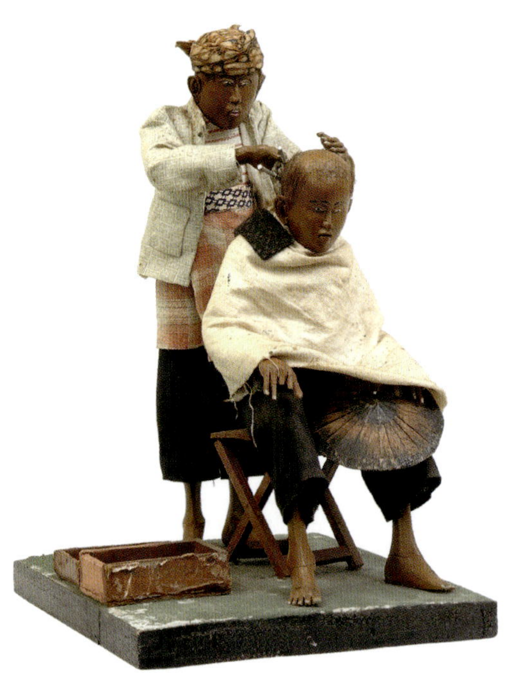

Left page, left to right
201
Model of a fisherman
Paint, wood, cotton
15 x 20 cm
Madiun, East Java
Early 20th century
887-5. Gift: J.G. Sluyp, 1934

202
Model of a fruit seller
Paint, wood, cotton
25.5 x 15.5 x 32 cm
Madiun, East Java
Early 20th century
887-4. On loan J.G. Sluyp, 1934

203
Model of a sate seller
Paint, wood, cotton
16.2 x 35.5 x 16.5 cm
Madiun, East Java.
Early 20th century
887-2. On loan:
J.G. Sluyp, 1934

204
Model of barber
Paint, wood, cotton
25 x 15 x 18 cm
Java. Early 20th century
3391-3. Gift: KIT Tropical Products, 1964

Right page, left to right
205
Model of portable restaurant
Paint, wood, cotton
20 x 30.5 x 24.5 cm
Java
3391-5. Gift: KIT Tropical Products, 1964

206
Model of a bird seller
Metal, wood, cotton
23 x 15 x 14 cm
Madiun, East Java.
Early 20th century
887-7. On loan:
J.G. Sluyp, 1934

207
Model of a watch-house with two guards
Cotton, wood, bamboo
30.8 x 23.5 x 26.5 cm
Madiun, East Java.
Early 20th century
887-1. On loan:
J.G. Sluyp, 1934

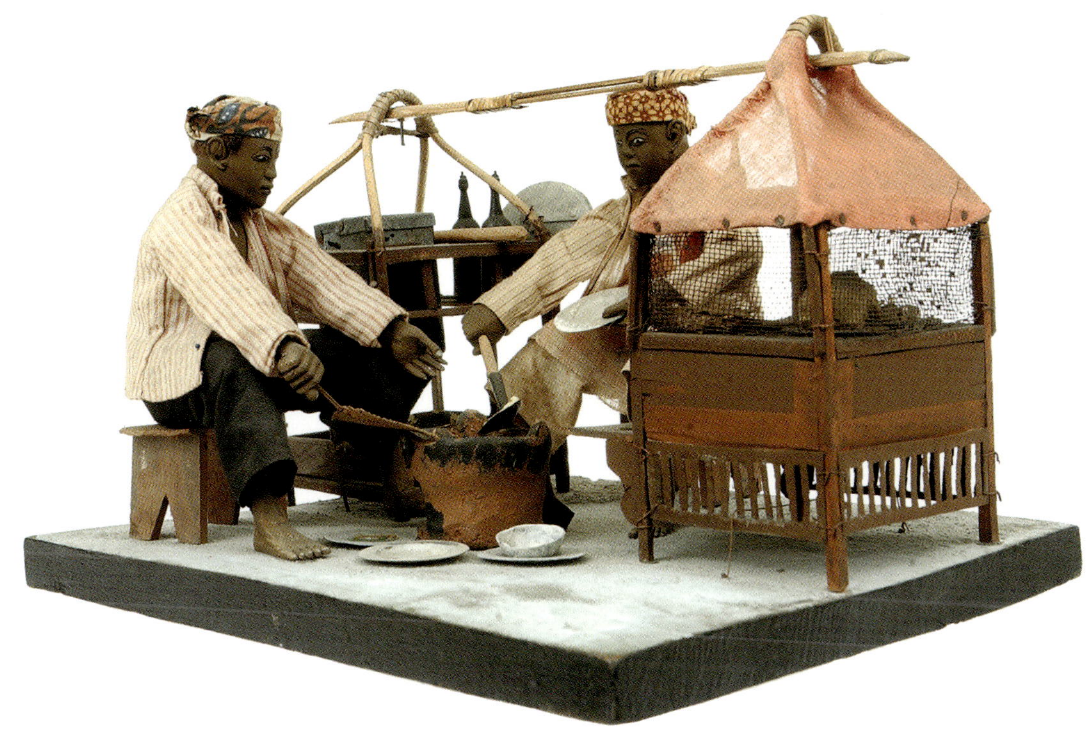

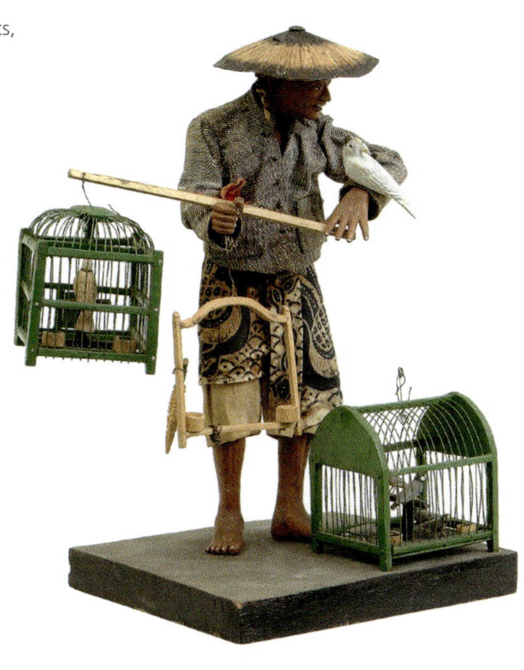

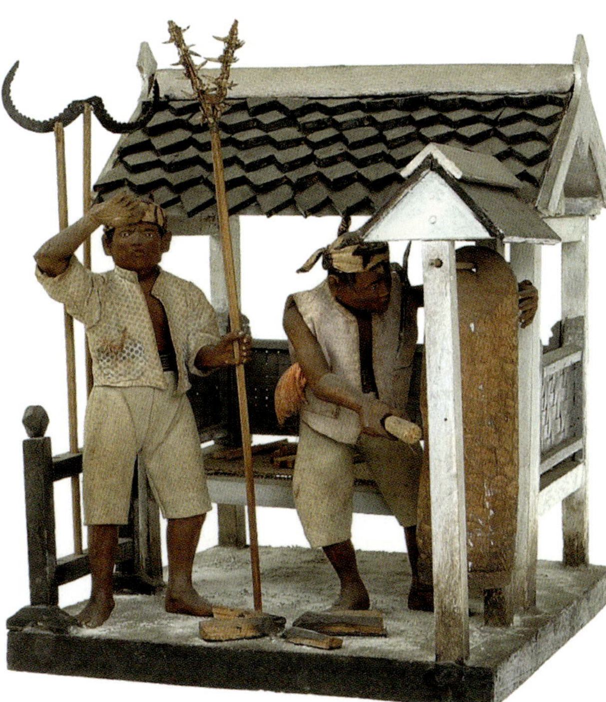

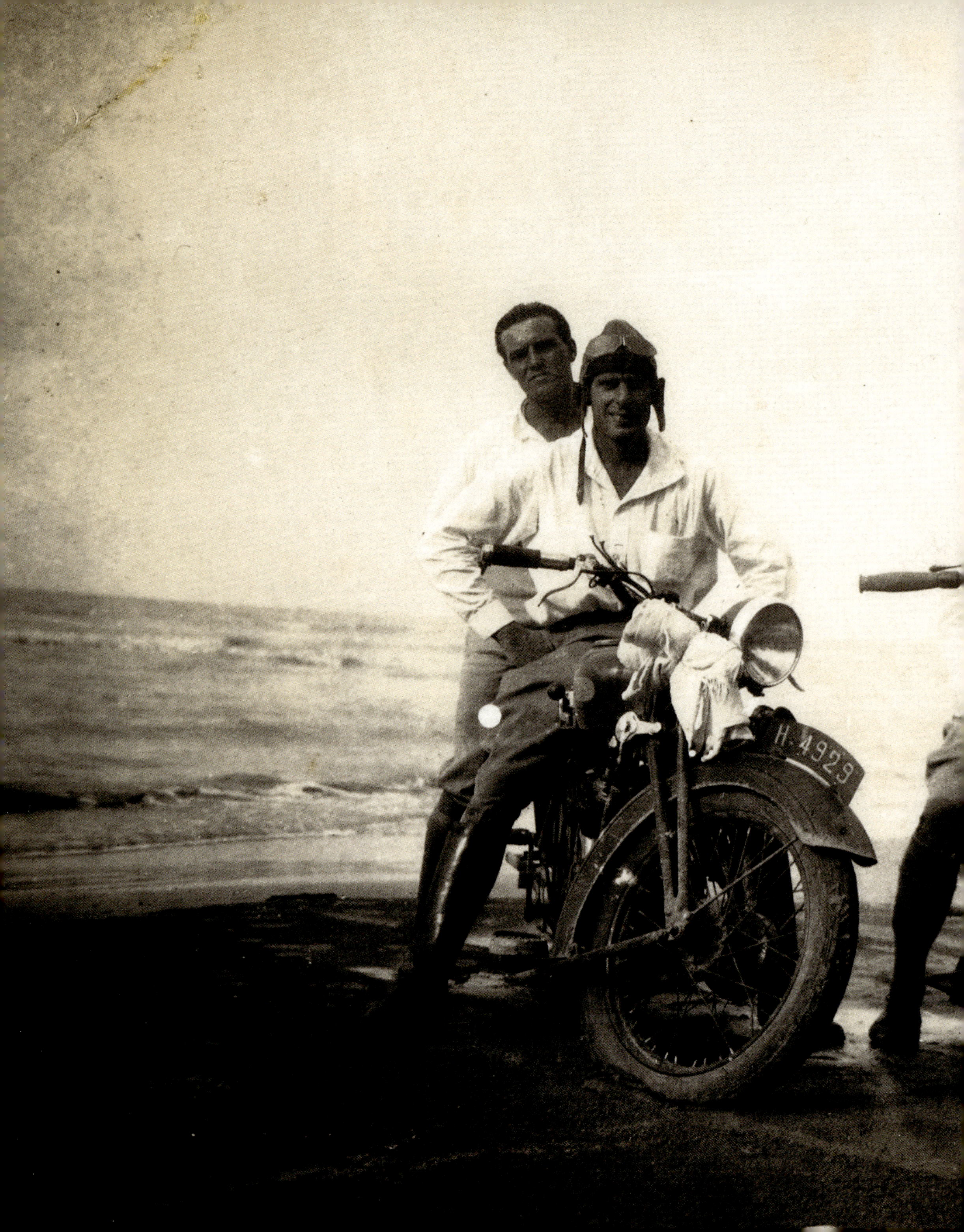
H-4929

COLONIAL IMAGINATION AND REFLECTION

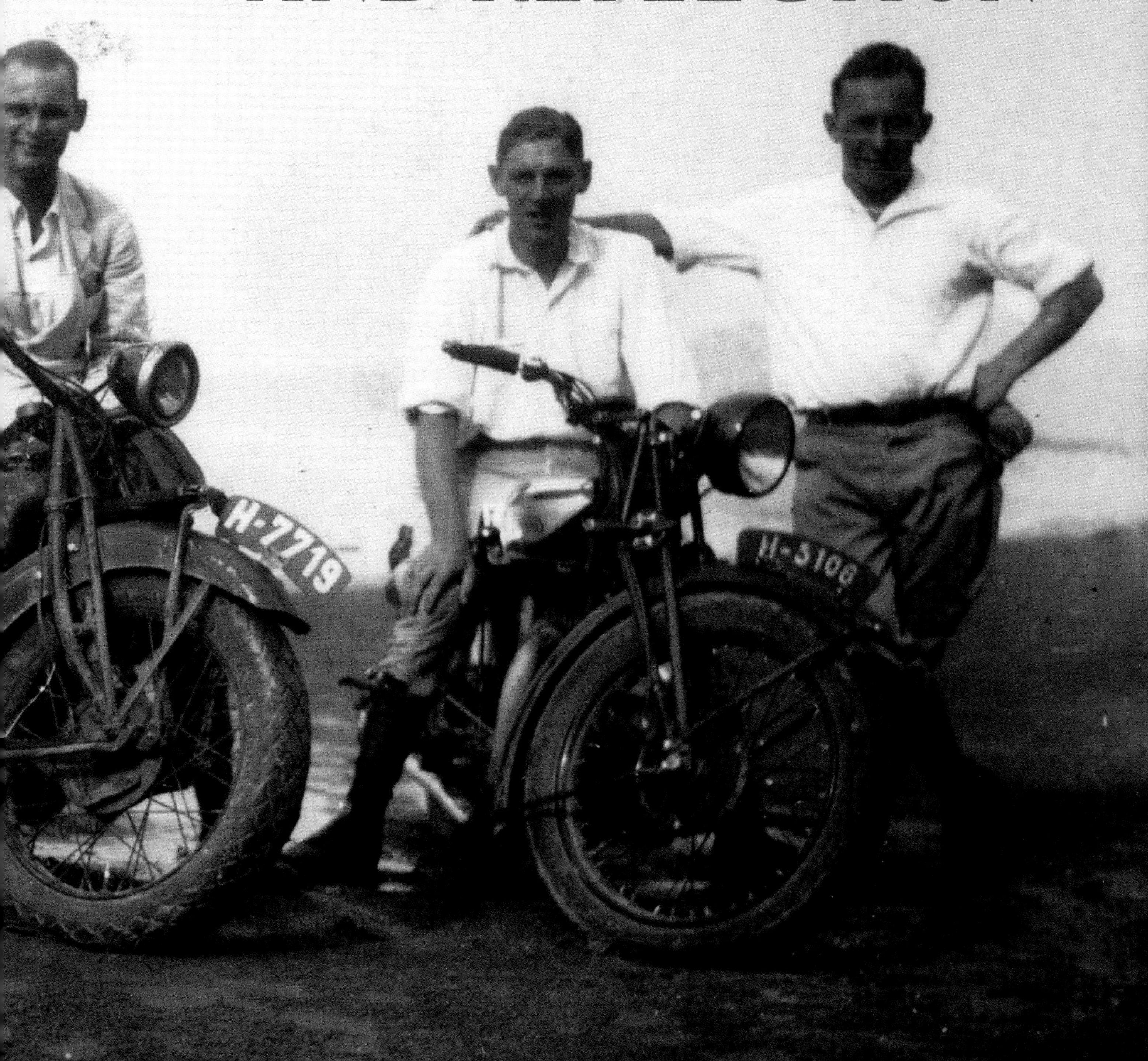

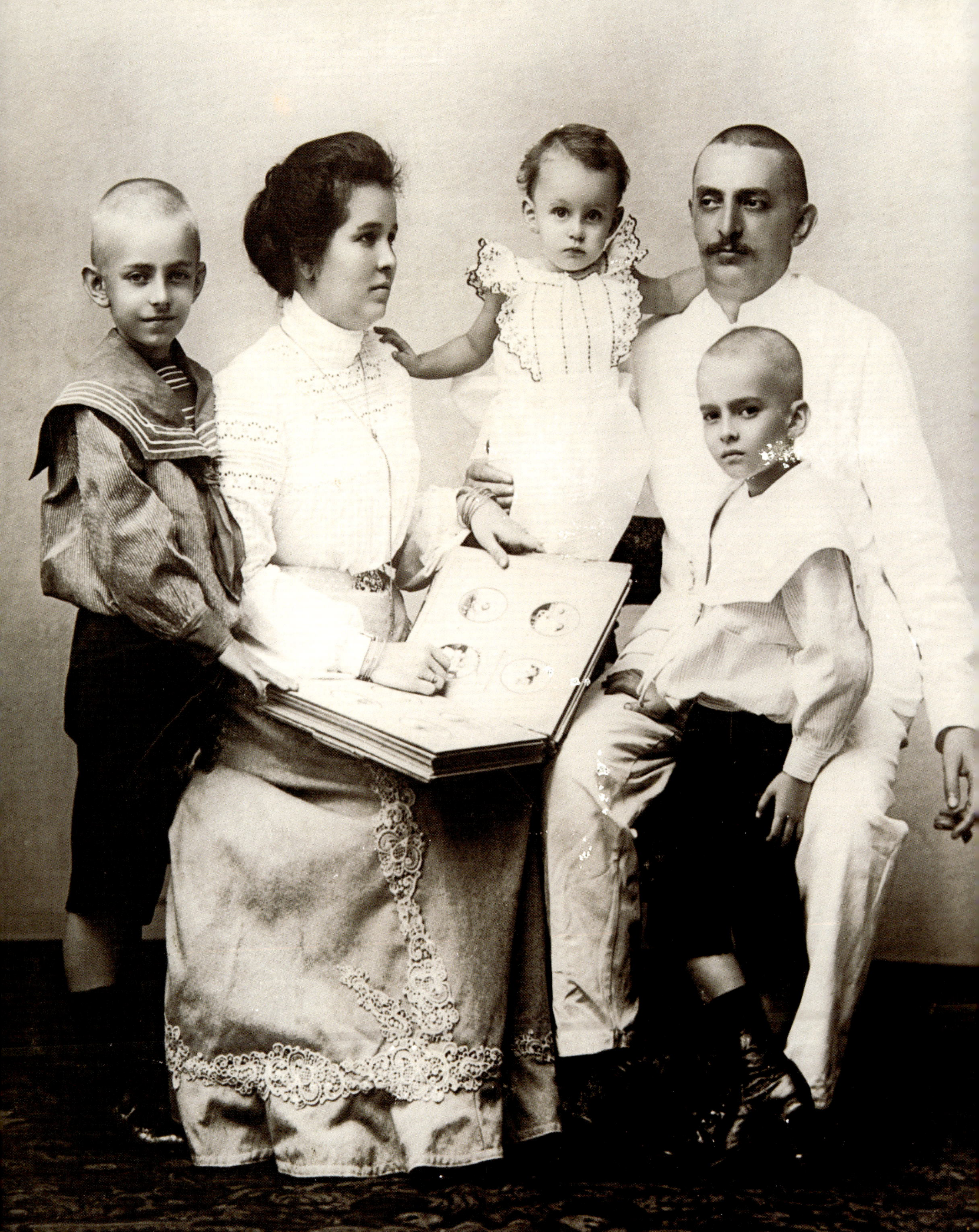

COLLECTIVE MEMORY
The interactions between literature, museums, cinema and photography

PAMELA PATTYNAMA

Introduction

The Tropenmuseum is a treasure house of stories and memories. Each of its collected objects tells its own story and embodies memories which afford us a glance into the past. Although museum objects may be considered static and solid, the stories they convey may be transformed over time according to the changing interests and ambitions of the Tropenmuseum. By organising collections in new and unorthodox ways museums can correct or alter dated stories or changed meanings. When aspects other than the customary ones are allowed to dominate, different stories will be told. The history of the Tropenmuseum shows a number of such processes of turning the lens and introducing 'other' perspectives on the past. What was collected during colonial times has, for example, long been dominated by the Dutch view of the past: the coloniser determined what history would be. Yet, in this postcolonial era voices from the locations where the museum objects originated from are increasingly being heard in the metropole. Interestingly, it is because of their similar capability to transform stories, that museums can be compared to literature, films and even to photography. Many of the postcolonial stories that are passed on via literature, museums, or the cinema are narratives that interact with each other and are in this way revised. Together they contribute to the Dutch cultural heritage and form a postcolonial 'collective memory' about the Dutch colonial past. This collective memory consists of stories that overlap and reinforce each other, but also clash and contradict one another. It is this continuously changing collective memory which influences our perception of the colonial past. In the following I would like to submit three examples to illustrate these postcolonial interactions of memory processes.

<< See Fig. 221

208
Studio portrait of the Spruyt-Laurens family, Buitenzorg, Java
c. 1902
Gelatin printing-out paper
27.1 x 22 cm
60027293
Gift: E.G. Spruyt

Eastward Bound!

In one of the permanent expositions of 'Eastward Bound!' in the Tropenmuseum a special section exhibits wax figures in 'natural settings'. Museums have, of course, a long tradition of creating imitations of human figures, often stereotypes, to bring unknown peoples and strange situations to the attention of the astonished public. The figures in the 'Eastward Bound!' exhibition continue in this tradition; they represent a past that is unknown to many of today's museum visitors. Yet, as these figures were made slightly different, they seem to be deliberately made un-lifelike. The fact that they are not 'real' is foregrounded by technical means. This makes it look as if they invite the visitors of the museum to consider the meaning of colonial 'reality'.

One of these life-size figures, labelled Toean Anwar, is an eye-catching object. (Fig. 209) Toean Anwar first appeared as a character, called Toewan Anwar (Mr Anwar), in the 1958 short novel *De raadsman* by H.J. Friedericy (1900-62). Like much literature set in the Netherlands East Indies, *De raadsman* is autobiographical fiction. Friedericy was a civil servant in the colonial administration of the Netherlands East Indies during the first half of the 20th century and it is this era that inspired his story. *De raadsman* is about the close collaboration between Toewan Anwar, an elderly native civil servant working for the colonial administration, and a young Dutch assistant-resident. The Dutchman recalls how he and Toewan Anwar came to appreciate one another, primarily because he adopted a modest, even humble approach to the local man whom he considers to be a fatherly mentor and confidant:

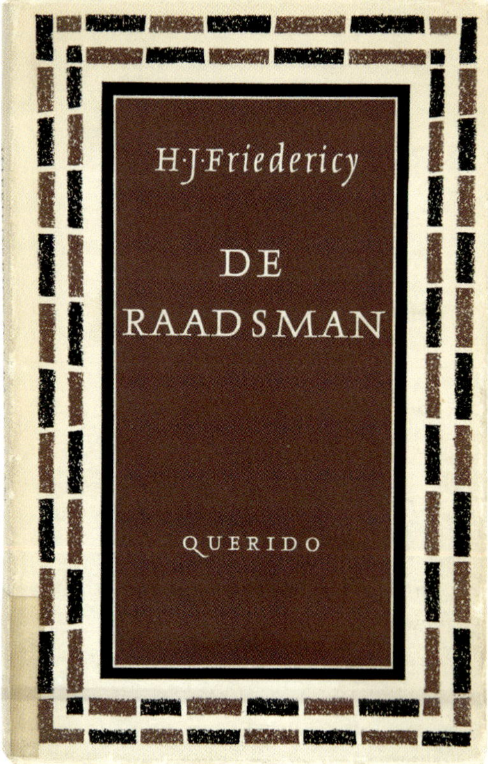

209
Book cover of *De Raadsman*
Published by Querido, Amsterdam, 1958

'Look – I am young; you are older and very experienced. Although I was appointed as your superior, will you please help me wherever you can? Would you be my teacher whenever possible? I am willing to be your pupil.' [translation by the author]

At the end of the novel, after Indonesian independence has been won and Toewan Anwar is long dead, the former assistant-resident has a conversation with two young Indonesian students. The name of an Indonesian minister, Moesa Anwar, is mentioned. 'His father', says the former assistant-resident, 'was the best East Indies civil servant I have ever known.' The students, however, see things very differently and mercilessly criticise Toewan Anwar: 'I beg your pardon, Sir… but in our view Moesa's father was a collaborator and a sell-out who did great harm to our country.'

Even though this conversation may suggest otherwise, Toewan Anwar is a fictional character, an amalgam of two people the author used to know. The Toean Anwar figure displayed in the Tropenmuseum is based on this literary character and is therefore a double fictionalisation. What makes Toean Anwar even more ambiguous is that, just as the figures positioned around him, he has a transparent limb that immediately draws one's attention. His right hand is luminous. It is a hand that both surprises and confuses the onlooker: is Toean Anwar supposed to be a 'real' historical person, a character from a fictional story or a replica, such as the almost human androids that we know from science-fiction movies? Does he stand for the colonial civil servant or does he represent the postcolonial memory of the Indonesian student? In other words, does he depict a fatherly mentor or a collaborator? These questions cannot be answered with certainty one way or the other. The answers will have to come from the onlookers in the museum. Their view of the colonial past will determine what they 'see' when looking at Toean Anwar. What is clear is that the Toean Anwar in the Tropenmuseum retells a story blurring the line between fiction and reality even more than Friedericy did. This makes him a part of our postcolonial collective memory.

TOEAN ('MISTER') ANWAR (C. 1880–1948)

He was the son of a former prince in South-west Sulawesi. After several years in primary school, his father brought him to the office of the Dutch colonial administration and asked them to 'educate' him. The type of education was not stipulated.
From being a jack-of-all-trades, he became an assistant writer. He moved from being an assistant writer to the position of writer, then from writer to administrative assistant: 'Toean Assistèn'. Finally he became an administrative assistant first class in the service of the Dutch government. He was a man of high standing.
Toean Anwar is included in the exhibition 'The Netherlands East Indies' as the archetypical Indonesian civil servant working for the domestic colonial administration. The person of Toean Anwar is based on the short novel *De raadsman* by H.J. Friedericy (1958). JDJ

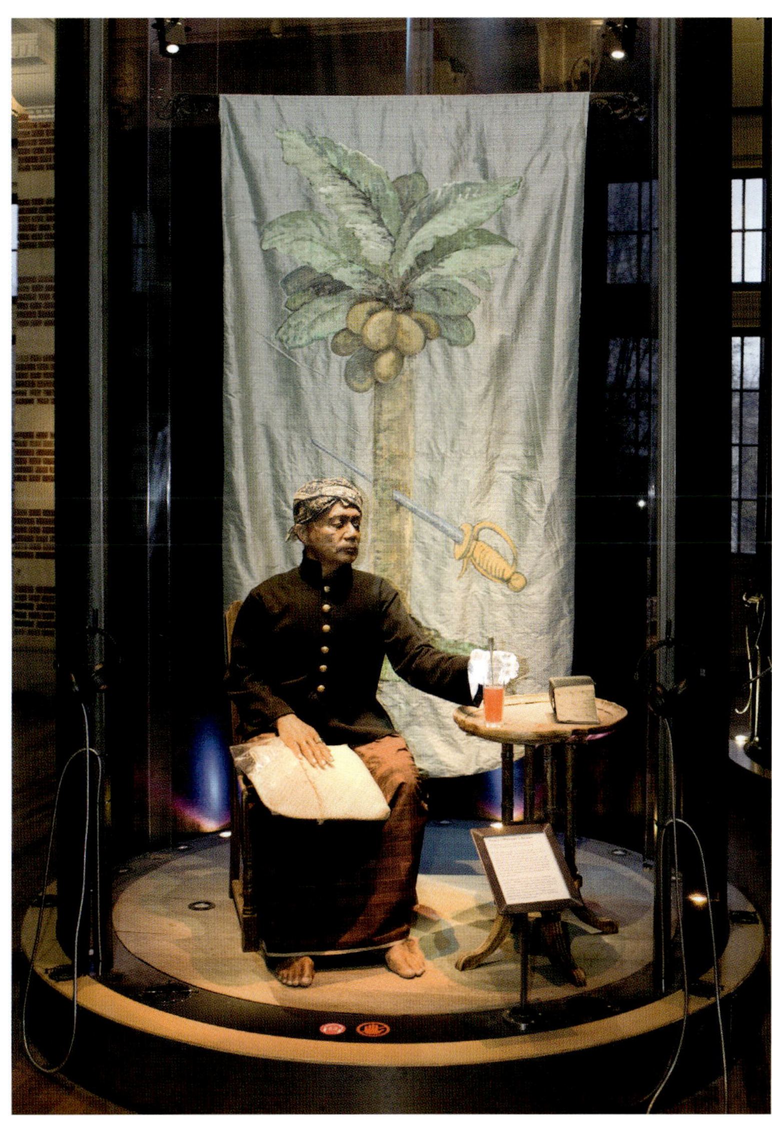

Mixed culture of the Netherlands East Indies

At least three other figures that are on display in the 'Eastward Bound!' exhibition also represent ambiguous images of the colonial past: Himpies, Rumphius and Sayers.
Just like Anwar, Himpies has stepped from the pages of fiction. He is the charismatic son of Felicia, the central character in Maria Dermoût's novel *De tienduizend dingen* (1955). In the novel he dies from a poisonous arrow shot by a *Bergalfoer*, a native inhabitant of the Arafura islands where Himpies patrols with the Dutch Colonial Army at the beginning of the 20th century. The museum figure of Himpies encapsulates the shocking moment during which the lethal arrow flies through the air. Maria Dermoût's fictional Himpies is a reference to an even older phase of the colonial past. Because he had a small collection of shells and other curiosities as a young boy and grew up in a beautiful Moluccan

garden he is an echo of a famous naturalist, the German-born Georg Everhard (or Georgius Everhardus) Rumphius (1626-1702).

Upon entering the exhibition from the east side visitors had already met this legend when they found themselves surrounded by an impressive collection of curiosities. The wax figure of Rumphius is seated behind a desk. His fame was established by the beautiful way in which he described the Moluccan Islands and the submerged sea gardens surrounding them, despite his blindness in old-age. In two amazing books, *d'Amboinsche Rariteitkamer* (1705) and *Het Amboinsche Kruidboek* (1741), he named and brought to life the creatures he had seen so that even the most unsightly jellyfish lives on in our memory. This naturalist appears as 'Mr Rumphius' in Dermoût's *De tienduizend dingen*; it is however, specifically his spirit that inspires her stories as this quote illustrates: 'Still, it seems that in these gardens something has remained of days long vanished, of images from the distant past.' Through the imaginary world Maria Dermoût has inscribed in the Dutch cultural heritage, both the fictional Himpies and Rumphius who was a real person, have become part of our collective memory. She created and recreated them as a series of memories of memories.

A few yards further in the exhibition Charles Sayers (1901-43) sits on his motor bike, handsome, perspiring in the tropical heat. Born and raised in the colony the young man is portrayed as the epitome of the Indo-Dutch macho man. As one of the most important representatives of East Indies art, Sayers brought together European and Asian influences in his art. Although Himpies is 'merely' a literary character, both he and the real-life Sayers were members of the Indo-Dutch population in the Netherlands East Indies, the people of mixed descend who formed the majority of the European colonial society in the former colony. On display in the Tropenmuseum, Himpies and Sayers remind us that such a group of people existed, even though this historical fact is often 'forgotten' in stories told about the colonial era.

Each of the figures on display in the 'Eastward Bound!' exhibition illuminates the complexity of the colonial past, both individually and together. Himpies and Sayers point emphatically to the often forgotten mixed culture of peoples in the Netherlands East Indies. The Dutch civil servant Toean Anwar has transgressed the colonial boundaries between indigenous and European people and reminds us of racial segregation. The German naturalist Rumphius who made the Moluccans his 'home' tells a narrative of displacement and shifting identity. Together they demonstrate that the past is never final, that although official history might for decades be told as a single story, history contains many, often clashing stories. Recently, the Tropenmuseum has shown that, as time moves on, other stories keep coming up. Sacred cows of one era are slaughtered in the next. Population groups who were marginalised in the past take centre stage in a subsequent era. Due to shifting interests and questions, the past is continually given a different meaning. Interestingly, previous marks and old stories do not, however, disappear entirely from our memory.

Nostalgie tropique

The volume *Met andere ogen* (1998) is a recent example of how old stories live on. *Met andere ogen* is a collection of stories written by friends of Rob Nieuwenhuys (1908-99), renowned doyen of East Indies literature. The stories written by Nieuwenhuys' friends are based on his four books of melancholic, annotated photographs (1961-88) of European life in the East Indies. These books in which the decline of old East Indies families plays a large role have had a large impact on the collective memory about the colony. The photographs look like authentic 'documents', but as a collection they exude an atmosphere of what Nieuwenhuys labelled as *nostalgie tropique* (nostalgia for the tropics). His choice of sepia family photographs and his evocative tales have created an East Indies as a world lost forever. This mythical world never really existed. Etched into our collective memory, it is nevertheless this nostalgic colony, which many people now fondly recall and yearn for. (Fig. 210, 211) *Met andere ogen* illustrates how Nieuwenhuys' memories impact on the memories of others. Confronted with his selection of photographs, his friends are occasionally carried away by their own memories; they sometimes tell stories that have nothing to do with what appears in the photographs. Even more intriguing is that the pictures remind some friends of an East Indies they have never ever personally experienced. It is Nieuwenhuys' mythical crea-

GEORG EVERHARD RUMPHIUS – RESEARCHER (1627–1702)

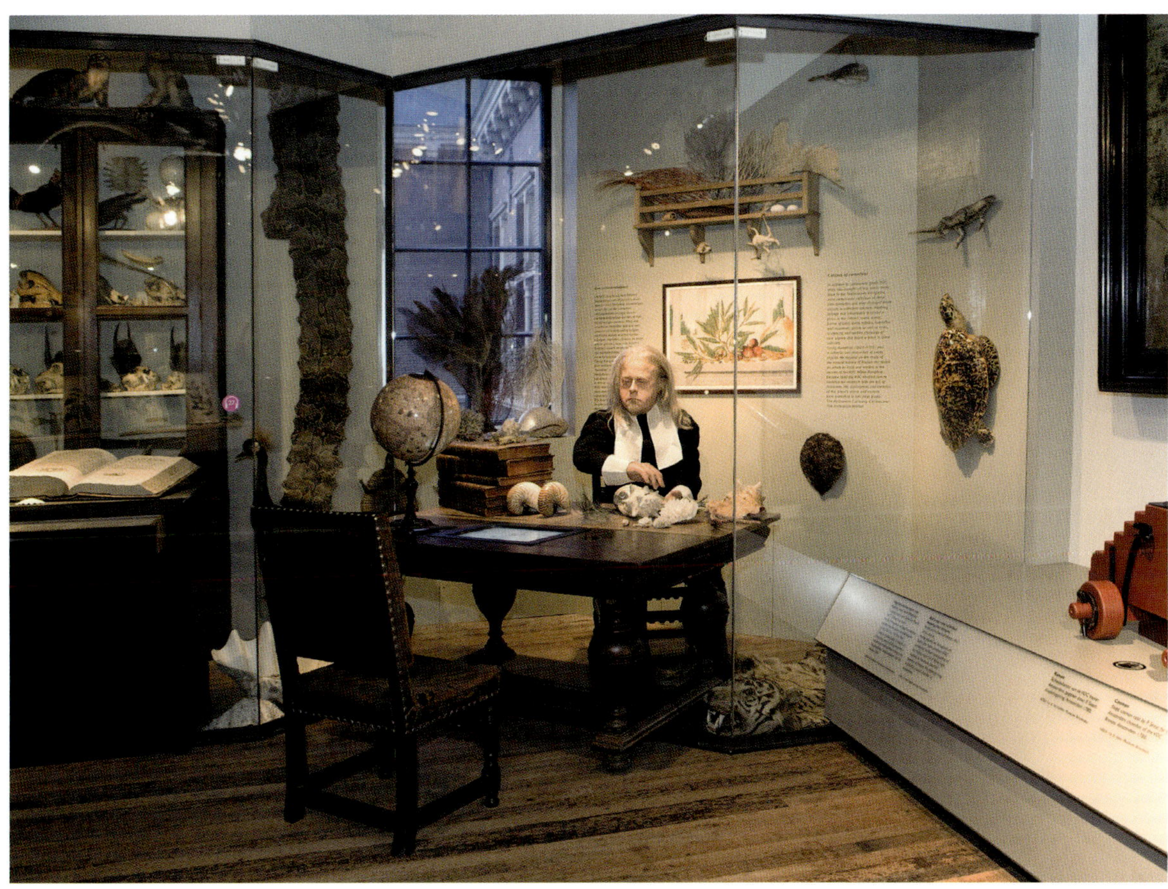

In 1652 he entered the service of the Verenigde Oostindische Compagnie (VOC) and was stationed on Ambon. There he became fascinated by the natural environment; he began to make a systematic and detailed log of the plants and animals he found on the island. He suffered misfortune in 1670. As a result of cataract, Rumphius became completely blind. From that moment on, he dictated his writings to his son Paulus, who was also an excellent illustrator. In 1674 Rumphius suffered grave misfortune yet again: during a massive earthquake, he lost his wife and youngest daughter. The VOC recognised the importance of his studies by placing a clerk and assistant at his disposal. But the Company did not allow him to publish his important research. So Rumphius made use of his international contacts to get around this publishing ban. He sent his detailed notes on molluscs and crustaceans in the waters around Ambon to the Delft mayor and collector Hendrik d'Acquet. D'Acquet made sure that Rumphius' findings were published after his death under the title of *d'Amboinsche Rariteitkamer* in 1705. The much more comprehensive *Het Amboinsche Kruidboek* was published between 1741 and 1752 in six volumes with nearly 700 pictures, thanks to the persuasive powers of Amsterdam professor Burmann, who convinced the administrators that Rumphius' knowledge could not be withheld from the science. Still today, Rumphius is an important source of information on the flora and fauna of the island of Ambon. JDJ

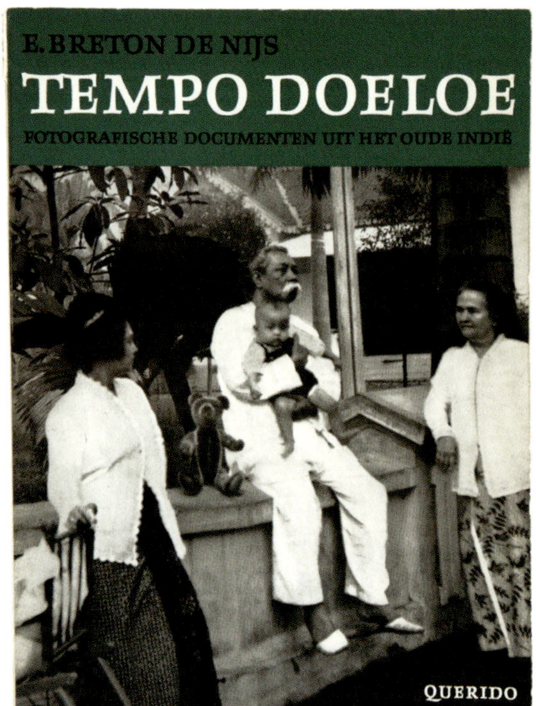

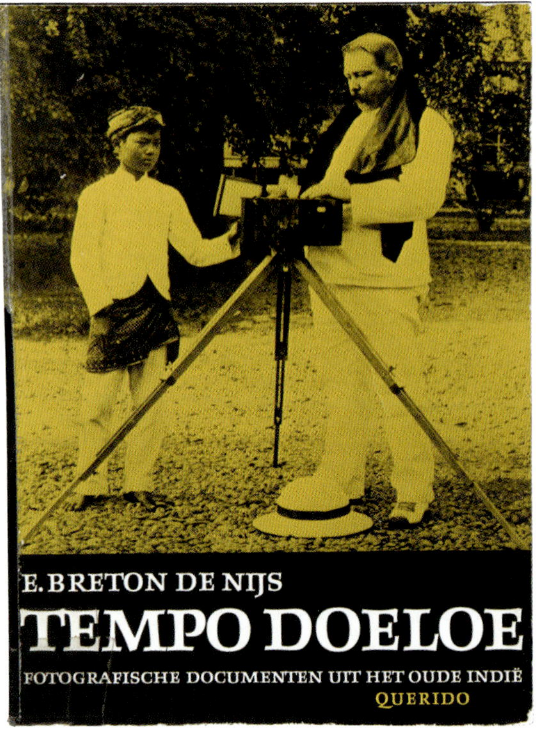

210
Tempo Doeloe, **fotografische documenten uit het oude Indië 1870-1914**
E. Breton de Nijs. Amsterdam: Querido1961

211
Tempo Doeloe, **fotografische documenten uit het oude Indië 1870-1914**
E. Breton de Nijs. Amsterdam: Querido 1973 (2e revised edition)

tion that resonates. The visual power of his selection together with his melancholic annotations have influenced their personal, 'unique' memories. This amazing process whereby someone else's memories become a part of one's own memories has often been discussed by memory experts. One such expert, Dutch essayist Rudy Kousbroek, has aptly commented on it: 'One's own life becomes a part of the myth and the myth becomes a part of one's own life.'

Cinema of the Indies second generation

The process by which other people's memories become your own also happens in visual media. Present-day visual media strongly influence our opinions and views. Especially historical movies intended to appear true, have a dramatic effect on how we perceive the past. A number of documentaries made by the second generation of Indo-Dutch migrants have taken a different approach. The Indies second generation of filmmakers are children of migrants who were born and raised in the Netherlands East Indies, or who spent an important time of their lives in the colony. The filmmakers themselves were usually born in the Netherlands so that they have no personal experience of the Netherlands East Indies. Their work reveals how the experiences of their parents had a major influence on their lives, but their films go further. Instead of showing a realistic picture of the Indies, they tend to show the uneasy link between official history and alternative, individual memories. They also often discuss an issue that is relevant for people living today in the Netherlands. In *Kinderjaren* (2006) filmmaker Piet Oomes takes his mother to Indonesia to bring her back to the disconcerting locations of the Japanese internment camps in the East Indies where her life took a dramatic turn. In his film Oomes reveals his mother's experiences of the colonial past, yet it is not the past as such he is interested in. The issues that concern him are contemporary ones and address his own life in the present. An emotional sequence right after the beginning of the film explains his urge to understand what happens between generations: is the distant relationship between his mother and himself a result of traumas she had experienced during the colonial era? Does the Netherlands East Indies subsequently impact on the relationship of the filmmaker with his own small son? Framed by these questions, the documentary begins and ends with the small son tentatively playing the piano in a modern Dutch living room. Oomes' film not only shows how the colonial past is interwoven in present lives, and subsequently influences next generations. The film has initiated another story, in a changed context. Due to its public broadcast on television, the film had a wide audience and has been disseminated in unlikely new surroundings. Author Doeschka Meijsing (1947) – not a second generation East-Indies child herself – has included elements from the documentary in her price-winning novel about lesbian love *Over de liefde* (2008). In her novel, the mother's camp experiences have taken on a radically changed meaning. This case illustrates how the representation of the colonial past continually alters in order to reflect contemporary concerns.

When does the past end?

'I do not know where the present ends and the past begins. Nothing ever lies entirely in the past. History can be written and rewritten in a thousand different ways.' [translation by the author]

This quote is taken from *De tuinen van Bomarzo* (1968) by the popular and much-heralded author Hella S. Haasse (1918). Haasse's books about her country of birth, the Netherlands East Indies, have had a major impact on the Dutch collective memory. Through her semi-autobiographical works a series of different views on the East Indies can be traced. An example is the sequence of her debut novel, *Oeroeg* (1948), the film of the same name (1993) and her more recent novel *Sleuteloog* (2002).

In *Oeroeg*, two small boys grow up together. (Fig. 212, 213) The nameless Dutch narrator is the son of a well-to-do plantation owner, while his indigenous friend Oeroeg is the son of his father's foreman. They share an unlikely friendship in a colony that is divided by race and class. The two 'blood brothers' become estranged from each other when Oeroeg embraces nationalism and rejects his old friend who does not understand his friend's political aspirations. The film *Oeroeg*, which came out years later and is based on Haasse's novel, has two storylines. In a series of flashbacks, the story of the boys' friendship is told. The second storyline focuses on the return of the grown up white boy (Johan) to the East Indies during Indonesia's war of independence. As a soldier Johan is obliged to fight the Indonesian nationalists, but his personal objective is a search for Oeroeg. He is taken prisoner by the Indonesian armed forces and does not see his friend until near the film's ending he is exchanged for twelve Indonesian prisoners. One of them is Oeroeg. (Fig. 214)

Sleuteloog, too, is a memory novel on the colonial era in the Netherlands East Indies. It also focuses on an interracial friendship from a Dutch perspective. The aging Herma Warner receives a request to provide information on the shadowy activist Dee Meijers. Dee turns out to be the Indo-Dutch bosom friend with whom Warner grew up in the East Indies, but with whom she has long since lost contact. *Sleuteloog* consists largely of the flood of confusing memories that washes over Herma Warner.

The succession of Haasse's debut novel, the film adaptation and the later *Sleuteloog* with their diverse publication dates – 1948, 1993 and 2002 – form three so-called 'telling moments' in a national postcolonial process of coming to terms with the past. In the novel *Oeroeg* we recognise Rudyard Kipling's much-quoted vision: 'East is East, and West is West, and never the twain shall meet.' Although the Dutch narrator is painfully affected by the rejection by his friend and

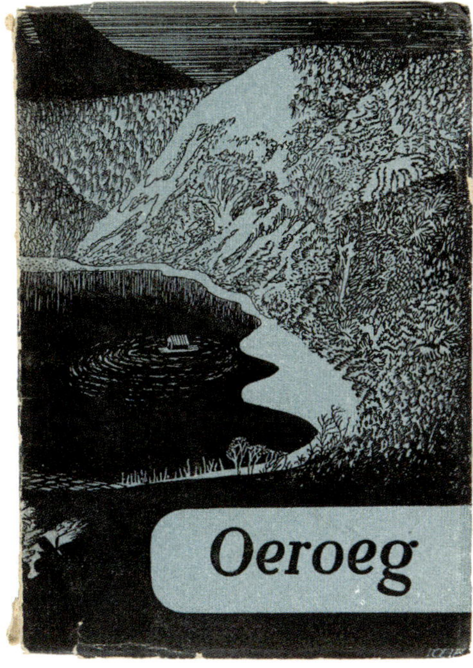

212
Oeroeg
H.S. Haasse. Vereening ter bevordering van de belangen des boekhandels, Amsterdam 1948

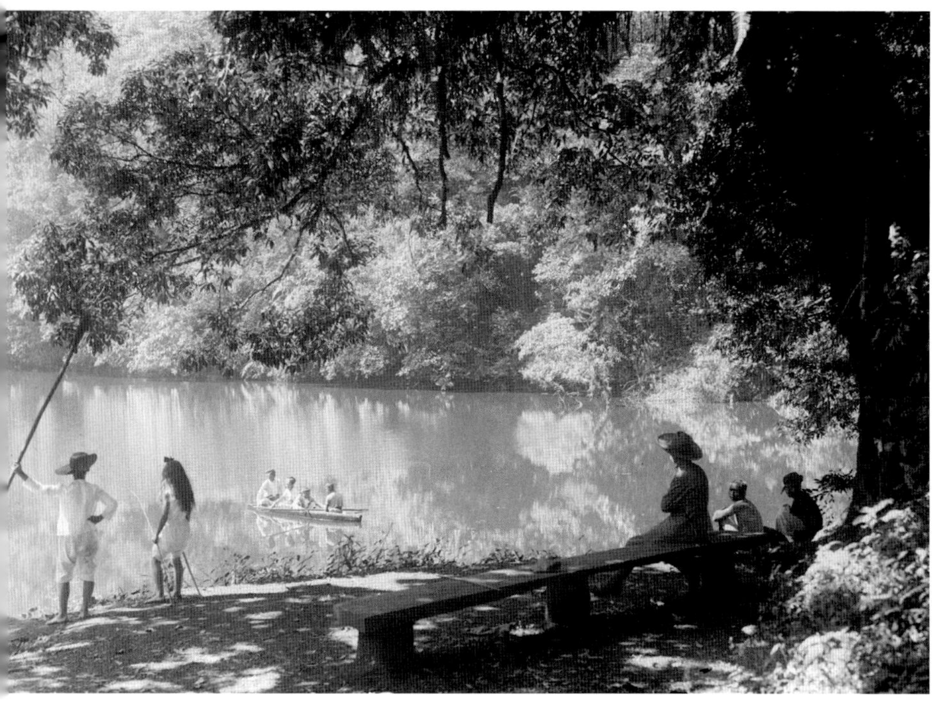

213
Lake Telaga Warna, Java
Lake Telaga Warna is referred to as Telaga Hideung in Hella Haasse's novel Oeroeg
c. 1910-1915
Glass negative
13 x 18 cm
10018387. Gift: Ph.S. van Ronkel

> 214
Film poster *Oeroeg*
Directed by Hans Hylkema, 1993
Collectie EYE Film instituut Nederland, Amsterdam

the loss of his native country, he never reflects on his own privileged position in the colony. Instead, he blames the 'unbridgeable' differences between himself and his native friend: 'I wanted to capture the image of those years, which have now disappeared into the past as though they were nothing more than smoke in the wind... I will never see Oeroeg again [...] I knew him, as I knew lake Telaga Hideung – a mirroring surface. Its depth I could never fathom.' [translation by the author]
Through the second storyline in the film, the search for Oeroeg is much more emphasized. This second line involves in fact a revision of memories of the colonial past. A clear example is a sequence in which Johan organises a military action and forces his way into the house of Oeroeg's family. Times have irrevocably changed, but, as if nothing had happened, Johan appeals to his past contact with the Sundanese family of his old friend. Oeroeg's sister Sati retorts: 'Your memories, Sinjo (young master) Johan, are different from ours.'
The film, which came out fifty years after the Netherlands East Indies became the Republic of Indonesia, does not simply reflect Dutch views of colonial relationships. The fact that an Indonesian voice is included in the story line is the direct result of an altered Dutch view of the colonial past. While Haasse's novel focused on unbridgeable racial differences, the film asks a postcolonial question: what happened, why did our friendship end? By zooming in on Herma Warners uneasy and painful self-examination, *Sleuteloog* (2002) highlights again another postcolonial moment. Through a hesitant and painful process, the white protagonist becomes aware of the privileged position she used to occupy in the colony. She is forced to correct her own memories and to revise her self-image, which makes her understand much more about her *Indo* friend Dee. This halting process of self-reflection can be compared to the reluctant course in which the Dutch nation has reviewed its own role in the past. Whilst the nation's loss of the East Indies predominates in *Oeroeg*, in *Sleuteloog* the East Indies is seen as a troubled past that has only begun to be reconsidered.
Noteworthy is another significant indicator of a changed view on the past, which involves the representation of Indo-Dutch people. The novel *Oeroeg* does not focus at all on the mixed culture of late colonial society with its majority of mixed-race people. Instead, without exception, East Indies people are portrayed as unreliable characters living on the fringes of colonial society. In *Sleuteloog*, the pluralistic, mixed East Indies society is the centre of focus and everything revolves around the Indo-Dutch figure Dee. This modified attitude in the writing of history is unmistakably the result of the increased awareness of voices of outsiders.

Conclusion

All the aforementioned examples show that Dutch museums, literature, films and photograph collections contribute not only to the formation of national cultural heritage, but also to the collective memory pertaining to the colonial past. As carriers of memory, they influence each other in their revisions of that haunting part of Dutch history. The stories they pass on overlap and authenticate but also contradict each other. By looking back on the Dutch past from a different perspective, new, postcolonial stories are continuously created and recreated within our collective memory. It is this changing collective memory which influences our perception of the colonial past all the time.

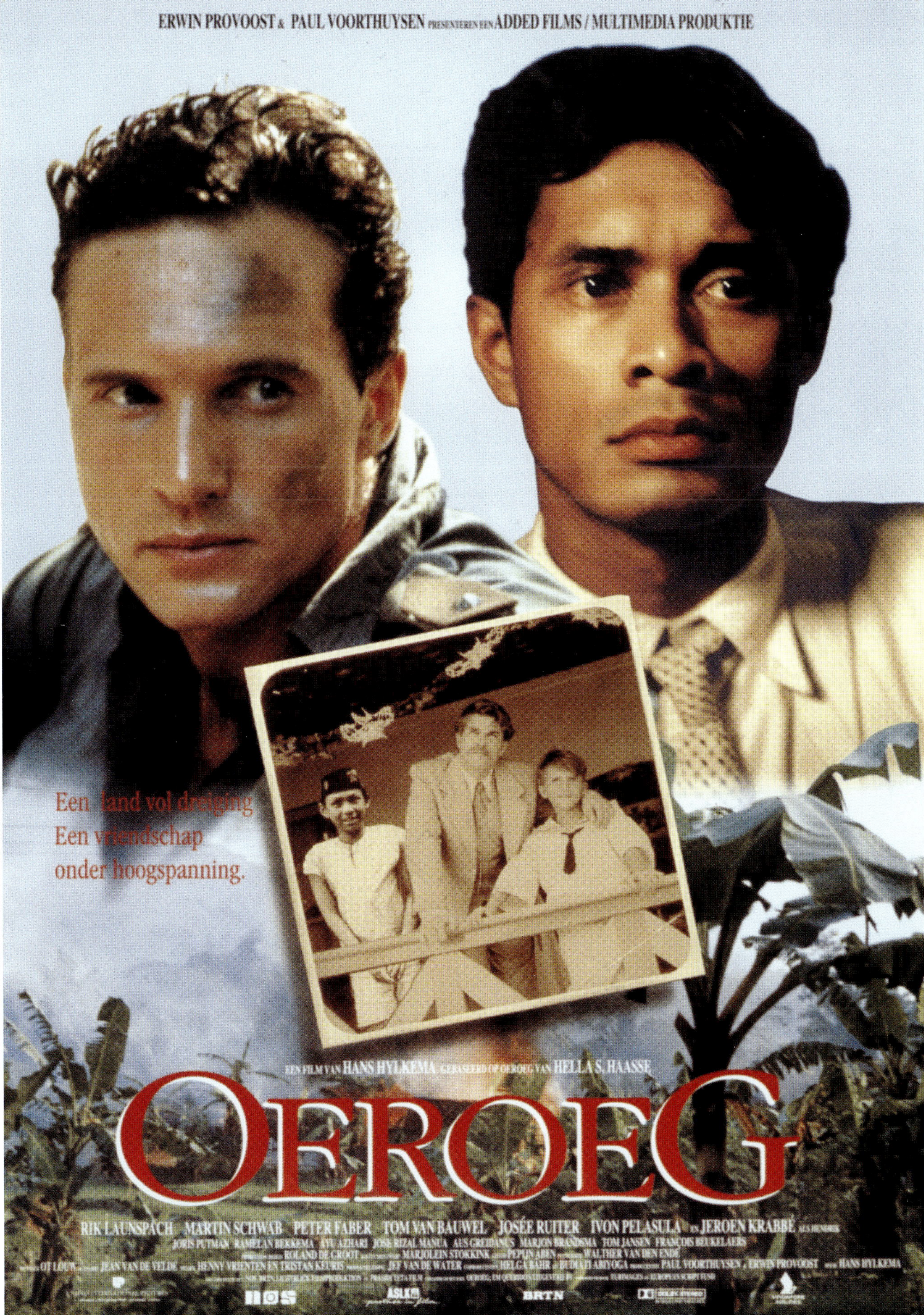
ERWIN PROVOOST & PAUL VOORTHUYSEN PRESENTEREN EEN ADDED FILMS / MULTIMEDIA PRODUKTIE
Een land vol dreiging
Een vriendschap
onder hoogspanning.
EEN FILM VAN HANS HYLKEMA GEBASEERD OP OEROEG VAN HELLA S. HAASSE
OEROEG
RIK LAUNSPACH MARTIN SCHWAB PETER FABER TOM VAN BAUWEL JOSÉE RUITER IVON PELASULA EN JEROEN KRABBÉ
JORIS PUTMAN RAMELAN BEKKEMA AYU AZHARI JOSE RIZAL MANUA AUS GREIDANUS MARJON BRANDSMA TOM JANSEN FRANÇOIS BEUKELAERS
ROLAND DE GROOT MARJOLEIN STOKKINK PEPIJN ABEN WALTHER VAN DEN ENDE
OT LOUW JEAN VAN DE VELDE HENNY VRIENTEN EN TRISTAN KEURIS JEF VAN DE WATER HELGA BAHR BUDIATI ABIYOGA PAUL VOORTHUYSEN ERWIN PROVOOST HANS HYLKEMA
NOS
ASLK
BRTN

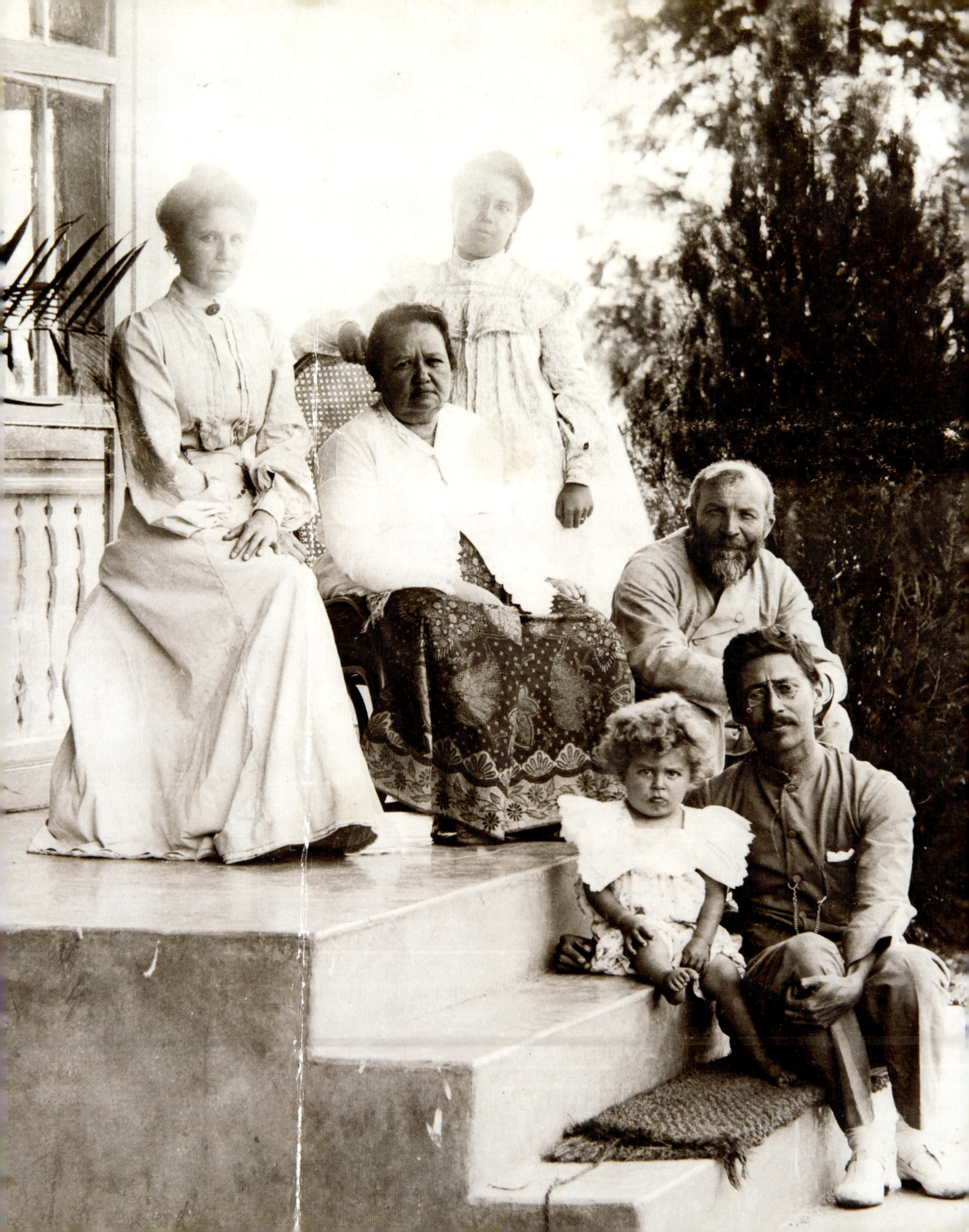

THE ARROWS AIM
Coloured comments on Dutch colonial drama

EDY SERIESE

Take the lift upstairs and step out into the midst of the exhibition. That's what I love to do when moving *Eastward Bound.* Instead of starting at Rumphius, I prefer to start at the end of Dutch colonial history, in the section of the exhibition called 'The Colonial Theatre'. It provides a good vantage point from which to look back on the era in Dutch and Indonesian history called the Netherlands East Indies. An era in which my own Indo-Dutch heritage has its roots. Here, where the Dutch colonial period is performed by actors in the form of mannequins-with-attributes, my presence seems natural. Not only as a visitor to the exhibition, but also as a participant in this history. Because the Colonial Theatre *proudly presents,* through a drama in different acts not only the Dutch and Indonesian presence, but also the Indo-Dutch presence in colonial history. That has not always been the case in the past.

Home

This history-inspired feeling of being at home in Dutch (colonial) history is one I do not often experience.[115] Dutch historical data, from sod hut to the Armada, reaches back far into the era of the Verenigde Oostindische Compagnie (VOC). Still it is information which I am only now taking in as an (interested) outsider because I felt 'incongruous' with the subject at school when I was young. It was some time in the 1950s, in The Hague, when a teacher once gave us the assignment of dressing up 'like our medieval ancestors'. It entirely unsettled me. How was I supposed to do that? In a then decolonising Netherlands, nothing more was known about Indies people than that they were the bastard children of Dutch soldiers and were often very poor. Of course, this view did not correspond with what we were told at home. But medieval? Did we, Indo-Dutch, even have Middle Ages in our history?[116]

Blind

The exhibition entitled 'Eastward Bound!' initially shows the traditional colonial answer to this question, saying East Indies people have no Middle Ages and did not even appear in history until, well, somewhere in the 19th century. The exhibition begins with a painting by Andries Beeckman, at a point when the VOC had successfully conquered the strategically important Portuguese forts along the ocean routes to 'the East'. (Fig. 216) The flourishing Mestizo cul-

215
Three generations of an Indo-Dutch family, Sumatra
1904
Gelatine silver print
12.8 x 17.9 cm
60011341. Gift: A. van Warmelo

BATAVIA CASTLE

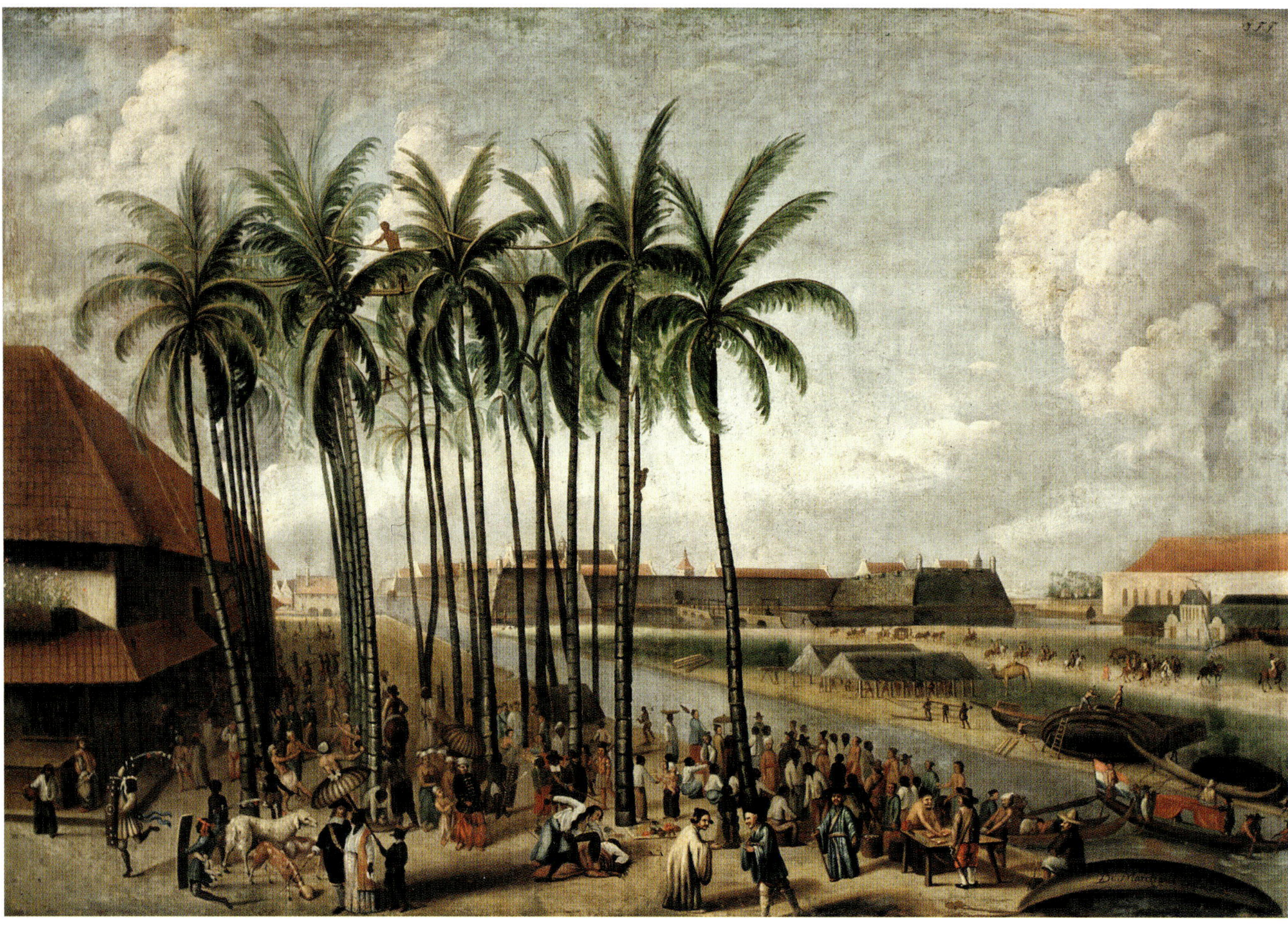

216
Batavia Castle
Andries Beeckman
Oil painting
144 x 209 cm
1656
118-167. Gift: J.W. IJzerman, 1921

The Governor General is preceded by a cavalry escort as he leaves the gate of the fort headed in the direction of the town hall. Trumpeters lead the way. To the right of the procession is the court house with the gallows and whipping posts. To the left are Chinese houses and, in the distance, a smithy (with smoke) beside the shipyard. In the centre is the fish market. Chinese traders are selling fish, an Ambonese dancer is performing a *Cakalele* (war dance) and a Dutch merchant is walking with his Javanese wife, while their servant or slave holds a parasol, a *payung*. Others are playing a ball game, some are fighting and a Timorese person is being arrested. The painting portrays people from every region. Beeckman's Batavia is a centre of commerce, a cultural and ethnic mix and a focus of international contacts. The dromedary and elephant, not normally seen on Java, reinforce this impression.
Two versions of this work were painted. The first, now at Amsterdam's Rijksmuseum, was displayed from 1663 at the East Indies House on Nieuwe Hoogstraat in Amsterdam above the fireplace in the council chamber of the directors – the Heren XVII – of the Verenigde Oostindische Compagnie (VOC). This second version may have been commissioned from Beeckman by a VOC governor, Arnold de Vlamingh van Outshoorn. (See also pp. 26,27) KVB

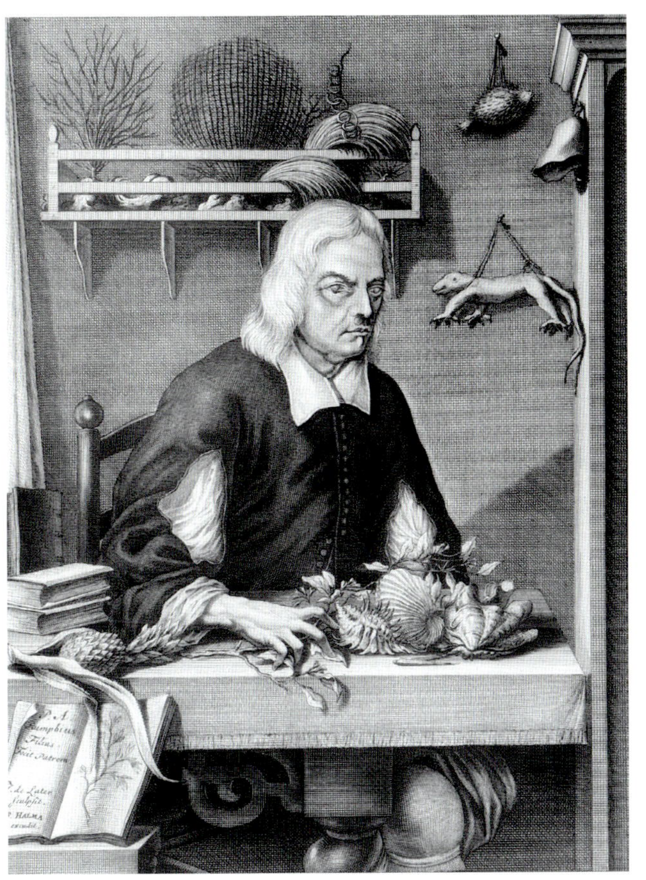

217
Engraved portrait of Rumphius
Gelatine negative
18 x 13 cm
10018692

218
A mestizo woman from Ternate
20.5 x 13.5 cm
1746-1789
3728-961. Gift: KIT Library

ture that was created there in the previous century, and which can be considered as the Middle Ages for Indies people, falls already outside the scope of the exhibition. But even for a long time thereafter, Indies people remained invisible. Not that they didn't exist. Rumphius, for instance, the Western botanist who brought together a true collection of curiosities from the East Indies in the 17th century and who – surrounded by his scientific attributes and the Dutch Authorised Version of the Bible – now oversees the entire exhibition, had children with an Asian woman, and he was not the only European to do so. (Fig. 217) But Indies people *avant la lettre*[117] such as Rumphius' children are at best only obliquely present in stories about their famous fathers. Such as in the story about the earthquake in which Rumphius grieves for his wife and daughter; and in the story that relates how one of his sons served as a personal assistant to Rumphius, by then entirely blind. [118] The world now would know nothing of Rumphius, had it not been for the efforts made by that East Indies child.[119]
Yet what do we know about this child? What did he look like? What did he wear at work, in his time off or when he slept? In short: what attributes surrounded him that defined him as an Indo? None what so ever. There are no historical descriptions of this son nor (literary) pieces of art devoted to him. Keeping 'the other' invisible, in addition to land-grabbing, was an effective instrument of modern colonialism. It was a means of conquering and mastering another people's image and self-image,[120] something Indies people experienced well into the mid 20th century. 'Eastward Bound!' mirrors this colonial blind spot in the first few halls. The combination of Beeckman's painting with the screen opposite it, which shows images of Javanese society, simply repeats the colonial view that the history of the Indo's does not begin until the *Hollander* appears on stage. Indies people themselves, called 'Mestizos' at the time, begin to appear when the art of portrait painting arises in the colony during the Golden Age of the East Indies. (Fig. 218)
Of course it takes a keen observer to recognise them as such in portraits from that time. Little can be gleaned from the names given to them because non-Westerners were forced to take a

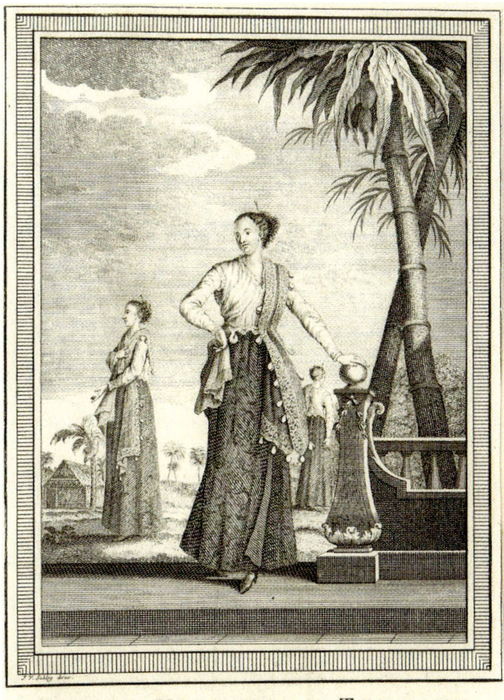

Christian name when being baptised or marrying a *Hollander*.[121] And the non-Westerner was difficult to discern from appearance, due to the Western clothing worn and the fact that their features were often shown as being more European than many family trees justify.[122] For anyone who cannot look with eyes different from those of the Western portrait painters and their Dutch-oriented clients, Indo-Dutch people in the 18th century look roughly the same as their Dutch parents, i.e. invisible as Indo's.

Seeing

Thus 'Eastward Bound!' pays little attention to Indo's in the first two scenes of the Dutch colonial drama. But in its final scene in the Colonial Theatre, focused on the late 19th and early 20th centuries, 'Eastward Bound!' clearly does not want to confirm this colonial view. Here the makers of the exhibition must have posed roughly the same question that was asked by this Indo-Dutch primary schoolgirl in the 1950s in The Hague. What did a housewife, schoolteacher, Governor General, planter, soldier, artist or native civil servant look like? What attributes had to adorn the mannequin actors to highlight them in their double roles as individuals and as colonial players in a historically accurate and convincing manner? By posing this concrete initial question, so necessary in a theatre, you can see at a glance that Indo's were a part of the cast. Because three of the seven mannequins are shown with a skin colour which – with a word affectionately used by East Indies people – is called *koelit langsep*, after the yellow-brown colour of a tropical fruit.

Colour

I felt exactly the same when, for the first time, I saw a historical reconstruction of Jesus of Nazareth: a brown-skinned man, just like Sayers, Anwar and Himpies are depicted here. The sight gave me an intense satisfaction about a historical correction being made. Yet it was a feeling mixed with curiosity because skin colour alone, of course, is beside the point. The question is 'what is the point?'. What is the function of this colour in this theatre production? What role do these dark-skinned mannequins play in a multi-cultural drama whose third act is played out here? What story does this eye-catching attribute tell about the history in which they play a role?
The mannequin depicting Charles Sayers (1901-43) shows that he is a painter.[123] At first glance, he is more a paragon of glamour than a cornerstone of Dutch colonialism.
As he stands there – slim, dark hair, with a painter's attributes on hand; one foot on the ground, the other on the treadle of his motorcycle, ready to disappear with a flash into the beckoning distance – he is clearly the type of dashing figure that schoolgirls would throw themselves at. His attributes reveal a bohemian artist, a phenomenon from Western culture that was also socially accepted in the colonial East Indies. So it is not the respectable paintings hanging elsewhere in 'Eastward Bound!' that give Sayers such a non-conformist image. That is the effect of his undeniably *eye-catching* attribute: the motorcycle.

Glance

Whether or not Sayers actually rode a motorcycle is less the point than the accent it places on freedom, which makes the vehicle the prominent means of transport of the *boedjang* (bachelor, young man) in the East Indies. In combination with the *koelit langsep*, the exhibition visitor is given a view of East Indies culture, the real cornerstone of this mannequin. It is a cornerstone that, in Sayers' time, robbed him of a large part of his ability to set standards. Though for many Indo-Dutch people, well into the 20th century, it was a realistic alternative to Western civilisation, so highly esteemed at the time. To see proof of this, you have to be familiar with the work of Jan Boon (1911-74). In the narratives of his alter ego, Vincent Mahieu, the motorcycle, which could take you out of Western culture into the direction of the primeval forest, is the token of the East Indies alternative.[124] In his *Bildung* novel about the East Indies boy in the Interbellum (which is spread over different narratives), Boon takes bikers (and boxers and hunters) as a role model for Indo-Dutch adolescents. They form the East Indies counterparts to the trio of skating, cycling and swimming which make a real 'Dutch boy'. All these Indo-Dutch boys, according to the author, once stood before the Werther-

CHARLES EUGÈNE HENRI SAYERS – PAINTER (1901–1943)

He was the son of an affluent sugar planter on Java who, after attending secondary school in the Netherlands, studied the art of painting at the Rijksacademie voor Beeldende Kunsten in Amsterdam (1920-23). He won the 'Mr. Cohen Godschalk award' (1923) and continued his studies at the Académie des Beaux Arts in Paris (1924-26). He held an exhibition of his work in Galerie Bernheim-Jeune, Paris (1928).
In 1931 he was commissioned by the Dutch government to produce three murals in the Dutch Colonial pavilion at the World Fair in Paris. In the same year, he married Olga Stern and returned with her to the East Indies. They lived on Bali, Java and Sumatra. He died in a Japanese internment camp in Thailand (1943).
For Sayers and for many artists, the art, culture and landscape of the island of Bali were great sources of inspiration. In their own way, his paintings contributed to the 'image' of the Netherlands East Indies. JDJ

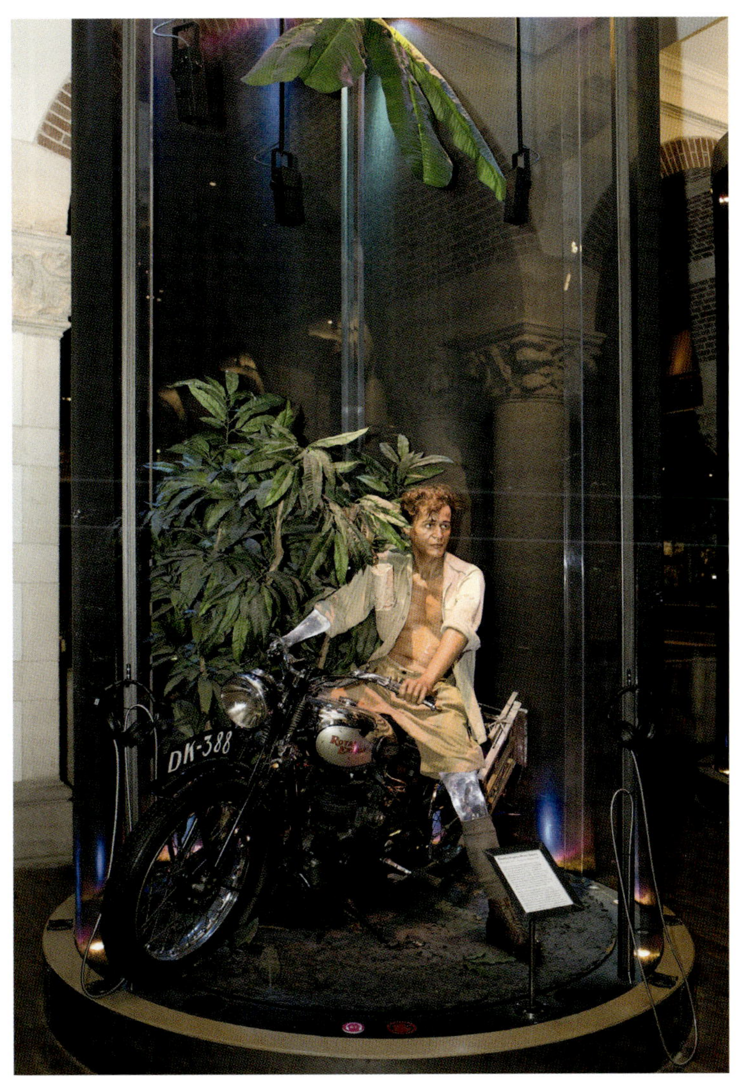

esque choice between a life of 'reflection' or 'reflexes'[125], that is to say, a life spent in Western culture while denying their own home culture. Bikers, hunters and boxers are a sign of this wicked either/or-choice. The sign posts to the social reality of a Western culture considered superior and an East Indies culture seen as inferior. For Boon, the motorcycle does not stand for artistic freedom only, but for the positive choice of a life on the colonial margins, without Western affluence, standing or recognition, let alone glamour. (Fig. 219, 220, 221)

Counterpart

Despite this, in Sayers' motorcycle I hear a contrasting call for the traditional colonial story about the small *Boeng* (lit: younger brother) that fails to become Westernised. From the wings of the Colonial Theatre other East Indies people with a 'different story' now appear by motorcycle in my minds eye. Ernst Douwes Dekker (1880-1950) for example, nephew of Multatuli, also a bohemian and writer, journalist, soldier in the Boer War, politician, edu-

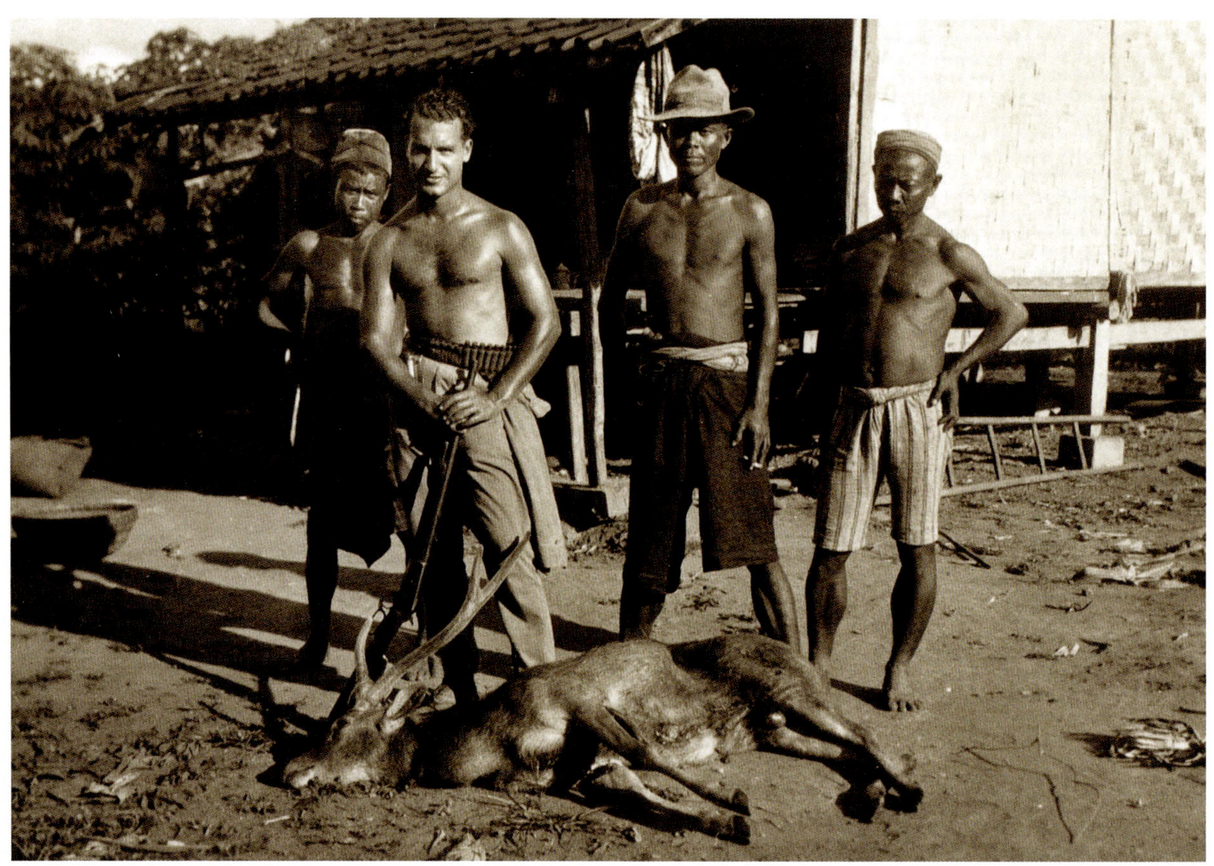

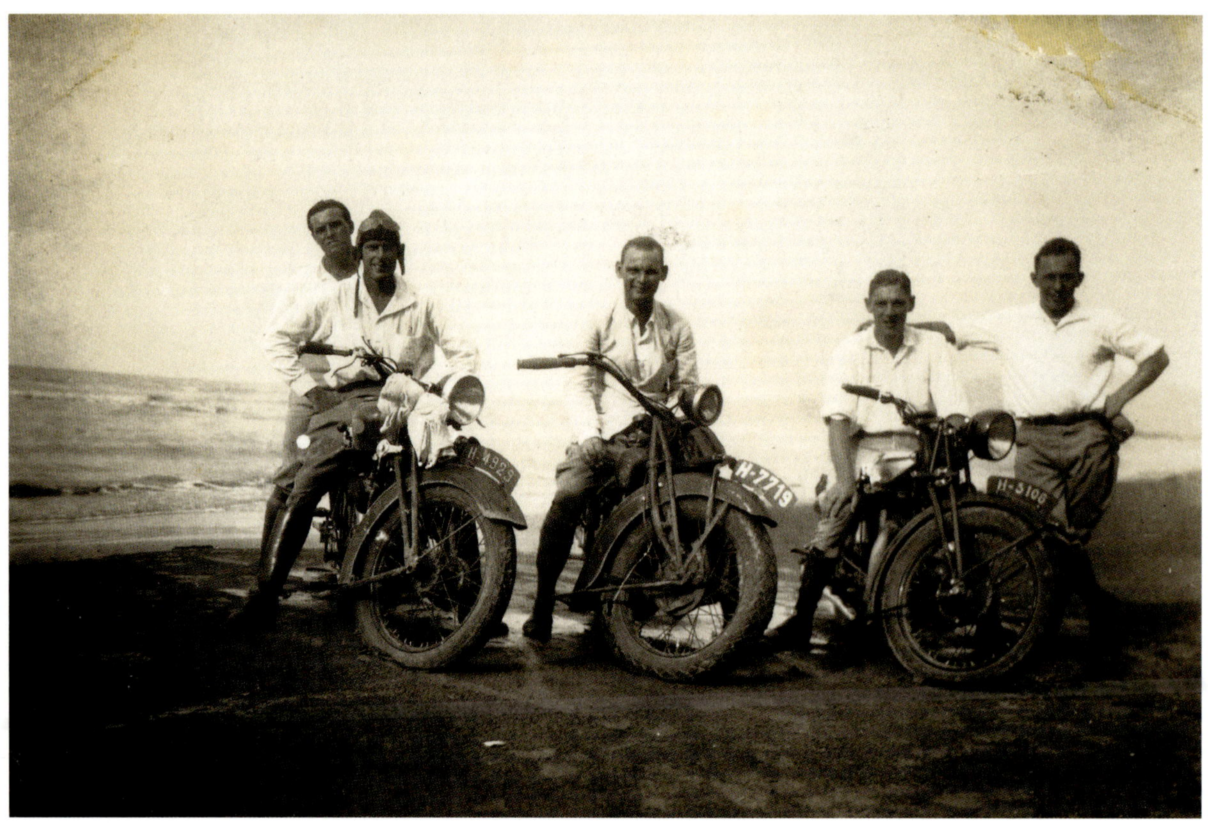
H-7719

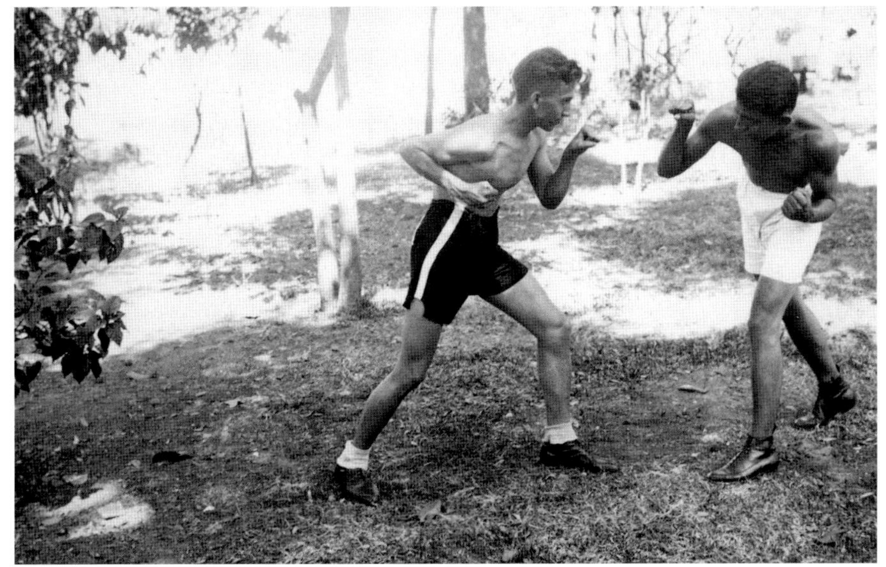

219
Charles Sayers with his hunting trophy, Bali, 1927
Private collection
T-2004-Say-39

220
Boys on motorcycles
Gelatin silver print
2.6 x 4 cm
1930- 1950
30050379. Former collection Indisch Wetenschappelijk Instituut, 2006

221
Boxing boys
Gelatin silver print
6 x 8.7 cm
c. 1935
60048946. Through mediation of M.J. Hillerström, 1970s

cator, exile, political prisoner in Suriname, and in Indonesia officially a *founding father* of the independent nation. Or Boon himself: writer-bohemian, educator at 'Wild Schools', journalist, urban vagabond, fervent biker, hunter and boxer, and unlike Douwes Dekker finally choosing to emigrate. Regardless of how quickly Boon's *outcasts* took the path to the socially acceptable Sayers, the role played by the Indies group in the colony are sufficiently highlighted by his *koelit langsep*: both oppositional and adapted, both marginal and constituent, invisible master and visibly marginalised. *Koelit langsep* as a sign of 'a different story'! Really, if the Indo ever becomes visible in Dutch history, it should happen in this way!

Contre-jour

Anwar looks much more tedious. His mannequin expresses calm, modesty and wisdom, a traditional colonial image of the 'Native'. Through the combination with other attributes such as the hipcloth and bare feet, his *koelit langsep*, unlike Sayers', is a reference to Indonesian culture. Anwar is – the civil code on his table bears witness to this – a 'Native civil servant'. Indonesians in Dutch government service like him were a considerable and important cornerstoneof colonialism. They were so important that, once they developed into nationalists as a *spin-off* of their Western education and the Dutch repression, Dutch rule soon came to an end. Anwar does perhaps look like an Indonesian who was extremely loyal to the colonial authorities, through thick and thin, until after the transfer of sovereignty. But he is much, much more.

In contrast to Sayers, Anwar is not a historical figure with literary connotations. He is the other way around, a character with historical pretensions: being the main character in *De raadsman* by H.J. Friedericy (1900-62). Novels like this provided the ideological justification of Western colonial rule by employing literary tricks such as the all-knowing narrator or an empathy-compelling main protagonist[126]. Thus the deep indignation of Max Havelaar concerning the colonial *bad practices* persuaded generations of new civil servants to be better colonisers than their forefathers. In *De raadsman*, too, the sympathetic protagonist, in this case the Indonesian Anwar, formulates the pro-colonial vision of the author. And in the Colonial Theatre, this vision is confirmed. Adorned with the intangible attributes of the 'loyal Native' from the novel, Anwar depicts *the Dutch image* of the Native civil servant corps. But due to the surprising choice of a literary figure rather than a historical one for this illusion, the Anwar mannequin highlights a true colonial *good practice:* the novelist's art.

Invisible

Regardless of how spectacular this effect is, the question that cautiously arose at Sayers is now even more pressing: how visible is it really? How much do you have to know about colonial literature and history to actually see 'the novelist's art' in this most apparent colonial cliché embodied in this Anwar character? Anwar is the only Indonesian in the Colonial Theatre. Aside from the modest historical film on the subject, the last act of Dutch colonialism, the war in which the Indonesians fought for their freedom and independence – remains unseen in the Colonial Theatre. Just as the exhibition for East Indies people began too late, for Indonesians 'Eastward Bound!' ends too early.[127] As a result, the colonial image presented obstructs our view rather than that it provides a perspective on a possible, underlying 'other' story. Without a double focus or (literary) foreknowledge, Anwar cannot, by lack of attributes on the matter, ever be connected to the creation of the sovereign

222
Children of the Van Lingen family
Text on photo: I have had two brooches made from this snapshot in lithograph, one for me and one for you. On arriving, I will give yours to you
Gelatin silver print
8.9 x 13.9 cm
c. 1930
60045815. Through mediation of M.J. Hillerström, 1970s

> 223
Wedding portrait of KNIL soldier and woman
Gelatin silver print
3.1 x 3.1 cm
c. 1910
30025446. Former collection Indisch Wetenschappelijk Instituut, 2006

state of Indonesia. Would the choice of another literary oeuvre without this pitfall, have done?[128] Or maybe the use of a historical figure?[129] Or was there simply no such purpose like using a colonial cliché that employs *koelit langsep* as a symbol for a 'different story'?

Black-and-white

These questions continued to nag us as we viewed the last brown-skinned mannequin. Like Anwar he is not a historical person, but a character from a novel. We are talking about Himpies, from the frame story *De tienduizend dingen* by Maria Dermoût (1888-1962).[130] Wearing military attire in the *full colour* of the profession that was the most important cornerstone of Dutch colonialism, smiling, against a décor of tropical plants, he is just as appealing as Sayers. With these two Indo's, 'Eastward Bound!' far surpasses the traditional colonial cliché of the Indo-Dutch as a sad *loser.* Yet, on second glance, something is not right about this Himpies. As is the case with Sayers, his attributes point both to the historical and to the literary source from which he is composed: his clothing and the décor refer to the army in which he was an officer, and the basket with a shell chain refers to Dermoût's novel. The small wooden arrow between the branches connects the two sources. From the literary source, we know that an arrow would kill Himpies on patrol by striking his 'unprotected neck'.[131] But Himpies in 'Eastward Bound!' is more like an innocent victim of a primitive object that happened to be flying through the air, rather than as a soldier on patrol. Standing in his fake primeval forest, he seems more a tourist than a player in a system in which some half a million Europeans suppressed more than 15 million Indonesians. Himpies is, in short, not as credible as Sayers (or Anwar). Also because the arrow is misdirected, and above all because Himpies' role in the Colonial Theatre – as a soldier – does not correspond with the role he fulfils in the literary source.
The colony was full of Himpies, people with a 'mixed spirit', as Aya Zikken referred to the divided cultural loyalty of Indo-Dutch children. [132] They grew up in the East Indies, in a culture that was focused on adopting Western culture as the standard. (see Fig. 222 and 223) They received a Western education and finally, to 'counter the East Indies influences', they were sent to Europe for further education. The desired result was a 'white' brown (wo)man, an Indo.

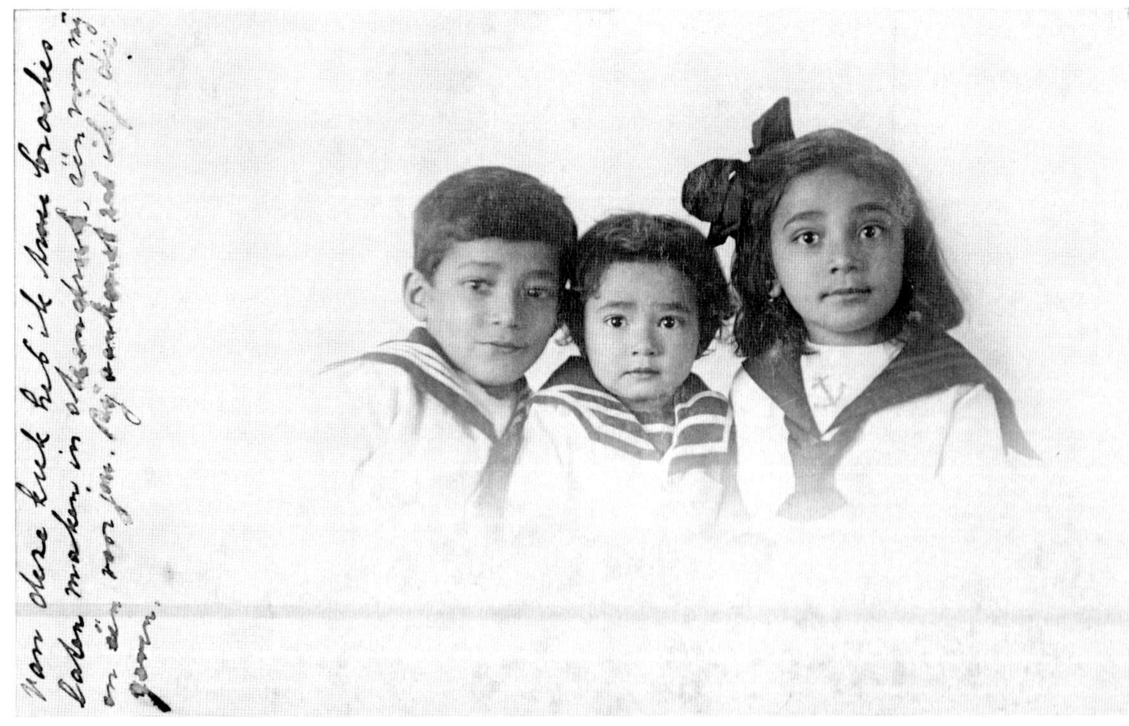

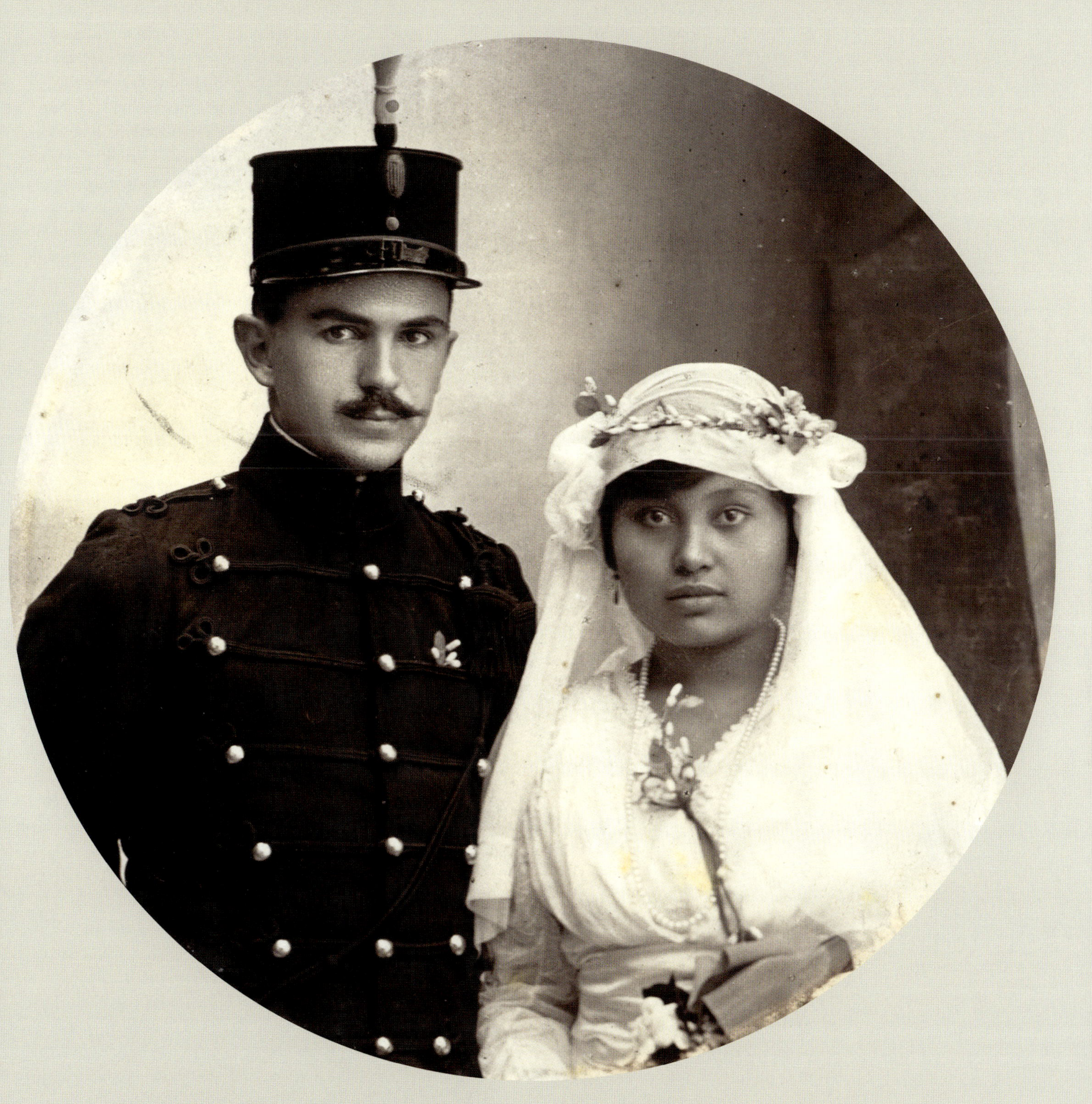

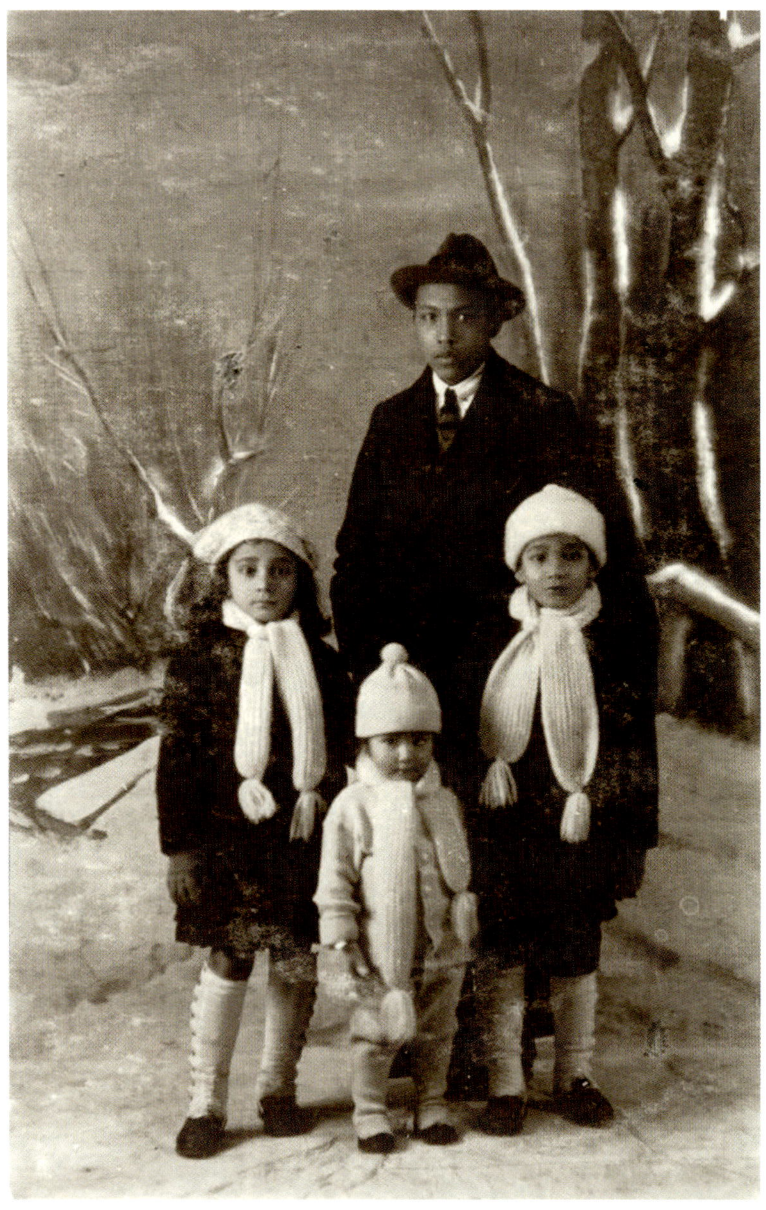

224
Van Lingen children and possibly their father during stay in the Netherlands
Gelatin silver print
14 x 8.9 cm
c. 1930
60050798. Through mediation of M.J. Hillerström, 1970s

In practice, he became either a Werther, in dramatic doubt about the loss of his East Indies culture, or a vivid Himpies. In Dermoût's book, Himpies is already dead. We see him only through the eyes of his mother Felicia, who searches her memory and conscience for a way to accept his death. *Contre coeur* but pragmatic, Dermoût's Himpies once in Europe, decided for the relatively short training programme for army officer, which would enable him to return as quickly as possible to his habitat in the East Indies without insulting his mother. Like Boon, Dermoût is an East Indies author. Unlike writers like Multatuli or Friedericy, Dermoût does not posit a vision of colonialism, or soldiers, or the colonial army through her protagonists. Instead, she formulates a value or idea from or about the Indies culture. Dermoût is focused on accepting life as it comes to us. Himpies' death was foreshadowed and determined by a series of past actions on the part of both Himpies and Felicia. Through his death, Himpies teaches Felicia, the protagonist in the frame story, that life and death are not incompatible quantities as they are viewed in Western civilization. She learns that the ten thousand things of life 'are not black OR white, not this way OR that way, but yes-AND-no [...] the one-AND-the-other, [...] side by side, touching one another [...], without any link, but at the same time always connected.'[133] Himpies' being a soldier in the story is an attribute to give shape to this idea, not a description of a real profession. The decision to use Himpies as a cornerstone of Dutch colonialism, is perhaps surprising, but wrong in literary historical terms, and therefore ultimately unconvincing.

Coloured

Himpies also does not ring true as a historical figure, as a soldier. Every time I meet this Himpies eye to eye, I always hear my father's voice calling him an 'amateur', or worse: 'a rookie'. He would then proceed to retell the story of that newcomer from Holland who was stabbed with a *kris* (Indonesian dagger) when he thought it was safe to drop his watchfulness in order to quench his thirst. 'Thirst', I hear him say in that typical tone used by KNILsoldiers, a tone that Hollanders referred to as a snarl. 'That amateur! Drinking like that, with his head tilted back, chest and belly unprotected. In enemy territory!' In fact, my father's experience with incompetent soldiers corresponds literally with the picture painted of Himpies by Dermoût as a non-soldier; Himpies in enemy territory acts just the same, drinking 'with his head tilted back'[134]. But 'Eastward Bound!' does not really want to present the truly seasoned army that the KNIL actually was, as being peopled with amateurs or toy soldiers, does it? Of course shortly after Himpies, the KNIL was unable to stand up to the modern guerrilla fighters of the TNI (National Indonesian Army). But in Dermoût's time, it was professionally armed to withstand any poisoned arrows of native East Indians (from the Arafura Islands).[135]

WILLEM ('HIMPIES') VAN KLEYNTJES-SOLDIER (C.1910–C.1930)

Himpies was the son of a family of clove planters on the island of Ambon. He was born in Nice during a trip his mother had taken with her parents, who were on leave. His father did a midnight flit. As a baby, he returned to Ambon with his mother. He attended secondary school in Surabaya (Java) and returned to the Netherlands to continue his studies. He first studied medicine and then enrolled for training at the Koninklijke Militaire Academie (Royal Military Academy) in Breda. As a second lieutenant in the Koninklijk Nederlandsch-Indisch Leger (Royal Dutch East Indian Army) (KNIL), he returned to the Netherlands East Indies, to Ambon. During a patrol on Ceram, he was fatally wounded by an arrow shot by a Bergalfoer (a native inhabitant of the Arafura islands). Himpies is a fictional character, based on a story by Maria Dermoût, *De tienduizend dingen*. JDJ

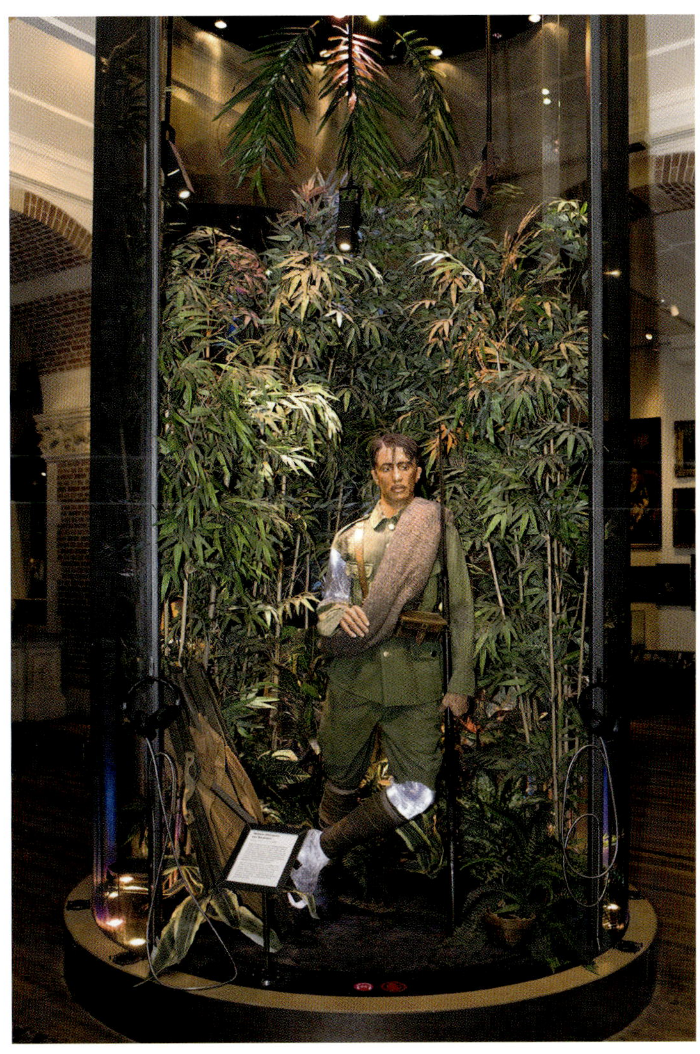

Why then was Himpies chosen as an example of a soldier? Is a literary character, in contrast to a historical figure, free to be used by third parties? Are the attributes that a novelist gives her characters less historical and therefore less respectable than those on which the historian focuses his attention? And why the use of *koelit langsep*? Dermoût never mentions the attribute. So why use Dermoût's work as a source, can one add or replace intangible attributes at will as the tenor of the narrative? 'Eastward Bound!' certainly does not want to typecast – in absolute contrast to my father's experience – the amateurs and non-soldiers of the KNIL as Indies people, does it? As a daughter of a father who served in that army, defending her father's experience and memories as a valuable source of historical knowledge, and maybe even more as a fan of Dermoût's work, I hope that Himpies perishes in 'Eastward Bound!' at some point.

JAVANESE STRIP CARTOON

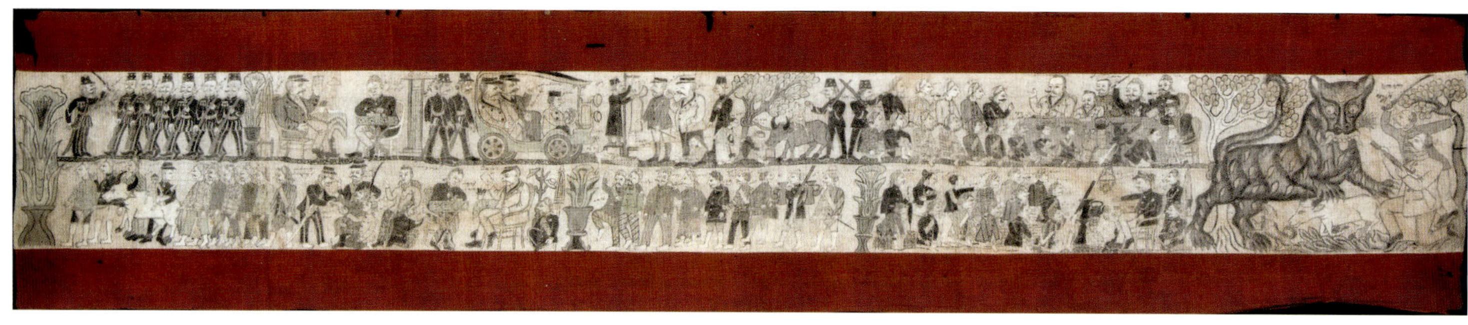

225
Javanese cartoon
Sitisiwan (1865-1948)
Linen, paint
703 x 145 cm
Gegesik, Java, Indonesia
c. 1920
5910-1. Purchase: Th. Murray, 2000

In nine scenes set in two rows one on top of the other, the arrest, trial and execution of a group of Javanese people by colonial officials are presented as a strip cartoon. The story probably begins at the lower right. What historical event is actually pictured here is not yet entirely clear. Research is still ongoing. Next to many people in the strip, a name or title is written in Javanese. They provide a way to further archival research into the legal proceedings depicted.
The canvas was painted in wayang (shadow puppet) style by Sitisiwan (1865-1948), an artist from Gegesik on Java. This village is still known as a centre of art and applied arts. Sitisiwan was well-known as a musician, wood carver and painter. He was the first to paint wayang stories and historical events on canvas in this manner. These canvases could be rented for ritual events; they either hung or they served as a canopy under which the guests were seated. This large narrative canvas is an example of folk art from areas in which the influence of the Javanese courts was less strong. Few of these canvases have survived. Traditionally, plants or animals were depicted, and sometimes also soldiers.
The representation of a narrative or an historical event, as appears on this canvas, is rare. (See also pp. 184-185) IVH

Full Colour

It must be said: the Colonial Theatre has done some clever casting. The mannequin actors unleash a torrent of associations and questions about the actors and the characters on which they are based. Questions that are focused on the choice of source and attributes, combined with the most precious attribute of the exhibition, the *koelit langsep*. In the context of the Colonial Theatre, this skincolour has taken on an unusual and risky effect. Unusual because the *koelit langsep* also colours the four other mannequins: they become 'white' instead of (quasi) neutral, subjective instead of (quasi) objective, co-actors instead of a single, all-knowing protagonist, thus breaking through a tenacious, colonial tradition. The attribute is also risky because in or throughout the colonial past 'colour' has been and still is, a sensitive subject. Here it functions as an eye-opener to the notion that 'history' might be written solely by and about 'white people' (with many subordinates of colour in the background), but is actually experienced in combination with those 'others'. In the Colonial Theatre, these 'others' are present, visible and co-actors. Seen from this perspective, 'Eastward Bound' throws a new light on the important role of Indo-Dutch and Indonesian groups in the colonial story. This feels really inviting to an involved 'other' like me, when I go in search of traces of the Indo-Dutch history within the Dutch stories.

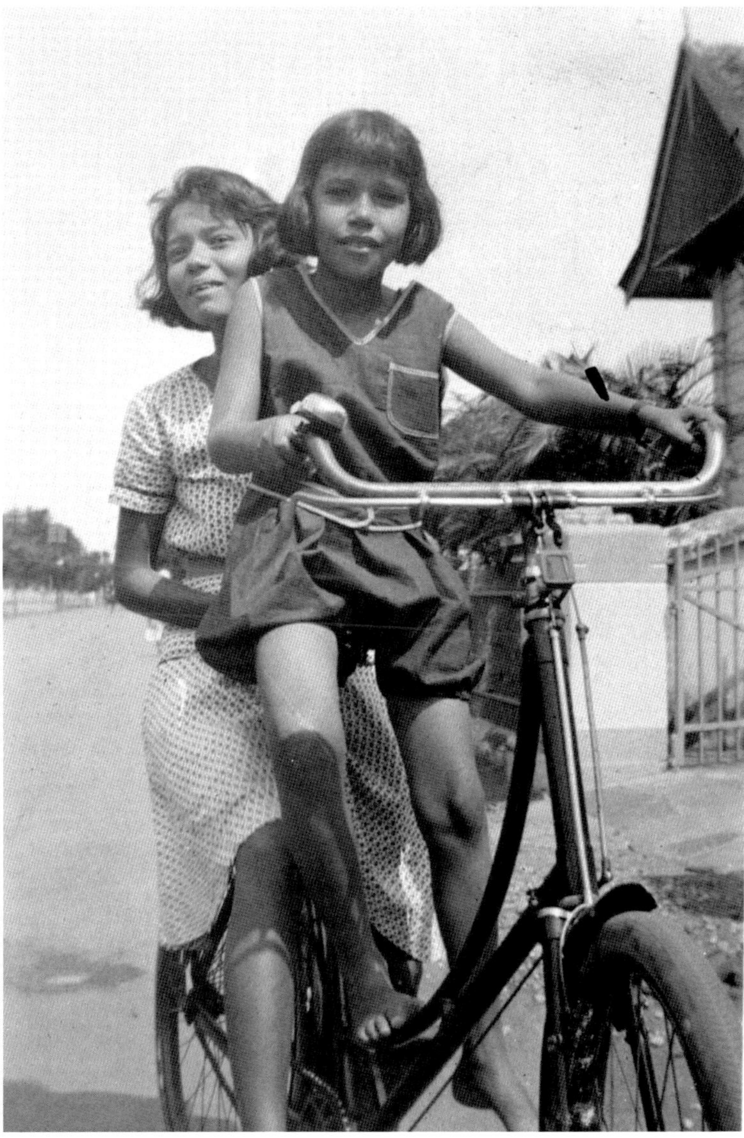

226
Two Indo-Dutch girls on a bicycle, Jakarta
Gelatin silver print
8.7 x 5.5 cm
1925-1935
60031712. Through mediation of M.J. M.J. Hillerström, 1970s

>> 227
Detail of Fig. 225

Multicoloured

It's just about whether this invitation really is there, that I'm not sure – in light of the best experiences of Indos in the 20th century. The poorly aimed arrow of the native East Indian hits the heart of 'Eastward Bound!' like a boomerang. The choice of Himpies as a cornerstone in the colonial drama activates the doubts already held with respect to Anwar and Sayers. Does the *koelit langsep* really refer to 'a different story'? Do the brown coloured mannequins really have an equal role to play? Or, along with their *koelit langsep*, do they only play a supporting role in a text written by the colonial director? On further inspection, it feels as though an invitation to a story told by many characters about the shared colonial history is being withdrawn. Yet without this invitation, 'Eastward Bound!' remains the usual – and closed-story of the ambitious 'Hollander' that plied the seas, in order – *right or wrong* – to perform something great. That is a story in which 'the others' – Indo-Dutchs and Indonesians, and even Germans such as Rumphius, vainly search for their own histories. The result would be the exact opposite of the brave choice to use *koelit langsep* as an attribute in the Colonial Theatre. For this reason, it is just as implausible as is Himpies.

Concord

The truth lies of course somewhere between the (rock-solid) concept of 'Eastward Bound!' and its realization in the Colonial Theatre, somewhere between the colours of the mannequins and the choice of additional attributes from the different sources, somewhere between fact and fiction, between literary and historical reality. 'Colour' in itself does not seem to be enough to provide a history told by many voices, not even when these 'others' have been consulted as was often done in 'Eastward Bound!'.[136] Multiple colours only become meaningful when many voices are heard, when actors are not relegated to supporting roles, but rather act out their 'own story'. If there is one story which deserves to be told by many voices, it is (Dutch) colonial history. Seen from this perspective, 'Eastward Bound!' will not be the last 'permanent' set-up of the Tropenmuseum, but the first step taken in that direction. The next step then is to continually surround 'Eastward Bound!' with (alternating) exhibitions full of 'other' stories. As the director of the IWI, the Indisch Wetenschappelijk Instituut (Indies Scientific Institute) which is putting together the 'own stories' of Indo-Dutch people, I feel especially invited to make a contribution to such a follow-up.

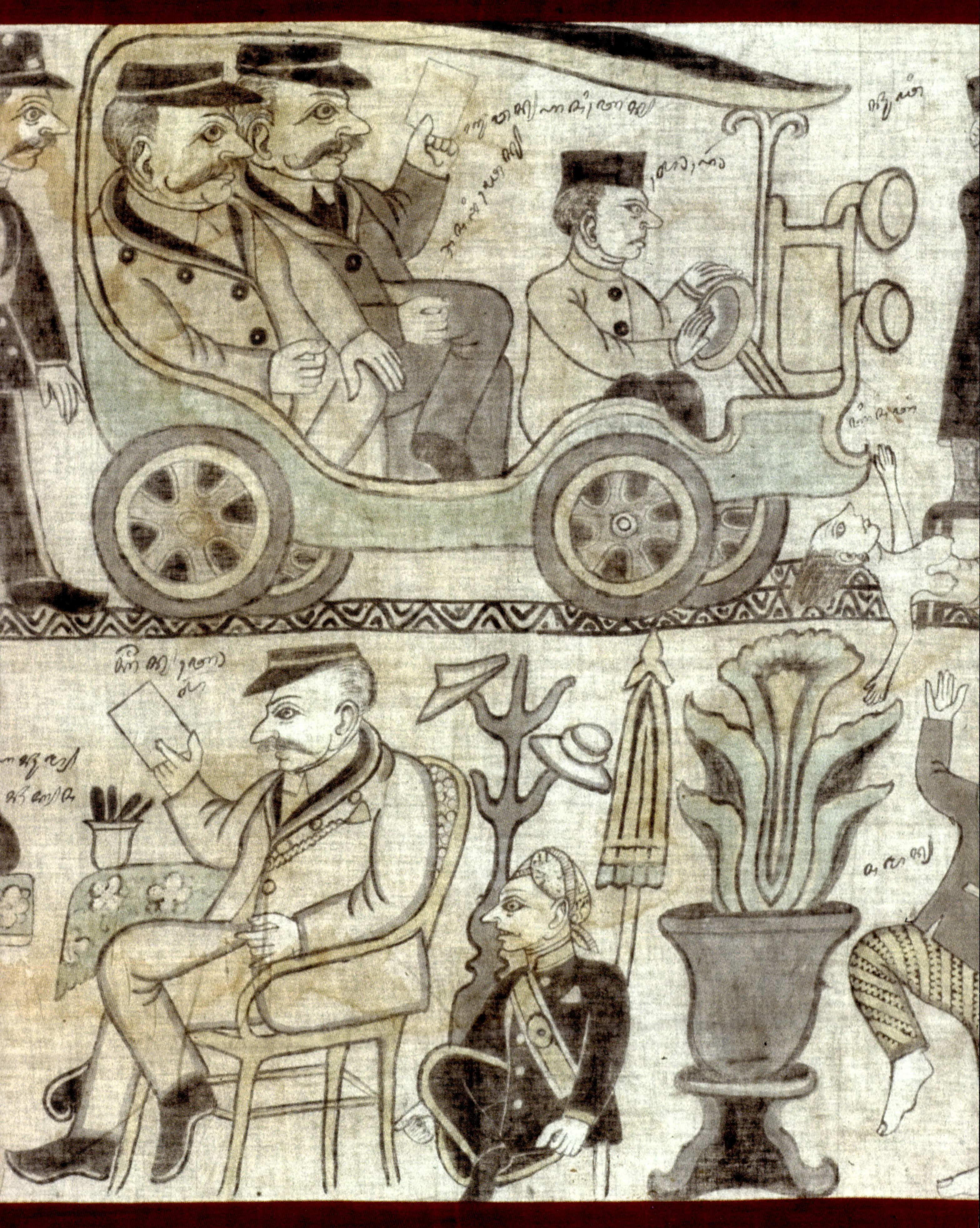

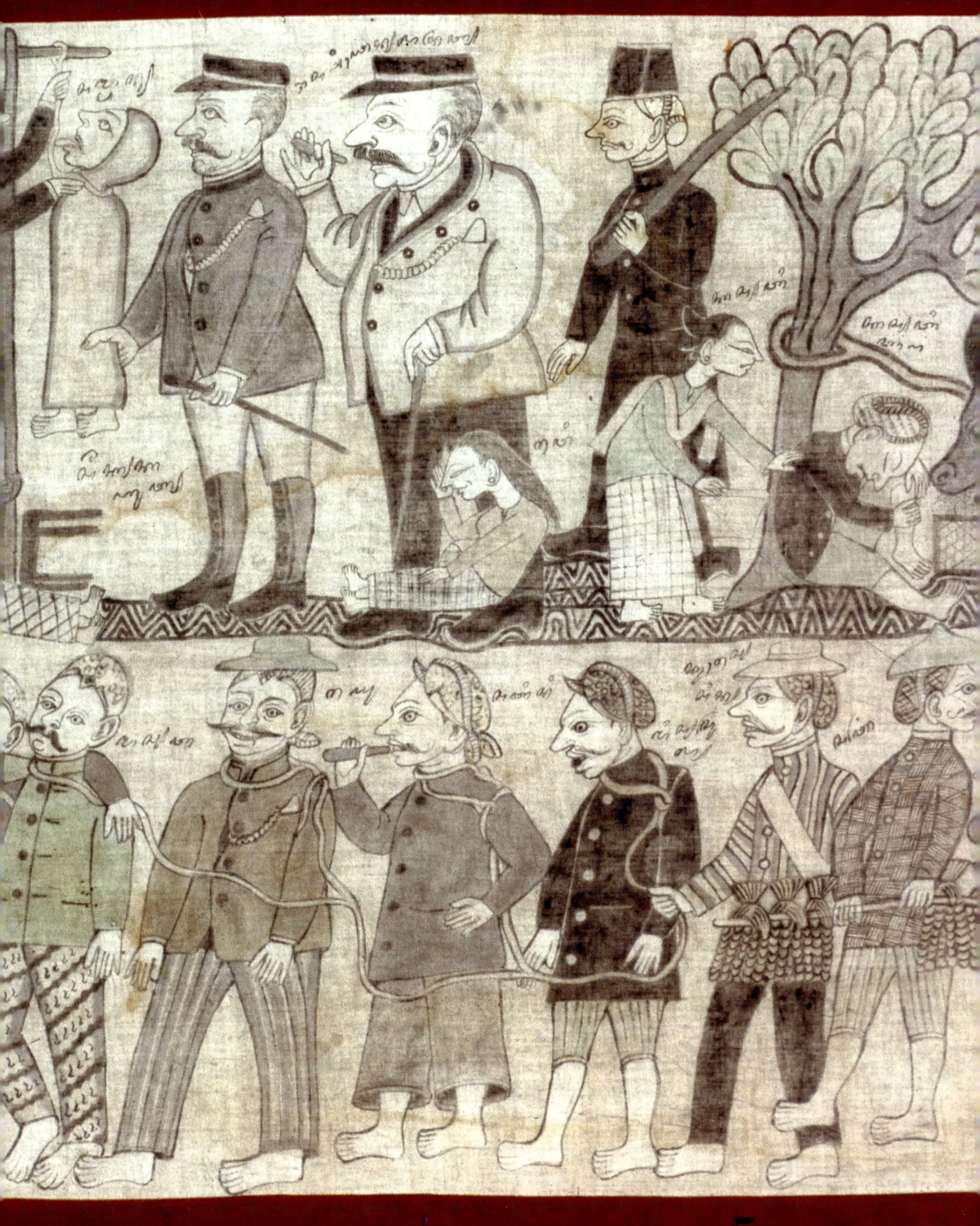

NOTES

1 Woudsma 1990.
2 Minutes of the Board, 9-5-1945; KIT archive inventory number s 566, 138; KIT Annual Report 1946.
3 Van Duuren 1990; Legêne & Postel-Coster 2000; Gortzak 2000.
4 On 'Whiteness'and 'Europeanness', Gouda 1995; Locher-Scholten 2000.
5 *Indonesische overpeinzingen*, 1945:22.
6 *Links Richten*, mei 1933:9. Poem 'Kolonial Instituut', by Jac van der Ster (our translation).
7 Schulte Nordholt 2002, p. 39.
8 'De onderwerping van den hoofd-muiteling Diepo Negoro aan den Luitenant Generaal De Kock. Einde van den oorlog op Java, 1825-1830'.
9 'Afgekapte hoofden van muitelingen'.
10 Kartini is also known as Raden Ajeng Kartini; Raden Ajeng is her title. Kartini 1987.
11 Soewarsih Djojopoespito 1986, 1940.
12 Groeneboer 1993.
13 Lelyveld 1992.
14 Bossenbroek e.a. 1995.
15 Statistisch Zakboekje voor Nederlandsch Indië 1939.
16 Quoted in Lelyveld, '"Geen overdaad", 290.
17 A vast corpus of literature exists concerning the subject of pre-war nationalism. See amongst others Shiraishi 1990, Bossenbroek 1995.
18 Székely 2007, p. 43.
19 Dick and others 2002, pp. 100-105.
20 Dick and others 2002, pp. 93-100.
21 Haasse 1992.
22 Knight 1996, p. 155.
23 NHM was later renamed ABN and has survived to this day as the ABN AMRO Bank.
24 Lindblad 1996, pp. 220-222; Breman 1987, p. 50.
25 The Ethical Policy was launched as a reaction to the substantial profits made by the colonial state in the 19th century and aimed at raising the prosperity of the Indonesians. Dick and others 2002, pp. 146-148.
26 Fasseur 1993, pp. 415-425.
27 Fasseur 1994, pp. 35-37.
28 Touwen 2001, pp. 163-183.
29 Dick and others 2002, pp. 141-142; original statistics in Creutzberg 1979.
30 Van der Eng 1996, pp. 212-213; Geertz 1963, pp. 74-82.
31 Breman 1987, pp. 30-35.
32 Taselaar 1998, pp. 165-170.
33 Van den Brand 1902, reprinted in Breman 1987, pp. 234-313.
34 Reprinted in Breman 1987, pp. 315-408.
35 Lindblad 1999, pp. 63-65.
36 Székely-Lulofs 1931, 1932.
37 BPM = Bataafsche Petroleum Maatschappij (Batavian Petroleum Company), a joint subsidiary of the Dutch 'Koninklijke' (Royal) and British Shell.
38 Van den Berge 1998.
39 Dick and others 2002, pp. 117-120.
40 Booth 1998, p. 273.
41 Lindblad 2008, p. 104.
42 Lindblad 2008, p. 149.
43 Lindblad 2008, pp. 161-163, 167-170.
44 Sluyterman 2003, p. 218.
45 Lindblad 2008, pp. 178-186.
46 Lindblad 2008, pp. 196-197, 208.
47 The Siau Giap 1958, p. 259.
48 Székely-Lulofs 1946.
49 Daum 2006.
50 Székely-Lulofs 1983.
51 Haase 1992.
52 Noordervliet 2004.
53 Baay 2008. See also Stoler and Strassler 2000.
54 Stoler 2002 p 230 fn.40; Taylor 1983, p 26.
55 Taylor 1996, pp. 225-248, Pollmann 1999, pp. 9-32, Baay 2008.
56 Milone 1967, p. 411.
57 Stoler 1996.
58 See www.kitlv.nl on how to obtain access to the interviews.
59 SMGI project. Interview 1372.2.
60 Abeyasekere 1987, p. 33.
61 Locher-Scholten 1998, p. 134.
62 Delden 1989, 25.
63 One project which is a source of information here is the research conducted under the framework of the Nederlands Instituut voor Oorlogsdocumentatie (NIOD) project entitled 'Van Indië tot Indonesië' ('Indonesia Across Orders') funded by the Dutch Ministry of Health, Welfare and Sport, 2001-2006. Ratna Saptari and Erwiza Erman were responsible for the theme 'Labour in the Decolonization Process'. Interviews were conducted between 2003-2005.
64 Interview conducted on 29 December 2003 as part of the NIOD project 'Indonesia Across Orders'.
65 Wijdeveld 1919, p. 3.
66 Rouffaer en IJzerman 1915, p. 129.
67 During the period that the Netherlands was occupied by Napoleon, the English took control of the administration of Dutch garrisons in the Indonesian archipelago.
68 Raffles 1830, p. 374
69 Ibid.

70 For a detailed explanation of the education system in the Netherlands East Indies, see pp.32-59 in this book.
71 Suwardi Surjaningrat 1919, pp. 4-7.
72 Raev 2004, p. 11.
73 Quoted in Raev 2004, p. 11.
74 Suwardi 1919, p. 6.
75 Van Lelyveld 1931, p. 29.
76 Van Lelyveld 1931, p. 25.
77 Quoted in Raev 2004, p. 11.
78 Wijdeveld 1911, p. 3.
79 Borel 1916, p. 123.
80 Van Lelyveld 1931, p. 32.
81 Van Lelyveld 1931, p. 32.
82 Artaud 1958, pp. 53-54.
83 Eliade 1949, p. 11.
84 This mask was collected by one J.A. Houbolt de St. Amand, of Dangin Puri, Badung (Badung) on Bali. In 1937, he lent a series of 57 masks to the then Koloniaal Instituut. These masks bear serial numbers 1156 1-57.
85 Groot 1932, pp. 56-56.
86 Quoted in Brakel 2004, p. 14.
87 Brakel 2004, p. 113.
88 Van Lelyveld 1931, p. 40.
89 Ballard, Vink and Ploeg 2001, pp. 17-25.
90 Ballard, Vink and Ploeg 2001, p. 29.
91 Wollaston 1912; Rawling 1913.
92 Kleiweg de Zwaan 1942, p. 55-57.
93 Here the seventh edition of 1913 was used.
94 De Jong 2003, p. 83.
95 Le Roux 1948- 1951.
96 Van Duuren et al. 2007.
97 Larson, Petch and Zeitlyn 2007.
98 Thomas 1991.
99 As stated on the accompanying documentation card 6046-1.
100 Van Brakel et al. 1996.
101 Kirshenblatt-Gimblett 1998.
102 Nias Tribal Treasures 1990, p. 31.
103 In the wing Arts d'Afrique, d'Asie, d'Océanie et des Amériques (Arts Premier).
104 Collection musée du quai Branly, col. no. 70.1999.3.1.
105 Van Brakel & Legêne 2008.
106 Locher-Scholten 2000; Stoler 2002.
107 For Paulides see Hamman 1997.
108 For Weissenborn, see Drissen 1983.
109 Also see Van Eerde 1914.
110 Also see Conrad 1901, Van Eeden 1883.
111 See also Heins, Den Otter, Lamsweerde, Kunst 1956 and Kunst 1994.
112 See Van Brakel et al. 1998.
113 Founded in 1902 on the two-hundredth anniversary of Rumphius' death to promote scientific research in the Netherlands East Indies.
114 See Van Duuren, Beks and Rogers 1998.
115 Also in the Nederlands Openlucht Museum (Netherlands Open-air Museum) in Arnhem where an East Indian backyard has been set up since 2004.
116 Pattynama 1996, p 59-66.
117 The term 'Indo' (Indo-European) dates from the early 20th century and in the 1980s became a name of affection in the Netherlands.
118 Nieuwenhuys, 1973 p. 56.
119 Literally: son Paulus Augustinus signed the only known portrait of Rumphius (Beekman 1999).
120 Morrison Playing in the dark 1993.
121 Taylor 1988 passim.
122 See prints from 'Met andere ogen' 1986, p. 18, fig 16, the Loos-Haaxman 1941, p. 87 fig 82.
123 Several of his paintings hang elsewhere in the exhibition.
124 Seriese 1994 in: Paasman e.a. 1994, p. 81-91.
125 Wharr, wharr, wharr, in: Mahieu VZ 1992, pp
126 Said 1994 in: Said Culture and Imperialism 1994, p. 95-115
127 Roughly at the death of Sayers in 1943
128 E.g. the work of Pramoedja Ananta Toer (1925-2006)
129 E.g. one of the Djajadaningrats or Hamenko Buwono IX (1924-1988), Sultan of Jokjakarta.
130 Dermoût VW 1974, pp.119-298.
131 Dermoût VW, p. 290.
132 In the novel 'De Atlasvlinder' (1958).
133 Dermoût VW, p 291, 296, 297.
134 Dermoût VW, p 207.
135 Literary and historical sources such as Lin Scholte, or one of the many story projects in which ex-KNIL soldiers recorded their personal experiences.
136 The choice of both Sayers and Himpies was made in consultation with experts from the Indische group, including the Director of the Indisch Wetenschappelijk Instituut (IWI).

REFERENCES

Abeyasekere, S. *Jakarta. A History*. Singapore: Oxford University Press, 1987

Adriani, N. *Verzamelde Geschriften*. Haarlem: De Erven F.Bohn, 1932

Akveld, L. & E.M. Jacobs. *De kleurrijke wereld van de* VOC. Bussum: Thoth, 2002

Artaud, A. *The Theater and its Double*. New York: Grove Press Inc. 1958 [Transl. of *Le Théâtre et son Double*, Paris: Gallimard 1938]

Avebury, Lord. *Prehistoric Times as illustrated by Ancient Remains and the Manners and Customs of Modern Savages*. London: Williams and Norgate, 1913

Baay, R. *De njai. Het concubinaat in Nederlands-Indië*. Amsterdam: Atheneum – Polak en Van Gennep, 2008

Ballard Chris, Steven Vink & Anton Ploeg. *Race to the Snow. Photography and the exploration of Dutch New Guinea, 1907 – 1936*. Amsterdam: KIT Publishers, 2001

Beekman, E.M. *Georgius Everhardus Rumphius. The Ambonese Curiosity Cabinet*. Translated, edited, annotated and with an introduction by E.M. Beekman. New Haven: Yale University Press, 1999

Berge, Tom van den. *Karel Frederik Holle. Theeplanter in Indië, 1829-1896*. Amsterdam: Bakker, 1998

Booth, Anne. *The Indonesian Economy in the Nineteenth and Twentieth Centuries. A History of Missed Opportunities*. Basingstoke, Macmillan, 1998

Borel, H. 'De Indische Kunstavond in den Haagschen schouwburg (15 en 17 maart 1916)'. *Nederlandsch-Indië Oud en Nieuw*. Maart 1916: pp. 119-124

Bossenbroek, Martin et al. (red). *Weerzien met Indië. 38: Taal en onderwijs. 44: De nationalistische beweging*. Zwolle: Waanders, 1995

Brakel, J.H. van, et al. *Indië omlijst. Vier eeuwen schilderkunst in Nederlands-Indië*. Amsterdam: KIT Publishers, 1998 [Transl. as *Paintings by Western artists during the Dutch colonial period in Indonesia*. Wijk en Aalburg: Pictures Publishers, 1998]

Brakel, K. van. *Charles Sayers 1901-1941. Pioneer painter in the Dutch East Indies*. Amsterdam: KIT Publishers, 2004

Brakel, Koos van, David van Duuren & Itie van Hout. *A Passion for Indonesian Art. The Georg Tillmann (1882-1941) Collection at the Tropenmuseum Amsterdam*. Amsterdam: KIT Publishers, 1996

Brakel, Koos van & Susan Legêne (eds). *Collecting at cultural crossroads. Collection policies and approaches (2008-2012) of the Tropenmuseum*. Bulletin 381. Amsterdam: KIT Publishers, 2008

Brand, J. van den. *De millioenen uit Deli*. Amsterdam: Höveker & Wormser, 1902

Breman, Jan. *Koelies, planters en koloniale politiek. Het arbeidsregime op de grootlandbouwondernemingen aan Sumatra's Oostkust in het begin van de twintigste eeuw*. Dordrecht/Providence: Foris Publications , 1987 [heruitgave Leiden: KITLV Uitgeverij 1992]

Bussy, J.H. de. *Gedenkboek Deli-Maatschappij 1916-1941. Gedenkschrift aangeboden aan den heer Herbert Cremer, directeur N.V. Deli Maatschappij, 15 februari 1941*. Amsterdam

Conrad, J.F.W. *F.W. van Eeden. Rede*. Haarlem: Nederlandsche Maatschappij ter bevordering van Nijverheid, 1901

Cremer, J.T. *Een Woord uit Deli tot de Tweede Kamer der Staten Generaal*. Amsterdam: Van Tijen, 1876

Cremer, J.T. *De Toekomst van Deli. Eenige Opmerkingen*. Leiden: Kolff, 1881

Cremer, J.T. *Jeugd en jongelingsjaren van Jacob Theodoor Cremer (30 juni 1847-14 augustus 1923) beschreven door hemzelf*. Den Haag: Leopold, 1924

Creutzberg, P. *Changing Economy in Indonesia. V. National Income*. The Hague, Nijhoff, 1979

Daum, P.A. *Uit de Suiker in de Tabak*. 's Gravenhage: Thomas & Eras Uitgevers, 1977 en 2002 [1st edition 1885]

Delden, M.C. 'Bersiap in Bandoeng: een onderzoek naar geweld in de periode van 17 augustus 1945 tot 24 maart 1946'. MA thesis, Universiteit van Amsterdam, 1989

Dermoût, Maria. *De tienduizend dingen*. Amsterdam: Querido, 1955 [Transl. as *The Ten Thousand Things*. New York: Simon & Schuster 1958]

Dermoût, Maria. *Maria Dermoût Verzameld Werk*. Amsterdam, 1974

Dick, Howard, Vincent J.H. Houben, J. Thomas Lindblad & Thee Kian Wie. *The Emergence of National Economy. An Economic History of Indonesia*. Crows Nest, NSW: Allen & Unwin, 2002

Djojopoespito, Soewarsih. *Buiten het gareel. Indonesische roman*. Den Haag: Nijgh en Van Ditmar, 1946 [eerste druk 1940]

Drissen, E. *Vastgelegd voor later: Indische foto's van Thilly Weissenborn*. Amsterdam: Sijthoff, 1983

Duuren, D.A.P. van. *125 Jaar verzamelen. Tropenmuseum Amsterdam*. Amsterdam: KIT Publishers, 1990

Duuren, D.A.P. van, K. Beks & T. Rogers. *The Kris: An Earthly Approach to a Cosmic Symbol*. Wijk en Aalburg: Pictures Publishers. 1998

Duuren, D.A.P. van *et al. Physical Anthropology reconsidered. Human Remains at the Tropenmuseum*. Bulletin 375. Amsterdam: KIT Publishers, 2007

Eeden, F.W. van. *Het Koloniaal Museum op het Paviljoen te Haarlem*. Haarlem, Nederlandsche Maatschappij ter bevordering van nijverheid, 1883

Eerde, J.C. van. *Koloniale Volkenkunde. Eerste stuk: Omgang met Inlanders.* Amsterdam: Koninklijk Koloniaal Instituut te Amsterdam – Mededeeling No. 1, Afdeeling Volkenkunde, 1914

Eliade, M. *Le mythe de l'éternel retour.* Paris: Librairie Gallimard, 1949

Eng, Pierre van der. *Agricultural Growth in Indonesia. Productivity Change and Policy Impact since 1880.* London: Macmillan, 1996

Fasseur, C. *De Indologen. Ambtenaren voor de Oost, 1825-1950.* Amsterdam: Bert Bakker, 1993

Fasseur, C. 'Cornerstone and stumbling block. Racial classification and the late colonial state in Indonesia'. In: Robert Cribb (ed.), *The Late Colonial State in Indonesia. Political and Economic Foundations of the Netherlands Indies, 1880-1942.* Leiden: KITLV Press, 1994, pp. 31-56

Fasseur, C. *De Weg naar het Paradijs en andere Indische geschiedenissen.* Amsterdam: Bert Bakker, 1995

Friedericy, H.J. *De raadsman.* Amsterdam: Querido, 1958 [Transl. as 'The counsellor' in: *Two Tales of the East [Indies].* Singapore: Periplus, 2000]

Geertz, Clifford. *Agricultural Involution. The Processes of Ecological Change in Indonesia.* Berkeley: University of California Press, 1963

Gortzak, H.J. 'Apports et contradictions du « tiers-mondisme ».' In: D. Taffin (red), *Du musée colonial au musée des cultures du monde. Actes du colloque organisé par le musée national des Arts d'Afrique et d' Océanie et le Centre Georges-Pompidou, 3-6 juin 1998.* Paris: musée national des Arts d'Afrique et d' Océanie, Maisonneuve et Larose, 2000, pp. 185-194

Gouda, F. *Dutch Culture Overseas. Colonial practice in the Netherlands Indies, 1900-1942.* Amsterdam: Amsterdam University Press, 1995

Groeneboer, Kees. *Weg tot het Westen. Het Nederlands voor Indië 1600-1950.* Leiden: KITLV Uitgeverij, 1993

Groot, J.H., de. 'Charley Sayers'. *Het Korenland, Maandblad voor cultuur en jeugdvorming.* Maart 1932, pp. 56-60

Haasse, Hella S. *Oeroeg.* Amsterdam: Vereeniging ter Bevordering van de Belangen des Boekhandels, 1948 [Transl. as *Forever a Stranger and Other Stories.* Oxford and New York: Oxford University Press]

Haasse, Hella S. *De tuinen van Bomarzo.* Amsterdam: Querido, 1968

Haasse, Hella S. *Heren van de thee.* Amsterdam: Querido, 1992

Haasse, Hella S. *Sleuteloog.* Amsterdam: Querido, 2002

Haga, A. *Nederlandsch Nieuw Guinea en de Papoesche Eilanden: een historische bijdrage. ±1500-1883.* Batavia: W. Bruining & co/ Den Haag: Martinus Nijhof, 1884

Hammann, Peter E.M. *Hendrik Paulides.* Haarlem: Hamman Fine Art Consultancy BV, 1997

Hazeu, G.A.J. *Bijdrage tot de Kennis van het Javaansche Tooneel.* Leiden: Brill, 1897

Heins, E., E. den Otter, F. van Lamsweerde & Jaap Kunst. *Indonesian music and dance.* Amsterdam, 1994

Jong, Ad de. 'Kleiweg de Zwaan'. In: Arnold Wentholt (red.), *In kaart gebracht met kapmes en kompas. Met het Koninklijk Nederlands Aardrijkskundig Genootschap op expeditie tussen 1873 en 1960.* Heerlen/Utrecht: ABP Public Affairs & KNAG, 2003, pp. 80-83

Jong, J.J.P. de. *De waaier van het fortuin: van handelscompagnie tot koloniaal imperium. De Nederlanders in Azië en de Indonesische Archipel, 1595-1950.* Den Haag: SDU, 1998

Kartini. *Brieven aan mevrouw R.M. Abendanon-Mandri en haar echtgenoot met andere documenten.* Bezorgd door F.G.P Jaquet. Dordrecht/Providence: Foris Publications, 1987 [Transl. as *Letters from Kartini. An Indonesian Feminist 1900-1904.* Clayton, Victoria: Monash Asia Institute, 1992]

Kerkhoff, G. *Louis J. Vreugde, 3 Januari 1868 – 3 November 1936.* Haarlem: Jaarboek 1936,pp. 20-25

Kinderjaren. Documentaire door Piet Oomes, 2006

Kirshenblatt-Gimblett, Barbara. *Destination Culture. Tourism, Museums, and Heritage.* Berkeley/London: University of California Press, 1998

Kleiweg de Zwaan, J. P. *De dwergvolken (anthropologisch beschouwd).* Den Haag: N.V. Servire, 1942

Klift-Snijder, A.C. van der & C.G.F. de Jong. *Geroepen, gezonden en gezegend. Memoires van een zendelingsvrouw in Zuidoost-Celebes.* Zoetermeer: Boekencentrum, 1996

Knight, G.R. 'Did "Dependency" really get it wrong? The Indonesian sugar industry, 1880-1942'. In: Thomas J. Lindblad (ed.) *Historical Foundations of a National Economy in Indonesia, 1890s-1990s.* Amsterdam: North-Holland, 1996, pp. 155-174

Kooy-van Zeggelen, M.C. *De Hollandse Vrouw in Indië. Indrukken van een zwervelinge.* Amsterdam: Scheltema&Holkema, 1910

Kousbroek, Rudy. 'Bij een foto'. In: Bert Paasman (ed), *Met andere ogen. Dertig vrienden over de fotoboeken van Rob Nieuwenhuys.* Amsterdam: Querido, 1998

Kruyt, J. *Het Zendingsveld Poso.* Kampen: Kok, 1970

Kunst, Jaap. Proeve van een autobiografie, 1956 (unpublished manuscript)

Kunst, Jaap. *Indonesian Music and Dance: Traditional Music and its Interaction with the West.* Amsterdam: Royal Tropical Institute, 1994

Larson, Frances, Alison Petch and David Zeitlyn. 'Social networks and the creation of the Pitt Rivers Museum.' *Journal of Material Culture.* 2007, vol. 12 (3): 211-239

Legêne, S. 'Enlightenment, Empathy and Retreat: The Cultural Heritage of the *Ethische Politiek*.' In: P. ter Keurs (ed), *Colonial Collections Revisited.* Leiden: CNWS Publications, 2007, pp. 220-245

Legêne, S., and E. Postel-Coster. 'Isn't it all Culture? Culture and Dutch development policy in the post-colonial period.' In: J.A. Nekkers & P.A.M. Malcontent (eds) *Fifty years of Dutch development cooperation 1949-1999.* The Hague: Sdu uitgevers, 2000, pp. 271-288

Lelyveld, J.E.A.M. Waarlijk geen overdaad, doch een dringende eisch. Koloniaal onderwijs en onderwijsbeleid in Nederlands-Indië 1893-1942. 1992 (unpublished PhD dissertation, Universiteit Utrecht)

Lelyveld, Th.B. van. *De Javaansche Danskunst*. Amsterdam: Van Holkema & Warendorf's Uitgevers-Mij, 1931
Lindblad, J. Thomas. 'Business Strategies in Late Colonial Indonesia'. In: J. Thomas Lindblad (ed.), *Historical Foundations of a National Economy in Indonesia, 1890s-1990s*. Amsterdam: North-Holland, 1996, pp. 207-227
Lindblad, J. Thomas. Coolies in Deli: Labour conditions in Western enterprises in East Sumatra, 1910-1938. In: Vincent J.H. Houben, J. Thomas Lindblad and others, *Coolie Labour in Colonial Indonesia. A Study of Labour Relations in the Outer Islands, c. 1900-1940*. Wiesbaden: Harrassowitz, 1999, pp. 43-78
Lindblad, J. Thomas. *Bridges to New Business. The Economic Decolonisation of Indonesia*. Leiden: KITLV Press, 2008
Links Richten, mei 1933:9 (introduction). Amsterdam: Van Gennip (complete reprint 1973)
Locher-Scholten, E. 'So Close and Yet So Far: The Ambivalence of Dutch Colonial Rhetoric on Javanese Servants in Indonesia, 1900-1942'. In: J. Clancy-Smith and F. Gouda (eds.), *Domesticating the Empire. Race, Gender and Family Life in French and Dutch Colonialism*. Charlottesville: University Press of Virginia, 1998, pp. 131-153
Locher-Scholten, E. *Women and the Colonial State. Essays on Gender and Modernity in the Netherlands Indies 1900-1942*. Amsterdam: Amsterdam University Press, 2000
Loos-Haaxman, J.M.C. de. *De landsverzameling schilderijen in Batavia. Landvoogdportretten en compagnieschilders*. Leiden: Sijthoff, 1941
Mahieu, Vincent. *Verzameld Werk*. Amsterdam: Querido, 1992 [Vincent Mahieu is ps. For Paup Boo, better known as Tjalie Robinson]
Meijsing, Doeschka. *Over de liefde*. Amsterdam: Querido, 2008
Milone, P.D. '*Indische* Culture, and its Relationship to Urban Life'. *Comparative Studies in Society and History*. 1967, Vol 9 no. 4, pp. 407-426
Mulder, M. 'Een Teeken Van Ons Gezag: een biografische schets van objectnummer 573-63, een Nederlands wapenbord afkomstig uit Nieuw-Guinea, in de collectie van het Tropenmuseum te Amsterdam.' Amsterdam, 2008. Unpublished manuscript
Nias Tribal Treasures. Cosmic Reflections in Stone, Wood and Gold. Delft: Volkenkundig Museum Nusantara, 1990
Nieuwenhuys, Rob. *Oost-Indische spiegel: wat Nederlandse schrijvers en dichters over Indonesië hebben geschreven, vanaf de eerste jaren der Compagnie tot op heden*. Amsterdam, Querido, 1973
Nieuwenhuys, Rob. *Met vreemde ogen. Tempo doeloe – een verzonken wereld. Fotografische documenten uit het oude Indië 1870-1920*. Amsterdam: Querido, 1988
Noordervliet, N. *Brieven van de thee: uit een Indisch familiearchief met originele foto's*. Amsterdam: Querido, 2004
Paasman, Bert (ed.) *Met andere ogen. Dertig vrienden over de fotoboeken van Rob Nieuwenhuys*. Amsterdam, Querido, 1998
Pattynama, P. 'Wat droeg een Indo in de Middeleeuwen.' In: *Onderbelicht, zwarte, migranten- en vluchtelingenvrouwen in Nederland, informatie-uitwisseling in perspectief*. Tentoonstelling en lezingcyclus van het Internationaal Informatiecentrum en Archief voor de vrouwenbeweging (IIAV), Amsterdam, 1996, pp. 59-66
Pollmann, T. 'Bruidstraantjes – De Koloniale roman, de njai en de apartheid'. In *Bruidstraantjes en andere Indische geschiedenissen*. Den Haag: Sdu uitgevers, 1999, pp. 9-32
Raev, A. 'In dienst van Diaghilev – Een Inleiding'. In: catalogus ter gelegenheid van de tentoonstelling 'In dienst van Diaghilev'. Groninger Museum, 2004
Raffles, T.S. *A History of Java*. London: John Murray, 1830. Internet: digitized by Google
Rawling, C.G. *The Land of the New Guinea Pygmies. An Account of a Story of a Pioneer Journey of Exploration into the Heart of New Guinea*. London: Seeley, Service & Co, 1913
Rouffaer, G.P. & J.W. IJzerman (eds.) *De eerste schipvaart der Nederlanders naar Oost-Indië onder Cornelis de Houtman, 1595-1597*. 's-Gravenhage: Martinus Nijhof, 1915
Le Roux, C.C.F.M. *De Bergpapoea's van Nieuw-Guinea en hun woongebied* (two volumes and a collection of prints). Leiden: E. J. Brill, 1948-1951
Rumphius, Georg Everhard. *d'Amboinsche Rariteitkamer* Amsterdam, 1705 [Transl. as *Rumphius, Georg Everard. The Ambonese Curiosity Cabinet*. New Haven: Yale University Press, 1999]
Rumphius, Georg Everhard. *Het Amboinsche Kruidboek*. Amsterdam, 1741
Rutten-Pekelharing, C.J. *Waaraan moet ik denken? Wat moet ik doen?: Wenken aan het Hollandsche meisje, dat als huisvrouw naar Indië gaat*. Gorinchem: Noordyn, 1923
Said, Edward W. Narratieve en maatschappelijke ruimte'. In: Edward W. Said, *Cultuur en imperialisme*. Amsterdam/Antwerpen, 1994, pp. 95-115
Scheffer, P. *Het land van aankomst*. Amsterdam: De Bezige Bij, 2007
Scholte, Lin. *Verzamelde romans en verhalen van Lin Scholte. Met een biografische inleiding door Vilan van de Loo*. Den Haag: Stichting Tong Tong, 2007
Schulte Nordholt, Henk. 'A genealogy of violence'. In: Freek Colombijn, Thomas Lindblad (eds), *Roots of violence in Indonesia. Contemporary violence in historical perspective*. Leiden: KITLV Press, 2002, pp. 33-61
Seriese, E. 'Jan Boon: een Indische jongen aan het werk'. In: B. Paasman (red), *Tjalie Robinson, de stem van Indisch Nederland*. Den Haag, Stichting Tong Tong, 1994, pp. 81-91
Shiraishi, Takashi. *An Age in Motion. Popular Radicalism in Java, 1912-1926*. Ithaca and London: Cornell University Press, 1990
Sjahrir, S. *Indonesische Overpeinzingen*. Amsterdam: De Bezige Bij, 1987
Sluyterman, Keetie E. *Kerende kansen. Het Nederlandse bedrijfsleven in de twintigste eeuw*. Amsterdam: Boom, 2003
Statistisch Zakboekje voor Nederlandsch Indië, 1939. Batavia: Kolff

Stoler, A. 'A Sentimental Education. Native Servants and the Cultivation of European Children in the Netherlands Indies'. In: L.J. Sears (ed.). *Fantasizing the Feminine in Indonesia*. Durham: Duke University Press, 1996

Stoler, A. *Carnal Knowledge and Imperial Power. Race and the Intimate in Colonial Rule*. Berkeley/Los Angeles/London: University of California Press, 2002

Stoler, A & K. Strassler. 'Castings for the Colonial: Memory Work in 'New Order' Java'. *Comparative Studies in Society and History*. Vol 42 no.1, 2000, pp. 4-48

Surjaningrat, Suwardi. 'De dans in het tooneel der Javanen.' *Wendingen* maart 1919: pp. 4-12

Székely, Lászlo. 'Het land der onmogelijkheden'. In: Lászlo Székely and István Radnai, *Dit altijd alleen zij. Verhalen over het leven van planters en koelies in Deli, 1914-1930*. Leiden: KITLV Uitgeverij, 2007, pp. 43-46

Székely-Lulofs, Madelon. *Rubber, roman uit Deli*. Amsterdam: Elsevier, 1931 [heruitgave Schoorl: Conserve, 1992]

Székely-Lulofs, Madelon. *Koelie*. Amsterdam: Elsevier, 1932

Székely-Lulofs, Madelon. *Onze Bedienden in Indië*. Deventer: Uitgeverij W. van Hoeve, 1946

Taselaar, Arjen. *De Nederlandse koloniale lobby. Ondernemers en de Indische politiek, 1914-1940*. Leiden: CNWS, 1998

Taylor, J. *The Social World of Batavia*. Madison: University of Wisconsin Press, 1983

Taylor, Jean Gelman. *Smeltkroes Batavia. Europeanen en Euraziaten in de Nederlandse vestingen in Azië*. Groningen: Wolters-Noordhoff, 1988

Taylor, Jean Gelman. 'Nyai Dasima. Portrait of a Mistress in Literature and Film'. In: Laurie J. Sears (ed) *Fantasizing the Feminine in Indonesia*. Durham: Duke University Press, 1996

The Siauw Giap. 'Urbanisatieproblemen in Indonesie'. *Bijdragen tot de Taal Land en Volkenkunde*. Vol. 115, 1958, pp. 249-276

Thomas, N. *Entangled Objects. Exchange, Material Culture and Colonialism in the Pacific*. Harvard: Harvard University Press, 1991

Touwen, Jeroen. *Extremes in the Archipelago. Trade and Economic Development in the Outer Islands of Indonesia, 1900-1942*. Leiden: KITLV Press, 2001

Wal, S.L. van der. *Herinneringen van Jhr. Mr. B.C. de Jonge: met brieven uit zijn nalatenschap*. Groningen: Wolters-Noordhoff, 1968

Wijdeveld, H.Th. 'De moderne dans in de rij der kunsten.' *Wendingen* maart 1919: p. 3

Wollaston, A.F.R. *Pygmies and Papuans. The Stone Age Today in Dutch New Guinea*. London: Smith Elder, 1912

Woudsma, C. *The Royal Tropical Institute, an Amsterdam landmark*. Amsterdam: KIT Publishers, 1990

INDEX

Aceh 22, 29, 33-37, 42, 58, 97, 135-136, 152
Aceh War 22, 35-36, 42
Acquet, Hendrik d' 141, 151, 165
administrator 21, 58, 62, 72, 98
Alor 9
Amboinsche Kruidboek, Het 164-165
Amboinsche Rariteitkamer, De 15, 151, 164-165
Ambon 46-47, 76, 135, 165, 181
ancestral figure 117
animism 9
anthropologist 21, 88, 103, 106-107, 113
anthropology 10-11, 35, 97, 102-103, 107-108, 113, 128, 134, 139
armes blanches 152
Art nouveau 130-131
art trade 114-115, 117
Artaud, Antonin 86
artisan 152
artist 5, 13-14, 21, 31, 121, 123-124, 128, 174, 182
Arts and Crafts movement 19, 120, 130
assistent-resident 29
avant-garde 81, 85, 94
Bali 9, 51, 87, 89, 91, 94-95, 97, 105, 128, 132, 145, 149-150, 175, 177, 187
Bank Indonesia 64
Bataafsche Petroleum Maatschappij (BPM) 47, 59, 63, 186
Batavia 42-44, 46, 54, 57, 62, 74, 87, 106-107, 118, 123, 126, 129-130, 139, 143, 150, 172
Bataviaasch Genootschap van Kunsten en Wetenschappen (Batavian Society of Arts and Sciences) 107, 139
batik 13, 19, 23, 69, 74, 120, 123, 130-131, 137, 148-150
batik belanda 149
Beeckman, Andries 150, 171-173
Benois, Alexandre 85
Bergpapoea's van Nieuw-Guinea en hun woongebied, De 106-107
Berlage, H.P. 13, 150
Bible 9, 119, 173
Bijdrage tot de Kennis van het Javaansche Tooneel 82
Billiton Maatschappij 59, 63
Boedi Oetomo (Lofty Intent) 46-47
Boon, C.J. 34, 36
Boon, J. (Vincent Mahieu) 34, 36, 174
Borel, Henri 85, 187
Borsumij 63
Boven-Digoel 48
Brand, J. van den 58, 186
Breton, André 118, 166
British India 46
British Ornithologists' Expedition 100
Bronner, J. 86, 142, 152
Buiten het gareel 39, 41, 188
Buitengewesten (Outer Regions) 43, 54, 58, 142
Cakranegara prince of 51
camera 21, 79, 106, 145
canon of ethnography (ethnographic canons) 113, 115, 188
capitalism 53
Carstensz, Johan 99
cartography 142
Chinese 17, 41-42, 45, 56-60, 62, 64, 67, 70, 77, 118, 149, 152, 172
Christianity 9, 118, 138
cinema 5, 146, 161, 166
civil servant 4, 45, 68, 121, 123, 162-164, 174, 177
clerk 21, 59, 65, 165, 188
Coen, Jan Pieterszn. 9, 22, 97
coffee 53, 72
Cold War 13
collaborator 162
collector(s) 4, 5, 14-15, 17-18, 20, 22, 24, 35, 95, 113-115, 117, 119-121, 123, 127, 129, 131, 133, 135, 137, 138, 139, 165
colonial administration 22, 29, 32, 44-45, 49, 97, 123, 148, 162-163
colonial art 18, 149
colonial civility 30-31, 33
colonial club 29-32, 34, 36-37
colonial collection 120
colonial culture 13, 15, 17, 19, 22, 118
colonial economy 53-56
colonial elite 15, 17, 21, 62
colonial government 30, 34, 40, 42-45, 47, 55-57, 59, 62, 97, 123, 148
colonial perspective 24-25
colonial society 10, 15, 17-18, 21-22, 24, 35, 41-43, 68, 113-115, 118, 120-121, 146, 148, 150, 164, 168
colonial supremacy 36
colonial system 15, 23
colonial theatre 17, 20-21, 171, 174-175, 177-178, 182-183
colonial troops 29, 34
communists 65
community of origin 114
community art 4, 81, 83, 85, 87, 89, 91, 93-95
controleur 123
cook 77-78
cornerstone 174, 178, 180, 183
Couperus, Louis 13, 15, 132
Cremer, Jacob Theodoor 16, 21, 58-59, 62, 113, 145, 188
crossover 119
cultural anthropology 10-11, 35, 102, 107, 128, 134, 139
cultural heritage 150, 161, 164, 168

Cultuurstelsel (Cultivation System) 54
Daalen, G.C. E. 36-37, 135
dalang 82, 84
dance 4, 81-87, 89, 91, 93-95, 150, 172
dance theatre 4, 81, 83-87, 89, 91, 93, 95
Dayak 99
Declaration of Independence 11
decolonisation 11, 13-14, 22, 24, 33, 65, 155
Deli 53, 55, 58-59, 62, 64-65, 144
Deli Planters Vereniging (Deli Planters Association) 58-59
Deli-Maatschappij (Deli Company) 55, 58, 65
Delprat, Theodore F.A. 4, 124, 126
depression 47, 56
Dermoût, Maria 21, 163-164, 178, 180-181, 187-188
desa 12, 42, 82
development cooperation 11-13, 146
Diponegoro, prince 30-32
Djojopoespito,Soewarsi 39-41, 46, 48, 113, 186, 188
domestic servant 75
Douwes Dekker, Ernst 175, 177
drama 5, 83-85, 88, 171, 174, 183
drawing 31, 45, 51, 78, 95, 128
dress 69, 128, 148-149
Durkheim, Emile 88
East Indian Party 47
Eastward Bound 4, 13-15, 18, 27, 29, 31, 34, 36-37, 40, 49, 161, 163-164, 171, 173-174, 177-178, 180-183
education 4, 23-24, 39-47, 49, 51, 55, 62, 65, 75, 82, 94, 113, 119, 136, 138-139, 163, 177-178, 187
Eeden, Frederik W. van 5, 137-138, 141-142, 187
Eerde, Joahn C. 5, 91, 98, 103, 128, 134, 152, 187
Eijkman, Christiaan 98
Eliade, Mircea 89, 95, 187
Elink-van Maarseveen, Anna 21, 25, 188
employee 58, 73, 103
employer 58, 69, 73-74, 77-78
Emulation 130
Emulation – Guide to Promote Homely Arts and Crafts 130
Engelen-Koets, Margaretha 21, 68, 188
enterprises 4, 11, 53, 55-57, 59, 61, 63, 65
entrepreneur 4, 63, 124
entrepreneurship 30, 53, 56, 59
equality 46
escutcheon 98
Ethische Politiek (Ethical Policy) 10, 18, 22, 24, 40, 47, 62, 68, 123, 134-135, 153, 186
ethnic group 65, 79, 108, 118
ethnomusicology 138-139
Eurasian 69, 73, 149
Europe 9, 17, 23, 53, 81, 85, 89, 120-121, 138-139, 150, 178, 180
Europese Lagere School(European Elementary School) 42
exhibition 13-18, 20-22, 24-25, 29, 31, 33-34, 37, 40, 42, 47, 58, 65, 79, 82, 89, 94-95, 105, 108, 114, 124, 128, 134, 136, 141-142, 155, 161, 163-164, 171, 173-175, 177, 182, 187
expansion 10, 22, 43, 54, 58, 64
exploration 10, 24, 33, 99, 105-106, 138
export 55-57, 59, 95, 137, 155
extremism 48
fairs 124, 129, 155
family life 79, 144
feminism 46
fiction 21, 162-163, 183
film 18, 100, 106, 145-146, 166-168, 177
First World War 10, 81
Foto Lux 132
Friedericy, H.J. 21, 162-163, 177, 180
Gamelan 82-83, 85, 87, 130, 138
Gamelanorkest 87
gardener 78
gender 46, 74
Geo Wehry 63
Germany 49
Gesseler Verschuir-Pownall, M.A. van 153-154
Governor General 21, 24, 35, 41-42, 47-48, 76, 128, 138, 143, 145, 172, 174
graduates 45
Greshoff 86, 151-152
guerrilla 49, 135, 180
Haarlem 9-10, 16, 86, 113, 121, 123-124, 130, 137, 141-142, 151-152
Haasse, Hella 54, 167-168, 186
Hatta, Mahammad 49
Hazeu, G.A.J. 82
Heeren van de thee 54
Heutsz, J.B. van 35-37, 42, 145
Hillerström 24, 144-145, 148, 177-178, 180
Himpies 163-164, 174, 178, 180-181, 183, 187-188
hinduism 9
History of Java 82-83
Hollands-Chinese School (Dutch Chinese School) 42
Hollands-Inlandse School (Dutch Native School) 42
Holle, Karel Frederik 59, 62-63
household 23, 67, 69, 73-74, 77-79, 119, 155
housekeeping 70
house wife 21
Houtman, Cornelis de 16, 82
Hubrecht, H.F. R. 16, 99
Huiselijke Kunst (Homely Arts) 130
human remains 102-103, 108, 130
IJzerman, J.W. 124, 172, 187
indigenous 17, 21, 53, 55-56, 62, 105, 123, 128, 130, 136-138, 145, 148, 164, 167
Indisch Instituut (Indies Institute) 11, 144
Indisch Museum (Indies Museum) 6, 11
Indisch Wetenschappelijk Instituut (Indies Scientific Institute) 145, 177-178, 183, 187
Indische partij 47
Indo 69, 129, 168, 173-174, 177-178, 187
Indo-Dutch community 15
indologist 134
Indonesian archipelago 10, 22, 49, 53, 97, 138, 187
Indonesian Communist Party (Partai Komunis Indonesia, PKI) 48
Indonesian Nationalist movement 10, 41

Indonesian Revolution 65
Indonesianisation 53, 63-64
infrastructure 59, 78
inlander 136
De Inlandsche Kunstnijverheid in Nederlandsch Indie 123
instruments 23, 102, 106, 119, 138-139
Internatio 63
Internationale Koloniale en Uitvoerhandeltentoonstelling (International Colonial and Export Trade Exhibition) 155
irrigation 56, 62
Islam 9, 42, 47
Israëls, Isaac 87, 150
Jacobson van den Berg 63
Japan 13, 46, 49
Japanese internment camp 123, 132, 175
jas tutup 148
Jasper, Johan Ernst 4, 123-124, 128
Java 9, 13, 17-18, 23, 29-32, 39-40, 43-45, 47, 53-56, 58, 60, 62, 64, 67-69, 71, 73-74, 76-79, 81-84, 87, 89, 91, 93-95, 98, 115, 119-120, 123-124, 128, 130-132, 135, 142, 144-146, 148-149, 154, 157, 161, 168, 172, 175, 181-182, 186
De Javaansche Danskunst 82, 85
Javanese elite 46, 75
Javasche Bank (Java Bank) 62
Jonge, B. de 21, 24, 41, 47-48, 188
Jubilee Exhibition 18, 20, 134
Juliana, queen 12, 49
Jung, Carl G. 89, 95
kain 69, 148
Kartini 39-42, 186
kebaya 69, 149
Kinderjaren 166
Kleiweg de Zwaan, J.P. 91, 103, 105, 108, 187
Kleyntjes, Willem 21, 188
KNIL, *See* Koninklijk Nederlandsch-Indisch Leger
Kock, Hendrik Markus de 30, 32, 186
Koelie-ordonnantie (Coolie Ordinance) 58, 62
Koelievraagstuk 58
koelit langsep 174, 177-178, 181-183
Koloniaal Instituut (Colonial Institute) 9-11, 16, 18-21, 24, 30, 35-36, 58, 62, 86-87, 103, 107-108, 120, 124, 126, 128-129, 134, 136, 139, 142, 145-146, 151-152, 155, 187
Koloniaal Museum (Colonial Museum) 5, 6, 9-10, 15, 18-19, 21, 23, 35, 41, 76, 86, 89, 105-107, 113, 116, 121, 124, 126, 128, 130, 134, 136-139, 141-142, 151
Koloniale Volkenkunde 134
Koninklijk Instituut voor de Tropen (KIT, Royal Tropical Institute) 6, 9, 68, 103
Koninklijk Nederlands Aardrijkskundig Genootschap (KNAG, Royal Dutch Geographical Society) 106, 126
Koninklijk Nederlandsch-Indisch Leger (KNIL, Royal Netherlands Indies Army) 21, 29, 35, 36, 51, 107, 145, 152, 178, 180, 181
Koninklijke Paketvaart Maatschappij (KPM) 64
Koninklijke Vereniging Indisch Instituut (Royal Indies Institute) 144
Koran 152
Krakatau 97
Krause, Gregor 81
Kretek 56
Krijnen, Quirien A.A. 5, 129-130
Krijnen's Maandblad 130
Krijnen-Surie, Petronella M.H. 5, 129-130
kris of Knaud 115
Krom, N.J. 82
Kudus 56, 74
Kunst, Jaap 5, 138-139
Kurkdjian 131
Lamster, J.C. 145-146
Lands Plantentuin, s' 98
Langen-Driyo 82, 85
League of Nations 57
Lelyveld, Th. B. van 82, 85-86, 187
Les Ballets Russes 81, 84-85, 89
Levi-Strauss, Claude 89
library 5, 10, 18, 54, 56, 74, 98, 120, 141, 151-152, 173
Lindeteves 63
Links Richten 18, 186
Lion Cachet, C.A. 19, 64, 91, 120
literacy 44-45
literature 5, 161-162, 164, 168, 177, 186
Lombok 51, 91, 97, 124, 152
Lord Avebury 102
Louvre 117-118
Mahabharata and Ramayana 83, 88
Mangkunegoro 74
mannequin 33, 174, 177-178, 182
map 97, 99, 120, 139, 142-143
Marind people 126
Markt in Klungkung 94
Mas Pirngadie 123
mask 83, 85, 89, 91, 187
Medical faculty 43
Mestizo culture 171
Met andere ogen 164, 187
migration 67, 69
military conflict 22
Millioenen uit Deli, De 58
Minangkabau 103, 124
miniature 23
Minister of Colonial Affairs 58
mission 9-11, 130
missionary 5, 9, 21, 25, 119, 121, 126, 128, 153
modernisation 12-13, 42, 64
Mooi-Indië-kunst 149-150
mosque 153
Mount Wilhelmina 99
Mountain Papuans 99-100
MULO 39, 41
mural 9, 11, 129
Museum van het Bataviaasch Genootschap van Kunsten en Wetenschap (Museum of the Batavian Society of Arts and Sciences) 106

music 5, 81-82, 84-86, 89, 119, 121, 138-139
myth 89, 166
nationalisation 65
nationalism 18, 40, 44, 46-49, 64, 167, 186
native elite 42, 45
native population 10, 17, 40, 103
native society 155
Natura Artis Magistra (Artis) 9, 15
Nederlandsche Handel-Maatschappij (Netherlands Trading Society) 55, 62, 138
Nederlandsche Maatschappij ter bevordering van Nijverheid (Dutch Society for the Advancement of Industry) 9, 137
Neeb, H.M. 36-37
New Guinea 4, 48, 64, 97-100, 102-108, 119, 126, 139
Nias 9, 115, 117, 121, 187
Nienhuys, Jacobus 55
Nieuwe Kunst (New Art) 81, 86
Nieuwenhuys, Rob 164, 187
njai, De 68
nobility 47, 62
Noto Soerotoe 87
Oceania 13, 15, 113
Oeroeg 167-168
Offerfeest te Besakih 94
Onze Bedienden in Indië 67
Oomes, Piet 166-167
opium 35, 57, 60
oral history 73
Ouborg, Piet 95, 150
pacification 68, 97
painting 30-31, 36-37, 47, 54, 63, 87-88, 94-95, 120-121, 124, 126, 128-129, 149-150, 171-173, 175
Panji cycle 83
Papua 9, 22, 134
Parang rusak 74
parliament 47-49, 58, 62, 65
Partai Nasional Indonesia (PNI) 48
Paulides, H. 5, 9-11, 18, 123, 128-129, 150, 187
peranakan 69
performance 81-85, 87
pesantren 42
Pesegem 100
photograph 15, 20, 23, 36, 79, 100, 168
photography 5, 13, 107, 144, 161
physical anthropology 102-103, 108
Pieneman, Nicolaas 30-31, 36-37
Pitt Rivers Museum 113
plantation 53-54, 58-59, 64, 72, 77, 113, 167
podang raja 33, 152-153
poenale sanctie (penal sanction) 58
Political Intelligence Service 41
postcolonial society 17
prehistory 102-103, 115
private investment 54
production 53, 55-56, 59, 64-65, 77, 124, 142, 146, 174, 200
productivity 55
Public education 42, 82
puppets 31, 82-83, 89, 118, 120, 136
pygmy 100
Raad van Indië (Council of Indies) 76
raadsman, De 21, 162-163, 177
race 68, 74, 85, 100, 108, 118, 167
Raden Mas Jodjana 87
Raden Saleh 150
Raffles, Sir Thomas Stamford 82
railway 51, 59, 75, 124, 130
recruitment 58
refurbishment 12-14
Regeeringsreglement (Government Regulation) 56
Regent 39-40, 74, 76, 148
Regent of Cianjur 76
Reinwardt, C.G.C. 98
relationship 19, 48, 65, 68, 75, 81, 88-89, 100, 117, 166
religious dance 85
Republic of Indonesia 34, 49, 53, 64, 168
resident 30, 34
rice 9, 54, 56, 84
Rijksakademie van Beeldende Kunsten (National Academy of Visual Arts) 86, 94, 128, 175
Rijkseenheidsgedachte 47
Rijksmuseum voor Volkenkunde (now Museum Volkenkunde, National Museum of Ethnology) 106-107
Round Table Conference 18
Roux, Charles C.F.M. le 21, 104, 106-107, 132, 187-188
Rubber 9, 53-56, 59, 70
Rumphius, George E. 15, 21-22, 33, 151, 163-165, 171, 173, 183, 187-188
Sarekat Islam 47
sarung 69, 146
Sayers, Charles 21, 88-89, 94-95, 150, 163-164, 174-175, 177-178, 183, 187-188
School voor Kunstnijverheid (School for Applied Arts) 16
Schoolplaten voor de Vaderlandse geschiedenis 51
Schulte Nordholt, Henk 29, 186
science 4, 9, 23, 97-103, 105, 107-109, 165
scientific research 23, 97, 113, 119, 187
scientist 5, 97, 121, 134
sculpture 9, 85, 94
seamstress 21, 77, 79, 188
Second South New Guinea Expedition 100
Second World War 18, 22, 45, 57, 97, 123, 130, 139
secondary education 39, 42-43, 65
servant 4, 45, 68-71, 74-75, 77-78, 93, 121, 123, 162-164, 172, 174, 177
Shell Oil 73
Si Singamangaraja 33-34, 113, 152-153
silver 5, 12, 23, 37, 39, 55, 59, 71-72, 74, 81, 85, 100, 104, 108, 119, 123, 126, 131-132, 137, 139, 142, 144-145, 148, 153-154, 171, 177-178, 180, 183
silversmith 153-154
Sitisiwan 120, 182
Sjahrir, S. 17, 41, 188
Sleuteloog 167-168

Stichting Mondelinge Geschiedenis Indonesië (SMGI) 73, 187
Soekarnoii 48-49, 65
soldier 5, 21, 23, 29, 35, 121, 132, 135, 145, 167, 174-175, 178, 180-181
South Asia 15
Southeast Asia 13, 15, 64, 100
Stadlmair, Victorina M.G. 5, 135-136
Staff 11, 18, 40, 55, 62, 74, 77, 103, 105, 120, 124
Stammeshaus, F.W. 34-35
status 56, 69-70, 78, 118, 145, 152
Stirling Expedition 106-107
Sudjojono, S. 150
sugar 9, 53-56, 94, 118, 150, 175
sultan 55, 74, 81, 85, 187
Sumatra 33, 35, 46, 53, 55-56, 58-59, 62-63, 68-72, 75, 88, 97, 103, 114-116, 124, 135, 142, 144, 152-153, 171, 175
Suriname 138, 141, 177
Surjaningrat, R.M. Suwardi 82, 187
Swart, Henri N.A. 5, 135-136
symbol 53, 89, 178
symbolism 116
Székely, L. 53, 186
Székely-Lulofs, Madelon 59, 186
Tak, captain 120
Taman Siswo (Pupil's Garden) 39-41, 82
Tapiro 100
tea 53-54, 57, 62, 118, 135
teacher-training college 39, 41, 62
Technical College 43
technology 23, 53, 55-56, 142
temple festivals 84
tempo doeloe 166
Teukoe Oemar Djohan 35
textiles 116, 124, 134, 136, 146
Theater and its Double, The 88
theatre 4, 17, 20-21, 32, 81-89, 91, 93, 95, 105, 171, 174-175, 177-178, 182-183
Third South New Guinea Expedition 100
Third World 11-13, 55
Thomas, Nicolas 4, 53, 82, 113, 187
tienduizend dingen, De 21, 163-164, 178
Tillmann, Georg 114, 116-117
Toean Anwar 21, 162-164, 174, 177-178, 183, 188
topeng 82-83, 89, 91, 95
Topografische Dienst (Topographical Service) 142-143, 145
totok 69
trade unions 64-65
tribe 100
Tropenmuseum 4, 9-15, 17-19, 21-22, 24-25, 29-30, 34-35, 37, 57-58, 89, 95, 105-106, 108, 111, 113-120, 124, 128, 131-132, 136-137, 141-142, 144-146, 148-150, 152-155, 161-162, 164, 183
tropical diseases 12, 98
tropical products 10, 57, 60, 120, 138, 141-142, 157
Uit de suiker in de tabak 68
United Nations 11
university 42-43, 45, 55, 103, 134, 138-139, 142
Verenigde Oostindische Compagnie (VOC, Dutch East India Company) 22, 57, 97, 99, 119, 165, 171-172
Vereniging Koloniaal Instituut (Colonial Institute Association) 6
Vertenten, P. 5, 119, 126, 128
violence 4, 29-31, 33-37, 54, 58-59
Volksraad 47
vreemde Oosterlingen (Foreign Orientals) 45, 56, 118
Vreugde, Louis J. 16
War on Java (Java War) 31-32
wax figure 164
wayang golek 83, 93, 95
wayang kulit purwa 82
wayang wong 81, 83, 85, 89
weapon 33-35, 152
weaving 9, 123, 136, 146
Weissenborn, Margaretha M. 5, 13, 131-132, 187
Wendingen 81-82, 84-85
'white-collar' proletariat 44
Wijdeveld, H.Th. 81-82, 84-85, 187
Wijck-de Kock van Leeuwen, van der 76
Wild Schools 39, 43, 48, 177
Wilhelmina, queen 10, 20, 34-35, 97, 99-100, 107, 115, 126, 128, 134, 188
wood 5, 10, 15, 19, 33, 36, 43, 55, 57, 86, 91, 93, 117-118, 120, 136-137, 141-142, 152, 157, 182
World Fair 124, 129, 175
Yogya 5, 23, 119, 153-154
Yogyakarta 31-32, 40, 74, 76, 81-82, 85, 87, 123, 128, 138, 153-154
Young people's movement 47

Mannequins

Concept and design: Paul Gallis
Models: Remie Bakker, Manimalworks
Costumes: Daan Wieman
Light design: Reinier Tweebeeke
Technical matters: Ground Zero – Rutger van Dijk, Sierk Jansen

Mannequins are based on the following sources:

Anna Elink-van Maarseveen (p. 25)
Adriani 1932, Kruyt 1970, Van der Klift-Snijder & C.G.F. de Jong 1996

Soewarsih Djojopoespito (p. 41)
Buiten het Gareel 1946

Jhr. Mr. Bonifacius Cornelis de Jonge (p. 47)
Van der Wal 1968, Sjahrir 1987, Fasseur 1995, De Jong 1998

J.C. Cremer (p. 62)
Cremer 1876, Cremer 1881, Cremer 1924, Breman 1987, De Bussy 1941

Margaretha Engelen-Koets (p. 68)
Kooy-van Zeggelen 1910, Several sentences were quoted from a radio talk given by the then Dutch Prime Minister H. Colijn, 1936

The seamstress (p. 79)
Rutten-Pekelharing 1923

Toean Anwar (p.163)
H.J. Friedericy 1958

Georg Everhard Rumphius (p. 165)
Akveld & E.M. Jacobs 2002

Charles Eugène Henri Sayers (p. 175)
Various newspaper articles and reviews, Memories of his daughter, Wilhelmina Eveline Sayers-Vonwiller, Van Brakel 2004

Willem ('Himpies') van Kleyntjes (p. 181)
Dermoût 2000

ABOUT THE AUTHORS

Janneke van Dijk is a freelance photo researcher specialized in colonial visual culture. For many years she was the curator of the photography collection at the Tropenmuseum. In this capacity, she was a member of the exhibition work group 'Netherlands East Indies, a colonial past' (Nederlands-Indië, een koloniaal verleden). She is the co-author of *Augusta Curiel, fotografe in Suriname 1904-1937* (2007) and *J.C. Lamster, een vroege filmer in Nederlands-Indië* (2010). She is also the co-author of *The photographs of the Nederlands East Indies and Indonesia at the Tropenmuseum,* the fourth of ten volumes in the series on the collections at the Tropenmuseum.

Margareta Dorila is an economist and works as an investment analyst at the ABN AMRO Bank. In addition to economics, she studied art history at the University of Amsterdam. As an art historian, she specialized in the influence of Javanese and Balinese art on art in Western Europe. During her studies, she published a thesis on this subject entitled *De originaliteit van de Nieuwe Kunst. Javaanse invloed op het werk van Dijsselhof en Lion Cache.*

David van Duuren is an anthropologist. He worked at the Tropenmuseum from 1970 to 2010, most recently as the curator for the Oceania and historical collections, and has published work on the history of collections. He is the author of books on the Indonesian *kris* and co-author of books on the collection of human remains and 18th-century Oceanic weapons in the Tropenmuseum. In collaboration with several colleagues, he wrote *Oceania at the Tropenmuseum,* the second of ten volumes in the series on the collections at the Tropenmuseum.

Susan Legêne is a historian. She was Head of the Curatorial Department of the Tropenmuseum, where she specialized in tangible and intangible heritage as historical sources for a comparative approach to colonialism, post-colonial state formation and citizenship. She has written a number of books and essays on this subject. A recent title is *Spiegelreflex. Culturele sporen van de koloniale ervaring* (2010), on cultural traces of the colonial experience in Dutch society. See also htpps://www.let.vu.nl/en/staff/s.legene. Since 2008 she has been Professor of Political History at VU University in Amsterdam, the Netherlands.

J. Thomas Lindblad is economic historian and teaches in the departments of history and Indonesian studies at the Leiden University. His area of expertise is the history of Indonesia – he is the co-author of a textbook, entitled *The emergence of a national economy; An economic history of Indonesia, 1800-2000* (2002). His most recent book is *Bridges to new business; The economic decolonization of Indonesia* (2008).

Elsbeth Locher-Scholten is a retired Associate Professor in the history of colonialism and senior researcher at the Research Institute for History and Culture, Utrecht University. She has published works on Dutch imperialism in Indonesia, the Ethical Policy, gender and colonial memories in the Netherlands. She also co-authored a biography on Governor General and diplomat J.P. Count van Limburg Stirum (2007). Some of her books have been translated into English: *Women and the Colonial State. Essays on Gender and Modernity in the Netherlands-Indies* (2000) and *Sumatran Sultanate and the Colonial State. Jambi and the Rise of Dutch Imperialism, 1830-1907* (2003).

Pamela Pattynama is Extraordinary Professor of Colonial and Post-colonial Literature and Cultural History, specifically Indies-Dutch literature and culture. She works in the Faculty of Humanities at the University of Amsterdam and has published internationally on the subjects of gender, cultural memory and post-colonial culture. At present, her area of focus is the transgenerational transfer of memories and the (visual) representation of the Netherlands East Indies in contemporary literature and films. Her book on this topic will be published soon.

Ratna Saptari is an anthropologist and is currently affiliated with the Institute of Cultural Anthropology and Development Sociology in the Faculty of Social Sciences at Leiden University. She is also a senior research fellow at the International Institute of Social History. Her past research has focused on the politics of labour, workers in the cigarette industry, household and family in Indonesia. She has also written an article (2006) and a number of reviews (2004, 2009) on Asian domestic workers, past and present. Currently she is involved in a research project on tobacco as a global commodity.

Edy Seriese is the Director of the Indisch Wetenschappelijk Instituut (IWI – East Indies Scientific Institute) and project leader of the Stichting Indische Cultuur (SiC – East Indian Culture Foundation). In both of these functions she collects stories from Indonesian people that she records in the series *Vertellingen uit de Indische cultuur* (Stories from East Indian culture). She is also the author of the double CD *Woorden die een leven maken* (2004), the double DVDs *10.000 dingen* (2006) and *Krontjongan* (2009) on East Indian music, as well as *Dooremigreren* (2011). She is writing a history of East Indian culture on the IWI website www.iwi-nu.nl based on these and other stories.

Harm Stevens is a historian. Since 2009 he has been curator of the Department of History at the Rijksmuseum in Amsterdam. Prior to this he was curator of edged weapons and armour at the Legermuseum (Army Museum) in Delft. He is also the author of a publication on colonial history: *De laatste Batakkoning. Koloniale kroniek in documenten 1883-1911* (2010).

The following authors have contributed to the text boxes and descriptions of mannequins, collections and collectors:

CD	Caroline Drieënhuizen
DVDa	Daan van Dartel
DVD	David van Duuren
EVD	Erwin van Delden
IVH	Itie van Hout
JDJ	Jaap de Jonge
JVD	Janneke van Dijk
MM	Mark Mulder
MTH	Marisca ter Horst
PW	Pim Westerkamp
RC	Rachida Chaouqui
SL	Susan Legêne
SV	Steven Vink

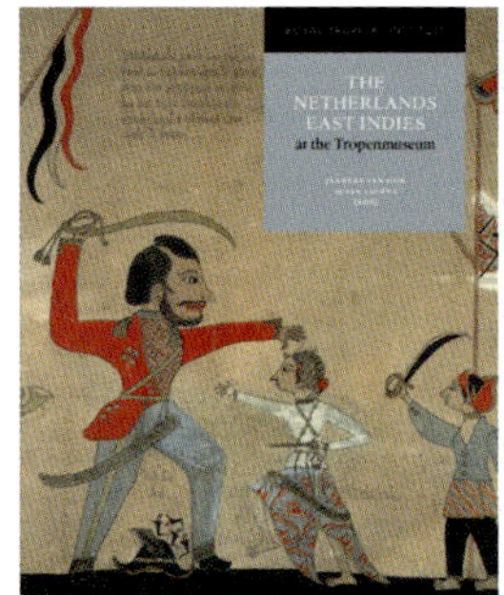

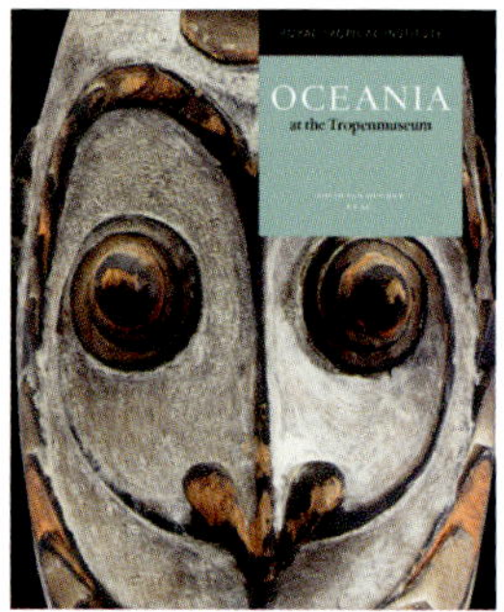

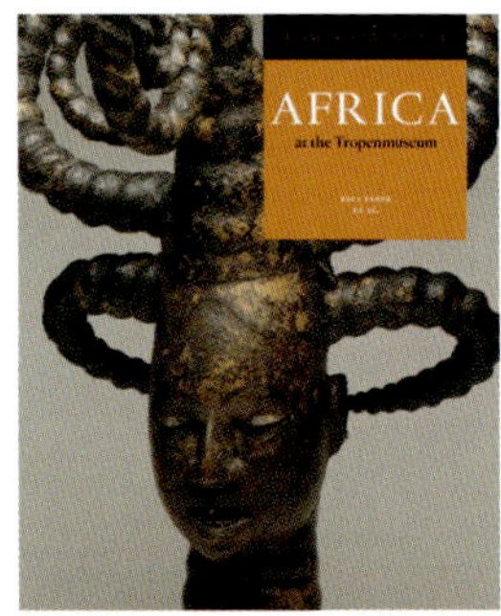

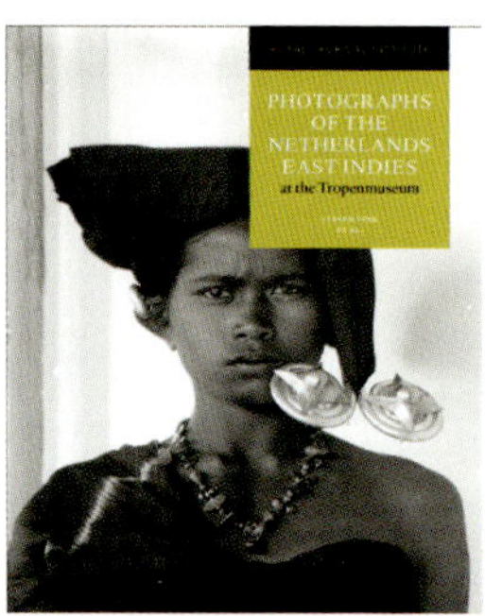

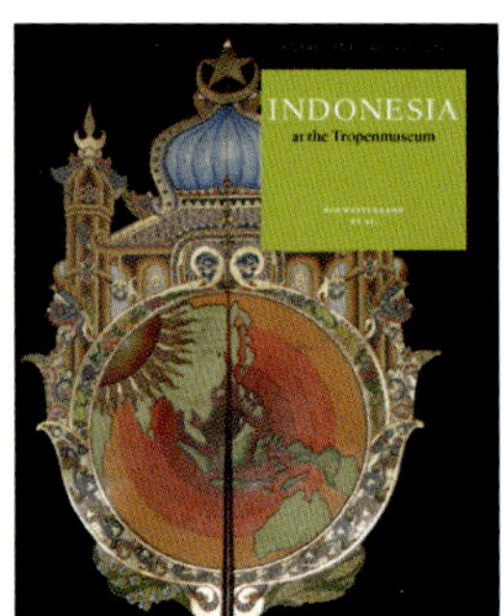

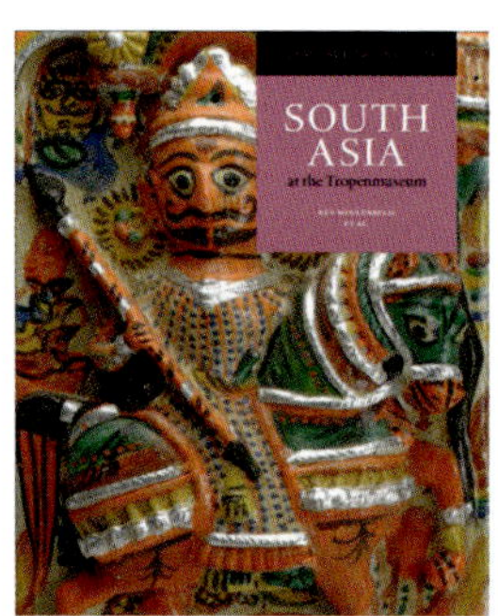

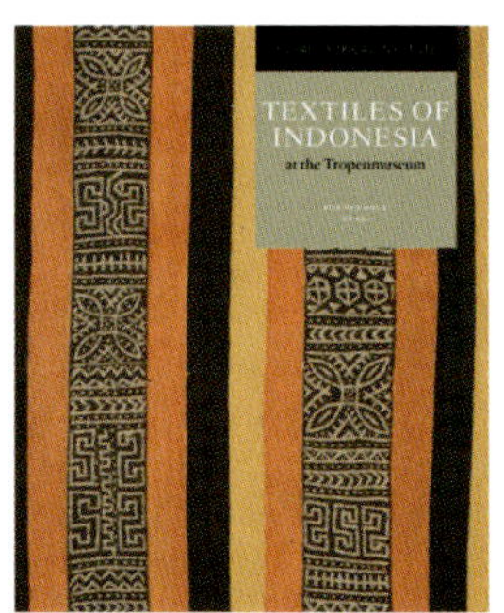

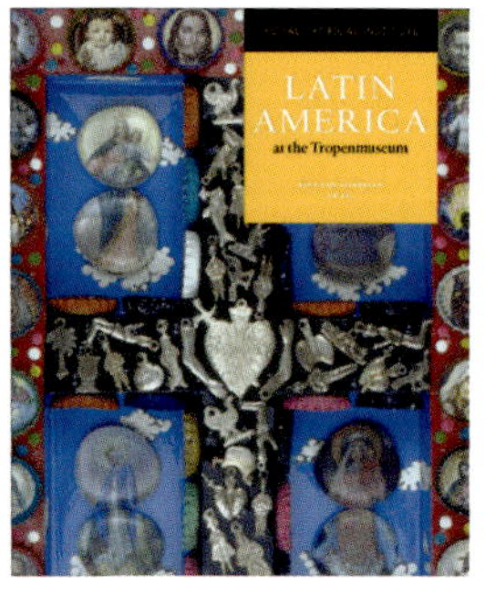

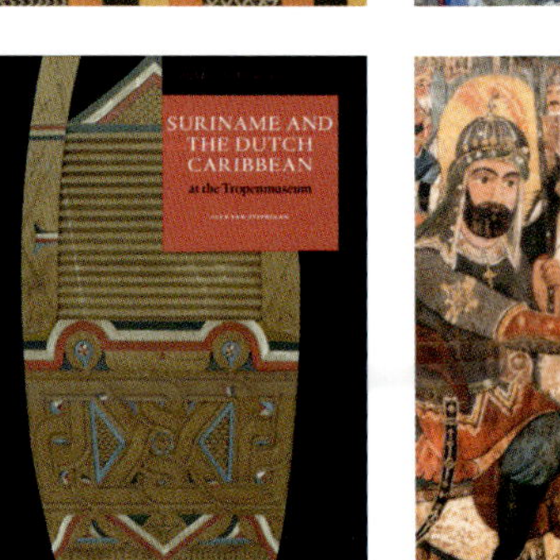

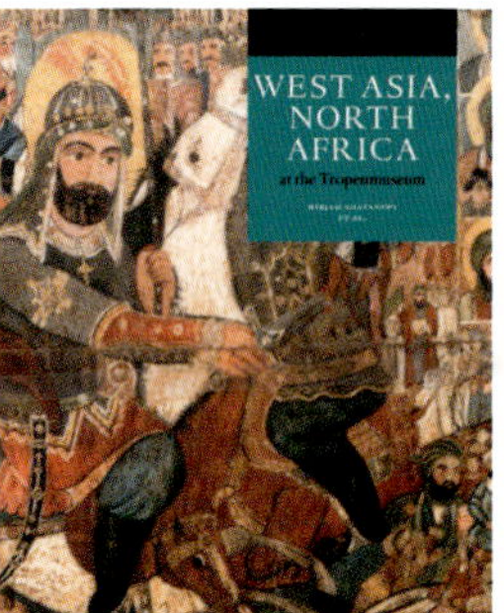

KIT Publishers
Mauritskade 63
P.O. Box 95001
1090 HA Amsterdam
The Netherlands
E-mail: publishers@kit.nl
www.kitpublishers.nl
www.tropenmuseum.nl

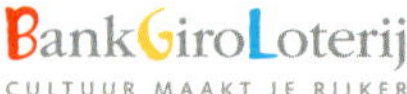

The publisher gratefully acknowledges the support of the BankGiroLoterij

Project managing
Kouwenhoven Publishing Services

Translation and editing
Spanjaard Boekproducties, Groningen, The Netherlands, Jessica Polak, Amsterdam, The Netherlands
Translation essay P. Pattynama: Ena Jansen
Editing captions Daan van Dartel and Sonja Wijs

Design
Studio Berry Slok, Amsterdam, The Netherlands

Production
High Trade BV, Zwolle, The Netherlands

Printed in Hungary

Cover illustration: detail Fig. 150
Illustration opposite title page: detail Fig. 56

ISBN 978 906832 7519
NUR 640

The Netherlands East Indies at the Tropenmuseum is volume one of a ten-volume series of the Royal Tropical Institute, published between 2011-2015.